Inside the System

Fourth Edition

Edited by
Charles Peters
and
Nicholas Lemann

Holt, Rinehart and Winston
New York   Chicago   San Francisco   Dallas
Montreal   Toronto   London   Sydney

Library of Congress Cataloging in Publication Data

Peters, Charles, 1926–   comp.
    Inside the system.

    1. United States—Politics and government—1945-
—Addresses, essays, lectures. I. Lemann, Nicholas.
II. Title.
E744.P43 1979   320.9'73'092   78-20870

ISBN 0-03-045101-9

Articles on the following pages are reprinted from the
Washington Monthly, copyright holder: p. 99, © 1969; p. 196,
© 1970; p. 27, ©1971; pp. 108, 237, © 1973; p. 205, © 1974;
pp. 132, 141, 161, 175, 180, 246, © 1975; pp. 15, 64, 227, 231,
©1976; pp. 19, 123, 214, 267, 289, 298, 315, © 1977; pp. 3,
80, 83, 189, © 1978. Article on p. 40 © 1969 by the *Washington
Monthly* and © 1977 by Prentice-Hall. Article on p. 276 © 1976 by Michael Wheeler.

Published 1979 by Holt, Rinehart and Winston

Foreword

Richard H. Rovere

These studies in anatomy, pathology, and therapy are the work of lucid clinicians and require no introduction by me or anyone else. The selection is a splendid one, and I would not detain the reader at all if it were not for my feeling that it might be useful to say something about how and why this book and *The Washington Monthly* came into being.

Some roundabout history is, thus, in order. It was never a secret that, when John F. Kennedy took office in 1961, neither he nor most of those who served him had much in the way of innovation to offer the country. I recall this as fact, not as criticism—though in another setting I might recall it as both. In general, however, no matter how many brilliant men a prince may surround himself with and no matter how receptive he may be to iconoclasm, "new ideas" in government are in short supply, and, of those that may be conceived and considered, some must for reasons of feasibility, finance, or certain other features of the reality of the day be shelved. At any rate, there was not much that was new on the New Frontier.

Institutionally, there was one true innovation: the Peace Corps. It was a new agency of government pursuing a new governmental activity. If, because of developments too well known to be cited here, its future is today problematical, it nevertheless endured for a number of years, and even if it is one day only a memory, it will still be recalled as among the noblest and most humane of American experiments.

The Peace Corps was an innovation and was itself in many ways innovative. It is with only one of its innovations that I am concerned here, because my purpose of the moment is to say something about this book and the magazine that gave it birth. When the Peace Corps was established, its director, Sargent Shriver, and his staff felt an urgent need to find effective ways of assessing the value of the work and the validity of their methods. Though what they were setting out to do was not altogether

Richard H. Rovere is the author of the *New Yorker* magazine's "Letter from Washington."

without precedent, the precedents were few and for the most part irrelevant.

It was therefore held to be enormously important to set up a system of evaluation that would bring from the field to Washington detailed and disinterested appraisals of the performance of the volunteers and the staff members supervising them. What were they doing? Was it worth doing? Was it being done well? Inspection is not, of course, a new idea in government. Every executive agency has some section within it charged with reporting on the efficacy and efficiency of its operations, and there are more or less independent agencies of government—the Office of Management and Budget comes to mind, as does the General Accounting Office and certain congressional committees—keeping tabs on the whole Executive branch. And then there are all those presidential commissions—generally a mix of government and nongovernment people—that report on, and make recommendations about, grave national issues. Even when the work of these bodies is not downright shoddy and biased, the tendencies are to quantify wherever possible and, when recommendations seem in order, to urge only procedural and structural reforms. This approach seemed inadequate to the Peace Corps founders. Their accomplishments, or lack thereof, might seldom be quantifiable (and, when they proved so, quantifiable on so small a scale as to breed only discouragement), and structural and procedural problems might be irrelevant, because structures and procedures were then practically nonexistent, the problem being not so much to have them criticized as to have them created.

But sound inspection, or evaluation, was essential, or so at least it was felt, and the development of a method was entrusted to a young lawyer and former member of the West Virginia legislature named Charles Peters, the founder and now the editor of *The Washington Monthly* and a coeditor of this volume. He put together a staff of full-time evaluators, some of them experienced journalists, and dispatched them to various points on the globe with instructions to cast a cold eye on what they saw and report back to Washington with a heavy emphasis on the critical, an accentuation of the negative. He was not much interested in good news —that tended to come to light rather quickly and to be useful mainly for purposes of sustaining morale. The bad news was the helpful kind; it could be turned into cease-and-desist and never-again orders—thus improving the ratio of good news, the kind that is rarely concealed, to bad news, the kind frequently concealed. To keep his staff on its toes, and to guard against the self-congratulatory tendency certain to arise in even the most enlightened of bureaucracies, he contracted with people with no governmental ties—some of them, indeed, harboring considerable resentment of government—for assignments similar to those undertaken by the members of his staff.

There was, I think, high imagination in Peters's work, but there was no magic, no secret about it. He knew what he wanted, and he knew how to get it. I have never been altogether sure about what the term "systems analysis" means—or, rather, about what it implies in terms of methodology—but systems analysis of a sort was what the Peace Corps needed in its early days and what, thanks to Peters and his evaluators, it got. The title of this volume may have led me into some obfuscation on this point, for, after all, "analysis" is analysis, and "systems," or the "system," merely one of the phenomena of life, like literature, that may be made subject to the analytical approach, or mood. "Criticism" is another word for it, and it has been practiced for some time, not only in arts and letters and philosophy but in politics and government as well. However that may be, it seemed a good idea to many of us when Peters decided to attempt to apply, in a magazine, the approach of the Peace Corps evaluators to a broad range of American institutions and, perhaps, even international ones. Today the Peace Corps, tomorrow the U.S. government, the day after that the world. So, with the moral support of some and the financial support of others, the magazine was born in the first month of 1969.

I think it has been a great success, maintaining a tone and temper that make it, I believe, the best thing of its kind in American life today. Still, I look, and with some confidence, to a day when it will fulfill its chosen function even more usefully than it does at present, and to explain this hope I must again revert briefly to Peace Corps history. Although, as I have said, Peters employed some outsiders like myself to provide competition for the evaluators who were part of the Peace Corps bureaucracy, my impression has always been that the best work was done by the full-time workers—those who were themselves "inside the system" and charged with the critical role. Several of them had earlier been quite deep inside the system—as volunteers or staff members abroad. A necessary assumption in founding the magazine was that there were people in other agencies and institutions who were or recently had been inside the system and could view it with objectivity and intelligence. Although it doubtless had more than its share of free and critical spirits, the Peace Corps was not, after all, the only part of the government that had attracted people of integrity and good sense. Even though at the moment there appears to be something of a premium on mediocrity, the long-range trend has been away from it, and what we all hoped was that Peters and his staff could find or draw to themselves present or recent members of the bureaucracy whose arteries had not become sclerotic and whose careers were more than a matter of careerism. To a great degree, possibly to a greater degree than we had any right to expect, the hope has been fulfilled, as the reader will note by the identifications of the contributors to be found with the articles in this anthology. But, as the reader will likewise note, it has not been completely fulfilled, with the consequence that the magazine has also been a vehicle for such professional journalists—all of them eminent —as David Broder and Russell Baker. It is a fortunate magazine that can attract such talents, and they have given it their best. The utopia I might seek, though—and I am sure they would agree—is one in which professional journalists, "outsiders" by definition, would be part of the magazine's constituency and broaden their perspectives by sharing those of insiders.

In any event, *The Washington Monthly* is with us, and with us, I trust, for good. I am proud of my own association with it, and I very much hope that the publication of this volume will bring it to the attention of a wider public.

Preface

This book is based on the assumption that in the American government, function does not follow form. It's our feeling that around every new agency, law, and program grows a subculture of people and practices whose existence would have been hard to predict in advance; we think the government on paper and the government in operation are two different things. Would the Founding Fathers have imagined that lobbyists would play as large a part in the operations of the Congress as they do today? Would Lyndon Johnson have thought his Great Society would do as much for lawyers and grantsmen as for poor people? American government is usually taught as if learning how it's supposed to work were all that's necessary; we want to show how it *does* work.

As will be clear in the following pages, this is a task largely ignored not only by teachers, but by reporters and even government officials themselves. Presidents, congressmen, and heads of agencies usually have little idea of what's going on in the government they're running. Reporters usually do their jobs by interviewing the Presidents, congressmen, and agency heads, so they don't know either. We've tried in this book to shed light on what's really happening—how policy is made, how it works, why it doesn't work.

There are two general points that emerge from the essays that follow. First, the experiences of the last ten years have shown that self-interest, always imagined by liberals to be the exclusive province of profit-hungry businessmen, is also an important factor in government. In seeking to understand the behavior of people in Washington, it's wise to place heavy emphasis on a congressman's urge for reelection, a bureaucrat's for safety, and a reporter's for space on the front page.

The second lesson is that the government ought to deal with its own complexity as a major issue and not just a side-effect. In most of the case studies in this book, the government is so large and diffuse that direct action is usually impossible; inefficiency and jurisdictional disputes are common; nobody understands what's really going on; and only a huge corps of government and nongovernment experts and explainers can make the whole thing go. These are important facts of life in Washington today, but they are almost never officially recognized.

Contents

part 1
THE SETTING

The way a government works is more than just the product of a combination of laws and economic forces. Governing has to be done in a place, and in the case of the American federal government the place is Washington, D.C.—mecca for the ambitious, the idealistic, the action-seeking, and the greedy; home of cautious bureaucrats, hangers-on, politicians, journalists, diplomats. In understanding what the government does, it's helpful first to understand the setting.

Right now there are two popular clichés about Washington, and both of them, like most clichés, have a lot of truth in them. The first is that Washington is a company town, where everything revolves around the federal government and there's always just one topic of conversation. The second is that Washington has become the national capital of affluence as well as of government.

It's true that government dominates Washington in the way that business dominates most cities. The capital is a city that's deserted during Christmas week because everybody's gone home for the holidays. For the most part Washington is run by people who moved there because they wanted the excitement and the opportunity for quick advancement that government work afforded. What brings them to Washington, specifically, is usually a job, which leads to another job, and another, until before long they are well settled and the desire to stay in town is overpoweringly strong.

Washingtonians assure their survival there by building up the kind of mutual protection networks described in the first article in this section. Because everyone is protecting everyone else, there is in Washington a powerful sense of shared enterprise that cuts across the supposed conflicts between the branches of government. How the apparently anti-Washington Carter administration fits into this set of networks is a still developing story, but James Fallows (who joined the Carter administration himself and then left it) offers some speculation about how the people around Carter will be brought into the fold in "The Seductions of Washington Society."

As for affluence, it's certainly there; Washington has the highest per-capita income of any metropolitan area in the country. But there are few really rich people there; the figures are high because of the vast number with upper-middle-class incomes. So despite the popular conception, Washington is not a city of Cadillacs and three-story mansions—it's a city of Volvos and two-story houses. "Money Doesn't Talk in Washington" explains that it's really power that motivates people, not conspicuous consumption. The only people Washington has made really rich are those in the private business of managing various aspects of the government relations of large corporations—consultants who interpret federal regulations, lawyers who can steer clients through agencies, lobbyists, grantsmen, and tax specialists. They live off their access to upper-middle-class government employees, whom they can't afford to offend by living the life of the rich.

Survival Networks: Staying in Washington

Nicholas Lemann

In 1962 Coates Redmon was in Colorado Springs, Colorado, and not a bit happy about it. Her husband Hayes was teaching Russian history at the Air Force Academy, which was a good step in his career; but she hated the military in general and the Academy particularly. There were many other things she would rather have been doing, but one that especially caught her eye was the Peace Corps, which had been set up the year before. "That was the greatest thing I ever heard of," she says now. "I wanted to come and be a part of it. But I thought, that's impossible, and I forgot about it."

One day, by chance, her husband happened to be given the assignment of showing a visiting colonel from the Pentagon around the Academy. Hayes Redmon so impressed the colonel that he was invited, on the spot, to come back to Washington and join his staff. Hayes called his wife right away and asked her if she'd like to move there. "I'm packing," Coates Redmon said.

They arrived in the fall of '62, not knowing a soul. One day in the first month they were in Washington the Redmons went to Hechinger's, an upper-middle-class lumberyard, to buy some planks for a bookcase. It was one of those moments in life of unexpected opportunity. Across the store Coates happened to see Dick Nelson, a young man who had been editor of the Princeton humor magazine, the *Tiger*. She had met him years earlier, in New York, when they had collaborated on a couple of projects while she was working at *Glamour* magazine.

Nicholas Lemann is a contributing editor of *The Washington Monthly*.

Nelson and the Redmons got to talking. He said he was now working at the Peace Corps as assistant to Bill Moyers, the already celebratedly bright and charming protege of Lyndon Johnson's who was then the Peace Corps' deputy director. Coates' heart leapt when she heard Peace Corps. "Oh," she said, "you're working for the wonder boy of Washington. Is he really that great?"

Nelson said yes, Moyers was that great, and that in fact Moyers and his wife were giving him a going-away party because he had been inducted and why didn't the Redmons come. They went—the next week, to a small dinner at the Moyers', where Coates emphatically let it be known that she was interested in working at the Peace Corps.

The Redmons couldn't have known it then, but bumping into Dick Nelson that day at Hechinger's would change both their lives. It was the watershed after which everything began to flow in a different direction. They had become Washington survivors.

THE CREST OF THE WAVE

Washington is a city to which many people come and few people leave. They come because of a specific job; because they want an outlet for their idealism; because they are interested in being involved in government and politics; because Washington offers more opportunity for quick advancement than do most American cities; and because they want to be at the center of things, to ride the crest of the wave. Usually it's some sort of break that brings them here—a chance meeting, a good score on the civil service test, a successful political campaign, friends, family, money.

Most people who live in Washington don't want to leave. It's a pleasant, pretty city, and after a few years their friends are here, their children firmly ensconced in school, their houses half paid for. Even those who don't mind leaving the city itself are loath to leave Washington in the figurative sense—that is, the world of public affairs, be it here or at the Council on Foreign Relations or the Fletcher School of Law and Diplomacy or the RAND Corporation or *The Atlantic Monthly*. And indeed, although jobs end, elections are lost, and agency budgets are sometimes cut, almost nobody ever has to leave Washington and go back home. Of the few who do go back, a high proportion are doing so only to "build a base" that will enable them to win a seat in the House or Senate and return to Washington in a more exalted position than they occupied formerly.

The reason why nobody has to leave is that almost everybody soon learns how to survive in the complex and perilous world of Washington. It's done by making contacts, by building a reputation, by establishing a network in which the unstated ethic is one of mutual protection. In other words, you turn your own part of Washington into a small town, with all the stability and resistance to change and to outsiders that that implies. Survival networks, of course, exist everywhere, and everywhere they help shape the communities they're in. But in Washington, besides all that, they also are an important factor in the governing of the nation.

Civil servants have tenure and survival is easiest for them, but still they have budget cuts to fear, so the high-ranking among them make sure to provide the President with programs and congressmen with constituent services. Those elected officials are grateful for that, because it helps them survive at election time; and they in turn help the bureaucrats and private lobbyists survive by listening to their entreaties. Even if the elected don't survive at the polls, of course, they can and almost always do stay in Washington, usually as lobbyists—in fact, it's partly by building up a survival network among both fellow elected officials and lobbyists that they can assure their futures in Washington.

Most adept of all at the art of survival are the political appointees at the top of government. These are people who build careers out of switching jobs every two or three years, and who in that fluid and uncertain situation have found a way to get de facto tenure. They have done so by building strong networks among the elected officials, the bureaucrats, the lobbyists, the co-workers, and the various constituent groups with which they deal in the course of their jobs. These networks will be the most important element in all the future jobs they get. An assistant secretary in the education branch of the Department of Health, Education, and Welfare, for instance, might go from there to a higher post in the department; to an education-policy job in the White House; to a partnership in a law firm; to the head of a foundation having to do with education; to the head of a university; or to a high position at an interest group like the American Council on Education. Since the average tenure of assistant secretaries is now less than two years, it's not too much to say that a prudent one must go about building all these bridges almost from the moment he takes office.

The result is that although Washington is supposed to be a city where power is carefully balanced between groups with contradictory interests, in fact it's a place with a strong sense of shared enterprise, a place where every person you deal with is someone who is either helping you survive now or might conceivably later on. The most remarked-upon case in point is the reporter who accords his sources kid-glove treatment so that they will remain his sources. If they stopped talking to him, he'd be out of a job. What isn't so well known is that that ethic exists for politicians and bureaucrats and political appointees too.

Thus when Rep. John Anderson, the prominent liberal Republican from Illinois, faced a tough primary campaign this year, Rep. Jack Kemp, the prominent conservative Republican from New York, went out to campaign for him—their survival bond was far stronger than their ideological

differences. Thus White House staff members, GS-16s, and corporate lobbyists alike are reluctant to do anything that will mark them as apart from
the shared enterprise, because that might mean their non-survival.

Of course, along with the survival instinct comes a genuine empathy
with other people in Washington that reinforces the bonds and makes
severe criticism a rarity. The same deep understanding that makes it hard
for you to believe that your cousin who's a lush should be fired also makes
it hard for you to condemn your friend Henry Kissinger with the vocifer-
ousness he deserves. The atmosphere, at any rate, is one that has made
some badly needed qualities—strong dissent, for instance, or ideological
passion—largely absent from federal policy.

CERTAIN REQUIREMENTS

Through the Moyers connection, Coates Redmon got her first Washington job, in the special projects division of the Peace Corps. In a first job
in Washington, there are certain requirements for survival that don't exist
later on. You have to prove your ability to do valuable work, and you have
to establish the network of contacts that will see you through the coming
years. In an outfit like the Peace Corps most people had come in through
some personal contact and were thus trained to be on the lookout for
more; and the group was made up of hard-working, like-minded people
who didn't need any prodding to form close friendships. For Coates,
finding some real work to do—making herself indispensable—was harder.
She eventually wangled the assignment of helping write the Peace Corps'
annual report to Congress, a task that had fallen to her division because
nobody else wanted to do it. Writing the annual report was the main skill
by which she was to survive in the Peace Corps.

Coates was flying back from a recruiting trip to Pittsburgh when President Kennedy was shot. At the Peace Corps, especially, the sorrow was
great. The organization had lost its founder and patron, and as a result it
also lost its brightest star. Moyers left right away to become Johnson's
right-hand man in the White House—and brought with him as his top
assistant, to everyone's surprise, Hayes Redmon from the Pentagon rather
than anyone from the Peace Corps. So besides having a needed skill,
Coates now had White House protection too. In 1965, when Shriver left
the Peace Corps, his successor, Jack Vaughn, told her to keep on doing
what she had done all along, writing the annual report. And Vaughn did
her a favor by putting over her a new boss named Bob Hatch, who would
later become a key figure in her survival network.

When Moyers left the White House in 1967 Hayes Redmon could hardly
stay on, so the Redmons soon moved to Cambridge, Massachusetts, where
Hayes took a job as assistant to Edwin Land at Polaroid. One day in

Cambridge, Coates got a call from Adam Yarmolinsky—former whiz kid at the Pentagon, close friend of Hayes and fellow member of a network of secret doves high in the government, and then a professor at Harvard Law School. Yarmolinsky was running the fellowship program at the Kennedy Institute of Politics at Harvard, and he asked Coates to come and help him part-time. On the one hand it was a lowly job, handling the paperwork and the details for the too-busy Yarmolinsky, but on the other it really required someone who had what was by now one of Coates' special skills: knowledge of Washington.

People in the world of public affairs would apply for the fellowships, and Coates would know how to find out how good, how promising, each applicant really was. She would call other members of her network—people like Joe Califano in the White House or Bob Wood at HUD. These people were helping Coates do her job, and she was giving them a chance to do a favor for some of their bright young acquaintances. It worked very well, and Coates stayed for a year and a half, until mid-1969, when she left to have a baby.

SUDDENLY VERY SERIOUS

Three years later, the process of survival, which until then had been pleasantly haphazard for Coates, became suddenly very serious. Hayes Redmon had a severe heart attack in 1972 and died shortly thereafter, leaving Coates with two kids to feed and very little money. She had to find a way to live right away.

Among many other tries, she asked Professor Richard Neustadt, part of her new network at the Kennedy Institute, to get her an appointment with someone at the Ford Foundation. Neustadt obliged, but at Ford they told her that because the recession was just starting and because there were a lot of applicants, her chances were slim. By the way, the man interviewing her said, I see by your resume that you were in the Peace Corps. Do you know Bob Hatch?

Sure, said Coates, I used to work for him. Where is he? He was at the Children's Television Workshop. She went right downstairs to a phone booth and called Hatch, and he said to come on over.

Hatch said the workshop was starting a new series on health and sent Coates to see its director, Bill Kobin. Kobin was looking over her resume and said, oh, I see you have Bill Moyers down here as a reference—I used to be his producer. Coates was hired, saved by the Peace Corps network.

The job was stimulating but Coates' heart was in Washington. Through the Peace Corps network she got a job with Senator Charles Percy, and some months after that ended she got a call from Bob Hatch in New York. There was a new project starting up at public TV, he said, sort of a quiz show for eggheads, and they needed somebody with Coates' special skill, someone who really knew Washington and could line up the right guests. She went to work there in September 1976—again, courtesy of the network.

JUST ABOUT EVERYBODY

That time, the late summer and early fall of 1976, was important for just about everybody playing the Washington survival game. When the Democrats left power in 1968, practically all of them survived. If you were, like Coates, a woman, widowed, from the middle levels of government, you got by okay. Few people got by worse and a lot got by better. By 1976 nobody Coates knew from the Peace Corps was away from the world of Washington, and some of them had been saved and eased into comfortable niches by their friends despite severe problems, alcoholism or utter incompetence in a job. Having proved themselves and established their network 15 years before, the Peace Corps people no longer had to perform to survive. It helped, but it wasn't necessary.

Some of the Peace Corps people had managed to stay on in government under the Republicans. Some had college presidencies. Some ran foundations. Some had ambassadorships. They were in business (but liberal business), labor unions, Capitol Hill offices, journalism—but all were still around and had survived on the strength of who they knew and what they knew.

Just about everybody had a network, often several. There are, for instance, networks built around almost every senator's office in Washington and around every major law school. There are networks of the proteges of powerful people, like the network of Theodore Hesburgh, president of Notre Dame, or of Chester Bowles, the former undersecretary of State, or of Robert Strauss, President Carter's special trade representative. There are cause networks made up of people who came to Washington to work for a cause and stayed on after the cause ended—like the network of Bobby Kennedy's Get-Hoffa Squad or Arnold Miller's Miners for Democracy. Network members stay in touch with one another. They help each other out in times of no jobs. A victory for one is a victory for all—one member's success puts him in a position to help the others more.

There are people who manage to survive forever in the appointive ranks of government, like Frank Carlucci (director of the Office of Economic Opportunity, deputy director of the Office of Management and Budget, undersecretary of HEW, and ambassador to Portugal under Nixon; deputy director of the CIA under Carter), but they are relatively rare. Some of those who haven't been able to work out the next job yet when they leave government are given the opportunity to spend a year

Survival in Washington is not a subject for polite conversation, usually less so than, say, sex. In my own research for this article I went through a string of canceled interview appointments, of secretaries telling me their bosses would be quite busy for the next four months and they'd get back to me after that. So it's no surprise that there are few published documents about survival.

One of the few—which is about survival unconsciously, but nonetheless centrally—is an odd little book called *Hope and Fear in Washington (The Early Seventies)*, an account of the Washington press corps by Barney Collier. Collier published the book in 1975, at which time he was an ex-*New York Herald Tribune*, ex-*New York Times* reporter who was down on his luck and trying to bounce back.

The theme of the book is this: Collier calls up important press people and asks them to lunch. In the meantime he ruminates a little about his own troubles. He goes to lunch and conducts strange conversations with his subjects, who obviously think they're talking off the record, although Collier will put it all in his book.

Now the reason all these people talked to Collier in the first place is that they were part of his survival network. Lunch with a friend who needs some help is an important, and worthy, ritual of survival in Washington.

Thus: "Dan Rather's opening words with me were: 'Sure, Barney, of course I'll do it. I'm sure it's a . . . worthwhile . . . project. I'll see you, sure. We'll have . . . lunch.' "

Thus: " 'I'll help you [says Art Buchwald]. I always like to help someone from the old *Herald Tribune*. We'll have lunch and talk about it.' "

But when it came time to write the book, Collier pulled out all the stops. In his preface he said, with masterful understatement, "This book was not written to be sober and respectable." In fact, it was *extremely irresponsible*, full of quotes like, "[John Chancellor] talked loudly in the nervously friendly way of a man who hasn't any true friends."

After publication there was a hail of vituperative abuse heaped on the book from all corners, and Collier, who was able to write it only because of his position in a survival network, has become a non-survivor. He is now said to be living quietly on a farm somewhere in Virginia.

decompressing and thinking and looking around on a fellowship. Coates gave out some of these at the Kennedy Institute; Robert O. Anderson, the ARCO tycoon, dispenses others at his Aspen Institute for Humanistic Studies, where distinguished men with titles like Director of Humanism and the Commonweal talk and write about such themes as From Independence to Interdependence. McGeorge Bundy at the Ford Foundation gave special one-year grants to some of Bobby Kennedy's closest staff after he was assassinated, people like Peter Edelman and Adam Walinsky, and a year later, to balance the ticket, Johnson aides like Califano and Walt Rostow got them too. These thinking fellowships are known collectively as The Leisure of the Theory Class.

But for the most part, survivors who leave government go into The Business—the access business, where you make a living by marketing your knowledge of the people and the processes of the federal government. The Business is sprawling. It includes the economist at the Brookings Institution who understands federal budgeting, the tax lawyer who knows who to see at the IRS about an exemption, the PR man who knows every reporter in town, the university president who knows how to shake grant money loose from HEW, and (its most familiar practitioner) the lobbyist who can call his old friend the assistant secretary and ask a favor. The smartest lobbyists know assistant secretaries and congressmen want to stay in Washington, and they imply as much as possible that they can be of help in the quest—which in turn helps them survive by getting access.

The Business is an easy way to survive because there's a lot of demand for it. How Washington really works is still largely a mystery to the rest of America—and an important one, since Washington affects the lives of most people and institutions. People who have been in the federal government can sell this knowledge to the rest of the country.

But The Business, because it is at one remove from the crest of the wave, is only second best to being in government. While just about everybody survives, very few are able to survive well enough to get back in in a good spot. As you get older the jobs you'd take dwindle, and it becomes harder to muster the time and energy to work in campaigns, which is the surest route to jobs in the government. The people who are still in their 20s and early 30s—the ones who can take time off for campaign work—are the ones who get most of the good jobs. Still, in a year like 1976, when it becomes clear the Democrats are returning to power, the thoughts of just about everybody, young and old, turned to the election. People in Congress had to run; bureaucrats had to worry about what a new President would try to do to them; people in Coates' generation thought about getting back in; and people a generation younger thought about getting in for the first time.

DROP EVERYTHING

Coates was happily at work on the TV show one day in November 1976 when she got a call from Mitzi Wertheim, yet another network member from the Peace Corps. Wertheim was in charge of the "foreign affairs cluster" in the Carter transition office. She asked Coates if she could drop everything and come over and work for two days, helping compile files on candidates for high appointive office. Coates would be perfect because she was a proven writer and she knew Washington. She said sure, she'd do it, and ended up staying for five weeks. During that time she was able to repay in a small way some of the people who had helped her survive by working up job files on them; she did this for people like Moyers and Shriver.

In that atmosphere of resumes you throw your own into the pile, which Coates did. Meanwhile, *another* member of the network, Mary Hoyt, who had shared an office with Coates at the Peace Corps, had run a PR business with some Peace Corps alumni, and had developed the sui generis talent of handling PR for the wives of important politicians, had surfaced as Rosalynn Carter's press secretary. One day Hoyt said to Coates, "Give me your resume and give it to me fast," and shortly thereafter she called back and offered Coates a job in the White House as "East Wing Writer." Almost all of the rest of the old Peace Corps crowd made some play for a job that never quite panned out. Most of them had shied away from Jimmy Carter for too long, had wanted jobs slightly out of their reach, and hadn't had the freedom to drop everything and join the campaign or the transition as Coates had.

At the same time, there was intense job-hunting activity on many other levels. One of the most intense was that of the bright young lawyers and Capitol Hill staff members and political academics, people in their late 20s and early 30s, full of energy and ambition, most wanting to be involved in formulating domestic policy. Few of these people went to work for the Carter primary campaign, but a group of them hopped aboard after it became clear Carter would be the Democratic nominee and spent the summer and fall working on issues in Atlanta.

After Carter was elected there was a second wave of domestic-policy hiring, and that wave included Joseph Onek. At 34, Onek had already survived in Washington for some years, having initially broken in through outstanding academic performance. Onek is from the Forest Hills section of Queens (no network potential there). He went from there to Harvard (that's one network), from there to England for two years on a Marshall scholarship (another network), and then to Yale Law School (yet another). There he did very well—well enough to become one of the top editors of the law review, which in turn was enough of a credential to get him a clerkship with Judge David Bazelon of the District of Columbia Circuit Court and then one with Justice William Brennan of the Supreme Court. It was these clerkships that brought Onek to Washington, and he didn't intend at the time to stay longer than the two years they would keep him here.

When the second clerkship ended Onek went to work for Senator Edward Kennedy's Administrative Practices Subcommittee (working for Kennedy is one of the best survival jobs on Capitol Hill; others are working for Senator Henry Jackson and, when he was still there, Senator Walter Mondale). Onek took the place of a Yale classmate who was going to clerk on the Supreme Court; and the subcommittee's chief counsel, Jim Flug, was a member of two of Onek's networks—they had gone to Harvard together and had both been clerks for Bazelon. Meanwhile another friend from Harvard, who had also gone to Yale Law School and clerked on the D.C. Circuit, Charles Halpern, had founded the Center for Law and Social Policy, a public interest law firm respectable enough to be funded by the Ford Foundation. Onek went there from Kennedy's subcommittee, and by 1976, five years later, he was running the firm.

Onek had stayed pretty clear of the campaign, but the network none-theless reached out for him. Ten days before the election he got a call from Harrison Wellford, a former aide to Ralph Nader (whose former aides now comprise one of the most successful networks in government). Onek and Wellford had been Marshall scholars together and had had some contact through the Nader organization, so they were fellow network members. Wellford asked Onek if he would take some time off and work in the transition on health issues—a field Onek had practiced in and taught a course in at Maryland Law School, where the dean was a friend from Yale. Onek said sure he would.

During the transition Onek worked partly with Stu Eizenstat and partly with Joe Califano, just appointed secretary of HEW. Onek knew Califano in a variety of ways. Califano had been a staunch friend of the Center for Law and Social Policy. When the Ford Foundation would become itchy about its funding of the Center, Califano would sometimes step in and call Mac Bundy at the foundation (who, remember, had given Califano a fellowship after working in the White House with him) and save the day. They were on opposite sides of an issue sometimes and on the same side at other times.

BETTER THAN ANYONE

By this time it was clear who of the Kennedy-Johnson-era people was going to survive really well and who wasn't, and Califano had to be ac-corded the honor of having survived better than anyone in Washington. His career was a thing of beauty. In his early thirties he had held the best domestic policy job in the Johnson Administration, at the President's right hand. After that he went into The Business, but somehow he managed both to make more money at it than anyone else and to keep his public-affairs image impeccable. He had written two books, one on World Youth and the other on The Presidency. He had had some key prestige clients, such as *The Washington Post*, Daniel Schorr, and the Democratic National Committee. In his law firm he had surrounded himself with the brightest young legal talent in the country. He had managed the transition from staff-level government job to Cabinet-level government job beautifully, and here he was again in the best domestic-affairs job in the administration.

The competition for best survivor, junior division, was harder to judge, but certainly a leading candidate for the honor was Ben Heineman Jr., Califano's young executive assistant. Son of a Chicago tycoon, a man who could be doing any one of a hundred important things right now, Heineman had been a Rhodes Scholar, gone to Yale Law School, and eventually had come to be Califano's closest aide. He had also worked with Onek at the Center for Law and Social Policy, which had become quite a network of its own, sending half a dozen others into high government jobs in the Carter Administration. For his part, Onek decided after the transition to stay with the Eizenstat operation and moved on to the White House staff as an associate director of the domestic policy staff for health issues.

Onek and the other associate directors—bright, ambitious people in their early to mid-30s—are just where they want to be right now, right at the center of things, their lives for the most part unbroken strings of successes to date. But already that is beginning to change. Options are starting to close down. The time is coming, a year and a half into their new jobs, to start thinking about what comes next—about how to survive. Part of it is the natural desire (in Washington) to become restless after a couple of years. Part is that working for Jimmy Carter is fast losing its luster. Part is that the associate directors are approaching that key age where you ought really to shift from a staff job to a line job, like an assistant secretaryship. So they're at the place where surviving and governing are intertwined.

In that place, there are some networks where everyone is simon-pure and thinks only about doing the job at hand, never about what will come next. At the other end of the spectrum, there are some where every move is designed to improve later prospects in The Business. Just as back home some insurance agents join charity boards just to sell the other members policies, in Washington there are people who work in campaigns and take pro bono cases solely to make contacts, and who while in public office make sure to touch base with as many people as they can both in and out of government. "When LBJ said he wasn't going to run again," says one of his aides now, "I made damn sure to call all those agencies and departments. I tried to find out who those guys were and what they did. I wanted 'em to remember my name when I called 'em and it wasn't from the White House."

For the most part people in government fall into some middle ground, their survival process and their networks not explicitly corrupting (the way being in Bobby Baker's survival network would be), but always in mind. Most people in Washington know they will live on on the strengths of their contacts and their reputation, so as they go about their jobs they naturally build up their strengths in those two areas. As a result they're one degree blander, one degree more technocratic, than they might otherwise be—and so, therefore, is the federal government.

'WHO DO YOU ANSWER?'

Anybody with an important job in government deals constantly with two facts of life: that more people want to make contact with him than he has time for, and that he has a built-in constituency of interest groups that he must deal with. "I never understood the access issue before," says Onek, "but I began to notice it in the transition. On a busy day, which isn't every day, on those days, you see what it's like. I come back to my office and there are 20 phone messages on my desk and I don't have time to return them all. Who do you answer? Your friends. People who are well-known. People you have a professional relationship with. Staffers on the Hill. That experience has given me a sense of how Washington works."

Why grant access? That gets back to survival. In the simplest formulation, you might give access to those who can help you survive in the future. But Onek is certainly not going to leave his job to work for the American Medical Association, so it's subtler than that. First of all, you'll stay in touch with your community—the cluster of groups that have to do with your job, not only the businesses but the foundations and the trade press and the think tanks. Second, and more broadly, there's that pan-Washington sense of shared enterprise. When Clark Clifford calls the White House you'll probably call back, not because you want to work for his law firm but because he's just a long-standing part of Washington, somebody you'd like to know. Not many people of integrity will make a decision based solely on the expectation of a future favor. But just about everybody tries, in a general way, to be nice, because of a vague sense that anybody might, in the fluid world of Washington, be a good person to have a friendly relationship with.

Reputation is even more subtly managed than contacts, and probably even more important to the way government works. One White House aide, not Onek, asked how you build a reputation that will insure your survival, started to list adjectives. You want to be reasonable, he said. Cool. Cogent. Toughminded. Responsible. Pragmatic. Visible within government, though invisible in the press. Expert. Tolerant. You have to be able to size up complicated situations, to understand the forces coursing through Washington and make them work for you. The ability to compromise. The ability to move events.

What kind of reputation won't help you survive? You can't be a blatant self-aggrandizer. It's bad to be disloyal, the kind of person who testifies against the administration. People remember that kind of thing. It's bad to be partisan. Emotional. Uncontrolled. Irresponsible.

That last is really the key word, and those who don't survive well are usually those who have committed the sin of irresponsibility. Daniel Ellsberg, for instance, behaved very irresponsibily in the late 60s and early 70s, while Cyrus Vance was responsible, not popping off, working through channels. Look where each is now. Rep. Ken Hechler of West Virginia, who left his seat in 1976 to run unsuccessfully for governor, was one of the first politicians to stand up on the mine safety issue, but on the other hand he's flamboyant and a little strange. So when he recently tried (unsuccessfully) to win his old seat back, all Washington backed the incumbent, a responsible young man named Nick Joe Rahall.

"There's a sense," says one person high up in the government, "that the people and issues you deal with are all part of a world that you want to remain a part of." Everybody in Washington knows what it takes to stay in that world, and just about everybody plays by the rules.

The Seductions of Washington Society

James Fallows

"Too many have had to suffer at the hands of a political and economic elite who have shaped decisions and never had to account for mistakes nor to suffer from injustice. When unemployment prevails, they never stand in line looking for a job. When deprivation results from a confused welfare system, they never do without food or clothing or a place to sleep. When the public schools are inferior or torn by strife, their children go to exclusive private schools.

"And when the bureaucracy is bloated and confused the powerful always manage to discover and occupy niches of special influence and privilege."

James Fallows recently resigned as President Carter's chief speechwriter to become Washington editor of *The Atlantic.*

That is what Jimmy Carter says he's going to change in Washington, and God bless him for it. But as one surveys the wreckage of all the bright idealists who came to the capital determined to change it and never left because they had been seduced, one fears that there may be a few more obstacles than Carter has considered.

Some of them are obvious. But one of the most important, and least frequently discussed, is the power of social class.

In a nation nominally free of hereditary rank and privilege, the power of class rests on a kind of voluntary bondage. It is the power of those on the top to prey on the social and intellectual insecurities of those on the bottom; its goal is to make the lower orders believe in their own inferiority.

In Washington, the process is somewhat more delicate, since it is a minuet performed among different layers of the national upper class. But over the years, the city's upper crust has proved itself marvelously adept at using this weapon. One real life example may serve: a lawyer for a corporate firm holds salons, where the distinguished from several walks of life get together. At a typical gathering there might be one member of the White House staff, a liberal Democratic congressman, the editors of two respected magazines, a film director, and representatives of the city's old-rich and rich-rich elements. It is the many worlds of culture all in one place, and how mutually flattering it is to everyone involved.

Every member of such a group gets a little and gives a little as he rubs elbows with the wonderful. The White House staffers—the Jody Powells and Hamilton Jordans of the future—give the most, in terms of power and prestige, but they also get the most, in fulfillment of long-smothered dreams. There is no doubt no insecurity so painful, so deep, that someone in the group cannot at least temporarily assuage it. Was your wife frozen out by the Junior League in Atlanta? Well come right here, and meet the directors of the Washington Junior League. Have you silently chafed because your accent is bad and your college degree worse? Here are six famous professors, who are obviously flattered to be talking to you. Have you dreamed of being an intellectual and an author? Here is the editor of the magazine that used to leave you cowed, now asking your considered judgment about Carter's new populism. Have you lived in the valley and yearned for the house on the hill? Mr. Wellborn, who happens to own a bank, may help you out with your mortgage. Whatever impediments of ambition or insecurity that the Carter men bring into Washington, there are those in town who can give them relief.

It is possible that Jimmy Carter is immune to all blandishments. The man who ran for President because he lost his awe for the competition is not the one to need reassurance and flattery. It is possible, too, that his aides will work 20 hours a day for his cause and have no time left over for frivolity or socializing.

But if history and common sense are any guide, the Carter aides may find that they need some of the things that Washington's higher society can provide. At the convention, they trooped around with Hunter Thompson; they celebrated at 21. Hamilton Jordan has already tried (and as of the convention had failed), to get a book contract and extend his fame to the world of the intellect. Margot Hahn, a prominent local hostess, gave Rosalyn Carter hints on where to find *the* right dresses in New York, so that she would not run the risk of being embarrassed at the convention.

PERILOUS FRIENDS

If Carter's people do embrace the social groups, there are several dangers at hand. One is that they lose interest in challenging the group that offers them so much. It has happened to good men before; one first-rate reporter got a publisher's advance for a book about Washington's mighty figures, and several years later had to mail it back because the subjects had become his friends. It is both a matter of civility and a question of status; one is judged, often enough, by the quality of one's friends, and with friends that are the best in town, there is small reason to offend gratuitously.

There is a further delicious subtlety, which is that many of these new friends will be genuinely loyal. They are the people who will not let you down, when the dark hour arrives and it is time to go home again. Four years, eight years, may seem like forever when the administration is new, but all around are reminders that this glory too will pass. There, at the corner table, is the man who was a big shot in the Truman years. That man, holding his glasses and massaging the bridge of his nose, had the town at his feet when Kennedy was in the White House. They thought it would last too.

But it did not last, and when it was over they did not want it to end for them. California and Missouri and Texas might have been enough before, but not now. Friends were in Washington; the action was in Washington; the sense of belonging to the class that caused events rather than reacting to them, could only be found here, or in the metropolis stretching north to Boston. Walter Jenkins went home, and so did Bob Finch, but they were the exceptions. The Carter men will learn that it is a much longer trip from Washington to Georgia than it seemed on the way up.

Learning this, prudent men look for safety nets. They realize that a group of well-connected friends can keep them in town. Their friends will help them find the berths—in the good law firms, on the Hill, at the World Bank, with Brookings—that enable them to hang on. Without friends they might be left in the cold.

As they learn, the White House men step carefully. They are less willing to upset the applecart of the group. And there is a second danger, which is that exchanges are being made. Most of them are intangible—your political power for my intellectual prestige—but some involve hard trading as well. The basic pattern is one dear to our culture, in the form of the small town Rotary Club. You buy from the Rotarian druggist, he goes to the Rotarian lawyer, the lawyer comes to your Rotarian store. You all overcharge each other a little, but the group helps ensure the survival of each member. The problem that arises when the pattern is transferred to Washington is that some of the Rotarians are public servants. What they have to exchange is not theirs but the public's. The banker offers his preferential mortgages, and the lawyer his services, but only the men from the White House and the Hill have the public favors to dispense.

FRAILTIES OF THE SPIRIT

What hope, then, for the Carter men? One rule is that they should not allow it to become important to them to get invited *back,* to the Harrimans or the Fritcheys or the Grahams. They should not shut themselves off from social intercourse, in the fashion of H. R. (Bob) Haldeman or I. F. (Izzy) Stone; there is too much they lose in the process, it becomes too hard to know what other people think. But they must by wary of IOUs they are running up and the commitments they are making. The only gift they should let themselves give is their presence—and even that only with caution and control. Some Washingtonians are perfectly capable of parlaying that presence into the appearance of influence that they can then peddle, sometimes with such discretion that only another cynical Washingtonian will recognize what's going on.

These temptations are hard to own up to, let alone to control. In my first years at college I wasted a lot of money and even more time on a luncheon society for the more "creative" students. As soon as decency allowed, old members angling for your initiation fee pointed out that T. S. Eliot had been a member in his undergraduate days. The rest was left to Aristotelian syllogism: T. S. Eliot was a member; I am a member; therefore. . . . The same thing, of course, applies to the dinner parties that the luncheon society was meant to prepare me for, and to which Carter's people will no doubt be invited: Why, Averell Harriman's here, the thought will run, and Jackie Onassis is here, and over across the way is John Kenneth Galbraith, so that must mean that I. . . .

The reason for dwelling on these frailties of the spirit is that they do hold much of the key to Carter's success. If his men don't deal with these problems, they will become part of the "Washington" their leader wants to change. Once that happens, they are helpless to produce their reforms.

To end on a bright note, we might point out that so far the Carter staff has shown the right spirit. Richard Reeves has reported on an incident that, if its philosophy persists, will keep the newcomers out of trouble:

"Ann Pincus, a Washington hostess of some note, met Hamilton Jordan for the first time in an elevator at the Americana Hotel during the first day of the Democratic National Convention. 'We'll be getting to know each other much better in Washington,' she said. 'By the way, are you called Jordan or Jerdan?'

"'My friends call me Jerdan,' he said smiling. 'But you can call me Jordan.'"

Afterword

After a year and a half of the Carter Administration, it was clear that the President and the First Lady had almost no interest in social life and preferred to spend their rare non-working hours with their immediate family. The top White House staff members from Georgia, especially Hamilton Jordan, have gotten a reputation for aggressively ignoring, or going out of their way to spurn, Washington society—though this behavior is usually taken to mean that Washington society does have an effect on them, if a negative one. The majority of the White House staff lived in Washington before the 1976 election and has fit in better. The final chapter of the story—what Carter and the people around him will do after they leave the White House—has, of course, yet to unfold.

Money Doesn't Talk in Washington

Walter Shapiro

The inflated federal salary structure has made Washington a uniquely well-off community. Washington residents support some of the highest real estate prices in the country without visible strain. It isn't surprising to see young federal workers getting into Porsche convertibles when their workday ends at 4:45. Neiman-Marcus has just opened a new Washington

Walter Shapiro is a special Assistant to Ray Marshall, the Secretary of Labor.

branch. Even the lowly hamburger now routinely costs $3.95 in the plant-filled California-style bars that have become a Washington institution.

But Washington's affluence can be exaggerated. Money plays a different role here than it does in other prosperous American cities. To be sure, Washington is the easiest city in the country in which to make $30,000 a year, a sum most Americans can only dream of. To be sure, government executives get perquisites that the rest of us don't. Still, this is a city where the role models and celebrities, people like cabinet officers and Supreme Court justices, make around $65,000, a fraction of what the role models and celebrities in other cities make. The monetary distinctions between people are not as broad in Washington as they are in most places.

As a result, while government officials are well off by any overall standard, few have enough money to be able to flaunt it. The implications of this situation are important and they are little understood by outsiders. Bert Lance, for instance, is one outsider who never understood, and his financial behavior in Washington stood in sharp contrast to the prevailing ethic.

By all accounts, Lance is a paragon of conspicuous consumption. A *Washington Post* profile of him, written the day he was named director of the Office of Management and Budget, quoted one friend as saying, "He is a little too impressed by money and powerful people." Another described Lance as a "millionaire who enjoys being a millionaire." In Atlanta, Lance and his wife, LaBelle, had entertained lavishly at their 50-room mansion, Butterfly Manna. Atlantans still talk about one dinner party at which the guests were invited in shifts because the dining room at the Manna only sat 50 people. The Lances summered at a $100,000 vacation home in Sea Island, Georgia. There were occasional weekends at their $150,000 estate in Calhoun. And every spring, without fail, Bert and LaBelle went to Paris.

LaBelle is a key to understanding her husband. She is a banker's granddaughter whose family eventually allowed Bert to take over the Calhoun National Bank, and many of Lance's financial pyrotechnics seem little more than the efforts of an insecure man to prove to his in-laws that he was good enough to deserve to marry into the family. It is revealing that many of the overdrafts that later caused Lance trouble were on checks written by LaBelle's relatives. For example, LaBelle's brother Claude is estimated to have had $300,000 in overdrafts at the Calhoun National Bank. Another brother, Beverly, had—when he committed suicide—$70,000 in overdrafts and $170,000 in loans. LaBelle's mother and stepfather also had sizable loans and overdrafts. The same intra-family insecurity may have lain behind the zeal of Lance's conspicuous consumption in Atlanta.

But Atlanta was surely part of it too. It's a city where only two things really matter—family and money (or, at least, the appearance of having money). Because Lance's family lacked pedigree, the money, and its display, became even more important. What Lance didn't realize when he came into the government is that Washington is worlds removed from Atlanta. While no one spurns money or family here, those attributes pale in comparison to political power. Washington hostesses have endured—even pandered to—some of the world's most graceless boors because they were senators, Cabinet members, or friends of the President.

ALL HE COULD EVER WANT

So Lance didn't really need to try to impress anyone when he came to Washington—his friendship with Jimmy Carter gave him all the glamour he could ever want. But it's clear that he and LaBelle sincerely believed that because of his position he had to live a certain way. No matter that his governmnet salary was a far cry from his income as the president of the National Bank of Georgia. No matter that he was in debt to his eyebrows. No matter that the value of his stock was plummeting daily.

Lance was one of the rare Carter Administration officials who decided to live in Georgetown. He rented a house on Dumbarton Street from Washington socialite and former Miss America Yolande Fox. This was an unnecessary extravagance because Lance didn't understand that Washington has created an environment designed to make high government officials feel confortable on upper-middle-class incomes.

It would be impossible to enjoy fully all the luxuries of New York or Atlanta or Dallas or Los Angeles on an income comparable to a government salary. These are cities that belong to upper-level business executives and people with accumulated capital; each of them has stores, restaurants, neighborhoods, and private clubs that are out of the reach of people who live on $65,000 a year. There are few such barriers in Washington.

Look at some members of the ruling class here. Hamilton Jordan or Tim Kraft would be a priceless ornament at any Washington party, but neither seems to have anything in the bank. Patrick Leahy is a senator from Vermont who chairs the Senate subcommittee that determines the city of Washington's budget. Earlier in 1977 Leahy opened his personal financial records to *The Wall Street Journal,* which reported that his monthly after-tax income is $2,673. After retirement and other deductions, Leahy's take-home pay shrinks to $2,119. People like this cannot be made to feel uncomfortable in the city that they rule, so even those few Washingtonians who really are wealthy generally don't broadcast it.

The absence of the obviously rich has spawned a few democratic customs in Washington that tend to startle outsiders. New York businessmen arriving in Washington on the Metroliner often unfavorably compare the taxicab situation at Union Station to that of a developing country. Other cities have a one-man-one-cab policy; Washington encourages group riding. Arriving train passengers are shoved into waiting taxis in groups of five to wend their way through downtown Washington as if they were on a lost jitney bus. Even those lucky few who get a cab to themselves are accustomed to having it pull over in the middle of the ride to pick up another fare or two. Group riding may not be elegant, but it is one mechanism that Washington uses to maintain some of the lowest cab fares in the country.

A STATE OF NEAR-HYSTERIA

New York restaurants and businessmen are currently in a state of near-hysteria about President Carter's determination to curb the tax deduction for expense-account lunches. That change will have a far less devastating impact on Washington's lunch habits. No one in the federal government has an expense account, (although the best-known can be taken out by journalists on *their* expense accounts) and the lunch prices of even the best restaurants are pegged toward what high government officials can afford out of their own pockets.

Washington's servant problem is that most high government officials can't afford them. In a rare gesture of financial realism, even LaBelle Lance did without them in her nine months in Washington. She did, however, complain to Sally Quinn of *The Washington Post* about how difficult it is to live without help. Democratic ideology, perhaps born out of financial necessity, plays a role as well. If you were to tell a prominent banker or lawyer in New Orleans, for example, that it is possible to dine at the home of one of the most powerful people in Washington and be expected to help clear the table, he would be shocked. (It is true, however, that part-time cleaning ladies are popular here.)

THE OPEN CITY

The increasingly prominent social role of the press adds a further democratic leavening to Washington. Prominent journalists are people whose social entree depends on the institutions they represent, rather than on their income or social prominence of their families. In fact, because your status depends mostly on your job, Washington is generally a very open city socially. New York bankers and Grosse Pointe auto executives live in tight social spheres that are difficult for outsiders to penetrate. But one friend of mine arrived in Washington a few months ago, immediately crashed a reception, and found himself chattering amiably with Clark

Clifford, that impeccable symbol of status and authority in Washington. Clifford saw nothing odd in patiently answering the questions of a total stranger at a Washington cocktail party.

Not only does Washington not demand most of the conventional badges of having made it big—it outright frowns on some of them. This is not, for example, a city of flashy dressers. Some White House aides don't have to wear a tie to work, and even a Cabinet officer needs nothing more than three or four suits, purchased off the rack, and a serviceable tuxedo. Taste in Washington is dictated by department stores, not expensive designers. Dressing too well can stimulate as much comment as dressing badly. Ron Dellums, who has a large wardrobe of designer clothes, is the continuing object of jokes about his tailor.

In most American cities, private schools for your children are another determinant of social status. That at first appears to be true in the Washington area too—even the presence of Amy Carter hasn't stimulated much interest among middle-class parents, black or white, in sending their children to public schools in the District of Columbia. But this isn't due to snobbery; in fact, Washington may be the only city in the country where sending children to private schools is a source of embarrassment for parents. It's just that the District's public schools are the worst in the country. In the Maryland and Virginia suburbs, most parents great and small send their children to public schools, and these schools are of high quality.

PRIVATE CLUBS

Then there's the matter of private clubs. Griffin Bell's long-standing membership in two Atlanta clubs (the Piedmont Driving Club and the Capital City Club) stirred up a controversy because these clubs discriminated against Jews and blacks. At the time, Bell expressed concern over resigning because he feared losing the $10,000 he had paid in initiation fees.

Clubs play a role in Washington society as well, but any prominent political figure is practically guaranteed admission to every club in town, aside from a couple of isolated islands of snobbery. And high initiation fees are rare in Washington. When Tongsun Park (with the help of Washington luminaries like Tommy Corcoran and Anna Chennault) established The Georgetown Club in 1966 as a base for his lobbying efforts, he kept dues artificially low. Even today, with Park gone from the scene, the club's initiation fee is $800 for a couple and the annual dues are $450. Dining at Pisces, another club in Georgetown that Park helped found, is a sure-fire way to get mentioned in the society columns of *The Washington Post* and *The Washington Star,* but initiation costs only about as much as a color television set.

So here we have a city that's a paradise for the upper reaches of the middle class. If the will of the people has placed limits on the salaries of major government officials, the local ambiance has compensated by making cabs and clubs inexpensive and servants, private schools, and custom-made suits unnecessary. Washington is a city where it's easy to keep up with the Joneses.

This climate has some salutary effects on government. Despite the multitude of scandals in Washington in recent years, there have been relatively few cases of large sums of money changing hands for personal, rather than campaign, use. The scandals have involved alcoholism, sex, free plane rides, illegal campaign contributions, and expensive gifts from mysterious Koreans. But it is an index of the relative unimportance of money in Washington that there have been few cases of outright bribery.

Smart lobbyists know that attitudes toward money in Washington are hopelessly middle-class. If a congressman took a cash bribe, he would probably feel compelled to put the money aside for his children's college education. The way to a public official's heart is through his ego, not his wallet. The best lobbyists influence officials by making them feel that they're important, that they've arrived, that they have legions of warm and admiring friends. Park is infamous for his outright gifts, but whatever success he achieved probably came more from his dispersing of club memberships and sponsorship of warm and elegant parties. Cynics often claim that money talks, but in Washington it just mumbles, barely audible under the din of power and prestige.

part 2
THE PRESIDENT
AND HIS MEN

The state of the Presidency under Jimmy Carter is a little confusing. Under Presidents Kennedy, Johnson, and Nixon, we realized how immensely powerful the office had become. To use the most obvious example from those years, it became clear that a President could wage a war if he wanted to without extensive consultation with anyone else in the government. So it was clearly important to understand the little world in which the President operated.

This pursuit led, first, to the disturbing conclusions that Russell Baker and Charles Peters draw in their "The Prince and His Courtiers: At the White House, the Kremlin, and the Reichschancellery." The White House is in many ways like any other court—proximity to the king is so alluring that people will do anything to get and keep it. Those closest to the President thus will become craven flatterers, sealing him off from whatever enemies and failures lurk beyond the walls, constantly reminding him of his assets, serving his every whim, intriguing against one another, never disagreeing with the chief. So before long a President has very little knowledge about the true nature of the problems he's supposed to be solving, and tremendous power to act according to the misinformation he does have.

This is the culture of the White House, and interacting with it are the characters of the individual Presidents. James David Barber, after carefully studying the lives of the twentieth-century Presidents, has concluded that each one's experiences and his character have had an important effect on how he governs—and that we are governed worst when negative-minded men are able, because of the power of the office, to govern in isolation and paranoia.

Carter was well aware of these hazards when he took office. He told reporters that Arthur Schlesinger's "The Imperial Presidency" and Barber's "The Presidential Character" were two of his favorite books, and he made a great effort in the first months of his administration to do away with the White House's imperial trappings. Of course, Carter is still isolated, and his administration to date is very much a product of his character; what has changed is that he seems much less powerful than his predecessors.

There are several reasons for this apparent powerlessness, but perhaps the most important is that Carter has not been able to take control of the workings of the departments and agencies of the executive branch of the government. The way a President can do this is through the 2000 or so people he is allowed to appoint to top-level positions in the government. Carter hasn't got those people under his control.

These political appointees have a character and a culture all their own. In "Gentlemen in Waiting" Tom Bethell describes one group of them maneuvering for jobs in the next administration during the 1976 campaign (successfully, as it turned out). They are experts whose desire to serve in the high reaches of government is far stronger than their commitment to any particular candidate or set of policies. And once they take office, they encounter a situation where it's hard to get anything at all done —the situation Walter Shapiro (a special assistant to a Cabinet secretary, writing under a pseudonym) describes in "Strangers in a Strange Land."

To borrow Professor Barber's terminology, Carter is an active President who runs a passive administration. As the essay on Carter that closes this section shows, the White House is a beehive of activity. Carter, fanatically organized and a stickler for detail, spends his days in a whirlwind of briefings and memos, deciding on thousands of policy options, putting forth major programs every month or so according to a clockwork schedule. The problem is, after that disappointingly little happens.

The Prince and His Courtiers: At the White House, the Kremlin, and the Reichschancellery

Russell Baker and Charles Peters

The analogy between the modern presidency and the royal European court, bewigged, bejeweled, and beset with intrigue, is not original with George Reedy, but he is the first to alarm us with notice that court government is undergoing a 20th-century rebirth in the White House. This renaissance of the princely court, Reedy insists, is breeding immense danger for American government, for much the same reason that the 17th- and 18th-century courts of Western Europe contributed to the development of violent revolutions.

In both France and England, our immediate political forebears, kings lost their heads because they had become unable to sense or hear the intent and passion of their peoples through the barriers of courts erected to glorify and, ironically, to protect them. Reedy suggests that the presidency is in somewhat the same danger, and for essentially the same reasons.

The president, needing "access to reality" in order to govern effectively, too often has access, instead, only to a self-serving court of flunkeys, knights, earls, and dukes in business suits, whose best chances of advancing their separate fortunes usually lie in diverting reality before it can reach the president. The result is a dangerous presidential isolation, which may be compounded in its peril because court life works to persuade the president that he is more closely in touch with reality than anyone else in the realm.

Russell Baker writes the "Observer" column in *The New York Times*. Charles Peters is editor of *The Washington Monthly*.

Thus, we had those repeated assertions from Lyndon Johnson that only the president had all the facts on which to base decisions about Vietnam, when in truth he lacked the first fact that was most essential of all for a leader and easiest to learn outside the White House court: to wit, that his people were not behind him as he waded deeper and deeper into the quagmire. This isolation from reality kept Lyndon Johnson and Richard Nixon obsessed with Southeast Asia as a prime problem of government at a time when very few among the people could sustain more than a flickering interest in it, and then only when aroused by White House theatrics.

Reedy suggests that the presidency may be confronted, if not with the headsman or guillotinist, with an institutional arteriosclerosis no less fatal at a time when the interests of government seem increasingly alien to the interests of the governed.

When Reedy's book was first published, its importance as a work of political science was discounted by some reviewers on grounds that Reedy, as a member of the Johnson staff, had based his treatise on a singularly peculiar presidency, one in which parallels to the Sun King were ludicrously easy to draw.

Reedy's discussion of courtiers insulating the president against reality was taken by many readers as sour grapes, a subtle intellectual's way of taking his vengeance upon the cleverer players of the court game who had eased him into retirement. John Roche, who stayed with President Johnson's staff to the end, refers with mild contempt to the notion that presidential staff aides can seriously be likened to royal courtiers.

Members of the Kennedy circle—that strange, apparently indissoluble court in search of a king—contend that Johnson was, of course, susceptible to royal isolation by slick courtiers. But not their man, not Jack. The court analogy had no validity when applied to a president of superior competence.

And yet. . . . And yet. . . .

There were signs, not altogether superficial, that the development of something remarkably like court life had been rapidly accelerating at the White House since the arrival of Franklin Roosevelt. With Roosevelt, the presidency—for reasons not too difficult to understand in an era that was dotting the rest of the earth with strutting Caesars—entered a period of apotheosis. There had been strong presidents before, but now we were embarked on the time of the strong presidency, a time which is still with us.

THE TRAPPINGS OF COURT

In sheer body density alone, the insulation around the presidency has thickened rapidly. Herbert Hoover had a staff of only 42 persons. A generation later, General Eisenhower, who prided himself on taut administration, had more than 2,000. Under Kennedy and Johnson, foreign-policy management groups were moved into the White House, and institutional divisions between domestic- and foreign-policy barons began to develop. In the Nixon White House, an expanding foreign policy dukedom was established under Henry Kissinger with a staff of his own moving in independent orbit around Kissinger, who simultaneously maintains a great-lord's orbit around the president in the larger White House universe.

The trappings of court began, simultaneously, to multiply. The custom-built carriages, magnificently engineered automobiles built expressly for the White House. Great ocean-spanning jets kept constantly at the ready. Special helicopters. Presidential appearances were preceded and surrounded by the inevitable, ineffectual showing of the private presidential bodyguard. Security at the White House thickened. First, there were the gates through which ordinary mortals might not step. Inside, the lobbies swarmed with hangers-on, most especially the press, waiting for some emanation to filter out from the ruler burrowed deep behind offices occupied by gentlemen of ascending importance. The elite might have entree to the Oval Room, equivalent of the Royal Bedchamber. For the sub-elite there were certain Presence Chambers where the Presidential Magnificence might be seen in the flesh, might indeed grant the boon of a smile, of a casual "Hi, there!" to the fortunate. And there was the White House Mess, where the etiquette of who might eat at what table was of an intricacy that would surely have bemused Louis XIV.

American fears of monarchy at the head of government are familiar to schoolboys—the debate at the beginning about how the leader of the new country should be styled, the fears of the more republican founders that the president might develop into a king and that the seat of government might develop into a court.

These fears survived from memories of the abuses of the English court of the 17th and 18th centuries, at which people and Parliament were frequently dealt with according to the advice of some royal favorite, whose grasp of statecraft ended with a mastery of sycophancy. The most notoriously inept of the courtiers whimsically given power by kings was perhaps the Duke of Buckingham, who seems to have bewitched King James I with his male beauty and skills at flattery and royal companionship. Buckingham survived James to continue incompetent government into the reign of King Charles I. When Buckingham was eventually murdered, all England lit bonfires to honor his murderer. The experience of such government, repeated in differing degrees in the reigns of Charles II and James II and later under the Hanovers, was part of the intellectual heritage of the men who founded the Republic. Hence, the distaste for courts.

Reedy's thesis holds that the time the Founders feared may have arrived at last, unnoted under all the mock-serious political uproar about kings, tyrants, and courtiers that has been part of the currency of political campaigning throughout American history. Reedy, in fact, gives us a full-length portrait of the courtier's life at the modern presidential court.

And what is a courtier's life like at the White House? Why, surprising to tell, not terribly different from court life at the Reichschancellery in the reign of Adolf Hitler, where a courtier's life was surprisingly like life in the Kremlin, at the court of Josef Stalin.

SERVILITY BECOMES ENDEMIC

By an extraordinary publishing coincidence, Reedy's memoir appeared in the same year (1970) that Albert Speer and Nikita Khrushchev gave us their memoirs of life at the top in Germany and Russia.* Neither the Speer nor Khrushchev book concerns itself consciously with court life under Hitler and Stalin; yet, when they are read in context with Reedy, we are startled to discover that the styles of government being described by all three are remarkably alike.

At each court, for example, we find the leader, or prince, treated with a deference approaching reverence, which must inevitably tempt all but the humblest souls (who are rarely to be found running large aggressive states) to assume they possess a superiority bordering on divinity. In time, the man treated with such distinction begins to expect it as his due. The sycophantic Buckingham repeatedly signed his notes to the king, "Your faithful slave and dog," and James seems never to have told him that a friend's groveling was embarrassing to the king. Jack Valenti, who knew his man as well as anyone in Washington, knew that Lyndon Johnson would not bridle if Valenti told the world he slept better for knowing Johnson was in the White House. Princes, whether monarchist, fascist, communist, or democratic, become accustomed to feeling like very special people.

Reedy writes of the White House:

There is built into the presidency a series of devices that tend to remove the occupant of the Oval Room from all of the forces which require most men to rub up against the hard facts of life on a daily basis. The life of the White House is the life of a court. It is a structure designed for one purpose and one purpose only—to serve the material needs and the desires of a single man. . . .

He is treated with all the reverence due a monarch. No one interrupts presidential contemplation for anything less than a major catastrophe somewhere on the globe. No one speaks to him unless spoken to first. No one ever

The Twilight of the Presidency by George E. Reedy—World Publishing, 197 pages. *Inside the Third Reich*, Memoirs by Albert Speer—The Macmillan Company, 675 pages. *Khrushchev Remembers*, translated and edited by Strobe Talbott—Little, Brown and Company, 618 pages.

invites him to "go soak your head" when his demands become petulant and unreasonable.

Speer found a similar condition under Hitler. He writes:

There is a special trap for every holder of power. . . . His favor is so desirable to his subordinates that they will sue for it by every means possible. Servility becomes endemic among his entourage, who compete among themselves in their show of devotion. This exercises a sway over the ruler who becomes corrupted in turn.

And in Moscow, at about the same time Speer and colleagues were competing to persuade the Fuehrer of his surpassing excellence, Khrushchev and comrades in Moscow were busily laboring to show Stalin that there was no duty more vital for them than humoring his whims. At the end of a brutally exhausting day, Khrushchev recalls:

We would meet either in his study at the Kremlin or, more often, in the Kremlin movie theater. Stalin used to select the movies himself. . . . When a movie ended, Stalin would suggest, "Well, let's go get something to eat, why don't we?" By now it was usually one or two o'clock in the morning. It was time to go to bed. . . . But everyone would say, yes, he was hungry, too. This lie was like a reflex. We would all get into our cars and drive to the dacha.

UNCOMFORTABLE TRUTHS

The prince, having become accustomed through the assurances of the courtiers to the sensation of being an extraordinary human being, becomes more difficult to deal with at certain times. One such time is the moment when an uncomfortable truth is delievered at the palace door. A courtier's first instinct is to protect the prince, and there are rationalizations for doing so in the unwritten court protocols, as Reedy notes:

It is felt that this man is grappling with problems of such tremendous consequence that every effort must be made to relieve him of the irritations that vex the average citizen.

It vexes the average citizen, fully aware of his own incompetence, to be forced to dwell upon the fact that in life, things frequently don't work out. Imagine, then, the difficulty of having to confront a prince, conditioned to believe in his peculiarly excellent superiority, with the fact that his policy is failing. There must be many of Lyndon Johnson's dukes and earls who, remembering the Vietnam years, would find it possible to sympathize with Hermann Goering's lines in an anecdote by Speer.

About to board his train to leave Berlin, Goering was visited by General Adolf Galland. Goering took the occasion to reprimand Galland for having told Hitler that American fighter planes had penetrated German territory. Galland said they would soon be flying even deeper into Germany. "Fantasies!" Goering said. Galland said American fighters had already been shot down at Aachen. "Impossible!" said Goering. And yet, Galland insisted, the downed planes were at Aachen.

> Goering finally declared: "What must have happened is that they were shot down much farther to the west. I mean, if they were very high when they were shot down they could have glided quite a distance farther before they crashed."
> Not a muscle moved in Galland's face. "Glided to the east, sir? If my plane were shot up. . . ."
> "Now then, Herr Galland," Goering fulminated, trying to put an end to the debate, "I officially assert that the American fighter planes did not reach Aachen."
> The General ventured a last statement. "But, sir, they were there!"
> At this point Goering's self-control gave way. "I herewith give you an official order that they weren't there! Do you understand? The American fighters were not there! Get that! I intend to report that to the Fuehrer."

It can't happen here? After the Sontay raid failed to discover a single American prisoner of war, much less rescue one, Secretary of Defense Laird went to the White House. What was this? A failure? Not at all, Laird explained. It had been a triumph for American intelligence.

Communism occasionally has the bad news problem, too; and apparently deals with it just as fascists and democrats do.

Khrushchev tells a story that had been told to him by Mikoyan. Demchenko, a member of the Ukrainian Politburo, called on Mikoyan in Moscow.

> Here's what Demchenko said: "Anastas Ivanovich, does Comrade Stalin—for that matter, does anyone in the Politburo—know what's happening in the Ukraine? A train recently pulled into Kiev loaded with corpses of people who had starved to death. It had picked up corpses all the way from Poltava to Kiev. I think somebody had better inform Stalin about this situation."
> You can see what an abnormal state of affairs had developed when someone like Demchenko, a member of the Ukrainian Politboro, was afraid to go see Stalin himself.

Actually, according to the evidence of our three memoirists, it wasn't abnormal at all. Rather than disturb the prince by becoming the delivery agent for bad news, and thus perhaps lose favor, the courtier elects to withhold from him information essential to realistic policy decisions. Or, to put it more bluntly, his own interests are placed above the interests of the prince and the state he professes to serve.

Experienced courtsmen may find it naive that anyone should expect them to behave otherwise. The rationale has been finely worked out; it has been articulated many times by men explaining why they chose not to voice their dissent from the Johnson war policy. Open dissent ends one's chance to exercise his benign influence within the government, and creates job openings to be filled by less high-minded men. In brief, he who runs away shall live to run away another day.

THE KEYS TO THE KINGDOM

Reedy, Khrushchev, and Speer give us comparable pictures of the advancing corruption created in the courtiers by their impulse to establish and protect their intimacy with the leader.

The White House assistants, writes Reedy, constitute "the greatest of all barriers to presidential access to reality." For them:

> ... there is only one fixed goal in life. It is somehow to gain and maintain access to the President. This is a process which resembles nothing else known in the world except possibly the Japanese game of *go*, a contest in which there are very few fixed rules and the playing consists of laying down alternating counters in patterns that permit flexibility but seek to deny that flexibility to the opponent. The success of the player depends upon the whim of the President. Consequently, the President's psychology is studied minutely, and a working day in the White House is marked by innumerable probes to determine which routes to the Oval Room are open and which end in a blind alley.

This world sounds remarkably like the court of King James I, at which the Catholic faction, finding the King between favorites and knowing his weakness for handsome young men, kept thrusting a lovely young man of their choosing across the King's path, in hopes of obtaining the keys to the kingdom.

In Johnson's White House, the technique at least must have been rather duller. The basic method, Reedy reports, was "to be present either personally or by a proxy piece of paper when 'good news' arrives and to be certain that someone else is present when the news is bad."

Speer found precisely the same principle at work around Hitler. Writing of Martin Bormann, his *bête noire,* he states:

> Bormann followed the simple principle of always remaining in closest proximity to the source of all grace and favor. He accompanied Hitler to the Berghof

and on trips, and in the Chancellery never left his side until Hitler went to bed in the early morning hours. . . .

The powerful men under Hitler were already jealously watching one another like so many pretenders to the throne. Quite early there were struggles for position among Goebbels, Goering, Rosenberg, Ley, Himmler, Ribbentrop, and Hess. . . . But none of them recognized a threat in the shape of trusty Borman. He had succeeded in representing himself as insignificant while imperceptibly building up his bastions.

"To be close to Stalin," Khurshchev remembers, "this seemed to be the crowning moment of my career."

And elsewhere, "I believed that everything Stalin said in the name of the party was inspired by genius, and that I had only to apply it to my own life." As this comment suggests, the courtier may, at some early stage in the relationship, develop such a psychological identity with his particular prince that he will abandon his own judgment and, like a lover, submerge his identity in that of the prince. The sweet delirium of ecstasy is produced when the prince returns the worship with some small gesture of recognition.

"For me to speak with the idol of a nation," writes Speer, "to discuss building plans with him, sit beside him in the theater, or eat ravioli with him in the Osteria" was simply "overwhelming."

"Now I was completely under Hitler's spell, unreservedly and unthinkingly held by him. I was ready to follow him anywhere."

On occasion, when Speer would greet Hitler with, "Heil, Mein Fuehrer!" Hitler would reply with, "Heil, Speer!" At such moments, Speer recalls, he felt "as if a medal had been conferred upon me. . . . All the intrigues and struggles for power were directed toward eliciting such a word, or what it stood for."

YES MR. PRESIDENT, I AGREE

Receiving the recognition and approval of the leader becomes a pleasure so powerful that the strongest of courtiers find it difficult to deny themselves. The empty-headed thrills which the younger Khrushchev and Speer derived from the notice of their leaders may be dismissed as the natural response of innocence in the presence of a celebrity. But what are we to make of the account of a National Security Council meeting under Lyndon Johnson, as recounted by Chester Cooper in *The Lost Crusade?* Cooper writes:

The President, in due course, would announce his decision and then poll everyone in the room—Council members, their assistants, and members of the White House and NSC staffs. "Mr. Secretary, do you agree with the decision?" "Yes, Mr. President." "Mr. X, do you agree?" "I agree, Mr. President." During the process I would frequently fall into a Walter Mitty-like fantasy: When my turn came I would rise to my feet slowly, look around the room and then directly at the President, and say very quietly and emphatically, "Mr. President, gentlemen, I most definitely do *not* agree." But I was removed from my trance when I heard the President's voice saying, "Mr. Cooper, do you agree?" And out would come a "Yes, Mr. President, I agree."

The courtier's need to please his leader often has disastrous consequences for the people on the other end of royal decisions. When the Russians surrounded Hitler's Sixth Army at Stalingrad, at a critical moment in World War II, a black reality began to threaten the Fuehrer's notion that the Wehrmacht could not be defeated. At the timed suggestion of a general, he was even considering an effort to save the Army by breaking out into a retreat until Reichsmarshal Goering entered the room:

> Depressed, with a beseeching note in his voice, Hitler asked him: "What about supplying Stalingrad by air?" Goering snapped to attention and declared solemnly: "My leader! I personally guarantee the supplying of Stalingrad by air. You can rely on that."

His delusion of invincibility thus restored, Hitler would hear no more talk of retreat. He ordered the Sixth Army to stay and fight it out in Stalingrad, where it slowly faced extinction when Goering's promise proved totally fabricated—as everyone on the General Staff knew it would. Finally, a group of generals persuaded Chief of Staff Keitel to recommend to Hitler an evacuation to the Army's helpless survivors. It was the only sane thing to do, and Keitel promised that he would. The courtier's instinct, however, overwhelmed him at the critical moment, as Speer recounts:

> But at the situation conference, when Hitler once again stressed the necessity of holding out in Stalingrad, Keitel strode emotionally toward him, pointed to the map, where a small remnant of the city was surrounded by thick red rings, and declared: "Mein Fuehrer, we will hold that!"

It is enough to make one sympathize with a tyrant, for the determination of his courtiers to deceive him for their own personal ends—if he is aware of it—confronts him with problems as baffling as those posed by an enemy state's diplomacy.

Rarely is combat among the courtiers pursued to much political purpose in these 20th-century courts. Old scores are settled. There is intrigue, jealousy. One may win prerogatives that can be gloated upon. There is the satisfaction of public recognition, of being written about with awe in the press, and other small chaff. On great issues, however, the court is rarely a court in the Elizabethan sense, but rather more like that self-applauding cheering section which modern American politicians like to call a "team." Members are permitted to work out personal rivalries behind the arras, but on issues of substance every man must shape up, and work with the team.

With court struggle fought out along petty personal lines, the courtiers are inevitably reduced to demeaning little maneuvers to protect their backs, while working into good knife position vis-à-vis their immediate opponents.

Bormann, Speer recalls, avoided long business trips and vacations for fear another would insinuate himself during the absence into Bormann's place. "The man with the hedge clippers," Speer calls Bormann. "He was forever using all his energy, cunning, and brutality to prevent anyone from rising above a certain level."

Speer himself was not without skill at the struggle. Hitler often explained the elimination of important men on grounds that they were in ill health. Politicians, therefore, "pricked up their ears" when they heard of Hitler's associates being "sick." And so, to keep his profile discreetly low, Speer, even when he became "really sick," deemed it "advisable to remain as active as possible."

Khrushchev, referring to personal competition for favor in the Kremlin, describes Stalin's men as "tearing at each other's throats." Indeed, as his version of the Beria story reveals, Khrushchev himself, by the time of Stalin's death, had become superbly adept at tearing throats.

"The life of a courtier," Reedy comments, "is to be Sammy Glick or to fight Sammy Glick."

KENNEDY AND O'DONNELL

This composite portrait of the new courts which seem to flourish around great political power in our century explains a great deal about why things go wrong in modern governments. The court imbues the prince with both religious and nationalistic characteristics that make him a figure of awe. ("I support the president," Americans will say, on most issues in which they have no immediate financial or blood interest. It is closely akin to saying, "I support the flag.")

The courtiers tend to identify the prince with the state. ("What is good for Josef Stalin is good for the Soviet Union," to paraphrase the young Khrushchev in American.) To help the state, the courtier must reach a position of intimacy with the prince, and to do this he must block or eliminate other courtiers moving toward the same goal. Above all, he must please the prince. And a prince who has been conditioned to consider himself a quasi-divine blend of flag, cause, and country is most unlikely to be pleased at being exposed too frequently to reality.

The danger becomes obvious, and Reedy has stated it. Our leaders, whatever their ideology, may very possibly be out of touch with the world that the rest of us live in. That hostile grille fence which keeps us away from the White House has two sides. The other seals off the president from the country he thinks he is governing.

As all this suggests, the courtier-prince relationship is almost inevitably corrupting to both parties. Consider the relationship of John Kennedy and one of his finest courtiers, Kenneth O'Donnell. In his memoirs published (last year) in *Life*, O'Donnell stated that Kennedy planned in 1963 to end the Vietnam war in 1965, after his reelection had been assured. O'Donnell, with his courtier's tendency to identify prince with state and place the welfare of ruler above all, saw nothing morally wrong, and to this day apparently fails to see anything out of order, with Kennedy's willingness to let men continue dying through 1963 and 1964 because it was politically awkward to end the war before assuring his own reelection.

What motivates the courtier? Money has something to do with it. Throughout history, the non-rich have tended to seek the patronage and protection of the rich. But money is far from the whole story. Another factor is the need to function, the opportunity the courtier gets to use his talents, to prove his mastery of special skills. Men wielding the pen or the brush naturally gravitate to the castle. Italian artists, for example, were given liberal use of church walls and domes to turn their talents to issues of ethereal importance in return for ignoring the rapacity and decadence of the princes who gave them their chance. Likewise, Albert Speer was able to blur away Hitler's final solution for the Jews as he focused on his own job performance. "I often ask myself what I would have done if I had recognized Hitler's real face and the true nature of the regime he had established," Speer said. "The answer was . . . my position as Hitler's architect had become indispensable. . . . I was in accord with the system so long as it permitted me to function effectively."

But the need to function is not the whole story, either. Note that Speer did not say "my position as architect," but rather, "my position as *Hitler's* architect" (our emphasis). This is finally what is most depressing of all: the compulsion of men to seek their identities in the gaudier identity of someone they perceive to be greater than they. It is the religious impulse perverted so that one's allegiance is to LBJ rather than to an idea of what the president should be.

THE PRINCE-SUBSTITUTE

Of course, most of us do not have a real prince to have faith in. We have evolved something like a prince-substitute, however, in the governmental and corporate bureaucracies; the universities, organized labor, foundations, with which so many of us are so unhappily familiar. Here we see working most of the same principles which animate life at the great political courts. Speer's willingness to overlook Hitler's mass murders as irrelevant to his specialty is similar to Khrushchev's position on Stalin's purges, as Khrushchev recalls:

> A list was put together of the people who should be exiled from the city. I don't know where these people were sent. I never asked. If you weren't told something, that meant it didn't concern you.

And although these examples are perhaps more dramatic, the attitudes are identical to those of today's corporate specialist—say the advertising men at General Motors, who didn't feel responsible for the unsafe cars produced by their company. Modern institutions remind us in other ways of the court—the elevation of the organization to suprahuman importance, the minuet of the courtiers, the increasing difficulty of perceiving reality.

The universities, for example, are still puzzled about "what the kids really want." AT&T is still trying to figure out why it didn't anticipate a rising demand for phone service in New York. Penn Central executives are still amazed that there was no one around the office who knew how to run a railroad. The unions are irritated because blacks excluded from jobs by union policy accuse them of racism. And so on, and on, and on. The organization man has already become the characteristic man of our time, the man who shapes our destiny after the princes have finished reciting their ghost-written (by organization men) speeches.

A prophetic article in *The Observer* of London, written about Speer in 1944, is worth recalling, for what it says about our own time.

> Speer is, in a sense, more important for Germany than Hitler, Himmler, Goering, Goebbels, or the generals. They all have, in a way, become the mere auxiliaries of the man who actually directs the giant power machine—charged with drawing from it the maximum effort under maximum strain. . . . In him is the very epitome of the "managerial revolution."
>
> Speer is not one of the flamboyant and picturesque Nazis. Whether he has any other than conventional political opinions at all is unknown. He might have joined any other political party which gave him a job and a career. He is very much the successful average man, well dressed, civil, noncorrupt, very middle class in his style of life, with a wife and six children. . . . [He] symbolizes a type which is becoming increasingly important in all belligerent countries: the pure technician, the classless bright young man without background, with no other original aim than to make his way in the world and no other means than his technical and managerial ability. It is the lack of psychological and spiritual ballast and the ease with which he handles the terrifying technical and organizational machinery of our age, which makes this slight type go

extremely far nowadays. . . . This is their age; the Hitlers and Himmlers we may get rid of, but the Speers, whatever happens to this particular special man, will long be with us.

And so they are, the new courtiers, rising at their most efficient to heights where they seem very close to becoming the organization, but never quite. One day, we are surprised that the organization has sloughed off one brilliant young man and found another immediately to replace him.

In a thousand conference rooms, where the smell of moral sterility is as strong as ether in a hospital corridor, the new courtiers do their minuet each day and the organizations slip further and further from reality.

How many of us [Reedy asks] have sat without protest through meetings where glorified nonentities expounded profound platitudes in the non-thought and the "innovative" non-proposal? How many of us have writhed in secret agony while "dedicated" mediocrities have responded with the organization man's version of Alleluia: "That grabs me. Run it up the flagpole and I'll salute it"?

These obscenities have become the condition of life in the modern world —in business, in labor, in liberal and conservative organizations, in publishing, in education, and even in our churches. And when they reach government, where decisions are life and death for hundreds of millions of people, they reach the ultimate of the intolerable. . . .

Somehow this thing must be made human again. Somehow we must learn to govern our people from an office that is secular and not from a court that is sanctified. If our destruction comes, it will be because we placed our faith —our unquestioning faith—in institutions that were only brick and wood and in men who were only flesh and blood and this seems to be the condition of the last half of the twentieth century.

Speer's personal lament may already apply to thousands who have never dreamed of Nazism and serve as epitaph for generations to come. "Years later, in Spandau," he writes, "I read Ernst Cassirer's comment on the men who of their own accord threw away man's highest privilege: to be an autonomous person.

"Now I was one of them."

Analyzing Presidents: From Passive-Positive Taft to Active-Negative Nixon

James David Barber

The President is a lonely figure in a crowd of helpers: he must share the work; he cannot share the responsibility. He may try, as Harding did, to escape this tension by surrounding himself with advisors he can give in to; but if he does, he will find no way out when their counsel is divided. He may, as Wilson did, seek escape by turning inward, with a private declaration of independence; but if he does, he will risk mistake and failure in ventures where cooperation is imperative.

Now as before, the endless speculation about who has a President's confidence—and who is losing it or gaining it as issues shift—reflects a general recognition that the way a President defines and relates to his close circle of confidants influences policy significantly. Detailed studies of such relationships as Wilson with House, Franklin Roosevelt with Howe and Hopkins, and Eisenhower with Sherman Adams, tend to confirm this view.

How, then, might we go about predicting a President's strengths and weaknesses in his personal relations? I think a close examination of his *style*—the political habits he brings to the office—and his *character*—his basic orientation toward his own life—can reveal a good deal.

Through his style, a President relates himself to three main elements: the national audience (through rhetoric): his advisors, enemies, and subordinates (through personal relations); and the details of policy-making (through what I shall call decision management). In other words, Presi-

From the book *The Presidential Character,* second edition, by James David Barber. © 1977 by James David Barber. Published by Prentice-Hall, Inc., Englewood Cliffs, New Jersey 07632.

James David Barber is chairman of the political science department at Duke University.

dents have to make speeches, conduct negotiations, and solve problems. Each President distributes his energies differently among these tasks, and each shapes his style in a distinctive way. No President is born again on Inauguration Day. Like most people past middle age, a President tries to use his experience; he draws from what has worked for him before in coping with new work.

Where in a man's past are the best clues to his Presidential style? Strangely, they may not come from the way he has acted in immediately pre-Presidential roles. One thinks of Truman as Vice President, Kennedy as Senator, Hoover as Secretary of Commerce. As President, a man emerges as sole king of the mountain—suddenly on top all by himself, no longer one of the many climbing the ladder. His reactions are highly individualized: elements of his old Eriksonian identity crisis jump out of the past. He tends to hark back to that time when he had an analogous emergence—to his first independent political success, usually in early adulthood, when he developed a personal style that worked well for him.

Character has deeper and much less visible roots than style. But two gross dimensions outline the main types. First, divide the Presidents into the more active and the less active. Then cut across that with a division between those who seemed generally happy and optimistic and those who gave an impression of sadness and irritation. These crude clues tend to symptomize character packages. The "active-positive" type tends to show confidence, flexibility, and a focus on producing results through rational mastery. The "active-negative" tends to emphasize ambitious striving, aggressiveness, and a focus on the struggle for power against a hostile environment. "Passive-positive" types come through as receptive, compliant, other-directed persons whose superficial hopefulness masks much inner doubt. The "passive-negative" character tends to withdraw from conflict and uncertainty, to think in terms of vague principles of duty and regular procedure.

WILLIAM HOWARD TAFT: PASSIVE-POSITIVE

What lends drama to Presidential performances is the interplay of character and style. Consider William Howard Taft. In character, Taft was from the beginning a genial, agreeable, friendly, compliant person, much in need of affection from wife, family, and friends. He fits the passive-positive category most closely, with his slow-moving pace and his optimistic grin. Taft endured several illnesses and a severe accident during childhood. His family was remarkable for its close, affectionate relationships. I think he was spoiled. His father expected his children to do well in school, and Will did. By his Yale days he was a big, handsome campus favorite, with many friends but no really intimate ones. By his twenties he was a fat man. Always sensitive to criticism and anxious for approval, he repeatedly entered new offices with a feeling of personal inadequacy to the tasks before him. He was a humane friend of the men and women around him. His mother often said that "the love of approval was Will's besetting fault." As Secretary of War under Theodore Roosevelt, he won the President's approval by complying willingly with every assignment and by repeatedly expressing his devotion to him.

Taft's political style developed in his career as a lawyer and judge. By a series of family connections and historical accidents (Taft said he always had his plate turned right side up when offices were being handed out), he found his way into the judiciary and adopted the style of the legalist, the law-worshipper. He found the bench comfortable and secure, stable and safe, honorable and respected. He developed a decision-management style based firmly in a narrow, literal, conservative concept of a judge's relationship to the law. Principles were applied to cases to give verdicts, period.

The conflict between Taft's character and style was largely latent until after he became President in 1909. In the White House he had to choose between loyalty and law. His biographer, Henry F. Pringle, wrote that:

> Indeed, one of the astonishing things about Taft's four years in the White House was the almost total lack of men, related or otherwise, upon whom he could lean. He had no Cabot Lodge. He had no Colonel House. For the most part he faced his troubles alone.

Again there is the pattern of his earlier years: many friends, no intimates. And from his character came also his worshipful, submissive orientation toward Theodore Roosevelt, which he continued to express in letters and conversation as President. "I can never forget," he wrote to Roosevelt from the White House, "that the power that I now exercise was a voluntary transfer from you to me, and that I am under obligation to you to see to it that your judgment in selecting me as your successor and in bringing about the succession shall be vindicated according to the standards which you and I in conversation have always formulated."

Taft saw himself as a follower of TR—but not as an imitator of the TR style. "There is no use trying to be William Howard Taft with Roosevelt's ways," he wrote. Taft had learned, as a lawyer and judge, to manage decisions by the application of legal principles: "Our President has no initiative in respect to legislation given to him by law except that of mere recommendation, and no legal or formal method of entering into argument and discussion of the proposed legislation while pending in Congress," Taft said in a post-Presidential lecture in which he disagreed explicitly with Roosevelt's view that the "executive power was limited only by specific restrictions and prohibitions appearing in the Constitution." This was more than a matter of intellectual principle. Taft's judicial

stance worked—as long as he was in judicial roles—to protect him from
the fires of controversy. But in the White House, he abhorred the heat of
the kitchen. As his Presidential aide wrote, "I have never known a man
to dislike discord as much as the President. He wants every man's approval, and a row of any kind is repugnant to him."

President Taft had once told an aide that "if I only knew what the
President [i.e., Roosevelt—for a long time Taft referred to TR this way]
wanted . . . I would do it, but you know he has held himself so aloof that
I am absolutely in the dark. I am deeply wounded." But Taft's character-
rooted affectionate loyalty to Roosevelt inevitably came into conflict with
Taft's legalistic style. The initial issue was the Ballinger-Pinchot controversy over conservation policy. The details are not important here. What
is significant to this discussion is that Taft attempted to solve a broad but
intensely political conflict within his Administration through a strict application of the law. As he wrote of the controversy at the time: "I get very
impatient at criticism by men who do not know what the law is, who have
not looked it up, and yet ascribe all sorts of motives to those who live
within it."

Slowly he began to see the Roosevelt Presidency as less than perfection,
flawed by irregular procedures. He tried to find a way out which would
not offend TR. But as criticisms from TR's followers mounted, negative
references to Roosevelt crept into Taft's correspondence. The two
managed to maintain a surface amiability in their meeting when Roosevelt
returned from Africa, but as Roosevelt began making speeches, Taft found
more and more cause for Constitutional alarm. When Roosevelt attacked
property rights and then the Supreme Court, Taft became edgy and nervous. He lost his temper on the golf links. He began criticizing Roosevelt
in less and less private circles. The man who had written in 1909 that "My
coming into office was exactly as if Roosevelt had succeeded himself,"
wrote in 1912 of "facing as I do a crisis with Mr. Roosevelt."

The crisis came a piece at a time. In 1911, Taft still hoped to avoid a
fight, though he saw Roosevelt as "so lacking in legal knowledge that his
reasoning is just as deficient as Lodge's." Roosevelt continued to criticize.
Taft stuck by his legal guns. However, he confided to his chief aide, Archie
Butt: "It is hard, very hard, Archie, to see a devoted friendship going to
pieces like a rope of sand."

By the end of 1911, it was clear that TR would not support Taft for
re-election. As Pringle says of Taft's mood:

He was heartsick and unhappy. "If I am defeated," he wrote, "I hope that
somebody, sometime, will recognize the agony of spirit that I have under-
gone." Yet Taft remained in the contest. He fought to the limit of his too-
tranquil nature because he envisioned the issue as more than a personal one.
The "whole fate of constitutional government," he said, was at stake.

Roosevelt attacked "legalistic justice" as "a dead thing" and called on the people to "never forget that the judge is as much a servant of the people as any other official." At first Taft refrained from answering what he privately called TR's "lies and unblushing misrepresentations," but in April of 1912, confessing that "this wrenches my soul" and "I do not want to fight Theodore Roosevelt," he defended himself in public:

> Neither in thought nor word nor action have I been disloyal to the friendship I owe Theodore Roosevelt.... I propose to examine the charges he makes against me, and to ask you whether in making them he is giving me a square deal.

Taft's nerves were shattered by the ordeal of attacking TR, that man "who so lightly regards constitutional principles, and especially the independence of the judiciary, one who is so naturally impatient of legal restraints, and of due legal procedure, and who has so misunderstood what liberty regulated by law is. . . ." Exhausted, depressed and shaken, Taft was found by a reporter with his head in his hands. He looked up to say, "Roosevelt was my closest friend," and began to weep.

In 1912 the Republican party split apart and the Democrats captured the government.

The break between Taft and Roosevelt had numerous levels and dimensions; one of those was clearly the conflict within Taft between his legalistic style and his submissive character. Taft's decision-management approach—the application of principles to cases—served him well both before and after he was President. It failed him as President. If he had had a different character, he might have pushed Roosevelt aside as soon as he won the Presidency, as Woodrow Wilson did the New Jersey bosses when he won his governorship. As it was, Taft nearly tore himself apart—and did help tear his party apart—by hanging onto his leader long after Roosevelt had, in Taft's eyes, broken the law.

HARRY S. TRUMAN: ACTIVE-POSITIVE

Harry S. Truman belongs among the active-positive Presidents. His activity is evident; beginning with a brisk walk early in the morning, he went at the job with all his might. And despite occasional discouragement, he relished his experience. His first memory was of his laughter while chasing a frog across the backyard; his grandmother said, "It's very strange that a two-year-old has such a sense of humor." When Democratic spirits hit the bottom in the 1948 campaign, Truman said, "Everybody around here seems to be nervous but me." And he played the piano.

Although he was in his sixties throughout his long stay in the White

House, he put in 16 to 18 hours a day at Presidenting, but "was fresher at the end than I was at the beginning," according to Charles Ross. Truman often got angry but rarely depressed. Once he compared the criticism he got with the "vicious slanders" against Washington, Lincoln, and Andrew Johnson. Truman expressed his bouyancy under attack in these words (quoted in William Hillman's *Mr. President*):

> So I don't let these things bother me for the simple reason that I know that I am trying to do the right thing and eventually the facts will come out. I'll probably be holding a conference with Saint Peter when that happens. I never give much weight or attention to the brickbats that are thrown my way. The people that cause me trouble are the good men who have to take these brickbats for me.

And then there is that ultimate, almost implausible indication of persistent optimism: he is said to have enjoyed being Vice President. The White House staff called him "Billie Spunk."

Truman had a strong father (nick-named "Peanuts" for his short stature) and an affectionate mother. The family had more than its share of difficulties, especially financial ones. They moved several times in Harry's early years. His severe vision problem kept him out of school until he was eight, and at nine he nearly died of diphtheria. But he appears to have come through it with an unusually strong store of self-confidence, ready to endure what had to be, ready to reach out when opportunities presented themselves. He drew on a home in which the rules said: Do the right thing, Love one another, and By their fruits shall ye know them. When he telephone his mother to ask if she had listened to his inauguration as Vice President on the radio, she answered: "Yes. I heard it all. Now you behave yourself up there, Harry. You behave yourself!"

Truman's drive for decisions, his emphasis on results, his faith in rational persuasion, his confidence in his own values, his humor about himself, and his ability to grow into responsibility all fit the active-positive character. The character shows itself as an orientation, a broad direction of energy and affect, a tendency to experience self and others in a certain way. Truman attacked life; he was not withdrawn. He emphasized his independence; he was not compliant. He laughed at himself: he was not compulsive (though he showed some tendencies in that direction). His character thus provided a foundation for the transcendence of his defenses, for devoting his attention to the realities beyond himself.

Style is what he built on those foundations. Truman's style developed in two main spurts. "So far as its effect on Harry Truman was concerned," his biographer writes, "World War I released the genie from the bottle." He had worked in a bank, farmed, taken a flier on an oil-drilling enterprise, joined the Masons, and fallen in love with Bess Wallace. The family was having financial difficulties again. His father died in 1914, when Harry was 30. At the outbreak of the war, he joined the National Guard and was elected lieutenant by his friends. Sent away from home to Oklahoma, he became regimental canteen officer, with Eddie Jacobson as his assistant. The other Ft. Sill canteens had heavy losses, but the Truman-Jacobson enterprise returned 666 per cent on the initial investment in six months. In charge for the first time, Truman had shown that he could succeed through careful management. Later in France, he was put in charge of a rowdy flock of Irish pranksters loosely organized as a field-artillery battery. One former officer who could not control the men had been thrown out of the Army; another had broken down under the strain. Upon assuming command, Truman recalled later, "I was the most thoroughly scared individual in that camp. Never on the front or anywhere else have I been so nervous." Alfred Steinberg, in *The Man from Missouri,* gives this account of how Truman handled himself:

> "Men," he told the sergeants and corporals, "I know you've been making trouble for your previous commanders. From now on, you're going to be responsible for maintaining discipline in your squads and sections. And if there are any of you who can't, speak up right now and I'll bust you back right now."

Truman did his own reconnaissance at the front, to get his information firsthand. When his troops broke and ran under fire in "The Battle of Who Run":

> "I got up and called them everything I knew," said Truman. The curses that poured out contained some of the vilest four-letter words heard on the Western Front. Said Father Curtis Tiernan, the regiment's Catholic chaplain, who was on the scene, "It took the skin off the ears of those boys." The effect was amazing. Padre Tiernan recalled with pleasure. "It turned those boys right around."

"Captain Harry" came out of the war with the respect and admiration of his men. He had learned that his angry voice could turn the tide and that he could decide what to do if he got the facts himself and paid attention to the details. Most important, his style developed around intense loyalty in personal relations: everything depended on the stick-togetherness of imperfect allies.

After the war, Truman and Jacobson opened their famous haberdashery, serving mostly old Army buddies. An Army friend who happened to be a Missouri Pendergast got him into politics—not against his will. He ran for county judge and won: his performance in that office reconfirmed his faith in hard personal campaigning and in careful, honest business practice. During the campaign he was charged with voting for a member of the other party and he answered with this speech:

You have heard it said that I voted for John Miles for county marshal. I'll have to plead guilty to that charge, along with 5,000 ex-soldiers. I was closer to John Miles than a brother. I have seen him in places that made hell look like a playground. I have seen him stick to his guns when Frenchmen were falling back. I have seen him hold the American line when only John Miles and his three batteries were between the Germans and a successful counterattack. He was of the right stuff, and a man who wouldn't vote for his comrade under circumstances such as these would be untrue to his country. I know that every soldier understands it. I have no apology to make for it.

These experiences reinforced and confirmed an emphasis Truman had grown up with. "If Mamma Truman was for you," he said, "she was for you, and as long as she lived I always knew there was one person who was in my corner." Throughout his political life Truman reiterated this for-me-or-against-me theme:

"We don't play halfway politics in Missouri. When we start out with a man, if he is any good at all, we always stay with him to the end. Sometimes people quit me but I never quit people when I start to back them up."

[To Admiral Leahy:] "Of course, I will make the decisions, and after a decision is made, I will expect you to be loyal."

[Margaret Truman, on her father's philosophy:] ". . . 'the friends thou hast and their adoption tried, grapple them to thy soul with hoops of steel'. . . ."

[From Truman's own memoirs:] "Vinson was gifted with a sense of personal and political loyalty seldom found among the top men in Washington. Too often loyalties are breached in Washington in the rivalries for political advantage."

[Truman on Tom Pendergast:] "I never deserted him when he needed friends. Many for whom he'd done much more than he ever did for me ran out on him when the going was rough. I didn't do that—and I am President of the United States in my own right!"

[Truman to Harry Vaughn:] "Harry, they're just trying to use you to embarrass me. You go up there, and tell 'em to go to hell. We came in here together and, God damn it, we're going out together!"

[Of Eisenhower's refusal to stand up for Marshall:] "You don't kick the man who made you."

What did this emphasis on loyalty mean for the Truman Presidency? The story of Truman's wrangles with aides high and low is well known.

Conflicts, misunderstandings, scandals, and dismissals piled up: Byrnes, Wallace, Ickes, Louis Johnson, J. Howard McGrath, Morgenthau, MacArthur, Baruch, Clifford vs. Steelman, and the ragtag crew of cronies and influenceables typified by Harry Vaughan. The landscape of the Truman administration was littered with political corpses. Both Presidential candidates in 1952 promised to clean up what Eisenhower called "the mess in Washington."

I think Patrick Anderson, in *The President's Men,* is right when he sees the key to Truman's loyalty troubles "in the man himself, not in those who so poorly served him." Anderson continues:

Truman once said that his entire political career was based upon his World War I experience, upon the friends he made and the lessons he learned. It was as an army captain under fire in France that Harry Truman first learned that he was as brave and as capable as the next man. He learned, too, the rule that says an officer must always stand by his men. Perhaps he learned that rule too well: in later years he seemed to confuse standing by Harry Vaughan when he was under fire from Drew Pearson with standing by the men of the 35th Division when they were under fire from the Germans at Meuse-Argonne and Verdun.

After the war, he was a failure as a businessman; his success came in politics. It must have galled Truman that he owed his political success to the corruption-ridden Pendergast machine. But he kept quiet, he kept his hands clean, he learned to mind his own business. That may be another lesson he learned too well. The most simple, most harsh explanation of Truman's tolerance is just this: You can take the politician out of the county courthouse, but you can't take the county courthouse out of the politician.

But it is not that simple. Another reason Truman stood by Vaughan and the others was no doubt simple political tactics: If you fire a man, you in effect admit wrongdoing; if you keep him, you can continue to deny it. More than by politics, however, Truman seems to have been motivated by stubborn loyalty to his friends. It was a sadly misguided loyalty, for Presidents owe a loyalty to the nation that transcends any allegiance to erring friends. Roosevelt understood this instinctively; Truman would not recognize it. Truman's dilemma was complicated by the fact that his nature was more sentimental than that of any of the other recent Presidents. It is often helpful for a President to be a ruthless son-of-a-bitch, particularly in his personal relationships; this, for better or worse, Truman was not.

There appears to have been a lapse in communication in each of Truman's "breaks" with such high-level personages as Wallace, Byrnes, Baruch, and MacArthur. Truman believed that he had made clear to the other fellow just how he must change his behavior; each of the others believed that Truman had endorsed him in the course he was pursuing. Truman seems to have been slowly, and then radically; disillusioned with men in whom he had placed his trust. He was not able to realize that the loyalties around a President are not black and white—as they are in battle or in a Missouri political campaign—but rather shade off from Vaughan-like sycophancy at one end of the spectrum to MacArthur-like independence at the other. For Truman, loyalties were hard and brittle; when they broke they broke. Before he became President, he had, after all, been the chief of loyal subordinates only twice: in the Army and as a "judge" in Missouri. It was natural for him to revert back to those times when he was again in charge.

In terms of our character and style analysis, Truman shows one form of danger inherent in the political adaptation of the active-positive type. To oversimplify what is really much more complicated: the character who has overcome his own hang-ups, who has leaped over the barriers between himself and the real world, whose bent is toward rational mastery of the environment, is likely to forget, from time to time, that other persons, publics, and institutions maintain themselves in rather messier ways. In another context I have said this type may want a political institution "to deliberate like Plato's Academy and then take action like Caesar's army," neglecting the necessities of emotional inspiration and peaceful procedure. The type is also vulnerable to betrayal when he assumes that others who seem to share his purposes will see those purposes precisely as he does and govern their actions accordingly. He is especially prone to this mistake with respect to the active-negative type who is, on the surface, like him in many ways.

Truman's style exaggerated these characteristic vulnerabilities. What he had learned of himself when he was under 20 was shaped and channeled by what he learned of life when he was over 30. Character fed style, style digested character. Amid many Presidential successes, most of his failures can be traced to a particular way in which style reinforced character trends.

DWIGHT D. EISENHOWER: PASSIVE-NEGATIVE

Eisenhower as President is best approximated in the passive-negative category, in which tendencies to withdraw predominate. On a great many occasions in the biographies, Eisenhower is found asserting himself by denying himself; that is, by taking a strong stand against the suggestion that he take a strong stand.

No, he would not get down in the gutter with Joseph McCarthy; no, he would not stop the Cohn and Schine highjinks. Franklin Roosevelt had usurped Congressional powers, he thought, and he would not do that: "I want to say with all the emphasis at my command that this Administration has absolutely no personal choice for a new Majority Leader. We are not going to get into *their* business." When "those damn monkeys on the Hill" acted up, he would stay out of it. Press conferences were another Rooseveltian mistake: "I keep telling you fellows I don't like to do this sort of thing." Was he under attack in the press? "Listen," Eisenhower said, "anyone who has time to listen to commentators or read columnists obviously doesn't have enough work to do." Should he engage in personal summitry on the international front? "This idea of the President of the United States going personally abroad to negotiate—it's just damn stupid."

With a new Cabinet, wouldn't it make sense to oversee them rather carefully? "I guess you know about as much about the job as I do," he told George Humphrey. His friend Arthur Larson wrote that Eisenhower found patronage "nauseating" and "partisan political effect was not only at the bottom of the list—indeed, it did not exist as a motive at all." In 1958 the President said, "Frankly, I don't care too much about the Congressional elections." Eisenhower disliked speechmaking (he had once been struck by lightning while delivering a lecture). Urged to address some meeting, he would typically say, "Well, all right, but not over 20 minutes." Sherman Adams writes that Eisenhower "focused his mind completely on the big and important aspects of the questions we discussed, shutting out with a strongly self-disciplined firmness the smaller and petty side issues when they crept into the conversation." In other words, he did not so much select problems upon which to concentrate as he selected an *aspect* of all problems—the aspect of principle.

When someone aggravated Eisenhower, he would "write his name on a piece of paper, put it in my lower desk drawer, and shut the drawer." When it came time to end his four-pack-a-day cigarette habit, "I found that the easiest way was just to put it out of your mind."

Eisenhower's tendency to move away from involvements, to avoid personal commitments, was supported by belief: "My personal convictions, no matter how strong, cannot be the final answer," he said. The definition of democracy he liked best was "simply the opportunity for self-discipline." As a military man he had detested and avoided politics at least since his first command, when a Congressman had pressed him for a favor. His beliefs were carved into epigrams:

He that conquereth his own soul is greater than he who taketh a city.
Forget yourself and personal fortunes.
Belligerence is the hallmark of insecurity.
Never lose your temper except intentionally.

It is the tone, the flavor, the aura of self-denial and refusal that counts in these comments. Eisenhower is not attacking or rejecting others; he is simply turning away from them, leaving them alone, refusing to interfere.

His character is further illuminated by his complaints, which cluster around the theme of being bothered. His temper flared whenever he felt that he was either being imposed upon or interfered with on matters he wanted others to handle. He heatedly gave the Cabinet to understand that he was sick and tired of being bothered about patronage. "When does anybody get any time to think around here?" he complained to Adams. Robert Donovan said of Eisenhower: "Nothing gets him out of sorts faster than for a subordinate to come in and start to hem and haw about a decision. He wants the decision and not the thinking out loud." Eisenhower felt that his 1955 heart attack was triggered when he was repeatedly interrupted on the golf links by unnecessary phone calls from the State Department. In 1948, when he finally managed to stop the boomlet for his nomination, he said he felt "as if I've had an abscessed tooth pulled." He told a persistent reporter as the 1948 speculations continued: "Look, son, I cannot conceive of any circumstance that could drag out of me permission to consider me for any political post from dogcatcher to Grand High Supreme King of the Universe."

Why, then, did Eisenhower bother to become President? Why did he answer those phone calls on the golf links? Because he thought he ought to. He was a sucker for duty and always had been. Sentiments which would sound false for most political leaders ring true for Eisenhower:

> My only satisfaction in life is to hope that my effort means something to the other fellow. What can I do to repay society for the wonderful opportunities it has given me?

> ... a decision that I have never recanted or regretted [was the decision] to perform every duty given me in the Army to the best of my ability and to do the best I could to make a creditable record, no matter what the nature of the duty.

> ... in trying to explain to you a situation that has been tossed in my teeth more than once (my lack of extended troop duty in recent years), all I accomplished was to pass up something I wanted to do, in favor of something I thought I ought to do.

He did not feel a duty to save the world or to become a great hero, but simply to contribute what he could, in the best way he was able. From the family Bible readings, from the sportsmanship of a boy who wanted nothing more than to be a first-rate athlete, from the West Point creed, Eisenhower felt, amid questions about many other things, that duty was a certainty.

In all these respects, and also in his personal comradeliness, Eisenhower fits the passive-negative (or "reluctant") type. The orientation is toward performing duty with modesty; the political adaptation is characterized by protective retreats to principle, ritual, and personal virtue. The political strength of this character is its legitimacy. It inspires trust in the incorruptibility and the good intentions of the man. Its political weakness is its inability to produce, though it may contribute by preventing. Typically, the passive-negative character presides over drift and confusion, partially concealed by the apparent orderliness of the formalities. Samuel Lubell caught the crux of this character when he saw in Eisenhower "one man's struggle between a passion for active duty and a dream of quiet retirement."

Eisenhower's political style, particularly his style in personal relations, channeled these character forces in an interesting way. At West Point he was a minor hellraiser (eventually ranking 125th in a class of 164 in "conduct") and a dedicated athlete until an injury, incurred because he would not tell a sadistic riding instructor that he had a weak knee, removed him from competition. He missed combat in World War I and kicked around for a good many years in staff jobs and football coaching; he served seven years on the staff of that flamboyant self-dramatist, Douglas MacArthur, for whom Eisenhower learned to make a newly-developing kind of military administration work.

The old structure of military command—the hierarchy—was giving way to a system less like a pyramid, more like a floating crap game, a system of interdependent functional specialities—teams—that had to be brought together around new technological and strategic concepts. Eisenhower mastered the skills this system increasingly demanded, particularly the ability to coordinate, to gather together the right threads into the right knot. It was *this* style, the style of the modern administrative team-coordinator, that stuck with Eisenhower on into his White House years. The danger of his "military mind" was not that he would be a martinet, a MacArthur; here Harry Truman misestimated him. It was Eisenhower's command habit of central coordination that shaped his behavior. The President, he said:

> must know the general purpose of everything that is going on, the general problem that is there, whether or not it is being solved or the solution is going ahead according to principles in which he believes and which he has promulgated; and, finally, he must say "yes" or "no."

The well-known staff system Eisenhower put into the Presidency was designed to leave him free to coordinate at the highest level. The trouble was that the level got higher and higher, more and more removed from the political battlefield, until, in his second term, Eisenhower had to break through a good many layers and circles to get at the controls of policy.

In the Army, Eisenhower's brand of coordination went forward in a context of command; the colonels were dependent on the generals. An order announced (after however much coordination) was an order to be executed. Not so in politics, where promulgation is just the beginning. In an Army at war, coordination takes place behind the advancing flag: the overriding purposes are not in question. Not so in the political "order" where the national purpose is continually questioned and redefined.

When Eisenhower had to deal with military matters as President, such as Lebanon and the Suez crisis, he could act with celerity and precision. He took his greatest pride in the fact that there had been eight years of peace during his administration. But at the same time his character and style fit together to contribute—along with many external factors—to a long list of less happy incidents and trends (Dixon-Yates, Dullesian brinksmanship, the Faubus and U-2 bumbles, the McCarthy contagion). He didn't mean it this way, but when Eisenhower said that "our system demands the Supreme Being," he was probably right.

LYNDON B. JOHNSON: ACTIVE-NEGATIVE

For this generation of President-watchers, it would be tedious to document President Lyndon B. Johnson's difficulties in personal relations. The bully-ragging, the humiliations visited upon the men around him, are nearly as familiar as his rages against the Kennedy clan. By mid-1966 it was hard to find an independent voice among his intimate advisors. What had happened to a political style whose cornerstone was the expert manipulation of personal relations?

Johnson experienced his first independent political success as a student at Southwest Texas State Teachers College. Lyndon's mother pushed the boy to get an education; when he was four years old she persuaded the local school-teacher to let him attend classes. In 1924, he graduated from high school at 15, the youngest of the six-member senior class as well as its president. That year he had lost an important debating contest ("I was so disappointed I went right into the bathroom and was sick."). The year before the family had moved back to a farm in Johnson City and stayed "just long enough for Daddy to go broke," Lyndon's sister recalled.

After high school, Lyndon told all his friends he was through with school forever, despite his mother's urgings to go on. That summer he tried a clerical job for a few weeks but got discouraged and came home. Then Lyndon and two friends left home for California in an old car. A year and a half later, thin, broke, and hungry, he came back and found a job on a road gang for a dollar a day. There was some beer and girls and fights; once his mother looked at his bloodied face and said, "To think that my eldest-born should turn out like this." By February, 1927, Lyndon had had enough: "I'm sick of working with just my hands, and I'm ready to try working with my brain. If you and Daddy can get me into a college, I'll go as soon as I can." On borrowed money, he set off for San Marcos.

Johnson's intense ambition—and his style in personal relations, rhetoric, and decision management—took shape in his college years. The academic side of life did not trouble him much at unaccredited Southwest Texas Teachers; he attacked his courses "with an intensity he had never before revealed." But his main energies went into operating, getting on top of the institution. President Evans got him a job collecting trash, but Lyndon soon cajoled his way into a position as assistant to the President's secretary, with a desk in the outer office. In *Sam Johnson's Boy,* Alfred Steinberg continues the story:

> According to Nichols [the secretary], what next unfolded was flabbergasting. Lyndon jumped up to talk to everyone who came to the office to see Evans, and before days passed, he was asking the purpose of the visit and offering solutions to problems. The notion soon spread that it was necessary to get Lyndon's approval first in order to see Dr. Evans. At the same time, faculty members came to the conclusion that it was essential for them to be friendly to Lyndon, for they believed he could influence the president on their behalf. This erroneous idea developed because the school lacked a telephone system tying President Evans' office with those of department heads, and when the president wanted to send a message to a department head or a professor, he asked his part-time aide, rather than Nichols, to run over with a note. Lyndon's tone and attitude somehow gave the impression he was far more than a messenger.

Soon this student assistant was slapping the president on the back, accompanying him to the state capital, answering mail, and writing reports to state agencies. "Lyndon," President Evans said, "I declare you hadn't been in my office a month before I could hardly tell who was president of the school—you or me."

Johnson was off and running. Black-balled by the dominant fraternity, he helped start a rival one, the White Stars, who won campus elections in part by Johnson's energetic behind-the-scenes campaigning and in part by fancy parliamentary tactics. Johnson sold more Real Silk socks than his customers had use for. He became a star debater, significantly in a system where he and his partner had to prepare both sides of each question because the assignment of negative or affirmative turned on the flip of a coin just before the debate. Johnson's strength was in finding the opponents' key weakness, and then exploiting it to the hilt. Later he began to win office: president of the press club, senior legislator of his class, student council member, secretary of the Schoolmakers Club, editor of the newspaper. His editorials were full of positive thinking. They came out for courtesy, "honesty of soul," and the Fourth of July, along with some more personal sentiments:

> Personality is power; the man with a striking personality can accomplish greater deeds in life than a man of equal abilities but less personality.

> The great men of the world are those who have never faltered. They had the glowing vision of a noble work to inspire them to press forward, but they also

had the inflexible will, the resolute determination, the perfectly attuned spiritual forces for the execution of the work planned.

The successful man has a well-trained will. He has under absolute control his passions and desires, his habits and his deeds.

There are no tyrannies like those that human passions and weaknesses exercise. No master is so cruelly exacting as an indulged appetite. To govern self is a greater feat than to control armies and forces.

Ambition is an uncomfortable companion many times. He creates discontent with present surroundings and achievements; he is never satisfied but always pressing forward to better things in the future. Restless, energetic, purposeful, it is ambition that makes of a creature a real man.

In 1928, Johnson left college with a two-year teaching certificate. He returned a year later after having served, at the age of 20, as principal of an elementary school in Cotulla, Texas. As principal (over five teachers and a janitor), Lyndon was in his first chief executive position. His friendly biographers report he was "a firm administrator, a strict disciplinarian, and a good teacher." He insisted that Mexican children speak only English, and he required his teachers to keep constant supervision of the students. Laziness or misbehavior "was likely to bring some form of punishment. A hard worker himself, Johnson expected others to work with equal energy and determination. He was persistent; sometimes high-tempered, energetic, aggressive, and creative." His march into the classroom each morning was the signal for the students to sing out:

How do you do, Mr. Johnson.
How do you do?
How do you do, Mr. Johnson.
How are you?
We'll do it if we can,
We'll stand by you to a man.
How do you do, Mr. Johnson.
How are you?

Mr. Johnson spanked at least one boy who ridiculed his walk. His energy was incredible. He introduced school assemblies, inter-school public-speaking contests, spelldowns, baseball games, track meets, parental car pools for transporting children, coached debating and basketball at the high school, organized a literary society, courted a girl who taught 35 miles away, and took courses at the Cotulla extension center.

Enough, Johnson's style—the whirlwind energy, the operator-dominator personal relations, the idealistic rhetoric, the use of information as an instrument—all of it was there when he emerged from road-gang bum to big wheel in the world of San Marcos and Cotulla. Obviously personal relations was at the core of his style. It displayed itself in two interesting variations: Johnson on the make, and Johnson in charge. In the first he was the operator who repeated, as secretary to a conservative Congressman and as Senate party leader, the story of his San Marcos takeover, showing a remarkable ability to expand his roles—and his influence—through energetic social manipulation. Johnson in charge used domination successfully, forcing subordinates into conformity.

I think Johnson's character infused this stylistic pattern with a compulsive quality, so that he was virtually unable to alter it when it proved unproductive. Clearly Johnson belongs among the active-negative characters. His fantastic pace of action in the Presidency was obvious. He was also characteristically discouraged much of the time. On the wall of his Senate office he hung this quotation from Edmund Burke:

> Those who would carry on great public schemes must be proof against the worst fatiguing delays, the most mortifying disappointments, the most shocking insults, and worst of all, the presumptuous judgment of the ignorant upon their designs.

He was, he said, "the loneliest man in the world," "the most denounced man in the world," for whom "nothing really seems to go right from early in the morning until late at night," who was "not sure whether I can lead this country and keep it together, with my background." Even at the height of his success—at the close of the remarkable first session of the 89th Congress—Johnson, convalescing from a gallstone operation, complained:

> What do they want—what *really* do they want? I am giving them boom times and more good legislation than anybody else did, and what do they do—attack and sneer! Could FDR do better? Could anybody do better? What *do* they want?

Johnson's remarkable effectiveness *in situations where the social environment provided direction* is not to be doubted. As Senate Democratic Leader he reached the high point of success in consensus-building by catching issues at the right stage of development, mapping the terrain of Senatorial opinion, and manipulating members' perceptions and expectations to get bills passed. The raw materials were given: Johnson did not take a stand, he worked with the range of stands he found among other members, pushing here, pulling there, until he had a workable configuration of votes. "I have always thought of myself as one who has been moderate in approaching problems," he said. But "moderation"—like Eisenhower's middle-of-the-road—is a relational concept definable only in terms of the positions others take. In the legislative setting, Johnson *had* to work that way. In the Presidency, Johnson had around him, not a circle of Senatorial barons, each with his own independence and authority, but a circle of subordinates. There his beseeching for knowledge of "what they *really* want," his feeling that "no President ever had a problem of doing what is right; the big problem is knowing what is right," and especially his plea to his advisors that "all you fellows must be prudent about what you encourage me to go for," indicated the disorientation of an expert middle-man elevated above the ordinary political marketplace.

Put crudely: Johnson's style failed him, so he fell back on character. There he found no clear-cut ideology, no particular direction other than the compulsion to secure and enhance his personal power. As his real troubles mounted, he compounded them by so dominating his advisors that he was eventually left even more alone, even more vulnerable to the exaggerations of his inner dramas until he took to wondering aloud: "Why don't people like me?" "Why do you want to destroy me?" "I can't trust anybody!" "What are you trying to do to me? Everybody is trying to cut me down, destroy me!"

RICHARD NIXON: ACTIVE-NEGATIVE

Strangely, no one seems to have suggested that Watergate (by which I mean the whole wash of woe that flooded forth after that gate was opened in June 1972) gave us a "new Nixon." Through so many even-numbered years in the past, the discovery of new Nixons seemed to have become a national pastime as observers hoped against hope that he was not what he had been. In the event, though, old reliable Nixon came through.

A clear continuity was Nixon's active-negative character. As he had before 1972, he poured on energy, night and day, at home and away; his presidential activities came to take up nearly all his waking hours, and, more and more frequently as his end approached, he woke and worked at night. "As long as I am physically able," he pledged in November 1973, "I am going to continue to work 16 to 18 hours a day. . . ." He was a man in motion, restlessly flying off to Camp David, Key Biscayne, or San Clemente, where he often asked his Secret Service guards to "drive somewhere, anywhere." By the end of November 1973, the President had stayed in the White House only four of the 44 weekends of his second term; in his last six weeks in office he spent only six days there.

'Joyless, Brooding'

Reliable Nixon continued also in his stance as a suffering martyr in the presidency. Even the version of the White House tapes he himself released to the public has him in continual complaint: "This damn case!" Even after his enormous victory in the 1972 election, Nixon conveyed a "joyless, brooding quality," one of his Cabinet members remembered, and talked of how all Presidents had gone downhill in their second terms. Even when he sat at ease in Washington while his bombers smashed out the lives of Vietnamese peasants, his sense of proportion and comparison deserted him: the Vietnam bombing became "my terrible personal ordeal."

Extensive data about Nixon's character appeared as the tragedy of his presidency deepened. His intimates had cause to blacken his name, but the detail and convergence of their stories lent them plausibility. Occasional visitors from Congress and the press gave shocking and similar accounts and the President's own voice—on tape heard by members of the House Judiciary Committee and in print read by the world at large—exhibited with unusual clarity the depth and nature of his struggle. Near the end, as his political defenses crumbled, so did his psychological defenses, and Nixon revealed the fragility of his self-esteem, the fear and trembling that hid behind his mask of stoic toughness. At the end, he was drinking heavily, sleeping sporadically, frequently out of touch with the reality gathering around him, often enraged and raging, at times a weeping, staggering, irrational man. Theodore White saw the task of the White House staff, as of August 1974, as "the management of an unstable personality," and others, similarly averse to hyperbolic diagnoses, used similarly strong language.

Nixon's own penchant for hyperbole lasted beyond 1972, as he dramatized his history, seeing his life as a series of sharp discontinuities. From "the largest dinner ever held at the White House" to "the greatest year of progress since World War II," Nixon zigged and zagged through wide varieties of "toughest" decisions, "most difficult crises," and "deepest valleys." He thought it "not too strong a statement to declare that this"— student demonstrations—"is the way civilizations begin to die." "All that we have risked," he said, "hangs in the balance," as he struggled with the Vietnam question. Now he told his friend Rabbi Korff that he could not resign, lest "foreign affairs . . . suffer irreparable harm." As Jonathan Schell put it in his *The Time of Illusion,* Nixon "invented crises and then he made 'great decisions' to resolve them." Clearly the Nixon who saw, as he wanted and needed to see, his life as a fascinating and heroic drama was still there in his time beyond 1972.

He was as insightful as ever about his own character. His speechwriter William Safire, aping Gertrude Stein, saw that "to the real Nixon, the real Nixon is not the real Nixon." "Ego is something we all have," Nixon admitted, "and either you grow out of it or it takes you over. I've grown out of it. It's really a compensation for an inferiority complex. Henry [Kissinger] has that of course. . . ." As he saw himself, "I could always get along with anybody . . . no matter what I thought of them." Just at the time he was refusing to obey subpoenas from the House Judiciary Committee, President Nixon issued his Law Day 1974 proclamation: "The law retains its value and force because every person knows that no man or woman is above the requirement of the law. Discussing the fate of John Mitchell with John Ehrlichman, Nixon, scoutmaster for the whole troop, says, "But what the hell, I am always kind." As for his stance toward the press, Nixon said, "The critics don't bother me, even though I have had the most unfriendly press in history, it has never bothered me, but it deeply bothers Pat and my daughters. They see it in personal terms whereas I see the press totally in impersonal terms." Again and again, Nixon demonstrated, as Safire put it, "the uncanny ability to step outside of himself and coolly misread the man he observed." As was the case during his years up to 1972, those who looked to Nixon's own statements for guidance to his character would soon be lost.

'The Easy Thing'

Like his active-negative predecessors, Nixon moralized his preferred line in such a way as to define alternatives as temptations, and thus his resisting them as virtuous. His "but-that-would-be-the-easy-way" habit continued: "The easiest course would be for me to blame those to whom I delegated the responsibility to run the campaign. But that would be a cowardly thing to do," he said in a television address, and then when the cameras were off, he told the crew: "It wasn't easy." As the end approached, Nixon said he would not resign because, "From a personal standpoint, resignation is an easy copout." To Senator Buckley's suggestion that he resign, Nixon replied sarcastically that, "While it might take an act of courage to run away from a job that you were elected to do, it also takes courage to stand and fight for what you believe is right, and that's what I intend to do." He told the Cabinet that he could not resign because that would change the Constitution, and so "I will go through this with my head high—right up to the end, if it comes."

The temptation was always toward weakness, relaxation, collapse: "All these people have come in here crying. I ought to be the one crying. I don't want anyone crying." He wanted others to know that "I sometimes feel like I'd like to resign. Let Agnew be President for a while. He'd love it." (To which Henry Petersen gave the desired response: "I don't even know why you want the job.") And earlier, when discussing the cover-up with Ehrlichman, Nixon equated "being forthcoming" with "caving [in]."

The point is clear: although Nixon eventually does all the things he is "tempted" to do in these passages, he does them long after they would have done him any good. Along the way, the temptations—to cry or quit or talk—must be resisted with all his moral force and fervor.

The other side of the temptation coin is the exhausted face of the gladiator straining upward, lost in his quest, experiencing the sufferer's confirmation that he cannot be doing *this* from any selfish motive. We have seen the suffering and striving Nixon already: working to all hours, exhausted, constantly complaining and reaching for sympathy, all the while denying that he needs any of that. The tapes are full of presidential metaphors of masochism: having to "bite the Dean bullet today," to "prick the boil and take the heat," "to get beat on the head and shoulders," "to be nibbled to death by a thousand hurts," not to mention numerous variants of Nixon's "scabflicking" simile. But far from passive acquiescence, Nixon would do unto others as he expected they would try to do unto him, by sharp, disciplined struggle, however "painful." As the "crisis" deepened in the fall of 1973, Julie Nixon wrote on her calendar, "Fight. Fight. Fight."

The Lone Struggle

As far back as January 1971, Nixon realized isolation was a part of his public image and proclamed "Open Door Hours." Statistics were to be gathered on how many people saw the President, and aides were to "build on the theme that he's the most 'Open Door' President in history." It did not work and could not last, because Nixon simply was not an Open Door person. As Watergate deepened, this famous loner of a President got loner and loner. His contacts with the press had already been in steep decline and became even rarer. Not only did his Cabinet members have trouble seeing him, his own lawyers were sometimes cut out—James St. Clair confessing he had not heard the crucial tapes, Leonard Garment complaining, at the end, "We had no access to our client." Nixon spent hours alone in the Lincoln room, which is furnished for one, the air-conditioning on high, the fire ablaze at the hearth, pondering his fate to the strains of "Victory at Sea." Cynics said that when he wanted to be alone, he brought along Bebe Rebozo, and they would sit together, talkless, for long stretches. Your average politician would rather talk than eat, argue than sleep, continue to converse than go the bathroom—and with the more the merrier. Nixon by Christmas 1973 "didn't want to see anyone and no one really wanted to see the President."

The President's physical separation from others, dangerous as that was, was only part of the picture. When he *was* with others, he kept them away, psychologically, by dominating the conversation or by just not listening. He jabbered on to Gerald Ford, driving him "close to distraction," according to John Osborne. As part of "Operation Candor," in November 1973, Nixon went into a social blitz with Congress: in eight meetings in six days, he met with nearly all of the 234 House and Senate Republicans and with 46 Democrats. Senator Barry Goldwater saw what those meetings amounted to:

"I've never known a man to be so much a loner in any field. . . . The President, I think, thinks of himself as the supreme politician in this country. And being a loner, I think he sits by himself and tells himself what he's going to do. Now we went through this gesture period of having congressmen and senators down to see him—but it seems to have ended. . . .

And as a result he's not getting advice. That's his problem, he's not getting it. And when he gets it, he won't listen to it. . . . My God, we've never had so many serious problems in the history of this nation."

That propinquity may not impel communication was evident in one of these "gesture period" meetings, when Republican Senator Robert Packwood looked his President in the eye and gave him a civics lesson:

"All of us, Mr. President, whether we're in politics or not, have weaknesses. For some, it's drinking. For others it's gambling. For still others, it's women. None of these weaknesses applies to you. Your weakness is credibility. This has always been your short suit with the news media and the general public. The problem with the public is that they no longer believe you. They no longer trust the integrity of the administration. . . .

"Congress has come to expect that many people who testify before it lie. It's an entirely different matter, however, when one person gives his word to another. That is a bond which those of us in politics revere highly. Those who breach that bond suffer an incalculable loss of credibility. . . .

"For too long, this administration has given the public the impression that its standard of conduct was not that it must be above suspicion but that it must merely be above criminal guilt. Mr. President, that is not an adequate standard of conduct for those who have been accorded the privilege of governing this country."

Nixon's reply was to say, "Thank you," and move on to the next man. You can lead a President to conversation, but you can't make him listen. Nixon was in an important sense "alone" even in the midst of company; this was especially so after Watergate gripped him.

The fact of Nixon's isolation is evident; what it meant to him is summed up in his comment to his then-friend John Dean, on March 13, 1974: "Bullshit: Nobody is a friend of ours." By April of that year, J. Anthony Lukas reports, "nobody trusted anybody in the Nixon camp. Haldeman, Ehrlichman, and Dean were routinely taping their conversations with each other and any other potential witness." At the end of April, Nixon at last fired these brittle and prideful counselors and took on a new crew. But the new aides, as Theodore White saw, "were loyal only to the public policies of Richard Nixon, his proclaimed purposes, the record that had won for him the largest popular election margin in American history. He could trust such men to serve such public purposes, but not to protect him personally. He was alone—all alone against. . . . 'the system.' "

So his rescue would be totally dependent on himself. Much as he felt that political leaders in the Middle East could rely "only on my words" and that agreements with the Soviet Union "were possible because of a personal relationship that was established between the General Secretary and the President of the United States," Nixon came to see Watergate as no one's but his:

"No man in public life," Nixon said in a speech, "has ever had a more loyal group of friends." In private, Nixon brooded over a biography of Napoleon, perhaps imagining his own Elba.

The Appeal to Faith

I will spare readers an extensive account of Nixon's litany of self-justifying idealisms called forth for protection from the prying eyes of reporters, courts, and special prosecutors. On the one hand, Watergate was one of those "petty, little, indecent things that seem to obsess us," one of "the murky, small, unimportant, vicious little things" contrasting so sharply with the high task of "building a better world." On the other hand, throughout his exhortations, Watergate threatened the presidency itself, the fundamental constitutional order, and the very peace of the world. Nothing is more familiar to those who lived attentively through those days than Nixon's extraordinary capacity to link his pettiest acts with his proudest purposes. The public could not be allowed to hear him plotting to fool them because "the President of the United States, under our Constitution, has a responsibility to this office to maintain the separation of power and also maintain the ability of not only this President but future Presidents to conduct the office in the interests of the people." The active-negative's enormous capacity for moralistic self-justification shone brightly through the Watergate miasmas.

The Emergent Enemy

"As you know, we're up against ruthless people," Nixon reminded Alexander Haig as the crisis persisted. Nixon was used to that. His aide Safire thought he was the first political paranoid with a majority. He lived in a generally dangerous world, as he saw and felt it, and he always had. He could sense the lurking ambushers: "I guess the Kennedy crowd is just laying in the bushes waiting to make their move," he told John Dean. Ruthless people laying for you in the bushes—that was Nixon's vision of the political landscape.

In an interesting passage, Nixon in February 1973 told his Cabinet what he had learned from another sovereign:

"I was talking to King Hussein of Jordan. When he was 16 years old, an assassin shot his grandfather, and he ran after the assassin and got shot himself. He made the point—if people throw rocks at you in a parade, you cannot sit down and look for protection. *The moment a leader shows timidity he encourages people to go after him.*

"People can sense when a leader is timid and they automatically attack. Remember, you are a member of the President's Cabinet. Try to be conciliatory when others are conciliatory toward you, but when the other side doesn't want to heal wounds, fight 'em—you get more respect."

In a world of piranhas, one had better be a shark.

As the Watergate crisis failed to fade back into the wake of the Nixon progress, Nixon's enemies, so perceived, multiplied. There were the "Harvards" (of Special Prosecutor Archibald Cox's 37 staff lawyers, 36 were Ivy League graduates), the Kennedys (Nixon on tape: "I was reading a book last night. A fascinating book, although fun book . . . on Kennedy's Thirteen Mistakes, the great mistakes"), the "upper intellectual types," the "establishment" ("dying"), Jews (Nixon's oft-repeated comment: "The Jewish cabal is out to get me"), and Italians ("They're not like us. . . . They smell different, they look different, act different. . . . trouble is, you can't find one who is honest"). The famous "enemies lists" ran the gamut from James Reston to Robert Sherrill, and included such dangerous folk as Carol Channing, Steve McQueen, Gregory Peck, Bill Cosby, Joe Namath, Tony Randall, Barbara Streisand, Jane Fonda, Paul Newman, and Dick Gregory. Former friends (Dean, Magruder, Mitchell) and worshippers (Hunt, Liddy, Barker, et al.) became objects of disdain and derision, to be "stroked" or "nailed."

Elliot Richardson tried to get across to Nixon's aides that "if you're President, there isn't any 'they'; the President has to be first among 'us'." The lesson simply would not take. Nixon at the end was lashing out in nearly every direction at "the people who won't rest until they get me."

The other three active-negative Presidents I studied, Wilson, Hoover, and Johnson, eventually fastened their ire on a single, personal enemy. I believe Nixon would have done the same and that the person might well have been Senator Edward Kennedy, particularly if the Watergate investigation had developed in Kennedy's committee. But the truth is that Nixon, despite many castigations of Kennedy and the Kennedys (not to mention such Kennedyists as Archibald Cox), targeted his anger not primarily on a person but on the media. There were individual targets there, too, such as Daniel Schorr ("that son of a bitch") and Joseph Alsop (who described Nixon as "the armpit of humanity"), and individual collectivities like *The Washington Post* (scheduled by Nixon for "damnable, damnable problems" after the election). But it was the press in general—the sum of the specifics—that got to him. Nixon was practicing his reverse-of-the-facts rhetoric when he said, "The critics don't bother me . . . I see the press totally in impersonal terms." On the contrary, Safire, who had heard Nixon fulminate that "the press is the enemy" a dozen times, explained:

"In all the world of 'us against them,' the press was the quintessential 'them,' the font and succor of other 'thems.' In terms of power, the academic 'them' was insignificant; the social-cultural elitist 'them' was useful as a foil that would help attract workingmen to a Nixon coalition; the liberal, political 'them' was in the process of destroying itself by narrowing its base along severe ideological-faddist lines; but the journalistic 'them' was formidable and infuriating, a force to be feared in its own right, but even more important, a magnifying glass and public address system that gave strength and attention to all the other 'thems.' "

Specifically on Watergate, Nixon said he had "never heard or seen such outrageous, vicious, distorted reporting in my 27 years of public life."

Surely in the long view of historical hindsight, Nixon's press will be seen as charitable in the extreme. Whether because he learned to play the press like a violin, counting on its short attention span and shallow insight, or because the press was in the main, with a few national exceptions, attuned to his Republican rhetoric, Nixon came through, time and time again in his career, forgiven before he was explained. But from his point of view, the press was the essential hostile threat: "they" could present his drama "in a way" different from his way, could warp his intentions away from the ideal, could pervert his most well-meant initiatives, and, most important, could refuse that enthusiastic consent which, if granted, would make his way work.

Gentlemen-in-Waiting: The Democratic Shadow Cabinet

Tom Bethell

For the Gentlemen-in-Waiting it has been a long wait, and a treacherous one. But now, at last, after almost eight long years of Republican rule, it looked as though the exile might soon be at an end. The election was upon us again, and with any luck a Democrat would win in November, and so would restore the Gentlemen-in-Waiting from the nooks of Brookings and the crags of Carnegie, and other second-class accommodations in and among the liberal foundations, to a more commodious seat in the state-rooms of government.

Tom Bethell is a contributing editor of *The Washington Monthly* and a Washington editor of *Harper's*.

The Gentlemen-in-Waiting did not themselves run for office. That they left to the politicians, or whoever had the time and money and fortitude to undertake such a risky enterprise. The Gentlemen-in-Waiting were the courtiers who gave advice—highly trained professionals in many instances, expert in the preparation of a position paper, generous with their expertise, ready for consultation at any hour. They were, in the most apt phrase, an "available resource," the recipients of the best education available at the best schools, equipped with the finest brains, and they were ready to serve their country.

Mostly they were Democrats. It had many times been said of Washington that the Republicans lived there during Republican administrations, but that during Democratic administrations they returned to their homes in Wyoming or Kansas, or wherever it was that Republicans came from; whereas the Democrats lived there all the time. It was their city. During the Republican interludes the Democrats waited nearby, and if they could not find employment in government, they could often find employment criticizing government. It was the next best thing.

And so, after almost eight lean Republican years, the Gentlemen-in-Waiting were waiting hungrily.

They were ready with their advice, but there was a troublesome difficulty brewing this year, a minor matter, perhaps, but in any event a hazard of the primary process: whom to advise? So many Democrats were running, and it was tactically unsound, obviously, to become too visibly a part of the entourage of one candidate—who might not turn out to be the *right* candidate—just as it was tactically unsound to be too noticeably lingering in the wings. One could jump from one candidate to another, of course, but more than one jump was considered poor form. Perhaps the best approach was to give advice to as many candidates as possible—discreetly. Here the lawyers, especially, were adept at maintaining the degree of discretion that was politic.

Of course, among the candidates there were obvious favorites. Those with a good, solid working knowledge of Washington and its ways were clearly favored because they already carried around in their heads a Who's Who in Washington and would not, therefore, have to be laboriously instructed in this important matter; and there were *ideal* candidates—Senator Kennedy came to mind, but alas he was not running this year, he had said so over and over again, but many of the Gentlemen-in-Waiting did not want to believe him, especially the ones who were waiting in Cambridge, Massachusetts, which was perhaps the favored waiting place outside of Washington itself; and there were rather ominous candidates, such as Jimmy Carter, who was from Georgia, and who, as far as anyone knew, had hardly been to Washington and so had a rather limited knowledge of how things worked in the capital and who might not, therefore, make an ideal President. Running "against Washington" might be winning votes this year, but as far as the Gentlemen-in-Waiting were concerned it was considered a joke in rather dubious taste. Indeed, one young lady who knew a number of the Gentlemen-in-Waiting on a personal basis had been heard to express the opinion that governors of states, and especially ex-governors, should not be allowed to run for President because they didn't have the proper background or experience. Foreign policy, especially, had to be properly conducted according to canons already laid down: the Russians dealt with in the manner to which they had become accustomed, the mysteries of SALT comprehended, there was a military litany to be recited, a protocol to be observed. There was, in brief, a theology at stake, and herein lay the Gentlemen-in-Waiting's chief weapon, because, in indoctrinating the candidates into some of the theological mysteries, they could at the same time create the illusion that they were indispensable. Jimmy Carter would in the end, no doubt, be realistic enough to realize that assistant peanut farmers could not hope to become assistant secretaries of state.

It was in the area of foreign policy that the Gentlemen-in-Waiting especially tended to concentrate their advice. In part this was because of the theology. Foreign policy was a mystery not given to many mortals to understand—especially those who had not attended Harvard and Yale and Columbia. Many other jobs opened up with a change of administration, jobs in departments like Agriculture and HEW and HUD, but for the most part the gentlemen sniffed at them; they could safely be left to unknown arrivistes from the hinterland. The reason for this was partly historical, partly social. But primarily the latter.

The big new social welfare agencies like HUD and HEW lacked the prestige and social cachet that was an integral aspect of the departments dealing with foreign policy. And there was a good historical reason for this, too. The formulation and implementation of the nation's foreign policy, and its defense, constituted the most basic, the most traditional, and the most irreducible function of government in any country, and its custodianship was appropriately rewarded in terms of social prestige. Despite their massive budgets, recently acquired, the agencies of domestic welfare were essentially innovations in the realm of government, and therefore suspect. The founding fathers had not, after all, thought it a function of government to collect money from people when they worked so that it could be returned to them in retirement, nor to provide medical care for its citizens.

The foreign policy calling was a peculiar one, in some ways as intangible and abstract as power itself. It attracted a very talented, very competitive group of young men who often tended to devote a good deal of their energies to eliminating rivals to power in an ongoing, discreetly subterranean Washington dogfight. Hundreds of people were seeking dozens of jobs. They all tended to know one another; knew each others' positions, latest successes, latest gaffes; knew who was supporting whom, and would speak of one another very politely for the record, but often condescendingly in private. They were not necessarily the brightest of their generation, and very probably were not the best, but very likely they were the most ambitious of the young men aiming for careers in government. To be a participant in the realms of foreign and defense policy was to be in the limelight; that was what got onto the front page of *The New York Times,* that was where the heady action was. To invade? To bomb? To negotiate? Decide it at a breakfast meeting, amid the maps and blackboards. (Let others decide about home mortgage interest rates.)

Despite the intense rivalries, the foreign policy Gentlemen-in-Waiting in some respects resembled a club, if only because of their small numbers. According to an estimate by one member, there were fewer than 200 all told. Others said several hundred. As they became more senior they would be in and out of government, withdrawing at intervals to realms of influence that were both more discreet and more lucrative than government —into investment banking and the law firms near the White House, in the Grand tradition of the McCloys and the Stimsons—but the younger men had little to market but their foreign policy expertise, and, perhaps more important, a public awareness of their expertise.

This was the difficult part of the game and the essential part. One had to become known, to rise above the common herd, small though the herd was. And this was not easy, because in the broad area that was of interest to the public there was a fundamental agreement between all participants (all would agree, for example, that nuclear war with Russia was to be avoided), whereas in the detailed debates as to the ways and means of policy—which is what the Gentlemen-in-Waiting argued about, often with great displays of erudition—the general public tended not to take much notice or even to care very greatly. In the primary campaigns, for example, there was scarcely a mention of foreign policy, beyond a decision by President Ford to abolish the word detente. And so, in a field of arcane disputes, it was not easy to make a name for oneself—especially for gentlemen waiting in the wings.

BEHAVE LIKE A TEAM PLAYER

The wait, some called it exile, had been protracted; precarious for some, disastrous for others. Perhaps worst hurt had been those Democrats of John Kenneth Galbraith's generation, who, in the past decade, had gone from their late 50s to their late 60s, and so had missed the prime opportunity to join government as experienced and senior sages; for such people, the name of Nixon often tended to be anathema, even before Watergate. For others, the last ten years had been a minefield, and not many had traversed it without suffering some injury. There had been Vietnam, of course, which had taken a dreadful toll. Few of Kennedy's or Johnson's top advisers had emerged unscathed. Walt Rostow had been banished from Harvard to Texas. Dean Rusk was in exile in Georgia.

For the younger men Vietnam had created the familiar dilemma: to resign (and abandon the reins of power) or to stay on (and risk becoming entangled in the sinking wreckage). It was, once again, a problem of timing similar to the one now facing many of the same people in their re-enlistment efforts with the new candidates. To resign? (If so, not too late.) Having resigned, to speak out? James C. Thomson, a former National Security Council adviser who left government in 1966 and went to Harvard, there to write a letter to *The New York Times* protesting foreign policy, a daring move at the time, knew the unwritten rule, and hence the danger: *When you leave, you go quietly.* Later he went one step further and wrote an article for *The Atlantic.* He was soon warned that this was incorrect behavior.

In March 1968, after Thomson's article had appeared, McGeorge Bundy, former NSC adviser to President Kennedy but by then president of the Ford Foundation, prefaced a public debate with Stanley Hoffman, a professor at Harvard, with the remark that he would not talk about the past—period. He went on to say that those who had been entrusted with responsibility by a President had been handed a pistol along with that trust, and that those who later spoke out not merely broke their trust but turned that pistol onto the President and shot him in the head. Thomson's wife gave her husband a nudge in the ribs and said, "He's talking about you." No, Thomson whispered, he's talking about Arthur Schlesinger. But the next day Schlesinger denied this, saying that Bundy had been referring to Kenneth Galbraith and Richard Goodwin. Later evidence suggested that Thomson's wife had been right. Thomson knew the implications: *To be asked back, you must behave like a team player.*

In short, the last two years of the Johnson Administration had been a difficult time for the Gentlemen-in-Waiting with ambitions to last the course, and with the arrival of Nixon, of course, the minefield had stretched on further. But, at the outset, there had been a pleasant surprise. Nixon, disappointing some of his long-time aides, had selected as his top foreign policy adviser a club member in good standing, Henry Kissinger, a Harvard professor, to occupy the National Security Council position. And Kissinger, it turned out, was willing to sign on as aides just those Gentlemen-in-Waiting who might well have imagined that they would have to wait for Nixon's departure, four years away at best, perhaps eight, until they could return to the centers of power.

BEATING A TACTICAL RETREAT

When the call came from Kissinger, the Gentlemen-in-Waiting were happy to join the team. Among them was Morton H. Halperin, who became chief of the NSC planning group, and whose background, as J. Anthony Lukas would remark, was "certain to make H. R. Haldeman's crew cut stand up straight and quiver: a B.A. from Columbia, a Ph.D. from Yale, an assistant professorship of government at Harvard.... In other words, Halperin was a full-blooded Ivy League intellectual, who had written several books, hobnobbed with Democrats in Cambridge, served them in Washington...." Oddly enough, Halperin was a Republican, but a number of other liberals who were Democrats enrolled with Kissinger— Tony Lake for example, who had joined the Foreign Service in 1962 and worked as a staff assistant to Ambassador Henry Cabot Lodge in Vietnam, and Daniel Davidson, who had been a personal assistant to the grey eminence of the Democratic foreign policy establishment, W. Averell Harriman, during the 1968 Paris peace talks. Harriman's Georgetown mansion, as Nixon well knew and worried, would become the courtly venue where the Ambassador-at-Large, surrounded by footmen, retainers and Democrats-in-Exile, would plot a return to power.

But the honeymoon was over soon enough. In May 1969 a story by William Beecher appeared in *The New York Times* reporting B-52 bombing in Cambodia, a story that was regarded as a breach of governmental security, and very shortly thereafter wiretaps were installed on the home telephones of a number of Kissinger's associates, among them Halperin and Davidson. The war dragged on, despite the best efforts of the increasingly disillusioned Democratic holdovers, who had felt that they could be more effective in government than out, but found that they had little influence on Kissinger. After the Cambodian invasion, in the spring of 1970, most of them had gone back into exile, and their period of government service was subsequently used as a pretext to continue tapping their telephones, revealing, among other things, preliminary planning for Muskie's 1972 campaign.

Fortunately for the Gentlemen-in-Waiting, however, exile wasn't the end of everything. For some, the law firms provided a secure haven. One who had beaten a tactical retreat to the world of Washington law without making so much as a misguided step in the direction of the Nixon minefield was Paul Warnke. Warnke had already been a partner in the important law firm of Covington and Burling before becoming the Assistant Secretary of Defense for International Security Affairs in 1967. He quickly became skeptical and dovish on Vietnam, befriended Clark Clifford, who would soon become Secretary of Defense, and with the onset of the Nixon Administration he became a partner in the law firm of Clifford, Warnke, Glass, McIlwain and Finney. Here Warnke could wait in comfort, with an office suitably overlooking Lafayette Square and the White House. Along with Cyrus Vance, who had been Deputy Secretary of Defense under Johnson and had made a similar tactical withdrawal to the New York law firm of Simpson, Thacher and Bartlett, Warnke would become by 1976 one of the most eminent Gentlemen-in-Waiting, of just the right age and seniority and experience for a new Democratic administration, and, vying with Vance, he was a name at the top of almost everyone's short list—a strong possibility for the top job at Defense or State if the right candidate came along. The lawyerly background encouraged discretion, of course, and if Warnke was doing position papers for candidates, he was doing so discreetly, confining himself publicly to the statement that he "hadn't a clue" about Democratic politics this year; but everyone knew that he had, and that he was one of the brightest talents available, thoroughly honest, outspoken and courageous; he had been "humanised," some said; others remarked that his advice came from the left-hand edge of the acceptable spectrum of opinion—perfect for Udall or Kennedy; but no one doubted that he was ready to make the financial sacrifice that would in his case be necessary to serve his country once again.

For others, there was the less secure but nevertheless comfortable world of the foundations, those institutions where old capitalist money laboriously accumulated was spent, a generation or two later, in searching for a more perfect society than had hitherto existed. Here the Gentlemen-in-Waiting could find suitable interim employment. The Brookings Institution on Massachusetts Avenue in Washington was perhaps the prototype. It was also the flagship of the numerous extragovernmental enterprises that flourished in the Dupont Circle area of Washington, ranging from the Institute of Policy Studies on the left to the American Enterprise Institute on the right (but by far the majority were on the left, usually stressing anti-business and environmental themes). Brookings was in the center, ideologically, and prestigious enough to make an ambitious professor quiver with anticipation at the prospect of a research position there. Robert Brookings, a self-made millionaire from St. Louis, had public-spiritedly donated his fortune, which derived from the sale of woodenware (clothespins, it was said), for the creation of an institution where men could be stimulated to think over questions of government and economics and social relations. By the 1970s, 40 years after the founder's death, with his money wisely invested on Wall Street, the thinking was being done by men who tended to perceive the most beneficial society as one in which a certain "tradeoff" between equality and efficiency was desirable. In Robert Brookings' day, for example, there had been entirely too much efficiency and not enough equality. Making amends required fairly strong government control of the economy, of course, because people, if left to their own devices, tended to end up rather unequal, but this enhancement of the role of government was not incongenial to those economists and aspiring rulers at Brookings. So the institution had a decidedly Keynesian, "liberal," and Democratic bias, although every prospectus emphasized its objectivity. But that bias was, perhaps, inevitable. As one economist who worked there commented, the conservative economists who thought market forces were sufficient tended to talk themselves out of jobs.

Here then, was a welcome refuge. In the economics field, men like Charles Schulze, head of the Bureau of the Budget under Johnson, and Arthur Okun, chairman of the Council of Economic Advisers, had taken up senior positions at Brookings sufficiently comfortable that some observers felt nothing less than Secretary of the Treasury could entice them back into government (which, whatever its advantages, tended to be a good deal more exhausting than life at Brookings); and here, too, was a port in the storm for Morton Halperin after his short-lived National Security Council venture, and Leslie Gelb, a refugee from the Pentagon, where he had coordinated the Pentagon Papers project.

For men such as these, in mid-career and awaiting a new opportunity, Brookings provided a position, a salary (about $25,000-a-year for middle-level research fellows, about $36,000 for those at the senior level), research facilities without the bother of students, a platform from which to issue dissenting policy statements—statements which, during the Nixon years, were often prominently played up by a press which often found the Brookings position more to its taste than the Nixonian position.

Another important refuge was the Carnegie Endowment for International Peace, a well-heeled redoubt of Democratic liberalism, presided over by Thomas L. Hughes, a former assistant secretary of state, who was, like Warnke and Vance, a prominent Gentleman-in-Waiting, and, because of his job at Carnegie, also a prominently *displayed* Gentleman-in-Waiting. He could, for example, write an article about China for *The New Republic,* as he recently had, and its substance would be somehow subordinate to the fact that the president of Carnegie, Tom Hughes, was making a statement on foreign affairs in a popular forum. Although a detractor had described Hughes as a one-carat diamond endlessly repolished, whose decisions tended to be wait-and-see, no one could fault him for a lack of humanitarianism in the study-projects undertaken by Carnegie. If it were possible, they risked seeming *too* humanitarian, dealing with places like Biafra and Micronesia, and were beginning to look too "soft" at a time when the American will with regard to foreign policy appeared to be moving to the right, and threatened to make Hughes look too dovish, too supportive of the view that the State Department needed to be presided over by a Ralph Nader. Concepts such as "public accountability" were bruited about at Carnegie, and there was even something called Project Dialogue—a "way within the American construct of values to explore different perspectives among people who don't trade views very often"— that smacked too much of Dupont Circle and not enough of Foggy Bottom. But even in his lifetime old Andrew Carnegie had seemed to want to make expiation for the harsh rigors of capitalism, and if so, his money ($50-odd million, at the mercy of the stock market), was clearly being spent in accordance with his intentions at the Carnegie Endowment.

The Carnegie Endowment also gave free office space to and paid off half the debts (about $60,000 annually) incurred by *Foreign Policy,* a quarterly publication wherein Gentlemen-in-Waiting could sound forth on foreign affairs to one another and anyone else who cared to listen. It had begun publication in 1970, under the editorial direction of Samuel Huntington, a professor of government at Harvard, and Warren Manshel, a public-spirited investment banker, both of whom felt that *rational discussion* of the new directions required of American foreign policy was *urgently needed.* Whether this was intended as a tiny rebuke of *Foreign Affairs,* it was hard to tell. *Foreign Affairs,* of course, was the quarterly publication of the Council on Foreign Relations in New York, presided over by Bayless Manning, edited by William Bundy, founded shortly after World War I, and frequently thought to be the spiritual home of "the establishment." (In 1961, Richard Rovere had half-humorously drawn attention to the Council as "a sort of Presidium for that part of the Establishment that guides our destiny as a nation.")

ZBIG THE HANKERER

Foreign Policy was not *anti-*establishment, exactly, but it was some-times irreverent, at least, while *Foreign Affairs* was always dusty dry. *Foreign Policy* seemed to suggest that cracks were beginning to appear in the old foreign affairs establishment, fragmenting it, and certainly it drew attention to the havoc wrought by Vietnam. In any event, the new publication was the perfect forum for Gentlemen-in-Waiting.

An editorial board was assembled which included such key courtiers to power as Zbigniew Brzezinski, a Polish immigrant who was director of the Institute of International Change at Columbia University, and who was inevitably compared with Kissinger as much because of his foreign accent as because of his teaching position at an Ivy League university. Brzezinski, it had been reported in *Newsweek,* "hankered after" Kissinger's job, too, but Brzezinski himself would only respond that he was too realistic to engage in such daydreaming. But he had been a most readily available resource, having advised nearly all the Democratic candidates, and re-cently he had invited a Jackson aide to one of the foreign policy get-togethers. The letter of invitation was dated the day of the Massachusetts primary, but postmarked two days later.

Brzezinski was a prominent Gentleman-in-Waiting, and another was George Ball, a former under secretary of state and a major figure in the foreign policy councils of Kennedy and Johnson, who was well known for having "spoken out" on Vietnam, for having published his "Skeptical Thoughts," even though, as detractors were not slow to point out, they had turned out to be ineffectual. Ball was now a partner in Lehman Brothers, an investment banking firm in New York, and the speculation was that he would be likely to return to Washington as Hubert Humphrey's Secretary of State—should the convention deadlock and the call go out to Waverly, Minnesota.

Another name frequently considered by Gentlemen-in-Waiting when they drew up lists of their rivals was Benjamin H. Read, the president of the German Marshall Fund and a respected member of the foreign policy establishment, also close to Humphrey. It was characteristic of the Gentlemen-in-Waiting that, when they drew up these lists, they also mentally decided who should get which precise job, as though they were at that moment President themselves. Read, it was felt, was *not* right for Kissinger's job, but *was* right for Brent Scowcroft's—the National Security Council Adviser, in other words—and those who felt they had a good chance of getting into the White House with Read in this new capacity especially tended to "recommend" him for the job.

LAKE AND HOLBROOKE

An important part of the life of the foreign policy courtiers was the schedule of conferences that could be attended and study groups that could be assembled. An example was the Trilateral Commission, which stressed that the U.S., Western Europe and Japan should work together closely—even more closely than they already did. It was said of these meetings that more thought was given to who attended them, and who spoke, in what order, than was given to the agenda. One of the most regular conference-attenders was also the managing editor of *Foreign Policy*, Richard Holbrooks, and his name came up so automatically whenever the Gentlemen-in-Waiting were mentioned that he sometimes seemed to be the principal courtier, whose achievement consisted primarily in being well known, rather than being well known for his achievements. Holbrooke's career seemed to consist, whether by design or accident it was hard to tell, of a series of delicately executed steps—a cautious (or fortuitous) negotiation of the recent mine-strewn years. If power itself was an intangible abstraction, so too, Holbrooke's history seemed to say, was its pursuit.

Both Richard Holbrooke and Tony Lake had entered the Foreign Service in 1962—a difficult time, in retrospect. It was said of both that they were the best of their class. Both had gone to Vietnam, and both had been staff assistants to U.S. Ambassador Henry Cabot Lodge. Back in the U.S.

Holbrooke became an assistant to Bob Komer, who headed up the misleadingly titled "Pacification Program" in Vietnam, and then to Nicholas Katzenbach, when he was under secretary of state. Holbrooke had gone on to be a member of the U.S. delegation to the Paris peace talks, where for two and a half months he helped grapple with the problem of the shape of the negotiating table (South Vietnam wanted a rectangular table, North Vietnam a square one, the U.S. a round one, and here at least, if not in Vietnam itself, the U.S. prevailed), and was able to observe admiringly and at first hand the Harriman approach to diplomacy, one of "creative ambiguity."

Both Holbrooke and Lake had then gone on to the Woodrow Wilson School at Princeton for a course of advanced international study. Lake got a masters degree in public affairs, and then joined the National Security Council staff at the beginning of the Nixon Administration. (He had met Kissinger in the mid-1960s.)

In May 1970, following the invasion of Cambodia, Lake resigned from government, an unusual event in foreign policy circles, and he then worked on his doctoral dissertation before assisting Edmund Muskie's short-lived 1972 presidential campaign. (Meanwhile, his telephone was being tapped, as a result of which he would sue Kissinger, Nixon, Haldeman, Ehrlichman and the FBI.) After a stint with the Carnegie Endowment in 1973, studying U.S. policy toward Rhodesia, Lake became director of an organization called International Voluntary Services, often described as a private Peace Corps. By 1976 he was advising a number of presidential candidates on foreign policy, but not Carter or Jackson. He had moved to the left of center, and he was becoming increasingly indifferent to playing the game by the rules, more ideologically committed to environmental and third-world themes. He was on the Foreign Policy Advisory Task Force for the Democratic National Committee, but he was looking more and more dependent on a Fred Harris long shot—or Udall possibly.

Holbrooke, in contrast, had proceeded more circumspectly.

In the fall of 1969 Holbrook, then only 28 years old, got a phone call from Samuel Huntington asking him if he would like to be managing editor of *Foreign Policy*, which was then gearing up for publication. It was something of a mystery to Holbrooke why he was made this offer, because he barely knew Huntington, but in any event he could not accept because he had already made arrangements to take a leave of absence from the Foreign Service and become the Peace Corps director in Morocco. Holbrooke was looking forward to getting away from Washington for a while, and in fact it was a good time to be gone. He recommended a replacement to Huntington, his good friend John Franklin Campbell, who had entered the Foreign Service in the same class with Lake and Holbrooke. Two years later, while Holbrooke was in Nepal on a trip, he received a cable from the Peace Corps informing him that Campbell had died very suddenly of an undiagnosed cancer.

Holbrooke returned to New York for the funeral, and, together with George Ball, made a brief speech in Campbell's memory. Afterwards, Warren Manshel came up to him and said he would like to speak to him in private. But even before he spoke, Holbrooke knew what he would say —it was that rare situation where you are offered the same job twice. This time Holbrooke accepted the job of putting out the magazine. Campbell had published five issues, had done a fine job, and circulation was up to 5,000.

From that point on the magazine provided Holbrooke with just the visibility that he needed to rise above the common run. It could hardly have been a better megaphone, far better than the relatively weak voice available to those at Brookings and Carnegie and the Kennedy Institute at Harvard (another foreign policy redoubt, where the proceeds of Joseph Kennedy's millions were carefully portioned out to worthy recipients). Under the aegis of *Foreign Policy,* Holbrooke could attend conferences, undertake tours of inspection, travel abroad (he had spent seven of the past 12 years abroad, and time spent abroad was an important credential for Gentlemen-in-Waiting; why, some of them, such as Mort Halperin, had not even spent one day in Vietnam) give speeches, and even, in the selection and encouragement of the articles that would appear in the magazine, maintain a semblance of influence over foreign policy itself.

By 1974 Holbrooke had been selected as one of *Time's* "200 Faces For the Future" (being one of those who exemplified "leadership with civic impact"), and by 1975 he had clearly become a member in good standing of the foreign policy "Quote Circuit," being tapped for a comment by *The New York Times* after the fall of Saigon, as were Lake and Halperin. (Holbrooke felt "sort of weary," Lake felt "glad the fighting is coming to an end," Halperin "relieved that it's over.") He was also making key appearances in those important instruments of visibility, the op-ed pages of the *Times* and *The Washington Post.* Here Holbrooke could animadvert upon Kissinger's performance, Nixon's world view, and detente, with one or two bold cultural diversifications thrown in, such as a description of meeting Pablo Casals, or reflecting upon snowfall in New York, which in sum demonstrated a breadth of outlook appropriate to the embryonic statesman.

So while Tony Lake was suing the Secretary of State, Dick Holbrooke was evaluating him—carefully—and to the impartial observer there could be no doubt which of the two had played his cards more cleverly in the past few years. There were, as James Thomson had remarked seven years earlier, rules in the foreign policy game. You did not get caught up too much in the Peace Corps mentality, you did not become too obviously involved with the "human rights" outlook; you certainly did not sue the Secretary of State; that was completely out of bounds, even though, as everyone remarked on Lake's behalf, he had done so out of principle, discreetly, quietly, without making too many waves, without an obvious intention to harass and embarrass his former boss.

They were thinking, of course, of Mort Halperin. By 1976 Halperin had changed direction considerably and had moved across town from Brookings to the Center for Strategic Studies, housed in an elegant building that was a part of General Motors heir Stewart Mott's counter-corporate conglomerate. The Center promulgated all the usual disclaimers about being independent and nonpartisan, but it was left wing in orientation, there was no getting away from it. Lake might or might not have gone too far, but there was no doubt that Halperin had. He too was suing Kissinger, Haig, the FBI, Haldeman, Ehrlichman, but in his case he was doing so noisily, which made it far worse. Halperin just kept on creating a great commotion of publicity about what he was doing. He spoke to friends about putting Kissinger in jail, in blithe disregard of the fact that the Secretary of State, whatever your opinion of Kissinger, was the high priest, and you did not subject him to such embarrassment. In the public arena, scarcely a week passed, it seemed, without a new article appearing by Halperin in *The New Republic,* or some civil liberties publication, about the outrage of wiretaps, leaks, and bugging, the incompetence of the CIA, the distortion of the truth, secrecy in government, possible perjury by Richard Helms; more and more Halperin was getting away from his former foreign policy beat and becoming a dissenter, growling at government from his third-floor perch in the Mott building, where plants dangled from almost every window.

By the time of the 1976 campaign, Halperin did not seem to be taking much notice of it. He was working with the American Civil Liberties Union, directing a project on national security and civil liberties—his new obsession. But he could still dare to conjure with the notion that he might someday return to government.

He knew he had broken several cardinal rules, of course, just as Daniel Ellsberg had. But like Ellsberg, who had wondered even after the Pentagon Papers leak if he could get his security clearance back and return to government in a fresh and more liberal administration (and had recently publicly endorsed the candidacy of Fred Harris, although whether with Harris' encouragement it was not clear), so Halperin entertained similar hopes—not the Pentagon, no doubt, not the National Security Council, but conceivably there was a slot, if someone from the left wing of the party was nominated, in the vaguely defined area where civil liberties and national security overlapped.

COURTIERS AND THEIR KING

There were, in fact, quite a number of rules to the foreign policy game, Halperin reflected. Not suing was one, certainly. There was a non-leak rule, which of course Ellsberg had egregiously broken. The point was, you didn't leave government and then go around telling everything—especially people's *positions*—Kissinger's position on Vietnam, Nixon's position on China, and so on. You didn't make personal attacks, that was another rule—you didn't call Dick Helms a liar. And you didn't make irresponsible proposals, either, like testifying before the Church committee that covert activities should be entirely abolished, as Halperin had recently done.

To some extent, it depended who you were and what your position was, Halperin thought. Thus, testifying on behalf of Ellsberg was all right for some, e.g. McGeorge Bundy, because it took on the appearance of atonement for him. He had been *for* the war, so it was all right for him. But it wasn't all right if you had been *against* the war—in that case testifying for Ellsberg identified one too much as an anti-war activist. Under differing circumstances, the rules could get quite esoteric.

But the gravitational pull, back to the centers of power was keenly felt, as the red telephone on Halperin's desk seemed to imply. Life in these liberal or left-of-center institutions dotted around Washington was fairly congenial and easy-going, it was true, but for those who had tasted power at the center, the sensations on the periphery tended to seem a bit attenuated at times. Take Brookings, for example. You had to have the purist mentality of a scholar to stay there for more than a few years. Its offices were more or less carrels, after all. And the research library with its dusty old treatises on economics, its cafeteria of the type where, at the end of the meal you pick up the tray and throw the whole remains, utensils and all, into a big plastic container, were more than a little reminiscent of life at Iowa State. Purely at the salary level, of course, there was a big pick-up if you went from Brookings middle-level into government at the deputy assistant level—from, say, $25,000 to $36,000. But there were additional perquisites of power. You could travel widely at government expense for four years, have access to chauffeur and car pool during working hours, and a large office with two secretaries in an outer room would be yours. *Wooden* furniture was available, courtesy of the General Services Administration, including an executive desk with 66-by-40-inch top dimensions (an $836 item), and perhaps a judge's rotary tilting chair (they recently went up from $234 to $380), a credenza, occasional tables, wall-to-wall carpets.

Plus the intangibles: an assured place on the social circuit, and, even better, breakfast meetings. Washington was perhaps the only city in the world where one could accrue greater status by attending a breakfast meeting than a cocktail party. In fact, it was probably the only city in the world where they *had* breakfast meetings, and where it was actually chic to work a 16-hour day. (No wonder it was necessary to rest up at places like Brookings from time to time!) And last, but not least, there was the perception—often illusory but no less heady for that—that one would be influencing the course of events in the nation.

By 1976, then, the Gentlemen-in-Waiting were well rested up, and they were getting restless. They were waiting on Capitol Hill, where one of the big developments in foreign policy had been the great increase in the number of foreign policy advisers attached to the Senators' staffs. During the Nixon years, the Congress had voted itself the necessary appropriations to create this alternative pool of expertise, and so now they waited; Richard Moose (in the Senate Foreign Relations Committee), Robert Hunter (on Senator Kennedy's staff), Richard Perle (on Senator Jackson's) and David Aaron (on Senator Mondale's). The new role the Hill was playing with respect to foreign policy was a problem the Gentlemen-in-Waiting would have to contend with if they were moved back into the executive branch.

They were waiting at Harvard, at the Kennedy Institute, and at the Harvard School of Government. Here Jonathan Moore and other professors were eagerly awaiting the opportunity to serve their country once again. The professoriat, it was said, would serve almost any master—it beat grading papers, after all. Perhaps, if all went according to plan, the Boston-Washington air shuttle service, discontinued in 1969, would be revived again next year; theory, airborne at last, would be put to the practical test. They were waiting in the law firms (patiently), and they were waiting in the foundations (impatiently). Enough time had been spent in the cubby holes and the carrels.

Now it was the season for the Democrats again. One had made one's pitch for prominence—in the pages of *The New Republic, Foreign Affairs, Foreign Policy,* on the editorial pages of the two papers.

Now it was time for the courtiers to find their king. Wallace was out, of course, and Henry Jackson was a serious problem, because he was threatening to enlist Daniel P. Moynihan, who was anathema to most Gentlemen-in-Waiting, as were Jackson's foreign policy advisers (the feeling was reciprocated), but almost any of the others were suitable. Udall was the big hope. Kennedy or Humphrey would be heavenly. And it was a mistake to imagine that Carter was a really serious threat. He could easily be swung toward the center, told what was what and who was who as others had been in the past.

If and when the time came, the boys from Macon and Athens and Augusta who had been working for Carter since he left the governor's mansion could be moved aside. It might even be worthwhile to include a few of them as leavening, but Carter himself would turn to the Gentlemen-in-Waiting for advice. He already had, in fact. He had already turned to exactly the same people as everyone else (among them Brzezinski, Milton Katz, Paul Nitze). "He had to," Richard Holbrooke would say, "there's no one else available." Holbrooke himself was realistic enough to know that the Gentlemen-in-Waiting were actually quite dispensable, that, as he put it, if they didn't exist, you wouldn't have to invent them, but others, such as Jimmy Carter, didn't see it this way, necessarily. Prominent advisers conferred a cachet that was much more important than the advice itself.

Carter had already come to Washington and dined at the home of Liz Stevens with Frank Mankiewicz, Holbrooke and a number of George McGovern's former advisers, and Carter had said that he needed them. Well, he was learning fast. There were rules in the foreign policy game, and it was nice to know that even an ex-governor from Georgia could so quickly learn the most basic rule of all, which was that, in the end, the king must come to the Gentlemen-in-Waiting, not vice-versa. He always had in the past, and he would this time, too. It had never failed. So in that sense Holbrooke was wrong. The Gentlemen-in-Waiting were indispensable after all, because every king needs a court and every court must have its courtiers.

Afterword

As it turned out, the change in governments that took place in January 1977 treated the Gentlemen-in-Waiting well, for the most part. Cyrus Vance is now Secretary of State, and among his highest-ranking assistants are Anthony Lake, director of the department's policy planning staff; Leslie Gelb, director of the Bureau of Politico-Military Affairs; Richard Holbrooke, assistant secretary of state for East Asian and Pacific Affairs; Benjamin H. Read, deputy undersecretary of state for management; and Richard Moose, assistant secretary of state for African affairs. Zbigniew Brzezinski is the President's national security advisor, and among his staff are David Aaron (his number-two man), Robert Hunter, and Samuel Huntington. Charles Schultze is the President's chief economic advisor. Warren Demian Manshel is the new United States ambassador to Denmark. A few of the Gentlemen-in-Waiting remain, alas, in their old jobs—among them Arthur Okun, Morton Halperin, Thomas L. Hughes, and George Ball.

Strangers in a Strange Land

Walter Shapiro

A Carter loyalist entering a Cabinet department at the beginning of the administration is like one of the handful of Spanish conquistadors who accompanied Pizzaro on his conquest of the Incas. Gunpower and European diseases like the measles were enough to make Pizzaro the ruler of a once-proud Indian people. The conquistadors found themselves the rulers of a people who spoke an incomprehensible language and practiced unfathomable customs. A conquistador could walk among the Incas and be treated with total deference, but he had little idea how the society worked, what glue held it together. For a while, life for the Incas went on pretty much as it had for centuries. It took two generations and a lot of priests for the Spaniards to decimate the native Indian culture.

Unfortunately, a political appointee does not have two generations to deal with the native bureaucratic population. In fact, with the average tenure of assistant secretaries running about 22 months, he does not even have a full four-year term.

A MYTHICAL DEPARTMENT

Let's examine for a moment the realities facing a political appointee in a mythical domestic Cabinet department with, say, a $30-billion budget and 150 patronage jobs. A ratio like that is bad enough, and it's made even worse than it looks because things usually work out so that there are barely a dozen Carter loyalists among the assistant secretaries, deputy assistant

Walter Shapiro is a special assistant to Ray Marshall, the Secretary of Labor.

secretaries, staff aides, and other political appointees. The reasons for this will take a moment to explain.

About 40 of these political appointees will have positions that are so technical or so minor that they can be of little help in carrying out the President's policies. Another 20 are total mediocrities who have been elevated to positions far beyond their competence in the hurried decision-making of a presidential transition.

Our 150 political appointees have been already reduced to 90. Probably about 50 of those are actually career civil servants who, for the moment, are holding political posts. (Heclo estimates that 20 to 40 per cent of all political jobs go to career bureaucrats in any administration.) Some of these careerists are holdovers from the previous administration who are kept around because it is necessary for someone to know where the keys to the men's room are kept; some are highly competent; many are apolitical; but almost all have developed a keen sense of loyalty to the way the department has been doing things for time immemorial.

One would assume that the remaining 40 political appointees are fierce loyalists who worked in the campaign and have a deep belief in the promise of Jimmy Carter. That may have been typical in prior administrations, but it isn't true in this new era of Cabinet government. Perhaps the most important decision that Jimmy Carter made during the transition was to take a laissez-faire attitude toward staffing the government; Cabinet secretaries, rather than the White House personnel office, chose most of the assistant secretaries and filled the Schedule C positions.

True, there were mounds of resumes sent over from the White House, but there were a few follow-up phone calls insisting that a certain person be placed in a certain slot. Only the President's keen interest in recruiting women and minorities provided a consistent exception to this general rule. Typically, fewer than half a dozen of the political appointees in our mythical department were active in the campaign or were early Carter supporters. Most of the others come from Capitol Hill or from one of the institutions that analyzes and feeds off the department's programs. The real Carter loyalists often feel like strangers in a strange land.

For those with a Common Cause world-view, this is a laudable development. Even school children now know that one of the sins of the Nixon administration was its determined effort to politicize the bureaucracy. Jack Anderson spoke for all good government zealots when he recently declared that if Nixon "had been able to pull it off, it would have amounted to almost a coup against our existing form of government." We have reached a point where trying to bring political accountability to the bureaucracy is widely regarded as a threat to the very fiber of the American way of life. Small wonder that Jimmy Carter took pains to assure the American people that the Cabinet secretaries could choose their subordinates.

This good-government gesture meant that the 180 key jobs that comprise the sub-Cabinet, as well as all the other political jobs, went to people whose primary loyalty was to the Cabinet secretary who appointed them, not to the President. An extreme example was Joseph Califano's selection of Hale Champion, a prominent Morris Udall supporter in 1976, to be undersecretary of Health, Education, and Welfare. Carter reputedly interviewed only two assistant secretaries before he sent their names to the Senate. Remember, these are the people who, day to day, run the government Carter is supposed to be reforming.

Little has happened in the last year to cement the loyalty of these assistant secretaries to the President they technically serve. Your typical assistant secretary finds out about presidential policies in three ways: reading *The Washington Post*, hearing a Cabinet secretary briefly summarize a meeting with the President, and dealing with the person on Stu Eizenstat's White House domestic staff responsible for their programs. An avid reader of *Time* and *Newsweek* knows as much about the inner workings of the White House as an assistant secretary running a $5-billion program.

Assistant secretaries have wide autonomy when it comes to administering programs or issuing regulations. President Carter began his term requiring four-page memos from his Cabinet secretaries each week detailing departmental activities. These memos were taken seriously, for, at times, the President would announce a major decision by scrawling marginal comments on the memos and sending them back to the Cabinet officers. The weekly memos continue, but they have become steadily truncated. Early this year the President announced at the Cabinet meeting that the memos should now be one-page efforts modeled after the "Kiplinger Letter."

GLOSSING OVER PROBLEMS

The handful of Carter loyalists who remain are the only people who feel compelled to do daily battle with a recalcitrant bureaucracy. They are the ones who constantly send back memos to be rewritten. They are the ones who worry that the careerists are hiding information and glossing over problems. They are the ones who chafe over the rigidities of civil service hiring practices.

The Carter loyalists are too short-handed to do much about these problems. Everything seems to have to be redone at the last minute. Decisions are made on the run. There seems to be at least one daily crisis. Their attention span suffers; soon they have the same powers of concentration as a wheeler-dealer literary agent with four telephones on his desk. Much of their time is absorbed by new programs and policies; they can't worry about the administration of programs they inherited. If something takes more than three hours of concentrated work, it doesn't get done.

Why Carter Fails: Taking the Politics Out of Government

Nicholas Lemann

Last summer and fall, President Carter undertook to learn the federal tax system. He had promised during his campaign that he would reform taxes, and the public had responded to that promise. Because he is very strongly a man of his word, the President now was determined to deliver to the American people what he had said he would. On the other hand, he hadn't given a lot of thought to what, exactly, he was going to do to the tax system. During the campaign there had been tantalizing glimpses of the Carter program, ideas like eliminating the home mortgage interest deduction, but these were not the tip of the iceberg they seemed to be at the time. Many times in 1976 reporters had asked about the specifics of the programs he was promising, and many times he had answered that he didn't know the specifics yet. At the time people doubted that, thought Carter really knew what he wanted but wouldn't reveal it for fear of alienating voters; but sincerer words were never spoken.

Two points seemed particularly to irk Carter about the tax system. One was that it was messy, full of loopholes and special provisions. Carter is a man who likes his government programs neat and orderly. The second bothersome point was that the tax system seemed to be set up to benefit unfairly the well-off, to allow them special little deals that would be far out of the reach of average working people. The President has a very keen sense of fairness, and although he is not an eloquent man, the tax situation has driven him to some genuinely impassioned remarks, like this one:

"Last year, one medical doctor, a surgeon, owns a yacht and he took a $14,000 tax credit, tax exemption, for entertaining other doctors on his

Nicholas Lemann is a contributing editor of *The Washington Monthly*. Research assistance was provided by Joseph Nocera and Frank Packard.

yacht. This is legal under the present law. Most American citizens don't have a yacht, and when they do go for a small pleasure ride, if they do have a small boat, they can't deduct it as an income tax deduction. And when that doctor didn't pay his $14,000 in taxes, other average American working families had to pay his taxes for him."

But beyond that, Carter didn't know much about how the tax system worked or what he wanted to do to it—surprisingly little, for a man who has been in public life for 15 years. So he held a series of meetings in the White House, at least six of them, none shorter than two hours and one four hours long, with officials of the Treasury, the Office of Management and Budget, and the White House Domestic Policy Staff in attendance. Few people can pay attention to anything for that long, let alone tax policy; Carter's alertness never flagged. Few presidents would get involved in anything but the broadest decisions on taxes; Carter discussed an endless series of details, matters as minor as why, since meals at country clubs aren't deductible, meals at downtown lunch clubs are.

While these long, detailed meetings were going on, there was at large in the land tremendous mistrust of government. One important reason Carter was elected is that Americans felt they were paying too much for their government and getting too little in return. In hindsight—the meetings having produced a complicated tax reform program that is not widely understood and is going nowhere—it's amazing that Carter didn't think to harness this public sentiment and stood by mutely while the "tax revolt" did so instead. He might have realized the tremendous opportunity he had to use the public's strongest feelings about politics. He might have had a clear idea of which laws and which organizations most needed changing, all balanced against a sense of the public mood, of the congressional leadership, of the proximity of the 1978 elections, of which interest groups' oxen would most likely be gored. As it was, he came to office knowing astoundingly little about how the federal government works or what new policies were needed.

Absent this knowledge, Carter's best course was to gather around him many talented and creative people and plumb them for information and ideas—to argue out the problems of government, to consult broadly, to balance out competing goals and parties, to arrive at a sure sense of what the major problems were and how they could be met.

This Carter is extremely loath, by nature, to do. He is a Navy man, a small businessman, a man whose experience is that of taking over a command, being told what the problems are, weighing the alternatives, then making a decision—giving the order, seeing it carried out down the chain. As is now obvious, that's not how the presidency works, and hence Carter's record of missed opportunities, programs that never went anywhere, lack of direction, and misuse of personnel. A close look at how the President prefers to conduct the business of governing—what he considers important, and what he doesn't—shows a lot about why his administration has been so disappointing.

MILD DEGREE OF INSECURITY

Jimmy Carter is in many ways the most admirable man to hold the office of president in years—possibly the smartest, certainly the most honest, the most upright, the hardest working. His White House has barely a trace of the culture that produced Watergate. He doesn't foster a slavish cult of personality among his staff. He has only a pale shadow of the insecurity and determination to prove himself that Lyndon Johnson and Richard Nixon had, perhaps most clear in the intensity of his Calvinism. He has told all of the several Rhodes Scholars on his staff, as a sort of joke, that he tried for the Rhodes his senior year at Annapolis and lost, but that he guesses it didn't do him much harm in the long run, did it? But compared to Johnson's and Nixon's obsessive raving about the Eastern Establishment, that's a mild degree of insecurity indeed.

It is obviously very important to him to be a good and moral man, a man who always does the right thing. Once he was given a long list of suggested winners of the Medal of Freedom, which under Johnson and Nixon had become an indiscriminately distributed reward to friends. He couldn't stomach that—this was, after all, the nation's highest civilian honor—so he tore up the list and gave out just two awards, to Dr. Jonas Salk and (posthumously) to Martin Luther King, Jr.

He is a perfectionist, a man who drives himself hard toward self-improvement and who wants to have every detail right. While doing his paperwork, he has his secretary play classical music and type up the program on a card so he can memorize it—no sense wasting that chance for a musical education. On vacation at Camp David for the Fourth of July, he decided to spend a day visiting the Civil War battlefields, and as preparation had Jody Powell bring in Shelby Foote, the novelist and Civil War historian, to give him a tutorial on the subject.

On matters that he gets personally involved in, he is almost physically unable to allow himself to be cursory, even when he ought to be. He once spent an hour and a half discussing the resurfacing of the White House tennis court. Last fall, his staff put together a lengthy memorandum for him (following lengthy negotiations) on reorganization of the government intelligence agencies—an unwieldy document, but one that all parties involved were satisfied with, except Jimmy Carter. It was illiterate, he said, unintelligible, not good enough. Two young lawyers on the White House staff spent a weekend rewriting it and sent it back in. Still not good enough, Carter said. They had to spend another weekend and do another rewrite before they could get it by Carter, though in substance it was virtually unchanged. Members of the White House staff say, generally, that it is amazingly easy to get paper in to Carter, and that often he has corrected the spelling, punctuation, and grammar—but seldom the ideas.

DECISION MEMOS

He is an organized man who would like to be remembered as a top-flight manager of the federal government. When a domestic-policy issue comes up, he never deals with it off-the-cuff with aides; he holds a series of meetings. Officials from the relevant Cabinet departments, from the Office of Management and Budget, from the Domestic Policy Staff, from the Council of Economic Advisors—all gather with the President at the White House. Before a meeting he has almost always read a lengthy memo giving him background on the subject, and on those rare occasions when he hasn't had time to prepare he says so. He is one of the few elected officials in Washington who will take the time to read enough to master complex material about government operations; the Senate and House are full of men who vote on the basis of 30 seconds' whispered summary from an assistant.

One person who has been in meetings with Carter calls him papal—a small, frail, almost delicate man, waxen in complexion, so soft-spoken that it's sometimes hard to hear him. He listens intently, sometimes asking a question, sometimes soliciting someone's views. He doesn't try to dominate. He talks as a real person would talk, calmly and knowledgeably, not in a politician's boilerplate phrases. He's low-key, impassive, and—on this everyone is quite emphatic—extremely intelligent and hard-working.

Meetings are usually followed by "decision memos," which are the procedural backbone of the White House. For the information of those who have lived lives away from managerial America, a decision memo is a bureaucratic art form in which an issue is presented succinctly and then a series of options and recommendations are offered forth. A simple one, like a cover memo for a minor executive order, might briefly describe the order and then say "Approve/Disapprove." More elaborate memos are carefully "staffed out" to anyone in the government who has an interest in their outcome, then reassembled with many options, pros and cons, and conflicting recommendations listed.

Very early on, Carter let it be known that he prefers to do business by decision memo, and he spends a good deal of every day (starting as early as 5:30) sitting alone in a small room adjacent to the Oval Office reading them and checking off options, very neatly, in a black felt-tipped pen. Occasionally he adds comments in the margins, such as "proceed with caution" or "move quickly on this." Carter plainly feels that this is the most useful way for him to spend his time as President. When John Chancellor and an NBC film crew followed him around for a day last year, they caught him saying at dinner, "And then I spent some time talking to Chancellor. Instead of doing an hour and a half's paperwork, I had an hour of conversation with him. Maybe it'll pay off." Even during those periods when his public relations advisors seem to have him on the road all the time, he still manages—through the exercise of even more than his usual self-discipline—to keep up with the memos.

Whereas his predecessors might have given their aides some broad outlines for a new policy and left the details to them, Carter likes to handle the details himself. He has received decision memos that proposed more than 100 matters for him to decide. The decision memo on urban policy for example (famous for its great length) handles one issue this way:

Under the heading "Program Coordination and Implementation" there are three subdivisions, each followed by a descriptive paragraph:

I.   The Problem.

II.   Existing Programs.

III.   Proposed Initiatives.

Under this third heading come the two options:

1)   Secretary Califano has suggested that a Special Representative for Domestic Assistance be created.

2)   OMB and IGR have developed a proposal utilizing an interagency committee headed by a senior White House or EOP staff person.

The memo then discusses the pros and cons of each option and ends with

Decision:

_____Support Option 1.

_____Support Option 2.

_____Do not have coordinating effort.

Thus is policy made in the Carter administration.

In the Cabinet meeting last year when welfare reform was first discussed, Joseph Califano made the opening presentation, explaining in a few minutes that a new welfare program would need so-and-so many dollars to work. Carter turned to him and said, "Joe, I don't want to spend any more money on this. How can we reform welfare without spending any more money? As far as I'm concerned, what you've just told me is that our welfare system can't get any better."

This caused Califano a rare moment of speechlessness, for which Carter must be admired, but otherwise it was a curious performance on the President's part. It's noteworthy that he seemed to have little idea what kind of welfare system we need—he was vague enough on the subject that the formulation of the welfare reform policy turned into a war, Califano and HEW vs. Ray Marshall and the Labor Department, negative income tax vs. public service jobs. Carter apparently didn't know before taking office where he stood on this question, though there is hardly a more pressing one in politics today. He just knew welfare was a mess, wanted very much to make it better, and figured that when he took office he'd make a rational study of the alternatives and choose the best one.

Carter did bring to his job a strong grounding in some broad principles that he applies to program after program. He is admirably concerned with reducing the size and cost of government. In any discussion, he's likely to ask whether the new policy will create more federal employees, more big government, more complication, more red tape. "If I see a memo saying that there is a unique problem in the area of relations with Puerto Rico," says one of Carter's aides, "and that we need a special White House office of Puerto Rican Affairs because the existing agencies can't handle the problem, I know he'll say no. Anything that says we need more staff he'll reject." The same goes for spending more money. The least believable of Carter's campaign promises—that he'll balance the budget—may be the one he most deeply wants to make come true. Hence his injunction to Califano.

What he didn't do, however, was ask Califano and Marshall what all the federal income supplements—Social Security, unemployment, welfare, food stamps, veterans benefits, pensions, and so on—cost and what they did. The President's mind does not comfortably embrace the idea of arguing out welfare program by program—inciting the kind of competitive presentation of views that would stimulate him to figure out where duplication exists, where money is being paid to people who don't need it or need less than they're getting. For another example, the idea of reforming the civil service came not from Carter but from Alan Campbell, the head of the Civil Service Commission; and while the President has been a dutiful pupil he has not been the originator or the instigator of sparks of insight about how to get control of the government. Occasionally Carter is said to have a firm idea about how a program might be improved, when he has had a directly related experience in Georgia; otherwise his suggestions, when they come at all, are along the lines of across-the-board budget cuts. He makes quantitative judgments where he should be making qualitative ones.

A sign of that lack of the instinctive ability to get to the heart of an issue, to extract the main points from knowledgeable people, and to synthesize them, is Carter's behavior in the face of enforced disorder. He is said at those times to be uncomfortable and unimpressive. He likes to discuss policy well prepared and outside the realm of what's politically feasible; he frequently enjoins his staff to bring him the best possible program, the ideal, and let him worry about selling it to the public and Congress. A crisis that precludes systematic consideration throws the President off. One Sunday back in March there was an emergency meeting on the coal strike for which Carter flew in from Camp David. So impressive in other meetings, so cool, so in command, in this one Carter let the discussion drift aimlessly and end with everyone convincing each other, erroneously, that the miners would go back to work if so ordered. The knack of either knowing how the miners might react or of finding that out very quickly, Carter didn't have.

A president who comes to office relatively undecided about what to do and uninformed about the ways of the federal government has to undertake a self-education, and this Carter has done, resolutely—through reading memos. A course he has avoided is the one Franklin D. Roosevelt (equally uninformed and undirected in 1932) took: surrounding himself with the best talent available, filling the government with it, and using these people, through argument, flattery, and cajolery, to find out what needs doing and to get it done. Carter is singularly unadept at the use of people—his own people no less than his adversaries. Apparently this is a matter of principle: the principle that using people is part of politics and that politics is something you use to get elected but not to govern. Carter's own view of governing is like a parody of a League of Women Voters pamphlet on efficient public administration. He takes his considerable charm out of the drawer only when he's in a situation where he can say to himself, "this is politics, not government."

For instance, at precisely 1:45 on the afternoon of March 16 the President strode into the Oval Office to greet Maury Gladman, a California banker who is president of Kiwanis International. Like most of the men in his organization, Gladman is not of the President's political persuasion, but he was nonetheless won over. He and Carter talked about service clubs—Carter himself is a past governor of the Lions—and the need for voluntarism and community service. The President mentioned that he was about to visit the aircraft carrier *Eisenhower,* and Gladman said that was a coincidence, his son was an assistant navigator on the *Eisenhower.* Well, said the President, you must write a note that I can carry to him, and Gladman did.

Carter has an impressive ability to inspire popeyed devotion in people on first meeting them—in fact, that ability is what won him the Iowa and New Hampshire primaries in 1976 and is why he is president today. Even now there are moments when the Carter magic can be seen. In the manner of a small town patriarch, the President is gracious and solicitous when someone he knows is ill or in trouble, or when he meets someone for the first time. But for the most part he seems to regard skill with people as something necessary to get the job but irrelevant or distasteful in performing it. So with his staff and with competing forces in the political world, such as congressmen and members of interest groups, he turns off the charm.

THE CELESTIAL WATCHMAKER

One departmental official remembers going to the Oval Office for a private meeting with Carter. The President walked in, precisely on time, said hello, and without further small talk asked the official to brief him. Carter sat listening, completely expressionless, leaving his visitor with no clue as to how he was reacting to what he was hearing. When the official was finished, Carter said softly, "Is there anything else you want to tell me?" "No," the official said. "Thank you," said the President.

A few weeks ago, *The New York Times* reported that Brock Adams, the Secretary of Transportation, was dissatisfied to the point of thinking about resigning. Adams denied it, but the *Times'* version of his woes rings true. A veteral of Capitol Hill serving a president in trouble on Capitol Hill, a former chairman of the House Budget Committee working for an ardent budget-cutter, Adams was consulted by the White House on narrow transportation issues exclusively. Carter's ethic is that those who work for him have a specific job—an area of operations, as they say in the military—and should be concerned with only that. If an aide in the Office of Management and Budget should have an inspiration about speechmaking, or an assistant secretary of Defense a brainstorm about welfare reform, it's possible he can get it to the President or his closest aides, where it will be read and ignored. Among all but the top staff, there's little sense of ferment, of being on the team, of knowing where the administration is going. Outside of the first and second floors of the West Wing, it's a government of hired hands. So although Carter's mastery of the workings of the government is growing with time, time has also brought a more and more restless staff, a staff full of people wondering whether they should get out before the administration's prestige sinks any lower.

And there's very little contact with Carter. Last Christmas he sponsored a reception for his staff—the reward for a year of hard work—but neither served any refreshments nor showed up. Carter is said to be bored with personnel matters. Besides the Cabinet secretaries, the political appointees in the departments are people he doesn't know, didn't appoint, never sees, and makes no effort to win over—apparently on the assumption that if he, the celestial watchmaker, gives the Cabinet members their orders, then everything will work fine down the line of authority. One department sent one of its assistant secretaries to the White House Columbus Day reception last year on the pretense that he was Italian, because that was likely to be his one and only chance to meet the President face to face.

One result of Carter's personal inaccessibility (as opposed to his tremendous accessibility on paper) is that any hint of where he stands, such as his scribblings on memos, is accepted as Gospel. An apparent mistake by the President causes a panic because it's so hard to get back to him and ask whether he really meant to check Option 2, and it's impossible to ask an aide to decide in lieu of Carter. A few handwritten words cause major tremors. In one department, the senior staff was meeting with the Secretary one day to discuss the recovery of some money the department had lost through fraud, when the secretary's assistant burst into the room, breathless and excited. The department's weekly summary memo had just come back from the White House, she said, and next to a brief description of the fraud case the President had written "continue to press on this" and she thought the Secretary would want to know that *right away*. Once on a memo Carter wrote, "We ought to do something to aid the third world," and a couple of months later, on another memo, "What ever happened to efforts to publicize aid to Latin America?" Shortly after that a major inter-agency briefing for press officers was held in the auditorium of the Executive Office Building, where John Gilligan, the director of the Agency for International Development, told the assembled masses about the activity swirling around this pressing concern of the President's.

There are a number of reasons for Carter's limited contacts. One is a fear of leaks, just as strong in this administration as in past ones (though in this administration, more is leaked). Another is Carter's faith in Cabinet government. One political appointee in a Cabinet department remembers Hamilton Jordan telling him, "Christ, to think that a campaign organization with few people who had more than a high school diploma could recruit people for key positions in HUD and State was ridiculous." Also, Carter doesn't like small talk—it's almost as if he considers it an abuse of the public trust to spend any of his time as President (as opposed to campaigning) shooting the breeze rather than reading briefing books.

Carter apparently doesn't see his dealings with his staff as a colossal missed opportunity for information, for the generation of ideas, and for control of the government; that's just not the way his mind works. So he's left with little firsthand knowledge or great forethought, relying on the government's notoriously bad regular channels of information to provide him with that.

On the other hand, the just-do-your-job-and-don't-expect-any-gratitude atmosphere has meant a White House remarkably free of internal politics, because nobody's likely to rise or fall. Phil Wise, the appointments secretary, and Rick Hutcheson, the staff secretary, are considered impartial in letting people and paper into Carter's presence. Carter has no one guru, as many senators and congressmen do, who makes all the decisions for him on some issue. On any domestic issue he will consult Stuart Eizenstat, the chief domestic policy advisor, a steady and reliable man with a surer sense of Democratic Party constituency than Carter has, a man who is sometimes spoken of admiringly as a "neutral broker," a presenter of ideas, a boiler down; Charles Schultze, the chief economic adviser, older, more intellectual and original of mind, with more influence than he is commonly given credit for; and James McIntyre, the budget director during Carter's governorship and now his presidency, a nice and earnest young man who is widely felt to be in over his head. Carter is relatively easy on the staff; some complain that he has been too easy and too loyal to old friends from Georgia who are not doing well in top White House jobs, men like McIntyre and Robert Lipshutz, the White House counsel. And among those who are not old friends, the next year will be crucial; if there is an exodus Carter will have little chance of using his increasing knowledge to turn the administration around.

REMINDERS AT KEY MOMENTS

With Congress, Carter's bad relations are usually blamed on Frank Moore, the chief of congressional liaison, just as his bad relations with interest groups were blamed before her demise on Midge Costanza. In fact, the bad blood is largely Carter's fault. He's not a man who likes to bargain, to trade favors, to form alliances, to control the Democratic Party —all that may be necessary in a campaign, but for Carter, campaigning and governing are two different matters. He needed until recently to be reminded which key congressmen to call at which key moments, and while his instinct for that is improving he still has to be reminded which interest-group members to call when.

He bewilders and infuriates politicians by casting his pleas to them not on the terms they're accustomed to——"Can you help me out on this?" —but on the only terms he is comfortable with—"This is for the good of the country." Political wooing and flattery don't come naturally to him. He flew back from the West once on Air Force One with Senator Warren Magnuson of Washington, the chairman of the Senate Appropriations Committee and a powerful politician in a region where Carter needs help —and spent the trip closeted in a private room with his precious memos, leaving Magnuson sitting all alone.

The experience of one first-term Democratic congressman from a Republican district is typical. The congressman (let's call him John) made his first trip to the White House with the House Government Operations Committee, which Carter was lobbying—via briefing, of course, not small talk or favors—for support on government reorganization. The President greeted him with a warm "Hello, Bill," and then said, "We followed your campaign and I think we were able to help each other"—though in fact Gerald Ford had carried John's district.

With the passing months this congressman compiled a record of voting with the administration more than almost any other member of the House —a fact the White House congressional liaison office appreciated but Carter himself couldn't have cared less about. Once, having never asked a favor of Carter before, he called the presidential appointments secretary and said he needed a letter from the President to read at a banquet in his district. A banquet in his district was small potatoes, he was told; the letter was out of the question. So the congressman called the congressional relations office and complained. The next morning he was awakened at home with a phone call from Frank Moore, who was on Air Force One flying to Panama; Moore just wanted to say he was sorry, and that the letter was on the way.

Similarly, Toby Moffett, a second-term Democrat from Connecticut, compiled an impressive record of support for the President in the early days of the Carter administration. Moffett's pet cause was an insulation bill —he wrote it, wooed all parties involved, followed its progress in the Senate as well as the House, got himself put on the relevant subcommittee. He worked on it for six months, and when it passed he began to call the White House to see when the President was going to sign it. Moffett figured that he might attend the signing, that some photographers might be there, that a picture of him watching the President signing his bill might grace the front pages in his district. Moore's office promised to cooperate. One evening Moffett started to get calls from his hometown papers—how do you feel, they wanted to know, about your bill being signed? Apparently Carter signed the bill in a free moment, thus not wasting any time, and didn't tell the liaison office about it.

With organized groups, Carter, no jawboner, is equally lacking in natural rapport. A few months back he had a meeting with the executive council of the AFL-CIO to discuss labor's role in his program of fighting inflation through voluntary restraint. Ray Marshall and Robert Strauss had done the spadework with the labor leaders. They had agreed to pledge overall support for the President's policy, special cooperation in certain areas like health care costs, and restraint on wage demands if prices stayed steady. That was the important word, restraint—the White House has wanted labor to promise wage "deceleration," but George Meany couldn't agree to that.

The meeting was held in the Executive Office Building. Carter walked in, smiled, and gave a little speech, saying how important fighting inflation was to him, how glad he was that he could count on the cooperation of labor, how crucial the policy of voluntary wage deceleration was. He then got up as if to go. Meany stood up and said, "Wait a minute, Mr. President, I want you to hear our response." Carter listened impassively to a lecture by Meany on how deceleration was out of the question, and at the end of it he stood up, said, "If you can't support me I'd rather not talk," and left the room.

"There are a lot of people in this town who could agree with Jimmy Carter," says one member of the White House staff. "He could make a coalition with them. Muskie. Udall. Chiles. Nunn. Why aren't these guys his best friends? Why does it always have to be Carter against the world? Does Carter have one person who would stick with him to the end? Even Nixon had people like that, and Carter doesn't. Because you're not going to get anybody to support an entire 40-point policy just because Carter thinks it's right and went through the decision memo carefully." In fact, that mixture of sincere belief and self-interest that constitutes political loyalty doesn't extend, in Carter's case, much beyond his immediate family and his four or five closest advisors. Certainly it's not unusual that Carter has enemies among the country's politicians—every President does. What's unusual is the blandness of his friends' positive feelings about him.

FINDING THE MORALLY SUPERIOR POSITION

Another member of the staff remembers having an argument with Carter during the campaign. Carter was accustomed to saying, over and over, that the United States is the first country in history where there is absolute compatibility between liberty and equality. The aide would say, liberty and equality aren't compatible, Governor, they're at each other's throats and the government has to balance them. No, Carter would insist, that may be true in other countries, but it's not true here in America.

That's vintage Carter. The President is a man who has an inclination toward, in the words of Joseph Kraft, "finding for each component part the morally superior position." Rather than compromise between two competing good causes, rather than strike bargains in quest of his goals, rather than carry out all his ideas to their logical conclusions, the President stands by his twin convictions that everything must be right and that everything must be neat. Thus he could in 1977 choose an energy plan that controls consumption through higher prices, and stick by it in 1978 while declaring himself to be battling inflation. Thus he could come out for harmony with the Congress, but refuse to bargain with or flatter its members. He prefers to make each initiative the sum of 40 or 50 small decisions, very difficult to paint in the kind of broad brush strokes that would be understandable to his staff, to Congress, to the public.

To the President and those closest to him, the problem is one of public relations and can be solved by two means. First, Carter can play tougher with his own government, making it clear that appointees should be loyal to him, that the departments should never publicly question his policies, that the Cabinet secretaries should go out and promote the administration's goals rather than their own pet programs, that congressmen who double-cross the administration will suffer the consequences. The other solution is to manage Carter's image better—hence the bringing on to the staff of Gerald Rafshoon to coordinate that effort. For the next several months, the staff has decided, every message from the President will concentrate on five key thrusts of his administration—inflation, energy, civil service reform, unemployment, and tax reform. But that attitude implies that a big picture can be imposed on the administration after the fact, so that Carter will not—horror of horrors—have to impose one in the doing of his daily business. Not long ago Rafshoon sent Carter a memo suggesting, among other things, that he address a joint session of Congress. "Let's do it," the President wrote in the margin. "We'll think of a topic later."

This kind of big-picture veneer won't change a man with a small-picture soul. The President continues to judge the programs and information his subordinates present to him, rather than arguing them out, and continues to govern by attention to detail and procedure rather than politics. It will be hard to make the world believe in a forceful, dynamic Jimmy Carter, a man with well-defined broad goals that he's moving impressively toward accomplishing, when in fact he continues to govern by sitting in his private office, listening to Bach, and checking off dozens of Option Ones and Option Twos, each of them, without a doubt, carefully considered and absolutely right.

part 3
THE CONGRESS

As the executive branch of government seems less like the dynamic juggernaut of the New Deal years and more like a fat, immovable monster, the attractiveness of Congress increases. Send a bureaucrat a letter and he won't write you back for months; write your congressman and you'll probably get a reply in a week. Congressmen feel some loyalty to the people; they're supposed to be (or at least appear to be) dynamic and fearless; they're aided by bright staffs of energetic bill drafters.

But Congress' bright potential to be the most creative part of government is so far unrealized, mostly because its responsiveness to the citizenry tends to be of the momentary, small-scale variety, with little attention paid to the big picture. A congressman's office can answer ten letters a day complaining about Social Security checks, and do it quickly and courteously, but never find out why there are so many complaints in the first place and try to find a solution to the underlying problem.

There are a number of reasons for this state of affairs. One is that the member himself is likely to be so overcommitted, pulled in so many different directions, that it's all he can do to keep all his appointments, let alone solve the grand problem of government. A recent study in the House showed that the average congressman spends 11 minutes a day on reading and reflection. As for the average senator, as the article by James Boyd that starts this section shows, he is so busy that he's only vaguely aware of the issues he's dealing with.

Lately political scientists have begun to speculate that this is no accident, but exactly what the members of Congress want. David Mayhew has argued that the best way to understand the behavior of congressmen is to assume that the motive behind everything they do is getting reelected. Morris Fiorina has taken Mayhew's theory one step further and said that the chaos of the government is actually a great help in Congressmen's struggle for reelection, since when the bureaucracy is unresponsive only congressmen can guide ordinary people through it. The congressman who gets ten people a day their Social Security checks is getting ten votes a day —votes he might not get if he solved the problem at its root.

If congressmen themselves aren't going to solve the larger problems, what about their assistants, who are usually bright, young, and dedicated? The two articles that close this section show why even the best assistants to the best senators are often ineffectual too. The chief aide to the late Senator Hubert Humphrey was severely constricted by the pileup of detail work and the short attention span of his boss; an investigator for Senator Thomas Eagleton found that Eagleton's urge to expose government inefficiency was usually overridden by his urge to keep in good order the political relationships necessary to passing legislation and advancing in the Senate.

"Legislate? Who, me?" What Happens to a Senator's Day

James Boyd

All but four of the 100 Senators' desks are unoccupied this afternoon. The debate on the pending amendment is sputtering along. In the visitors' galleries, groups of tourists, initially awed, then perplexed, have been filing in and out at the 15-minute intervals prescribed by the attendants. Now, after whispered consultations below, the debate ends and the voting bell sounds reverberating through the vast Senate complex of Capitol Hill buildings. Scores of Senators begin to converge upon the chamber.

Possessed of the prima donna's disdain for peers, compelled by their profession to fight one another on issues, they have often measured each other as enemies. But they are conscious, too, that they are brothers, that ambition makes them endure the same indignities, wage the same lonely struggle for career survival. And so they compensate for the mutual hostility inherent in their situation with the kind of exaggerated cordiality that is evident as they enter the doorways together.

But as the Senators approach their desks the cordial glow is fleetingly interrupted by a look of perplexity—what the hell is the vote about this time?

You have to watch closely or you'll miss this look. From living in the public eye in a frenetic environment, most Senators evolve an inpenetrable outer equanimity and confidence. They know that public embarrassment lies constantly in wait, and they must be prepared to sidestep it deftly whenever it confronts them. Does this loudspeaker system fail in the stadium? Does a convicted labor leader approach to shake hands while

James Boyd, author of Above the Law, worked on a Senator's staff for six years.

the cameras are poised? Are his statistics shown up as bogus by some college heckler? Does the ghost-written speech in his envelope turn out to be the wrong one? All must be fielded with public aplomb, if wrathfully avenged in private upon hapless subordinates. To men so skilled, the minute remaining before the roll call should be adequate to identify the issue and divine the safe vote.

Covertly, they case the situation through the particular strategem each has worked out over the years. Some have aides who now come forward to whisper a 30-second summary of the three-hour debate. Some just follow their party leader, who has minions stationed about the floor, to pass the word "aye" or "nay" to the faithful. Some, who are not faithful, follow the lead of their particular Senate guru—perhaps Jacob Javits or Edmund Muskie. Some, particularly those who are committee chairmen or near-chairmen, automatically support the position of the chairman who has jurisdiction over the measure—for they expect the same hierarchical support when they are piloting their own bill through the Senate.

And, too, there is last-second vote hustling on the floor. "Give me a vote, Bill, if you can," the sponsor of the pending amendment will say to an undecided Senator *he* has given a vote to in the past, and, if this is not one of those red-flagged issues of particular interest back home, the vote may well be given for "friendship's sake," with the donor carefully filing the incident away in his memory for future repayment.

By a variety of means, then, most of them substitutes for personal study and decision, the Senators work their will and the votes are counted. On occasion there is a concluding element of burlesque. Announcement of the vote is delayed, for the Chair has learned that a colleague, recently disembarked at National Airport, is somewhere in the corridors of the Capitol rushing toward the floor.

His brethren stall for time with parliamentary inquiries. Doorkeepers hold open the great doors in expectation. Breathless and unbriefed, the tardy solon enters, all eyes fixed amusedly on him. The clerk calls his name. "Aye," he says hopefully, and looks to his nearest deskmates for confirmation. But they shake their heads in disagreement. "Nay," he corrects himself, to a burst of understanding laughter. The result is officially announced. A new law is on the books. The world's greatest deliberative body has completed another deliberation.

The process just described recurs daily, not just on legislative trifles, but on major issues—such as military appropriations bills which swallow up almost half of the Federal revenue and have an incalculable effect on all aspects of American life. "All defense appropriations," Senator George McGovern has said, "sail through Congress almost automatically, without thoughtful consideration."

The precipitate and near-unanimous passage of the Gulf of Tonkin Resolution sums it all up. A Senate created by the Founding Fathers as a break against ill-considered action voted the nation into large-scale, undeclared war without individual study, without collective investigation, without true deliberation. Too late for the Chairman of the Foreign Relations Committee to announce that he was deceived. Too late for the thousands of lives, the hundred billion dollars, the half decade of lost time that was the Senate's responsibility.

Defenders of the system argue that the Tonkin Resolution was an exception and that usually the denouements on the Senate floor are not representative of the legislative process. The typical vote, they contend, is only a gesture of ratification, the predetermined end-product of an exhaustive and responsible deliberation. Wise men on Senate committees, they say, expert in their fields, have fashioned the legislation; and it survives, mostly intact, the chaotic finale of floor action. This faith in the inner workings of committees, most of which cannot be observed by outsiders, has long been invoked to assuage misgivings about the outer workings on the floor, which can be observed. Furthermore, they assert, the average Senator spends long hours with his staff studying issues in the privacy of the office.

Let us examine an average Senator's day to see how his time is spent.

The Senator starts his typical day tired. He returned very late last night from a speech back home, and he had to get up early this morning to present himself at a breakfast sponsored by utility executives. ("These guys come here mostly for a good time, but to make it look official, they nail me for an hour when I can't claim a conflicting engagement.") In the gray light of the cab he gives his *New York Times* a 10-minute reading, hoping that his aides will let him know if anything important happened yesterday. ("Bill Proxmire went to the Evelyn Wood fast-reading school and claims he reads four times faster now. Maybe I'll try that.") The breakfast is a bore, naturally, but he hopes he convinced those Republican businessmen that *he* is one Democrat who understands their problems.

He arrives at his office at 9:30, already 30 minutes late, grousing to himself about the three hurried minutes it takes to get down the long corridor. ("After another term, I'll be better situated.") He goes in through his private door, so visitors won't see him. He has the usual committee meeting scheduled at 10 o'clock, and he remembers that yesterday he tried to accommodate his legislative assistant by agreeing to be briefed for half an hour on everything under consideration by the committee.

But a check confirms his suspicion: his waiting room is crowded with people he can't ignore. He apologizes to his assistant and tells his secretary to "run them in." One of them helped him in an election back in the dim past. ("He just wants to say hello and show his wife that he has entree to a Senator's office.") Then there is a delegation of union people who contributed to his campaign last time. They want to let him know they are watching what he does on the compulsory arbitration bill.

By now the committee hearing has already started. But there are more constituents, or self-proclaimed representatives of constituents, to be seen. He greets them, one after another, listens, nodding agreeably for a few minutes and turns them over to his executive aides. But he worries. He gets a lot of votes by helping constituents, and this service is one of his major assets during campaigns. He knows it takes up half the time of his staff, time that he needs for help on the issues. And besides, even though he helps these people, he knows that most of the things they ask are wrong or antithetical to the public interest.

If a call from his office to the Veterans Administration causes the disability file of John Jones to be pulled from the middle of the pile and placed on top, it only means that all the others, who have patiently endured the normal procedures, are set back one. Jones doesn't care about the others, of course, and the others won't find out it was their own Senator who pushed them back one, but it's a funny way to run a country.

Then there is the recurring case of the foreign medical student. This one is from Nigeria. He was given a visa several years ago to study a medical specialty, under a State Department program. Now he has completed his course. But naturally he doesn't want to go back to Nigeria. He wants to be a specialist here in the United States, and the hospital he is attached to wants him to stay, too, for there is a shortage in his specialty. So a lot of people are writing letters. ("If I raise the roof enough, they'll let him stay, but it makes a mess of our foreign policy. Instead of gaining a specialist, Nigeria loses a general practitioner.") Once in a while, some humble citizen with a legitimate complaint *is* rescued from the toils of the bureaucracy, and this is duly written up in the monthly newsletter. But Senators know that the sum total of their efforts for constituents, instead of improving bureaucracy for the benefit of all, is lowering its efficiency for the sake of a few.

It is past 11 o'clock when he gets to the committee hearing. During the walk over, his legislative assistant gives him a hurried, capsule briefing, just enough to confuse him. In the hearings he asks the wrong questions. So do other Sentors who come and go every few minutes. The questions that get to the heart of the matter are so rare as to seem accidental, and the needed follow-up question is almost never asked. By 10 minutes of 12 he has picked up the thread, but it's time to get to the Senate floor to insert into the Congressional *Record* a number of press releases just handed him by his head speechwriter. ("If I get there late, I'll have to wait my turn, behind all the windbags, and then I'll be late for lunch with my campaign finance chairman. *He* can't be kept waiting.")

The luncheon, in the Senate dining room, takes an hour and a half because he has to take his guest around the room and introduce him to all the Senators.

It's now 2 o'clock. The Senator is back in his office, and the afternoon schedule shapes up like a nightmare. But somehow, alternately helped and hindered by his staff, he gets through it. He signs a week's accumulation of letters—the one per cent of the outgoing mail that commits him to things too important to be signed on the autograph machine. ("I wish I had time to read them carefully.") He worries about the 100,000 letters that got out over his name each year that he never sees. And every once in a while when he is back home, some constituent approaches him and complains that he wrote a month ago and never go an answer. He writes the name down and tries to get to the bottom of it, but usually he doesn't. ("I sure hope we've got the mail thing fixed. That can kill you.")

He misses one vote on the floor because he's taping a discussion program downtown, but he does make three votes. Each time, however, it takes 20 minutes to get over to the floor and back, so there goes an hour.

There are two afternoon committee sessions on his schedule. He goes to the one that's being televised. As for the other, a closed session where a piece of legislation is being drafted, he sends his proxy to the chairman. By 4 o'clock he leaves the televised hearing (the camera has been shut off) to have his picture taken on the steps of the Capitol with a high-school class from back home. Afterwards he takes them into the Senate Reception Room, makes a little speech, shakes hands, and presents each visitor with an embossed ball-point pen ("They'll all be voters in three or four years, and their parents are voters now.")

He is late for his 4:30 appointment at NASA, but he knows that the top men there will wait for a Senator. ("Come to think of it, why didn't I have the meeting scheduled in my own office?") He is accompanied by businessmen from his state who are bidding for a new government contract. The meeting is mercifully short. ("I loused up my presentation, but I think I pulled it out. I gave them that I'll-remember-at-appropriation-time look and I don't think they'll give me the run-around again.") Lobbying for businessmen eats up his time in great chunks. He sometimes feels that he is forever cajoling a government contracting agency, or appearing before a regulatory commission, or testifying before the Senate Appropriations Committee at the behest of some business or other.

Back in the office at 5:45 for some paper work—but his secretary hands him a list of 20 phone calls that must be returned. He goes through the list. He picks out six from the array of homestate politicians, reporters, and contributors; he turns the rest over to his administrative assistant. He finishes the calls at 6:30 and asks his staff in. They had been waiting for a crack at him all day on matters they think are urgent. But those matters must wait; today is the last day he can name his state's quota to West Point and Annapolis. So, awash in the papers assembled by his staff, he starts trying to balance the examination grades of boys he doesn't know against the recommendations from people he owes favors to. He finally scribbles down the prescribed number of names, and that's that.

By now his aides can tell from his gray countenance that he is bushed, so they don't press him for decisions. Everyone has a drink or two, the talk is pleasant and general, and gradually the chief's energy revives. His cleaning is brought in and he changes. He has dinner scheduled tonight with a columnist who has seven outlets in his state. ("I'd better not have that third drink.") And after that, he has promised to take his wife to an embassy party. He hates the thought of it, but he hasn't seen her for three nights, and tomorrow night he will be speaking for a $1,500 fee in Pennsylvania. ("She's always telling me how tired I look and how I ought to slow down and get some rest, but she sure likes those parties.") Maybe when he gets home, around midnight, he'll take an hour to dig into his briefcase, to read that material on the population explosion, on starvation in Mississippi, on a new idea for housing in the ghetto, on the missile defense system, on the currency crisis, on the nuclear proliferation treaty. Yes, he's been trying to get to that briefcase for days, and maybe he will tonight. But he knows he won't.

Deep in the interior of the Library of Congress there is a unit called the Legislative Reference Service. What has happened to it is symbolic of what has happened to the Congress itself. It was established long ago to give Congress expert research facilities on public issues and legislative lore. Thanks to the anonymous dedication of its staff, it continues to do good work to the extent that Congressmen let it. But there's the rub. Congress has its own priorities which it places above legislative research.

High-school students send their classroom assignments to their Senators, who forward them to the Library of Congress, where harried researchers are put to work writing term papers for the little scholars. Booster clubs ask for blurbs about one thing or another, and their requests are dumped on the Legislative Reference Service. Antiquaries ask their Senators for information on obscure topics, and over they go to the big library. But most of all, it is the speeches; the thousands and thousands of speeches for home-state appearances by Congressmen—some political, some ceremonial, some occasional, some undefinable—that have overwhelmed this perservering band of researchers and largely nullified their effectiveness.

Home-state appearances are the leading cause of absenteeism. Senators will righteously affirm that any time spent with the folks is time spent on official business, the most important hours they put in. They are educating the public on the issues, they say, or fostering the democratic dialogue. Obviously, this is true some of the time or more so with some Senators than with others. But all too often the Senator does not go home to educate or listen, but to speak words he thinks a special group wants to hear. Hence the dreary round of Columbus Day with the Italian-Americans, Pulaski Day with the Poles, civil rights with the Negroes, law and order with policemen's benevolent associations, pay-raise promises to postal unions, economy-in-government pleas to chambers of commerce, pro-Israel statements, delivered complete with yarmulke, at Jewish Community Centers.

For the sake of this kind of "education," the average Senator misses 25 per cent of his votes, and the House of Representatives can function regularly only three days a week.

Sometimes the speech has another purpose: additional income for the Senator. A Senator whose name commands even dim public recognition, or who serves on a committee that is important to any of the many organized interest groups in the land, can command $1,000, $2,000, even $3,000, plus expanses, for a speech in Las Vegas, or Dallas, or Miami, or Chicago, or even, in this day of the paid lecture boom, in the heart of the hinterlands.

Leaving nothing to chance, many Senators have signed up with professional booking agencies in New York and Boston, who, for one third of the take, line up tours and dispatch Senators across the country on one-night stands, like so many actors and acrobats of old. This sideline can bring in $20,000 or $30,000 a year or even more. And the lecture game is only one of many private sidelines, which include law practices, bank directorships, real estate and insurance businesses and many others. (As of 1979, restrictions on Senators' outside earned income will begin.)

When the Senator returns to Washington from his speechmaking, there is no assurance that he will get down to the business of legislation. Much of his time in Washington is devoted to getting news about himself sent home. To accommodate him, the Senate more and more has taken on the appearance of a vast publicity mill. Although it is sometimes a projection pad for presidential and vice presidential aspirants, it serves more often as a forum for incumbents seeking reelection.

In the lower reaches of the Capitol complex, government employees and government machines are ever at work stamping out addressograph plates which can endow a Senator with a personalized mailing list running into hundreds of thousands of names. Though this is the least visible and prestigious part of the Senator's establishment, it can be the most important. For with these lists, other government employees and other government machines can pour out a constant stream of mail-outs—circulars, reprints of speeches disguised as Christmas cards, newsletters, and the like —millions and millions per month which are carried by the mails free of charge. These lists become powerful campaign weapons. When the late Senator William Langer of North Dakota was too aged to campaign in person for reelection, he did so entirely through his mailing list and won by a whopping margin.

Senatorial newletters, generally thinly disguised political advertisements, are published regularly by most Senators. For days before publication date, part of a Senate office is immobilized. Whenever a quarter of a million newsletters are mailed out, as many as 25,000 will be returned, due to the turnover in addresses. Contemplate if you will the lives of quiet desperation led by Senate aides who might have done research on public issues, but who are doomed to wrestle forever with great stacks of returned newsletters.

Under the Capitol itself is a television and radio studio, maintained at government expense, where Senators for a token fee grind out regular television and radio programs. To play a Senator on the screen for half an hour against a painted backdrop of the Capitol a Senator may neglect his real-life duties for half a day.

Unfortunately, the publicity operation is not kept entirely underground. Senate hearings are increasingly designed not to gather information but to feature confrontations that might make Walter Cronkite. If a tourist were to make the rounds of all the open hearing rooms, the only ones he would be certain to find well-attended by Senators would be those where the television cameras are focused on such currently telegenic witnesses as an adolescent pacifist or black exhibitionist—and on the Senators.

Senators, it is said, used to talk to each other on the Senate floor; now they only read to empty seats. More and more the Senate chamber is used as a vehicle for covering press releases sent out days before to meet home-state deadlines. It is ironic that peak attendance on the floor, outside of voting periods, occurs during the so-called "morning hour" when, by agreement, no real business can be transacted. Senators are not assembled there to hear the opening prayers. They are allowed three minutes each to drone prepared statements into the *Record.* Frequently, they read only the first and last pages of a pre-released speech, and the clerks insert the whole thing into the *Record* as if it had been delivered with all the gusto of an Alben Barkley.

"Major" speeches, delivered later in the day, are also intended more for the press than for the Senate. The sight of a pageboy moving toward a Senator's desk with a speaking lectern will empty the floor automatically. Senator Wayne Morse openly acknowledged this by delaying his daily speeches.

Senators are part of a national phenomenon. Like successful professors who are so busy earning consulting fees that they do not teach, like successful lawyers who are so busy making contacts for the firm that they do not practice law, many Senators seldom cease being candidates long enough to become legislators.

Since most members of the House spend even more time being candidates, the work of the federal legislature receives astonishingly little attention from a large number of the men who are supposed to be doing it.

This fact is evident to every executive branch witness who sighs with relief when that right follow-up question is not asked.

What can be done?

For the Senate, the simplest solution would be to limit Senators, like Presidents, to two terms. This would mean that half of them would always be free to concentrate on legislative work. It would also do much to eliminate another serious problem, the combination of seniority and senility. But whatever the merits of such a system, its chances of passing the Senate are ridiculously slim.

Another improbable but needed reform is a prohibition on senatorial intervention with federal agencies to obtain favors for their constituents. Not only does this intervention consume a tremendous amount of the Senator's time, but the I'll-remember-you-at-appropriation-time look is demoralizing, demeaning, and corrupting to the government employees who must endure it, as far too many must. However, congressional intervention on behalf of constituents has its good side—the ombudsman role and the valuable clues it gives congressmen as to where the federal bureaucracy is malfunctioning. This role could be preserved in an office of congressional ombudsman, run by appointive officials but reporting to Congress.

The semi-fiction that the work of the Senate is done in its committees could progress toward reality if the number of memberships on committees and subcommittees were drastically reduced. For political reasons, and occasionally from genuine interest, Senators tend to spread themselves too thin with committee assignments. There is no reason why most subcommittees need have more than three members. The number of subcommittees could also be cut, since many have little reason for being, other than to honor a member with a chairmanship.

There is no pressure for this reform because the public doesn't know it's needed. This unawareness is a product of inadequate press coverage of the work of Congress.

The press should give much more attention to appraising the ways Congress goes about its work and the actual contribution of individual members to that work.

Such reporting would inspire better use of his time by the average member—the man who works hard but mostly on the wrong things or with the wrong priorities. It would also thoroughly expose the handful who make little effort to do anything. And it would give recognition to that other handful, the men who come to floor and committee prepared. Perhaps their number would increase. It certainly needs to.

Living through the Boss—
A Day in the Life
of a Senator's A.A.

Polly Toynbee

Seven A.M. Monday morning, Ken Gray arrives in his office. He has two hours before the office opens to deal with the mountain of memos to be written, letters answered, decisions made.

He is Senator Hubert Humphrey's administrative assistant, the man who runs everything behind the scenes, the invisible hand that passes over the right speech at the right time, the invisible mouth that whispers reminders at crucial moments, the invisible brain that prepares a statement and a view on anything and everything. He may not do it all himself, but he is the man responsible for seeing that it is done. He must see that his man gets through every appointment on his schedule properly briefed, equipped with speeches, and dressed right. In the words of another administrative assistant, "You blow their nose, dust and diaper them, and send them out there."

In Ken Gray's case, although he is in his mid-thirties, some 25 years younger than Humphrey, it's hard to see which of the two men is father and which is child. The roles seem to shift from one to the other. Some new senators hire old pros who know more about the system than they do and begin by being babied and tutored by their administrative assistants. But, although a man like Hubert Humphrey hasn't much to learn about politics, Ken advises him. Humphrey sometimes takes his advice.

These two men's lives are symbiotically intertwined. Without Ken and his staff, Humphrey is a big gun without a gunner, a knight in armor with no one to put him on his horse. And Ken, in turn, must depend on Hum-

Polly Toynbee is a columnist for the *Manchester Guardian*.

phrey. All the effort and the feeling of achievement to be had from the job is invested in the senator and his ability to put it all to good use. If in some way the senator fails, if he bungles something that's taken a lot of planning, if he changes his mind or gets something wrong, it's likely that Ken will not feel altogether forgiving. He has traded in all hope of personal recognition for the belief that he can achieve something through the senator. But there is even more to it than that. In some way Ken has taken on, as part of his own identity, the glamour and sparkle of the senator's image. He has, to some extent, merged, invested part of his own personality in that far stronger and more forceful public image of the man he serves. For this reason it is difficult to make him stand out and come alive as a man apart from the senator.

Arriving at seven, to make up for not having worked on Saturday, Ken has two hours in which to clear the letters and memos on his desk. He sits down to his dictaphone and begins at the top of the heap. There must be well over 200 letters. These are the first few:

A questionnaire from an assistant university professor in Fresno, asking for a detailed account of Humphrey's presidential campaign expenses. An angry though polite letter from a Houston oil transporter complaining about Humphrey's statements on the fuel shortage. A letter from Minnesota reading, "Sir, All you thinks about your selfs. You ain't for common people or farmers. . . . I like old time better I don't care for new time. You can't see that people living on farms they want the old time better." An official letter from the American Society of Mechanical Engineers enclosing their latest statements with regard to Humphrey's position on the new Office of Technological Assessment. A thank-you letter reading "Dear Chief, I want to express my thanks for your assistance in helping my son Ian get into Brown University." An anxious but friendly letter from someone who claimed that during the campaign last May he had used his father's Texaco credit card to hire cars, on the assurance he would be paid back, and was now being sued for $298.68 which he couldn't pay himself. The Young People's Socialist League wants a quote for its new magazine, but attached to this letter was a note from another staffer reading, "Ken, I assume I should just ignore?" A Minnesotan complaining about the Democrats in the Minnesota legislature: "If the Democrats can't be constructive why don't they shut up?" A large number of letters applying for a job in the office, which get the universal reply, that they have excellent qualifications for working in the Senate but alas, there are no openings. The welfare director from Knoxville, Tennessee wants to recommend a young man he knows to become the head of the FBI, "since he's done so well as safety director of the city of Knoxville." The League of Women Voters of Minnesota wishes to introduce a new lady in Washington with whom the senator's office should coordinate. Someone offers a little money towards Humphrey's presidential campaign deficit. A mimeographed questionnaire asks for Humphrey's views on heredity and intelligence. A letter thanks Humphrey for the tear sheet he sent her from the Congressional *Record,* which she encloses, "I now apply for the job of your secretary. You sure need one. Your remarks in the *Record* are sure a jumbled mess." Sure enough, the enclosed reprint is full of muddles and repeated paragraphs. Someone else writes to suggest a new FBI director: "A real good guy now working in the real estate business." Another thank-you letter saying, "Dear Hubey, I am really ashamed for my delay in saying THANKS for your time at our First District dance." Then another questionnaire from a kid in Moorhead, Minnesota who is writing a paper on "The Role of Administrative Assistants to U.S. Senators." And those are only the first few on the top of the heap.

By nine, the rest of the staff has arrived, 25 in all. Senator Humphrey's suite on the second floor of the Old Senate Office Building consists of four rooms with high ceilings and not enough floor space. (There is also an annex, a long way away, in a converted apartment building where three people do the first sorting of the mail.) The suite is on one of the many long marble corridors of the building. The great mahogany doors to the senatorial suites with their heavy senatorial seals look dark and forbidding. Not that they deter many chance tourists who, happening to be in Washington, take it as their constitutional right as taxpayers to call on their senator at any time of the day. Mostly these corridors are used by busy aides who hurry down them, their feet clack-clacking on the marble, like so many White Rabbits, looking at their watches and muttering over pieces of paper, passing the mail shafts where letters are continually puttering down from floors above.

Kathi Sezna, Ken's secretary, goes down to the carry-out in the basement as soon as she gets in, and fetches us each a cup of coffee. The telephone begins to ring. A mayor in Pennsylvania wants Humphrey to make a 25-second video-tape supporting him in an upcoming election. Dan Spiegel, the foreign affairs legislative assistant, comes in and says, a little indignantly, "I called you yesterday, you weren't there."

"Yesterday was Sunday. No, I wasn't in."

"I wanted to talk to you about Rhodesia," Dan says, and there is a brief discussion of a statement Dan will write for the senator to insert into the *Record.* At least six members of the staff are expected to produce three or four statements apiece each week for the *Record.* These will not often be read on the floor, but they will appear in the Congressional *Record* as if they had been. Since the *Record* isn't many people's bedtime reading, I ask what the point of all that work was. Ken explains that there is no money put aside for printing, but senators are entitled to reprints of anything that has appeared in the *Record,* so that when someone writes asking for Humphrey's views on any subject, there will always be a copy of a statement on hand on almost any conceivable matter. "Also," he says, "the few thousand most important people in the country will read the *Record* now and then and it makes him appear active on every front." The senator averages 20 such statements a week. "Another reason," Ken adds, "is that I love to think that in 10 years' time when people are doing research they will find that Hubert Humphrey was the first to put something in the *Record.*" It still seemed to me a remarkable waste of time and effort.

It is now 9:30. During the course of a normal day Ken will not see the senator very often. He hasn't yet spoken with Humphrey, although he is in an adjacent, though not adjoining, room. Their relationship is a controlled, rather than a natural, one. Ken feels that the less he has to see Humphrey, the more efficiently the office is running. There is not much natural empathy between these two men. Where Humphrey gives off an aura of hysterical energy, unable to keep still for a minute, quivering with an unnerving and unnatural bounce, Ken is slow, calm, deliberate, and thoughtful: but there is plenty of respect between them. Ken is a heavy man, dark, bespectacled, and dressed in large-size casual clothes. He moves slowly, appears unruffled, but can be sharp and authoritarian with members of his staff, although he doesn't lose his temper.

At this time Ken takes a tour around the different rooms of the office, partly to see that everyone is there, partly to show he is there, and partly to answer any questions. It is mostly a matter of routine.

Sitting in the room adjoining Humphrey's own office is the senator's personal staff, his personal secretary, scheduling secretary, and his press officer, who also schedules Muriel, Mrs. Humphrey. These three women seem to act as an independent group within the office. Although technically they are answerable to him, there is a certain amount of tension between the women and Ken. They tend to go their own way without consulting him. Ken likes to see everything that goes onto and comes off Humphrey's desk, but members of the personal staff are sometimes possessive. They often give Humphrey advice that conflicts with Ken's as will be seen in the bickering over the senator's TV appearance.

When Ken comes back to his office after his rounds, the telephone rings. Humphrey is invited to appear on the *Today* show to talk about Watergate. Ken is enthusiastic, but Betty South, the press secretary, is not. Humphrey can't make up his mind. Senators Alan Cranston and Thomas Eagleton have accepted, Muskie is dithering, and McGovern has refused. "I think he has a duty to appear at a time like this," Ken says. "A duty to himself, and a duty to the country to let them know where he stands." Humphrey, it appears, is not so sure. Betty feels he should stay well clear. The matter remains unresolved until the end of the day. The question does in fact turn into something of a battle between Ken and Betty—a quiet, unstated battle of the wills.

Next, someone from McGovern's office comes in and asks Ken whether

Humphrey can stand in for McGovern on the Nutrition Committee, as the senator is away at the funeral of his maid. "What's the subject?" Ken asks. "Sugar in the diet, diabetes, and heart trouble," the young man answers. Ken says that if no one else can be found he'll see what he can arrange. There is no problem about the fact that Humphrey probably knows nothing about sugar in the diet, as the staff of the Nutrition Committee will provide a statement and a set of relevant questions for him to ask the witnesses who will be testifying.

The witness list for an important hearing tomorrow is handed to Ken. Tomorrow Humphrey plans a hearing on the gasoline shortage, which he is particularly interested in. Ken OKs the list and sends it in to the senator. Ken OKs a letter for Humphrey to sign, a reply to a request by Senator Mike Gravel to co-sponsor a bill on the Airlines Mutual Aid Agreement, designed to stop airlines from receiving compensation when their employees strike, thereby destroying the incentive for airlines to resolve their disputes. Humphrey declines to put his name to this, saying the airline employees are "too highly paid already." However, there may have been more to Humphrey's decision than meets the eye. Northwest Airlines, noted for its protracted strikes and readiness to claim compensation even after one-man walkouts, has its head offices in Minneapolis, and it would not be unreasonable to suppose that the senator numbers several of its executives among his political friends.

The issue of a Watergate statement keeps reappearing. More startling Watergate revelations break, and soon the senator comes through to Ken again on the telephone. "Are you hesitant about making a statement on this business?" Ken says. "I hope you aren't." Ken suggests that Humphrey go down to the press gallery and make a statement. Humphrey agrees in principle.

No sooner has he put down the telephone than Hyman Bookbinder, an old Humphrey friend and adviser, is on the line urging Ken to persuade Humphrey to make a "ringing appeal for national unity so that government may continue to function," saying that if Nixon tells the truth, all will be forgiven, on the condition that he agrees to cooperate with Congress. Someone else calls up with the same idea, saying they had just bumped into Eric Sevareid, who also suggested the same course of action.

Ken is pleased to get this support for his own view on the matter.

A call comes in from a powerful man on a powerful senator's staff, asking Humphrey to speak for a minute to his daughter's sixth-grade class, which will be visiting the Capitol tomorrow. Ken says he'll try and tells the scheduling secretary to squeeze it in somehow. "I don't like that guy," he said, "but I guess it's good to have him owe us a favor or two."

Humphrey's position in the Senate doesn't allow for much wheeling and dealing and trading of favors. He has no seniority, no powerful committees. In the offices of more powerful men far more trading on a much deeper level takes up the time of the A.A.

At last it is lunch time. I am already exhausted from trying to keep up with the volume and variety of the morning's work.

We go down to the senators' dining room, where aides can eat when their senator isn't there. It wouldn't be described by many as one of the greatest privileges—regular canteen food and no liquor. It is the first time in the day that I have a chance to speak at any length with Ken. It is impossible to discuss his job, its frustrations and satisfactions, without discussing Humphrey himself in some detail.

"The trouble is that he still lives his life as an national candidate. He's been doing it for 20 years and it's very difficult to get a man to change. He used to be outspoken and very liberal, but as a national candidate he became less sharp. I guess that's been one disappointment in this job. But then, I really don't criticize him for becoming more moderate—that's the way the whole country's going. I really love Hubert Humphrey for having gone such a long, long way with good causes."

Ken began his career in politics as a legislative assistant to veteran liberal Senator Paul Douglas in 1961. His wife was hired as Humphrey's appointments secretary. In 1964 Ken became Humphrey's baggage man on his campaign plane, keeping track of everyone's luggage, "especially the reporters'." This also meant dealing with all the scheduling and travel plans on Humphrey's campaign. "He can be the most considerate man. Once, for no reason at all, he invited me, his baggage man, to attend some high-level campaign finance meetings in Florida." After the campaign Ken went back to Douglas' office, until the senator was defeated, in 1966, and in 1967 he became a legislative assistant to Humphrey, then vice-president. "But I quit after three months. There wasn't any legislating to do. It was like being in limbo." Ken went from limbo to work for Maryland Senator Joseph Tydings who was defeated in 1970.

But it seemed that Humphrey didn't hold this defection against him, for in 1970 he begged Ken to come back as his administrative assistant. "Why did he choose me? I don't know. It was a choice between the Minnesota Mafia he had always been surrounded by or a whole host of other applicants who had their own private agenda for Humphrey. They came from labor unions or business interest groups. Yes, I was surprised. We'd never had a close relationship. We still haven't. I don't think either of us feel that much at ease together socially, although I do go and have dinner there once every three weeks or so."

Munching his way through a plate of tasteless chicken and watery vegetables, Ken explained how hard life was for Humphrey and his staff having no seniority, no committee chairmanship, only a couple of not very important subcommittees, with no right to any committee staff. When Humphrey returned to the Senate after leaving the vice-presidency, he was forced to begin all over again as a freshman senator. Several kind senators had appealed to the power-that-be to give him back his seniority as far as possible, to put him back in the rank that he had left, but Senator Mike

Mansfield put his foot down and sent him to the bottom of the class. "That means he'll be dead before he qualifies for an important chairmanship," Ken said.

Ken has had important disagreements with Humphrey on how to maximize his power. "The trouble was that Humphrey still had all the old ideas about the Senate. He didn't see how things had changed. When something happened he expected to be able to go down on the floor and talk about it with the other senators. He really loves the Senate. It used to be a place where you could politely interrupt and say what was on your mind. It was a freewheeling outfit. But [Majority Whip Robert] Byrd has a tight grip on the Senate now. It's firmly in his custodial care and everything is scheduled. In the beginning Humphrey used to come back from the floor shaking mad. He used to say with terrible indignation, 'I went over there and wanted to talk, and I couldn't!' "

The important decision that Ken has never forgiven Humphrey for making was abandoning his place on the Government Operations Committee in exchange for a place on Foreign Relations. Ken had strongly advised him against it, pointing out that very shortly the senator would get an important subcommittee on Government Operations, but that he'd probably never get one on Foreign Relations. But Byrd had offered him the Foreign Relations job as a special favor, and Humphrey rememberd the good old times he had had on that committee. Now he regrets it terribly. Ken feels bitter, but tries not to remind the senator of this mistake. "If he'd stayed he'd have had the subcommittee on impoundment, a thing close to his heart. He wishes now that he'd listened to me."

Ken estimates that Humphrey would be listed as one of the 25 most important senators, but not as one of the top 10. "He has many friends, and he gets listened to. There is a chance he might become the Senate majority leader, as people are anxious not to have Byrd—just a chance." Humphrey's advancement is the only way that Ken himself can move on. He has come to the top of the ladder as an administrative assistant and would have nowhere to go, except to the office of a more powerful man.

In the Senate there are basically two types of administrative assistants. Some are old friends and colleagues who worked with their bosses long before they reached the Senate, coming from their home states and acting as emotional as well as official props to their man. They would never consider working for anyone else. Others, like Ken Gray, are professional aides who work their way through several senatorial offices in the course of their careers, soldiers of fortune who move freely from one senator to another, always hoping to move up the ladder in terms of working for more and more powerful men. Many of these aides tend to spend a good deal of time politicking for themselves, trying to do favors for the offices of great men for whom they aspire to work, building up personal contacts with people who will help them get on in the world. It seems likely that

Ken will decide to move on at some point. He is by nature far more issue-oriented than many A.A.s, but almost none of Humphrey's bills get passed, and what goes on in Humphrey's minor subcommittees could not be described as being of much importance. Also, rather to Ken's disapproval, Humphrey is determined to involve himself in every conceivable subject, and not to specialize. Although Humphrey has an enormous ability to absorb facts, Ken feels he really shouldn't spread himself so thin.

It is more than time now to hurry back to the office.

Waiting for Ken is a little pile of telephone messages. Ken's secretary has her lunch at her desk. Humphrey is asked to chair the Foreign Relations Committee on May 10, so Ken calls back and agrees with some alacrity. Someone from the Canal Zone has a query about voting rights. John Ehrlichman has, not surprisingly, canceled his debate with Humphrey at the Brookings Institution, will a substitute do? There is a bit more politicking to be done to get a Humphrey friend onto the Democratic Party's Vice Presidential Selection Commission. The Commission seems to be getting ridiculously huge. Will Humphrey co-host a conference on "Saving the Cities"? The answer is no, he won't have time. Ken calls back a Baltimore potentate ("I don't like that guy") and laughs and jokes with him for a minute or two. He has developed a habit common to most people who are used to working in crowded offices of making his end of the conversation completely discreet and incomprehensible. He glances through copies of letters Humphrey himself has just sent out, one to "Dear Willy," of Germany, another to Lady Bird, saying he is thinking of her in Washington in the spring now that all her daffodils are in bloom. An aide rushes in and asks could he put through a priority call to Teheran for a friend who needs to find her husband urgently.

The press secretary comes in, still worrying over Humphrey's Watergate position. "I've polled the office, and the majority are against his appearing on the *Today* show tomorrow morning." Ken nods and lets the matter drop for the time being. He intends to persuade Humphrey to do it.

Kathi has hurriedly finished her club sandwich and is licking her fingers. Above her is a notice board filled with pictures of the senator, a poster saying "Little People for Humphrey" showing him with some children, a picture of him bottle-feeding a lion cub, a picture of him looking sporty in a felt hat. On the mantlepiece is a sign saying "THINK MINNESOTA."

It is time to rush over to the Senate floor to give Humphrey a statement to insert into the *Record*. As we reach the senators' subway to catch a train over to the Senate, another train pulls in with Humphrey sitting in the front, as if he were driving the thing, also looking agitated at having to sit still doing nothing for a few moments. Ken hands him the document and Humphrey promises to squeeze it in later. They then set off at a racing speed down the corridors, Ken managing to keep up most of the time,

Humphrey talking very fast and loud, myself having difficulty staying with them without breaking into a run.

I could list another 2,000 things that came across Ken's desk that afternoon. He doesn't see the senator again, as Humphrey is in an agricultural committee hearing, but he does manage to persuade him to accept the *Today* show invitation, and he feels very pleased about that.

We leave the office at six and go down to the parking lot. One of the biggest privileges of being a senator or an A.A. turns out to be the right to a parking space of your own. For all the other thousands of Hill employees, the scramble in the morning to find a place to park is one of the main topics for conversation. We drive off to the Washington Hilton, where the Minnesota Chamber of Commerce, wives in evening dress, was holding a reception. The *pièce de résistance* was a gigantic ice flower vase full of real flowers.

Ken hates receptions and tries hard to melt into a corner, but he tends to be sought out. Everyone has a large lapel label which helps with the identification problem, as long as you don't appear to be looking at it. A man from Northwestern Bell, a Minnesota journalist, a Chamber of Commerce official, all hurry to greet him. This is a big, freeloading, holiday occasion, and everyone is out to enjoy himself. The canapes are vanishing and there is a fair bit of backslapping and joking about wives, most of whom are present. Then there is a bustle at the door, a flash of a few instamatic cameras, and Humphrey bounds into the room, hand outstretched to anyone who wants it. This is not an occasion where Ken is expected to stand behind his boss, discreetly reminding him who everyone is. Humphrey probably knows more people in the room than anyone else. It isn't often that Ken can be of much assistance to him in that way. Humphrey just knows and remembers every hand he's ever had the pleasure to pump.

By 7:45 Ken can slip away and go home, but it isn't the end of his official day. He and his wife are dining with the people from Northwestern Bell.

Next morning, 8:30 A.M., Ken arrives, not in the best of moods, but his moods don't show, unless you ask him how he feels. After Ken had left the office for the reception last night, the senator had been gotten to by his press secretary, and had been persuaded to cancel the *Today* show. Instead, he went to a Minnesota Grain Terminal Association breakfast. Ken is not pleased. But nothing more is said about it. That round was one up for the personal staff.

At nine, the phone rings, and Ken says, "Yes, sir," as if he had no quarrel with his boss. The senator is calling him into his office, together with a legislative assistant, to go over a speech to be made tomorrow on federalism at the Woodrow Wilson Center. "It's totally unnecessary for me to work on the speech," Ken says, "but Humphrey likes an audience." He returns shortly, having insisted that he was not really needed. The phone rings. A man in Albuquerque asks why Humphrey isn't shouting about Watergate. Ken explains quietly that the senator doesn't want to make too much of a partisan thing out of it. He could have jumped all over the president, but like other Democrats, he was holding back for fear of damaging the country. You would think Ken agreed with Humphrey's non-position from hearing him talk. That's the kind of restraint needed in that job.

More letters come off Humphrey's desk, already signed, saying things like, "It's always a pleasure to be with my friends the meatcutters." An old lady of 95 in a Minnesota nursing home gets a letter saying, "How grateful you must be for all the blessings that have been yours during these many years. May the days ahead bring you even greater joy." And "Dear Sister Hubertene. Thank you for remembering Mrs. Humphrey and me with your Easter greeting. We spent this meaningful time of the year with our family." He also promises to support any legislation that might come up against the slaughter of porpoises.

At 10:00 a call comes through saying that the Senate lacks three for a quorum. Ken promises to deliver Humphrey right away, but as he puts the phone down he says there is no rush, and he will wait until they've found the other two senators before sending Humphrey over.

At 10:30 Ken calls the weekly press and scheduling conference. When the senator is out, his office is used for meetings. The whole staff, apart from clerical workers, gathers, and Ken addresses them quite sternly. Some of them, notably the press secretary and the senator's personal secretary and scheduling secretary think these meetings are a waste of time. Probably this is only because they are constantly striving to wriggle out from under Ken's grip and make themselves into a separate group answerable only to the senator. The rift seems to be quite deep, and apparently is quite common in many Senate offices.

The press secretary is not particularly pleased to see me in the meeting, possibly only because she had not been consulted in the first place about my visit to the office. "Well," she said, laughing a little edgily, "So Ken's going to be a celebrity, ha, ha!"

Everyone is sitting around in a circle of chairs, no one daring to sit behind the boss's huge desk. They all are a little hushed, awed in this large, carpeted room which reeks of the aura of power. Big portraits on the wall of Johnson and Truman, none of Kennedy. A primitive painting of a farm above the mantle piece, presumably something to do with Minnesota, a great vice-presidential seal and a senatorial seal behind his chair, an elegant cut-glass jar full of peanuts on the coffee table. One of the less reverent women insists on eating some in spite of Ken's warning that it's against the rules.

"So what about Watergate?" Ken starts off.

"Just that piece on the op-ed page of *The Minneapolis Tribune* that may get printed in *The Washington Post.* That's all we feel necessary at the moment," the press secretary says quickly.

"Have we got anything on the Arts and Humanities Bill coming up today?" Ken asks.

"We have a statement for him and a memo on two amendments," says Al Saunders, the chief legislative assistant.

The scheduling secretary is then called upon to read out what the senator is already committed to for the next week in the way of speaking engagements outside all the Senate work. There are 12 speeches, ranging from Temple Israel to the 7th District PTA, and a file on each is ready to be distributed for people to work on.

Then there is the most exciting event of the week, Humphrey's hearings this afternoon on the gasoline shortage. "It's a fun hearing and a fun issue," Ken says, licking his lips. "He'll probably want to make a short speech putting some of the material in the *Record.* Are there any important Minnesota press men coming? We've really done well getting in first with these hearings."

In fact, the effort to get the gas hearings in before anyone else is an extraordinary waste of time. During the next few weeks there are at least five different sets of hearings scheduled on exactly this issue, each arranged by a different senator. The chief government spokesman on the matter is due to testify at each, presumably giving the same evidence five times over, for no better reason than that this is a politically sensitive issue, much in the public mind, and a number of senators want to be noticed for "doing something" about the situation.

There are at this meeting two new Congressional Fellows who had arrived this week to join the staff for four months. They are on loan from different branches of the government; the idea is that their experience on a senator's staff will help them deal more smoothly with Congress when they return to their regular jobs. They are treated exactly as if they are new legislative assistants.

Ken proceeds to brief the two newcomers, and most of the others drift back to their own offices, Humphrey's personal staff hurrying out with almost indecent haste.

"If you get a specific memo from the senator asking you to do something, you must let *me* know. Every so often he misdirects his memos, and I'll see that the work gets done by the right person. He believes in what's best described as controlled chaos. Sometimes he does it by mistake, sometimes because he thinks it's good to keep the office on its toes."

Ken then inquires what particularly interests the two. Wendy says she is interested in problems of the elderly. Tim says education. Ken then tells Wendy that since the senator has already put her on the gasoline shortage and the energy crisis, she'd better stay with it. She doesn't look altogether delighted. "Nutrition? Does that interest you?" Neither of them answered, but Ken gives it to Wendy, presumably because it sounds like the sort of thing a woman ought to be interested in. Tim is given a range of topics to study: the interior, land-use, and strip mining, most of public works, national growth and development, commerce, transportation, judiciary, consumer affairs, and District of Columbia affairs. Wendy is told that a third of her time will probably be taken up by energy. Her other responsibilities will be the judiciary, law enforcement, antitrust, the Post Office, the Civil Service, consumer economics, as well as nutrition and the elderly.

They are both aghast, though Wendy is the braver in expressing her horror at the amount of work. "But that's ridiculous! Are we trying to run a mini-government in this office or something?" she says, trying to make it sound as if she is half joking. "I mean, do just the few of us in this office have to cover the *entire* government?"

Ken explains that Humphrey "likes to have a policy on everything, and he likes to understand everything that's going on in the Senate."

When you imagine this much work being duplicated a hundred times, in each senator's office, when you consider that every senator feels he must have a policy somewhere on record on everything from porpoise hunting to strip mining, from sugar in the diet to arts and humanities, the whole Senate suddenly appears to be a kind of madhouse of hurried statements, spurious opinionating, and pointless duplication. This particular office is probably worse in this respect than most, first because Humphrey has no committee staff to take the weight off the shoulders of his staff on the things that are most important to him, and second, because Humphrey still acts like a presidential candidate out on the road, required to answer well every question from every stray heckler. He doesn't like to feel that anything is passing him by.

Most senators seem to have this feeling to some extent. In many cases it is probably disastrously bad for their effectiveness as knowledgeable and serious men. However, it's only fair to point out that a number of senators do try to specialize and thoroughly learn about the issues that interest them most. Among senators who like, trust, and on the whole agree with one another, it is common for them to defer to the senator who specializes in a certain subject and trust his opinion on how to vote. This helps reduce the amount of work and lets the senators learn about some things in depth.

Ken continues to instruct the newcomers. "I feel like a new member of the House being loaded with committees I don't want," Wendy says. "So what does all this really mean?"

Ken took a deep breath, "Well," he said slowly, "on a day-to-day basis it means the receptionist knows who to channel calls to when we get inquiries on a particular subject. We try to satisfy all callers who aren't crazy repeaters. We treat them with courtesy. We make almost no distinction between Minnesotans and non-Minnesotans. You don't *have* to see all the people who turn up and ask for you. You aren't totally vulnerable to chance visitors. If they're not from Minnesota you can give them the reprint of a speech and tell them to go away. If they are from Minnesota, you can get them to make an appointment to come back and see you when you aren't so busy.

"The senator doesn't care all that much about his committees. Otherwise, he particularly likes amendments, if you want to propose some. One of his maxims is, 'Some of our best legislation is non-germane.' He doesn't like to testify before anyone else's committee, he thinks it's a waste of time."

Cleaning out the ashtrays that had been used in the meeting, and putting the chairs in the senator's office back in position, Ken says to me, when the others have gone, "You know, I used to have a slogan on my desk which said, 'If you can keep your head while all about are losing theirs then you don't fully understand the situation.'" He explains that he had meant to hand out the week's speech files at the meeting, but "everyone was moaning and groaning so much that I thought it would be better to let it wait."

As we come out into the corridor, a loud crescendo of singing voices crashes around our ears. It turns out that senators take turns inviting choirs from their home state to sing in the rotunda at the end of the passageway; all right for those with offices on the other side of the building, not so good for those in easy earshot. Back in the office, someone calls up to ask what the president's decision to increase cheese imports means. The Martin Agronsky show calls, and Ken tells the press secretary that there just isn't room on the schedule today. "Anyway, we don't owe him a thing. Last time he was on that show Agronsky was as rotten as can be, gave him a really bad time." The phone rings again, "Yes, senator? Uhuh. Uhuh. Right." He turns to me and says, "The senator is grabbing a bowl of soup in the Senate dining room. We'll go over there and take him to his 1:30 gas hearings."

No time for lunch. We go over to the Senate. Wendy comes too, since she is dealing with gas. As we arrive, Humphrey comes bolting out of the dining room chewing deliberately on an indigestion tablet. We are all just about to set off when the phone beside us rings. It is Max Kampelman, a Washington attorney and longtime Humphrey adviser. He has something urgent to say. It is getting very close to time for the hearing and Ken is fidgeting a little with the file he is waiting to hand the senator. "I swear to God I haven't seen her for a month," Humphrey is saying down the telephone. He always talks as loud as if he were addressing a room full of deaf people. He puts down the telephone and dives toward the corridor, all of us following as best we can. He waves to some beaming nuns and calls out "Hi." A woman with an instamatic camera leaps out at him from behind a pillar, boldly introducing herself. Humphrey grins at her, shakes her hand, and says how very glad he is to see her. Ken and Wendy stand well back from this encounter. Humphrey suddenly stops seeming as if he's in a hurry. The woman produces her aunt, her husband, and her child from behind the same pillar and takes their photograph talking with him. Humphrey suggests that the aunt hold the camera and take another photo with the woman in the picture. Then he waves to them and moves on, having patted the baby. He dashes on around the corner and again we follow. Someone grabs his jacket as he passes and he waves again. A number of people call out "Hi, Senator." It's as if he were Santa Claus in a big department store, paid to be nice. But Ken says he enjoys this more than anything, cares little for privacy, and feels himself regenerated by every hand he shakes.

Arriving at the committee room, he sits down, shaking hands with the other people there, and right away launches into the statement Ken has just handed him, which he hasn't seen before. We stay for a little while to hear him. Having already read the statement, I recognize when it comes to an end and he continues to speak extempore on fuel shortage, with particular reference to Minnesota. He has no brief with him that tells him these things, but he does seem to know exactly how many independent gas stations have just closed down, exactly how many men are out of work, exactly which firms in the state own how many stations. Ken doesn't know where all this information came from, "Probably someone he talked to last night at that Chamber of Commerce reception."

Then, at 3:30, a call comes from the front office: did Ken remember that Humphrey had an appointment with an important contributor, to discuss a conference he was holding that the senator had promised to attend? Ken groans, vey silently. This man has been in Washington three times before and they had been unable to fit him in. And he is important. He says that in 10 minutes he will take him over to the gas hearings and hopes that they end soon.

Then we walk all the way back to the hearing room with the important contributor. Humphrey is not halfway through yet, and is still interrogating the first witnesses. He is clearly in full flight and not interruptible. So we stand outside in the corridor while the man explains to Ken exactly what he wants to say to the senator, and then asks if Ken will guide him to Wilbur Mills at the Ways and Means Committee. Weaving and wending our way through the passages and corridors, we hurry along, Ken having got used to Humphrey's walking pace, until we reach the great double doors of the Ways and Means palace. The man, knocking on the door rather nervously, looks not unlike Dorothy knocking on the door of the Wizard of Oz's audience chamber. The door opened a crack, and inside you could just catch a glimpse of the room, darkened by heavy yellow drapes across the window. He went in and the door closed again at once.

By the time we get back to the office and Ken has dealt with a few more phone calls, it is 4:30. The senator has to catch a plane to a Freemasons' dinner in New York at 5:30. There are still statements to be inserted into the *Record* before he goes. Also, he must change into a dinner jacket and get to the airport. "Well, it won't be the first time he misses a plane," Ken says, as we make the long journey back to the hearings. We wait 10 minutes while Humphrey winds up. He comes hurrying out, glances at the statements as he pounds along, and disappears into a "Senators Only" room with them in his hand. While he is gone, Ken goes to find his driver, who works during the days as a doorman outside the public gallery of the Senate. That is a patronage job, of which each senator is entitled three. Unfortunately, the driver has gone to repark the car and won't be back for 10 minutes. Humphrey has to fit in time for coffee with Willy Brandt and some other senators before he goes, and he now hurries off to that function.

Ken goes back to the office, the day almost over. He gets away at 6:00, more easily done when the senator is away. I still have to ask him about the real satisfactions of his job.

He says, "You don't understand the fascination of power, of being near where it all happens, of making history yourself, of making things happen. I wouldn't be in any other business. There's scarcely a day when I don't leave the office feeling that I have really achieved something that day, feeling I have really done something important."

But what is really being achieved out of that great mountain of trivia? Very few of Humphrey's bills ever get passed. Not many people read his statements in the *Record*. It isn't clear that the world is being made any better by the work in that office. The most important task that Humphrey has to perform is voting, and his time would be spent more profitably in reading and being briefed thoroughly on current legislation. For senators with more seniority and powerful committees, their most important work is done in the hearing room, where there is a large complement of extra staff to help them get some kind of grasp on what's going on. For a man like Humphrey, whose power is confined to his vote, devoting so much time to holding competitive, repetitive hearings and generating opinions on so many subjects isn't productive.

If all that great amount of work done in the office, if all the time all the energy of Humphrey and his men were channeled into something else, they could, among them, produce a daily newspaper, put on a big Broadway show every week, or probably govern a country the size of England. They are like a group of men on bicycling machines in a slimming salon, using maximum effort for minimum mileage. Worthy, noble, well-intentioned effort for the most part, but spun out so thin that the end result is scarcely visible to the human eye.

Why Senator Eagleton Fired Me

GREGORY G. RUSHFORD

By most standards my short career as a staff investigator for Senator Thomas F. Eagleton would have to be rated a success. During the first six months of this year, I probed the Carter administration's mishandling of the sale of radar planes to Iran, which became the focal point of congressional debate on arms sales. I investigated an $800-million Air Force computer scandal and exposed officials' lies. I started an inquiry into inefficiencies in our overseas Food for Peace program. I also helped persuade the Foreign Relations Committee to reconsider the War Powers Resolution, participated in negotiations with the administration on our policies toward Greece, Cyprus, and Turkey, and worked up amendments to the defense bill that will trim military waste.

One day in June 1977 Senator Eagleton called me into his office and fired me. It was the rational thing for him to do.

The reasons why it was rational go a long way towards explaining the pressures at work on a young (by Senate standards) legislator who wants to do the right thing and still win the esteem of his peers. They also make it clear why Congress does so little to investigate government wrongdoing.

In January 1977, Thomas Eagleton looked to me like the ideal boss. He was 48 years old and in his second term in the Senate; his seniority and influence were growing, especially because a new Democratic President and Congress were just coming into office. A native of St. Louis, Eagleton graduated from Amherst College and Harvard Law School. At 31 he

Gregory Rushford, a former congressional staff aide, is now a Washington writer.

became Missouri's attorney general and at 39 one of its senators. As chairman of the District of Columbia Committee he pushed home rule through the Senate. He was the chief sponsor of the resolution that stopped the Cambodia bombing in 1973. He led the effort to cut off military aid to Turkey after it invaded Cyprus in 1974. He has taken the knife to the Pentagon's budget. I met him in 1976 in the course of writing an article for a magazine about his successful effort to stop one waste of Defense Department money, the Navy's Condor missile.

ESTABLISHING OUR TURF

In January a member of Eagleton's staff got a job in the State Department and recommended me as a replacement. Eagleton offered me a job, and a few weeks later I accepted. My predecessor had been officially an employee of the District of Columbia Committee (disguising personal staff as committee staff is a common practice in the Senate) and so was I, although the committee had been reorganized into a Governmental Efficiency and the District of Columbia Subcommittee of the Governmental Affairs Committee. My job was to examine waste and inefficiency anywhere in the government.

Eagleton and I first set about establishing our turf, which is a tricky business. We had to pick issues that other senators didn't already consider their own. For instance, military issues were out—they would offend Henry Jackson and Sam Nunn, who had already claimed them. And Lawton Chiles chaired a sister subcommittee that was studying military procurement. Even more important, the late John McClellan had just granted Eagleton membership on his Defense Appropriations Subcommittee, and it would not be good manners for Eagleton to return the favor by using another subcommittee to investigate the military.

So my first idea—to look for evidence of corruption in the Pentagon's $10 billion research and development budget—got nowhere. "I can't look like I'm on a vendetta against the military," Eagleton said. "Get me a cripple. Some horrible wasteful weapon no reasonable person could endorse." Even then, it was better to hold off for a while, for fear of stirring up resentment on the McClellan subcommittee.

Eagleton taught me another lesson, one he had learned on the D.C. Committee. When he started to uncover the District's shoddy bookkeeping some years ago, he said, "it became a morass of work that threatened to tie up my time forever." This time, he wanted "quick and easy examples of waste to expose, so we don't get bogged down."

What Eagleton most wanted me to look into, he knew I couldn't. "I'd really like to have you investigate the Equal Employment Opportunities Commission," he told me. "That whole place is in a shambles. It breaks your heart to see the way people who have been discriminated against are treated. But I can't touch that one because I'd be called anti-black. I had enough of that when I criticized the D.C. government."

And now, of course, Eagleton was no longer in an adversary role with respect to the executive branch. His relations with the White House were (and still are) good. As he admitted to one audience, "I'm now mainly in the role of apologist" for the new team. Investigating the EEOCs of the federal government was primarily the task of the Republicans. It seemed that everything I looked into brought on some unacceptable political problem.

EASY TO DRAMATIZE

I first tried to look into the easy-to-dramatize issue of overseas private arms sales. The Foreign Relations Committee, of course, was already in charge of the larger question of the Defense Department's $10 billion in arms sales to foreign governments. Private commercial arms sales, far smaller than the government's sales, are licensed by an obscure State Department munitions control office. By several accounts, that office, understaffed and tucked away in a highrise across the Potomac from the State Department, performs inadequately. The papers have printed stories about widespread illegal international gunrunning; I got a tip myself that the munitions control office has in recent years downplayed the scope of its dealings in its reports to Congress. Members of the Foreign Relations Committee staff assured me that they had no time to investigate the office and would welcome a hand from Eagleton.

But Eagleton had to say no to the idea because of the political risks. A furious last-minute campaign by the gun lobby had nearly defeated him in his first Senate race in 1968, and he was afraid of stirring up the same opposition in the 1980 election. It was a stirring tribute to the lasting power of a few weeks of well-organized lobbying.

In April Eagleton agreed to tackle the Food for Peace program as his new subcommittee's first investigation. The program, established in 1954, is the vehicle by which we give and sell at generous terms food to other nations. Because it has several purposes (smoothing out diplomatic relations, helping the world's poor, disposing of surplus products, promoting farm exports), and because it is administered by two different agencies (the Agency for International Development and the Agriculture Department), it seemed like a logical candidate for an efficiency study.

I carefully laid the groundwork for my investigation by checking first with Senator Humphrey's staff to see if they had any objections. Eagleton himself made courtesy calls to Humphrey and Abraham Ribicoff. All this was necessary because Humphrey is known as "Mr. Food for Peace" and his feelings were important, while Ribicoff is chairman of the full Governmental Affairs Committee, under which our investigation was taking place. After these elaborate hedges against senatorial ill-will, Eagleton told me to get to work.

ROTTING ON THE DOCKS

The first thing I found was that Food for Peace food was rotting on docks and in granaries in Bangladesh. In September 1976, a subcommittee that Humphrey chaired reported that in the first nine months of that year, more than half of the $50 million worth of wheat, rice, and soybean oil Food for Peace sent Bangladesh would be "lost to insects, rodents, and mold" in inadequate storage facilities. The report said U.S. officials "knew or should have known that a substantial amount of food would spoil." The culprit was apparently the Agriculture Department, which, amid much haggling, had pushed AID to export too much food, especially rice. And why was that? My sources told me a delegation of congressmen had visited the White House early in 1976 to push hard for increased rice exports, and the White House had pushed Agriculture. The representatives from Arkansas and Louisiana, both rice-producing states, had lobbied with particular ardor.

Arkansas, of course, was the home state of John McClellan, a very special senator to Eagleton. One of my first instructions had been never to displease McClellan. In the Defense subcommittee, when Senator Proxmire urged the opening of unclassified hearings to the public, Eagleton supported McClellan's successful efforts to keep them closed. "You don't oppose the Chairman on little things," he told me. The situation was especially sensitive because just before I was hired, Eagleton had gotten into McClellan's doghouse by opposing the transfer of a Missouri military facility to Arkansas without the courtesy of advance consultation.

But if my first set of findings was ill-advised, my second big lead could have earned me the political rube of the year award.

I discovered that the most inefficient part of the Food for Peace bureaucracy was the innocuous-sounding Office of the General Sales Manager. The general sales manager apparently duplicates the work of other officials, bollixes up the administration of our food export policies, and acts as a thorn in the side of another Agriculture Department subsidiary, the Foreign Agricultural Service. Its annual budget is $3 million. The office seemed to be a God-given target for a set of hard-hitting hearings.

Unfortunately, that was not the case. The Office of the General Sales Manager had been created in 1955, over the objections of Agriculture

Secretary Ezra Taft Benson, by Rep. Jamie Whitten of Mississippi, the chairman of the House Agriculture Appropriations Subcommittee. Whitten, a shrewd and tough operator who has been in Congress since 1941, has been engaged for years in a battle with the Foreign Agriculture Service. He sees the Office of the General Sales Manager as his chief within-the-department weapon in that fight. In a recent report, Whitten complained that the Agriculture Department often leaves the position of general sales manager vacant, and that even when it is filled, it is "dominated by the Foreign Agriculture Service and its policies concerning sales in world markets."

So my investigation of Food for Peace had provided Eagleton with an opportunity to attack not only the chairman of the Senate Appropriations Committee, but also a Congressman who could destroy him in the House-Senate agriculture bill conference. Missouri grain interests would not have been pleased if in the name of reforming the bureaucracy Tom Eagleton had made Jamie Whitten hostile to them. Indeed, try as I might I could find no problems in Food for Peace that were truly its own fault rather than the fault of Eagleton's esteemed colleagues in Congress.

BLIND AMBITION

In late May I had a where-are-we-going talk with Eagleton. I said foreign agriculture is an important issue (our farm exports of $23 billion are of increasing diplomatic and economic magnitude) but one that would take several years' work to probe fully. I told him my situation reminded me of John Dean's, as Dean described it in *Blind Ambition,* a book both of us had read with total absorption. Like Dean, I had the sense that I was working for a boss who had no clear idea of what he wanted me to be doing, and like Dean I felt pressured to create work for myself as a way of making myself indispensable. Whether I went ahead on agricultural exports or not, I told Eagleton, "I want it to be your decision because you are interested in it, and not because it's something a John Dean has dreamed up. And we can find discreet ways to run the political minefield, or at least try our best." The Senator said he would puzzle the dilemma through.

A few weeks later, in mid-June, Eagleton called me into his office and said, "Greg, I think we must sever our relationship." It wasn't anything personal, he said, and he would recommend me to anyone as a good investigator. He just wasn't comfortable with me. As Eagleton's administrative assistant told me shortly afterwards, "I guess you're too much the investigative type." He was right.

Eagleton and I continued to have a pleasant working relationship over the next few months; he kindly offered to let me stay on his staff while I looked for another job. We even accomplished a few things. But there was constantly the specter of grave political liabilities if we pushed too hard.

THE ART OF POLITICS

The lesson of my story is that the art of politics is not compatible with the art of investigation. In the legislative process the best players are moderates, people with principles but not rigid ideology who know how to horsetrade, compromise, and temper disagreements. Eagleton is good at this, and I saw him accomplish several noteworthy things through its use. But to be effective an investigator has to follow the path wherever it leads—to Democrat or Republican, friend or foe.

Most government investigators learn to temper their zeal with political savvy, usually to the detriment of their investigative work. For instance, Henry Peterson of the Justice Department's criminal division got the message during the initial Watergate investigation that he was not to ask the White House tough questions, and he complied. My test of political loyalty came early in my association with Eagleton, and I failed: I didn't deliver on a request to find illegal campaign contributions to Charles Percy for a friend of Eagleton's who wants to run against Percy in 1978.

But I don't mean to sound self-righteous. Arguably, it might be possible to achieve a greater public good by not running completely frank investigations. By not pushing McClellan and Whitten, Eagleton staved off a possible loss for himself, and for his constituents, in the Appropriations Committee.

A better example comes from my experience a couple of years ago as an investigator for Rep. Otis Pike's House Intelligence Committee. Pike ran a no-holds-barred investigation. When he learned that Senator Henry Jackson had helped the CIA stave off an investigation of the ITT-Chile affair, Pike was willing to publish the information. In light of Jackson's national political power, that took great courage for Pike as it took great courage for Rep. Robert Giaimo to go along with Pike's decision even though Giaimo was chairman of Jackson's presidential campaign in Connecticut.

Senator Frank Church, who ran the Senate's intelligence investigation, had access to the same information on Jackson and, as he did on nearly every other sensitive political matter, he covered it up.

Here's the price of honesty: Pike was damaged politically for what he did. The House refused to establish a successor Intelligence Committee when the Pike committee's jurisdiction lapsed. Three members of the Pike committee who ran for the Senate lost. But Frank Church, who showed he could play along, went on to run a creditable presidential campaign. And the Senate established a follow-up Intelligence Committee, weaker than might have been hoped for but nevertheless alive.

It's a tough problem. People elect congressmen to perform both the legislative and investigative functions, but in practice those functions work at cross-purposes. Eagleton wasn't reluctant to investigate because he's an evil man—he's a good senator trying to pass good bills, and he saw investigating as standing in the way of that.

For most of American history, the cross-purposes problem has been present, but it hasn't had major bad effects. The federal government was small enough so that making sure it delivered the goods honestly and efficiently wasn't itself an issue of the utmost importance. But in the last 30 years that has changed, and it's no longer enough to stand by and cluck about the Senate's reluctance to investigate. We have to find an answer.

part 4
LAW
AND THE
COURTS

Even Jimmy Carter is alarmed about the state of the American legal and judicial system. We have clogged courts, technicalities substituting for justice, an uninspired Justice Department and Supreme Court, inadequate representation for the poor, and a host of other problems.

These are sweeping complaints, but they rise out of one very specific malady: any sensitive observer who spends any time in court these days comes away feeling that what goes on there has only a passing resemblance to the doing of justice. Judge Lois Forer, describing a day in her life, complains of feeling trapped by her caseload and by the constraints of the legal system. Tom Bethell, in "Criminals Belong in Jail," sees dangerous young men who have committed violent crimes being casually let free. In criminal courts today plea-bargaining is the rule and discussion of a case on its merits—whether the accused is innocent or guilty—is becoming a rarity.

What's wrong here? The standard reply is that we're suffering from a severe shortage of judges and lawyers, that if there were more of them everyone sued or accused could have a real fair trial. But it might be that the answer is the opposite. In "Thinking Like a Lawyer," Charles Peters and Michael Kinsley lay much of the blame for the problems of the legal system on the attitude (held mostly by lawyers) that law is the ideal solution to all of America's problems. As a result, we've become law-crazy. Every reform means more lawyers suing other lawyers. Every dispute and negotiation becomes a matter fit for litigation. Instead of moving toward mediation and simplicity, we're making the courts increasingly the central forum of our society, and as a result they're becoming even more unsatisfactory in that role.

View From the Bench: A Judge's Day

Judge Lois G. Forer

At 9:30 the court personnel begin to assemble. The crier opens court. "All rise. Oyez, oyez, all persons having business before the Court of Common Pleas Criminal Division come forth and they shall be heard. God save this honorable court. Be seated and stop all conversation. Good morning, Your Honor." The crier calls out the names of the defendants. Most of them are represented by the public defender. He checks his files. One or two names are not on his list. A quick phone call is made to his office to send up the missing files.

On one particular day when I was sitting in criminal motions court, three cases had private counsel. One had been retained by the defendant. The other two had been appointed by the court to represent indigents accused of homicide. Where are these lawyers?

As is customary, the court officer phones each of them and reminds his secretary that he has a case listed and he must appear. Several of the defendants are not present. The prison is called to locate the missing parties. The judge, if he wishes to get through his list, must find the lawyers and litigants and order them to come to court.

Frequently the prosecutor cannot find his files. When he does, he discovers that a necessary witness has not been subpoenaed. The case must be continued to another day. The other witnesses, who are present and have missed a day's work, are sent home. The defendant is returned to jail to

Lois G. Forer is a judge in the Philadelphia Court of Common Pleas. This article is adapted from her book, *The Death of the Law*. Reprinted by permission of Curtis Brown, Ltd., 575 Madison Avenue, New York. Copyright © 1975 by Lois G. Forer.

await another listing. Often cases are listed five and six times before they can be heard.

On this day there were three extraditions. Amos R. is wanted in South Carolina. Seven years ago he had escaped from jail and fled north. Since then he has been living in Philadelphia. He married here and now has two children. His wife and children are in the courtroom. He is employed. Amos has not been in trouble since leaving South Carolina, where 10 years ago he was convicted of stealing a car and sentenced to nine to 20 years in prison. He had no prior record. In Pennsylvania, for the same crime, he would probably have been placed on probation or at most received a maximum sentence of two years.

Now he testifies that he didn't steal the car, he only borrowed it. Moreover, he didn't have a lawyer. When he pleaded guilty he was told he could get six months. This is probably true. Also, he was undoubtedly indicted by a grand jury from which Negroes were systematically excluded. All of these allegations would be grounds for release in a postconviction hearing, for they are serious violations of constitutional rights. But they are irrelevant in extradition hearings. The only issues that the judge may consider before ordering this man to leave his family and shipping him off to serve 18 more years in prison are whether he is in fact the Amos R. named in the warrant and whether the papers are in order. There is little judicial discretion. One is often impelled by the system to be an instrument of injustice.

This is the dilemma of a judge and of many officials in the legal system. Following the rule of law may result in hardship and essential unfairness. Ignoring the law is a violation of one's oath of office, an illegal act, and a destruction of the system. Some choose to ignore the law in the interests of "justice." Others mechanically follow precedent. Neither course is satisfactory. The judge who frees a defendant knows that in most instances the state cannot appeal. Unless there is an election in the offing and the prosecutor chooses to use this case as a political issue, there will be no repercussions. But it is his duty, as it is that of the accused, to obey the law. If the judge is not restrained by the law, who will be? On the other hand, it is unrealistic to say, "Let the defendant appeal." In the long period between the trial judge's ruling and that of the higher court, if it hears the appeal, a human being will be in jail. One does not easily deprive a person of his liberty without very compelling reasons. Almost every day, the guardians of the law are torn between these conflicting pulls.

After hearing the life story of Amos R., as reported by the prosecutor, the young defender said, "Mr. R. wishes to waive a hearing."

I looked at the lawyer. "Mr. R., do you know that you have a right to a hearing?"

"Yes."

"Have you consulted with your attorney about waiving a hearing?"

"My attorney?" R. looks bewildered.

"Your lawyer, the defender," I pointed to the young man.

"Oh, him," R. replies. "Yes, I talked to him."

"How long?"

" 'Bout two minutes."

"Your Honor," says the defender, "I have spoken to the sheriff. There is no question that this is the Amos R. wanted. The papers are in order."

I search through the official-looking sheaf of documents with gold seals and red seals and the signatures of two governors, hoping to find a defect, a critical omission. At last I discover that Amos R. was arrested in New Jersey on a Friday night. He was not taken to Pennsylvania until the following Monday. It is 89 days that he has been in jail in Pennsylvania. The extradition hearing must by statute be held within 90 days of arrest. By adding on the three days he was in custody in New Jersey, I conclude that the 90-day time limit has not been met. Amos R. is once again a free man. This happy ending is unusual. Bureaucratic inefficiencies seldom redound to the benefit of the individual.

PRISONERS OF BUREAUCRACY

The next four matters are bail applications. All the defendants fit the stereotype. They are black males under the age of 30. Only one is in the courtroom. The others are in the detention center. It is too much trouble and too expensive to transport them to court for a bail hearing. I must decide whether to set free or keep locked up men whom I cannot see or talk to. If I don't release them, they may be in jail for as long as a year awaiting trial. The law presumes that they are innocent. I look at the applications. This is not the first arrest for any of them. For one there are records going back to age nine, when he was incarcerated for truancy.

"The defendant's juvenile record may not be used against him in adult court," I remind the prosecuting attorney.

"I know, Your Honor," he replies apologetically, "but the computer prints out all the arrests."

"How many convictions?"

The computer does not give the answer to that question.

One man is accused of rape. The record shows that his prior offenses were larceny of an automobile and, as a child, running away from home. The police report indicates that when the police arrived the defendant was in the complainant's apartment with his clothes off. He left so quickly that he abandoned his shoes and socks. The complainant admitted knowing him and gave his name and address to the police. No weapon was involved.

My usual rule of thumb is a simple one: "If he had time to take off his shoes, it wasn't rape."

Before releasing an alleged rapist from jail, possibly to prey on other victims, I want to speak with the accused. Although Lombroso's theory that one can tell a criminal by his physical appearance is out of fashion, I still want to see him, but he is not in the courtroom. Perhaps his lawyer, the defender, can give some helpful information. The defender, however, has never seen the accused. Someone else interviewed him on a routine prison visit. No one knows whether he has a family, a job, a home.

"Please have this defendant brought to court tomorrow and get me some information on him," I tell the defender.

He replies, "I'm sorry, Your Honor. I'll be working in a different court-room tomorrow. There is no way I can find out about this man."

"We're dealing with human beings, not pieces of paper," I expostulate. "You are his lawyer. You should know him.

The young defender sadly shakes his head. "Your Honor, I work for a bureaucracy."

So do I, I remind myself, as I look at the clock and see that it is past 11:00 and there are 14 more matters to be heard today.

FOUR UP, FOUR DOWN

I refuse bail for a 14-year-old accused of slaying another child in a gang rumble. Will he be safer in jail than on the street, where the rival gang is lying in wait for him? I do not know. The boy is small and slender. The warden will put him in the wing with the feminine homosexuals to save him from assault. I mark on the commitment sheet that the boy is to attend school while in prison awaiting trial. But if the warden does not honor my order, I will not know.

A 23-year-old heroin addict tells me that there is no drug treatment program in prison. "It's just like the street. Nothin' but drugs," he says. I try to move his case ahead so that he can plead guilty at an early date and be transferred to the federal drug treatment center. He, like so many others up for robbery and burglary, is a Vietnam veteran. He acquired his habit overseas and now must steal in order to pay for his daily fix.

The next matter is a petition to suppress a confession. Court appointed counsel alleges that the defendant did not make a knowing and intelligent waiver of his rights when he confessed three murders to the police. Cornelius takes the stand and describes his life. His history is typical. He was sent to a disciplinary school at 11, ran away at 12, and spent a year in juvenile jail. At 17, there was a conviction for larceny and another period of incarceration. He is married, two children, separated from his wife. He is vague about the ages of the children. Cornelius works as an orderly in a hospital earning $80 a week take-home pay. At the end of each week he divides his money in two parts: $40 for living expenses and $40 for methadrine, which costs $20 a spoon.

Where does he buy it? On any corner in the ghetto. He steals the syringes from the hospital. His expenses are minimal except for the precious methadrine. He is riddled with V.D. He seldom eats.

While on a high, he shot and killed three strangers. Why did he do it?

"There are these voices I hear. They're fightin'. One tells me to kill; the other tells me not to. Sometimes I get so scared I run out into the street. That's when I'm in a low. But when I'm in a high, I feel I can walk in the rain without getting wet. I don't feel sad, I ain't lonely. When I'm comin' down from a high, I got to get another shot."

Now he is in a low—sad, soft-spoken, withdrawn, disinterested in his own fate. I see his skinny brown arms pocked with little needle scars. The psychiatrist says that when Cornelius is on drugs he cannot gauge reality. He could not understand the meaning of the privilege against self-incrimination and make a knowing and intelligent waiver of his rights.

The earnest psychiatrist explains patiently. I watch Cornelius, wraith-thin, sitting in withdrawn disinterest, lost in some dream of flight. Is he mad or are we—the prosecutor, the defense lawyer, the psychiatrist, and the judge? After five hours of testimony, I rule that the confession must be suppressed. There are dozens of eye-witnesses. The confession is not necessary to convict Cornelius. After this hearing, and before trial, a psychiatrist for the defense will testify that Cornelius is not mentally competent to stand trial; he cannot cooperate with his lawyer in preparing his defense. A psychiatrist for the prosecution will testify that when Cornelius has withdrawn from drugs he will be able to participate intelligently in his defense. The motion to defer trial will probably be denied. At the trial itself, one psychiatrist will testify that at the time of the shootings Cornelius did not know the difference between right and wrong and the nature and quality of his act. Another will testify that he did. Neither psychiatrist saw Cornelius at the time of the crimes. Both of them examined him in prison months later. They are certain of their opinions.

A middle-aged, white, epicenely soft man is next on the list. His face is a pasty gray. He mutters under his breath. He is accused of committing sodomy on three teenaged boys. Most of his meager salary he spent on these boys, and now they have turned on him. I order a psychiatric examination simply because I don't know what else to do. A month later the report is sent to me. It follows a standard format: facts (gleaned from the accused), background, diagnostic formulation and summary, and recommendation. This report states: "Probable latent schizophrenia. We recommend a full examination 60-day commitment." At the end of 60 days and the expenditure of hundreds of dollars, the doctors will decide that he is or is not schizophrenic, possibly sociopathic. A long period in a "structured environment" will be recommended. But what will the judge do? There are only two choices: prison, where he will be tormented and perhaps beaten by strong young thugs, or the street.

LOST IN THE JAILHOUSE

Most of the prisoners brought before me are young—under 30. I also see children who are charged with homicide. They are denied even the nominal protections of the juvenile court and are "processed" as adults. The 14-year-old accused of slaying another child in a gang rumble; the 16-year-old dope addict who, surprised while burglarizing a house, panicked and shot the unwary owner; the girl lookout for the gang, who is accused of conspiracy and murder. Many of these children are themselves parents. Can they be turned back to the streets? I refuse bail for an illiterate 15-year-old accused of murder and note on the bill of indictment that he be required to attend school while in detention. I ask the court-appointed lawyer to check with the warden and see that the boy is sent to class. But is there a class in remedial reading at the detention center? Who would pay for it? Not the overburdened public schools or the understaffed prisons. It is not a project likely to find a foundation grant.

A perplexed lawyer petitions for a second psychiatric examination for his client. The court psychiatrist has found him competent to stand trial but the lawyer tells me his client cannot discuss the case with him. Randolph, who is accused of assault with intent to kill, attacked a stranger in a bar and strangled the man, almost killing him. Fortunately, bystanders dragged Randolph away. I ask to speak with Randolph. A big, neatly dressed Negro steps up to the bar of the court. He speaks softly, "Judge," he says, "I'm afraid. I need help."

Randolph is out on bail. This is his first offense. He has a good work record. He is married, has two children, and lives with his family. It is Friday morning. I fear what may happen to him over the weekend. The court psychiatric unit is called.

"We've got people backed up for a month," the doctor tells me. "Even if I took Randolph out of turn I couldn't see him until next week." When he does see Randolph it will be a 45-minute examination. A voluntary hospital commitment seems to be the only safeguard. But at least he will be watched for ten days. Gratefully, Randolph promises to go at once to the mental health clinic. What will happen to him after the ten-day period?

There is no time to wonder. The next case is waiting.

It is a sultry day. When the ancient air conditioner is turned on we cannot hear the testimony. When it is turned off the room is unbearable. At 4:45 p.m., I ask hopefully, "Have we finished the list?" But no, there is an application for a continuance on an extradition warrant. The papers from the demanding state have not arrived. It is a routine, daily occurrence.

I look around the courtroom. By this hour only the court personnel and a few policemen and detectives are present. "Where is the defendant?" I inquire. The prosecutor does not know. He is not responsible for producing him. The defender does not have him on his list. "Is he in custody?" I ask. We all search the records and discover that he was arrested more than five months ago. There is no notation that bail has ever been set. No private counsel has entered an appearance. A deputy sheriff checks and reports that he has not been brought up from the prison. The computerized records show that this man has never had a hearing. Hardened as we are, the prosecutor, the defender and I are horrified that someone should be sitting in jail all this time without ever having had an opportunity to say a word. Is he, in fact, the person wanted for an offense allegedly committed years ago and hundreds of miles away? Was he ever there? Is he a stable member of society? Has he a family, a job, a home? Is he a drug addict? No one knows. The papers do not indicate. No one in the courtroom has ever seen him. Each of us makes a note to check on this forgotten prisoner whom the computer may or may not print out for appearance on some other day in some other courtroom.

NOBODY WAIVED GOOD-BYE

The scene in criminal trial court is similar. Most of the cases are "waivers" and guilty pleas. The accused may waive his constitutional right to be tried by a jury of his peers and be tried by a judge alone. Fewer than five per cent of all cases are tried by jury. In most cases, the accused not only waives his right to a jury trial but also to any trial and pleads guilty. Before accepting a waiver or a plea, the accused is asked the routine questions. Day after day defense counsel recites the following formula to poor, semiliterate defendants, some of whom are old and infirm, others young and innocent. Read this quickly:

"Do you know that you are accused of [the statutory crimes are read to him from the indictment]?

"Do you know that you have a right to a trial by jury in which the state must prove by evidence beyond a reasonable doubt that you committed the offenses and that if one juror disagrees you will not be found guilty?

"Do you know that by pleading guilty you are giving up your right to appeal the decision of this court except for an appeal based on the jurisdiction of the court, the legality of the sentence and the voluntariness of your plea of guilty? [The accused is not told that by the asking and answering of these questions in open court he has for all practical purposes also given up this ground for appeal.]

"Do you know that the judge is not bound by the recommendation of the District Attorney as to sentence but can sentence you up to—years and impose a fine of—dollars? [The aggregate penalty is read to him. Judges may and often do give a heavier penalty than was recommended. They rarely give a lighter sentence.]

"Can you read and write the English language?

"Have you ever been in a mental hospital or under the care of a psychiatrist for a mental illness?

"Are you now under the influence of alcohol, drugs, or undergoing withdrawal symptoms?

"Have you been threatened, coerced, or promised anything for entering the plea of guilty other than the recommendation of sentence by the District Attorney?

"Are you satisfied with my representation?"

All this is asked quickly, routinely, as the prisoner stands before the bar of the court. He answers "Yes" to each question.

The final question is: "Are you pleading guilty because you are guilty?" The defendant looks at the defender, uncertainly.

"Have you consulted with your lawyer?" I inquire.

"Right now. 'Bout five minutes."

"We'll pass this case until afternoon. At the lunch recess, will you please confer with your client," I direct the defender.

In the afternoon, the accused, having talked with the lawyer for another ten minutes, again waives his right to a trial. He has been in jail more than eight months. The eight months in jail are applied to his sentence. He will be out by the end of the year—sooner than if he demanded a trial and was acquitted.

The plea has been negotiated by the assistant defender and the assistant prosecutor. The defendant says he was not promised anything other than a recommendation of sentence in return for the guilty plea. But the judge does not know what else the defendant has been told, whether his family and friends are willing to come and testify for him, whether his counsel has investigated the facts of the case to see whether indeed he does have a defense. The magic formula has been pronounced. The judge does not know what the facts are. Did the man really commit the offense? Even if there were a full-scale trial, truth might not emerge. Many of the witnesses have long since disappeared. How reliable will their memories be? The policeman will say he did not strike the accused. The accused will say that he did. Friends and relatives will say that the accused was with them at the time of the alleged crime. The victim, if he appears, will swear that this is the person whom he saw once briefly on a dark night eight months ago.

The lawyers are in almost equal ignorance. The prosecutor has the police report. The defender has only the vague and confused story of the accused. The judge is under pressure to "dispose" of the case. There is a score card for each judge kept by the computer. The judges have batting averages. Woe betide those who fail to keep pace in getting rid of cases. A long trial to determine guilt or innocence will put the judge at the bottom of the list. The prosecutors and public defenders also have their score cards of cases disposed of. Private defense counsel—whether paid by the accused or appointed by the court and paid by the public—has his own type of score card. For the fee paid, he can give only so many hours to the preparation and trial of this case. He must pay his rent, secretary and overhead. All of the persons involved in the justice system are bound by the iron laws of economics. What can the defendant afford for bail, counsel fees, witness fees, investigative expenses? All of these questions will inexorably determine the case that is presented to the court.

The National Conference on Criminal Justice, convened in January 1973 by Attorney General Kleindienst, recommends that plea bargaining be abolished within five years. What will replace it?

At the end of a day in which as a judge I have taken actions affecting for good or ill the lives of perhaps 15 or 20 litigants and their families, I am drained. I walk out of the stale-smelling, dusty courtroom into the fresh sunshine of a late spring day and feel as if I were released from prison. I breathe the soft air, but in my nostrils is the stench of the stifling cell blocks and detention rooms. While I sip my cool drink in the quiet of my garden, I cannot forget the prisoners, with their dry bologna sandwiches and only a drink of water provided at the pleasure of the hot and harried guards.

Was Cottle really guilty? I will never know. Fred made bail. Will he attack someone tonight or tomorrow? One reads the morning paper with apprehension. It is safer for the judge to keep them all locked up. There will be an outcry over the one prisoner released who commits a subsequent offense. Who will know or care about the scores of possibly innocent prisoners held in jail?

This is only one day in a diary. Replicate this by 260 times a year, at least 15,000 courts, and 10 or 20 or 30 years in the past. Can one doubt that the operation of the legal system is slowly but surely strangling the law?

I must sit only three and a half more weeks in criminal court. But there is a holiday. So with relief I realize that it is really only 17 more days that I must sit there this term. Next year I shall again have to take my turn.

I am reminded of Ivan Denisovich. Solzhenitsyn describes Ivan's bedtime thoughts in a Soviet prison. "Ivan Denisovich went to sleep content. He had been fortunate in many ways that day—and he hadn't fallen ill. He'd got over it. There were 3,653 days like this in his sentence. From the moment he woke to the moment he slept. The three extra days were for leap years."

Criminals Belong in Jail

Tom Bethell

"Can I offer you a ride home?" my host asked at the end of the evening, shortly after I had arrived in Washington, D.C. from New Orleans. I thought about it briefly and declined. It was a pleasant evening and I felt like walking. I knew about the D.C. crime problem, of course, the problem that besets not only the nation's capital but all other large American cities, but this was, after all, one of the safest areas of Washington—just off Embassy Row. Besides, wasn't the crime problem here gradually improving? The money that had been spent, the programs that had been forged, the good intentions that had been lavished upon the problem of crime— hadn't they begun to take effect finally? Weren't we "turning the corner," especially in Washington, D.C., the home of good intentions? I strode off confidently into the night.

I might have been less confident had I been reading *The Washington Post* or *Star* in recent months. Crime was going up, up, up, I would have read. Up 15 per cent in D.C. in 1975, up 17 per cent in the nation, according to FBI statistics. "Crime is increasing at a record rate," according to *The Washington Post*. About 5,000 serious crimes a month are reported in D.C. There are 8,000 robberies, 40,000 burglaries per annum in the capital city. Washington is second only to Cleveland in homicides, second only to Boston in robberies. Heroin purity is up, too—from two per cent in 1973 to five per cent in 1976. That would mean more addicts, more robberies.

Tom Bethell is a contributing editor of *The Washington Monthly* and a Washington editor of *Harper's*.

141

There are 4,586 police officers in the District of Columbia, costing each resident an average of $124 per year—double the national average. But crime was increasing at about the same rate as in the rest of the nation. The number of police seemed to be making no difference to the crime problem, nor did the amount of money spent. In fact a cynic could point out that the more money was spent on crime, the more crimes were committed. Young people were the worst offenders, with more than four-fifths of all serious crime being committed by those under 30.

Since 1966, the FBI's Index of Crimes (i.e. serious crimes) had increased 82 per cent, while the amount of money spent on trying to combat crime had more than doubled. In 1974, this sum, at the federal, state, and local levels, had reached $14 billion a year. The Law Enforcement Assistance Administration had spent $4 billion, and in doing so it had searched for ever more "innovative" solutions. But with each innovation, it seemed, there were ten more rapes, a dozen more armed robberies, several more murders, and a rash of muggings. Auto thefts alone were down, and that was because manufacturers had figured out how to make the new models practically burglar-proof.

Here's another item from *The Washington Post* I missed before setting off on my evening walk: "Recently revised park police statistics show intense criminal activity on the Monument grounds during the afternoon hours of Human Kindness Day.... Park Police reported 468 robberies alone on May 10 on the Washington Monument grounds—more than half the total of 733 robberies reported by D.C. police throughout the rest of the city for the entire month."

A couple of months after that Lawrence Meyer noted in the *Post* that "in contrast to the optimism of the 1960s that crime and other social problems could be brought under control, a consensus is developing among those who study crime that the little that can be done will have only a marginal effect.... In some circles, a mood of outright pessimism has taken hold."

Gallup polls have shown that one household in four was hit by crime in the past year, one American in two is afraid to walk in his neighborhood at night. But I was cheerfully ignorant of these figures as I walked along, until . . . hello, what's this . . . I'm walking close to the P Street Bridge and there's been an accident, apparently, the circling red light of an ambulance, police cars, a sheet on the road. . . .

It was a murder, not an accident, committed perhaps only minutes before I arrived. I read about it two days later in the *Post:*

"A minister's son, who came to Washington in July after his college graduation to work as a draftsman for Amtrak, was fatally stabbed Friday night, D.C. police said, as he walked along P Street N.W. near the bridge across Rock Creek Park.

"Duncan McCrea, 21, died shortly after 11 p.m. of a single stab wound in the chest, according to the D.C. medical examiner's office. Amtrak officials said they believed McCrea was on his way home when the apparently random killing occurred."

A man named Aubrey Dockery was soon arrested and charged with murder. He was arraigned the next day before D.C. Superior Court Judge Theodore Newman, Jr., and assistant U.S. Attorney John Gizzerelli asked the judge to hold Dockery on a $10,000 bond. But Newman released the man on his own recognizance—that is to say, set him free, without requiring him to pay any bail—until his trial date.

'I KNEW THEY WERE GOING TO FIRE'

When a criminal suspect is arrested in Washington, D.C., one of several courses of action may be followed: the accused may be released on his personal recognizance (this is by far the most common outcome), or the judge may require him to post bond, which can be of two types—cash or surety. With a cash bond, the suspect can put up the money himself. (Under certain circumstances, he may even be able to pay his bond with the money he has stolen from a robbery victim.) With a surety bond, a bonding company must agree to pay the bond. (As an indication of the relative affluence of many criminal suspects, this is regarded as being a much stricter parole condition.) Another—and very lenient—possibility is third-party custody; organizations such as Bonabond, founded by ex-convicts in 1966, may agree to accept custody of defendants awaiting trial. (But a recent study has shown that over a third of Bonabond's clients either fail to appear for trial or are rearrested for another crime before they appear in court.) Finally, in very rare cases, the defendant can be detained in jail until trial. Of course, if he fails to pay the cash or surety bond, he also goes to jail until trial.

A few days later I read a *Washington Post* editorial on the P Street Bridge incident. The newspaper discerned a "deeply troubling question" as a result of this murder and the subsequent pretrial release of the suspect, wherein both the judge and the prosecutor had been "following the law, literally and explicitly." The "deeply troubling question" was: "Does this procedure adequately protect the community?"

The answer, I should have thought, was so obvious that the question would give me no trouble at all. I began to feel that I had accidentally fallen into a topsy-turvy world, like Alice in Wonderland.

"The desirability of jailing murder suspects is not so obvious as it might look at first glance," the *Post* cautioned. "The suspect in the P Street case is far from the only person to be freed here in recent years while facing a trial that could end in a life sentence. The practice is, in fact, not uncommon. Experience has shown murder suspects to be well behaved while awaiting trial, particularly in comparison with suspects in certain other types of cases—for example armed robbery. It needs to be repeated that the suspect is presumed innocent until convicted, and being in jail makes it much more difficult for him to present an effective defense at his trial."

The information about "well behaved" murder suspects is highly misleading, however, because about half of all the murder cases the courts deal with involve a marital or domestic flare-up, a "crime of passion" (often helped along by a readily available handgun), in which it is generally safe to assume that the attacker does not have a criminal disposition, is immediately docile following his or her assault, and can be relied upon not to repeat it.

Also, the suggestion that defendants in jail find it difficult to present an effective defense is not plausible. Defendants don't "present" a defense at trial (or don't have to, at any rate), their lawyers do, and defense lawyers are entitled to interview their clients in prison.

But the most interesting revelation in the editorial was that the judge had, in fact, followed the letter of the law, which was itself complicated by the following turn of events: Originally, judges had the power to hold defendants in jail for trial in capital cases. But in 1972 the U.S. Supreme Court "effectively abolished capital punishment in the District of Columbia." Capital cases no longer exist. As a result, the *Post* editorial continued, "the most violent and wanton crimes are now handled under the extremely rigorous and restrictive standards that—altogether properly—were originally written for the less serious cases. These standards limit pretrial detention to those cases in which the suspect is a drug addict or had a prior record of violent crime."

With capital cases no longer in existence, then, the *Post* recommended that Congress "remedy this anomaly by reinstating the discretion [to] judges in cases involving the most serious crimes of violence." If this remedial step is taken, the *Post* said, "the public's right to reassurance will not necessarily outweigh the suspect's right to freedom before trial."

Why is it, I asked myself, that the rights of criminal suspects must *balance* the rights of those not suspected of crimes? Why shouldn't the latter *outweigh* the former?

About a month later I read another and in some ways more remarkable story by Ron Shaffer in the *Post* about a different case. A girl named Sally Ann Morris had been shot in Georgetown. The story went on:

"It was about 10:30 p.m., she recalled. She and her boyfriend, Henry Miller, were walking down 33rd Street, heading for an M Street restaurant . . . when two men approached. As they passed the couple, one of the men pulled out a gun, cocked it and stuck it in Sally Morris' back. 'I knew right away they were going to fire it because you just don't cock a gun without a reason,' Morris said.

"Instinctively, Miller grabbed her and they started to run. After a few steps, she said, she heard gunfire and felt a slap at her back. 'It felt like a burning needle that went through me real quick. It sort of numbed me.' . . . The bullet ripped through her intestinal tract and lodged in her lower abdomen. . . . Doctors had to perform a colostomy, rerouting the undamaged intestinal tract to a substitute opening in her lower abdomen. This type of operation allows body waste to be passed into a disposable plastic bag attached to the new opening."

And there was this: "Police said the two men had been committing armed robberies in Georgetown for several weeks before the Morris shooting, escaping by hiding in the back seat of a getaway car driven by the women."

And this unbelievable paragraph: "Compounding all this is the fear that the ordeal is not yet over and that her assailants may return to kill her. Four suspects arrested in the case, who were released on personal recognizance, pending trial, promptly disappeared and are at large today."

What was going on here? A *Washington Post* editorial soon followed, making three recommendations: "First of all, the District of Columbia needs legislation to compensate the victims. . . ."

First of all? This ordering of priorities disturbed me, with its implication that if only the victims of crime can be "paid off," then society and its criminals will once again be in a state of balance; and with its familiar suggestion that money can solve all problems, including criminal assault. Would money repair Sally Morris' intestinal tract? What about the suspects having been released? Did not that raise a more urgent issue?

In fact, this turned out to be the *Post's* second recommendation. "The time has come for Congress to hold oversight hearings on the Bail Reform Act and the way in which it is working in practice," the editorial continued. "Experience under it is beginning to raise questions as to whether the rights of the public are being adequately protected."

'MERE COMMUNITY SAFETY'

I decided to visit the D.C. Superior Court where, I hoped, I would be able to find out more about the Sally Ann Morris case, and the Bail Reform Act itself. The District of Columbia is a federal jurisdiction, and so it is important to bear in mind, in trying to understand D.C. crime, that what would be a state crime anywhere else becomes subject to federal court procedures in Washington. The prosecutors for local or "street" crime, as well as federal crime, are U.S. attorneys. Thus the Bail Reform Act of 1965, which applied to federal jurisdictions, applies to *all* crime in Washington.

I spoke first to assistant U.S. Attorney Judith Hetherton, who handled the Sally Ann Morris case in Arraignment Court. Here the presiding judge (they work in this court for a month on a rotating schedule) makes the decision as to whether the defendant shall be released on recognizance, or released on a money bond, or detained in jail while awaiting trial.

"I remember the case," said Judith Hetherton. "A girl was quite seriously injured. I argued for a money bond, but the judge didn't grant it. I take it that the suspects didn't show for a preliminary hearing?"

"Right."

"They were arrested on two separate charges that evening," she went on. "We took our strongest case and held them on that charge. The judge knew that they were suspects in the other case, but he has to consider their record of convictions, their ties to the community, their employment record, and so on, in determining their bond. You should talk to Lee Cross. She might be able to tell you more about the case, and about the Bail Reform Act."

Assistant U.S. Attorney Lee Gross, the deputy chief of the Grand Jury section, has worked in the U.S. Attorney's office for four-and-a-half years. The part of the Grand Jury section I saw had rooms where policemen were sitting playing cards, waiting to testify; other rooms with rows of seats bolted together, where waiting witnesses sometimes lay horizontally, giving the impression of a railway station at 2 a.m.; defense attorneys who occasionally strolled from room to room (generally they wore three-piece suits of an elegant cut); and prosecutors with piles of documents under their arms (generally they looked harassed).

Lee Cross sat behind her desk, which was laden with files. She had time to talk, as it turned out, because she was waiting for her 7 p.m. appointment.

"I don't know the details of the case," she said when I mentioned Sally Ann Morris. "But you could look up the 'jacket' in the Bench Warrant section. It's a public document. A warrant will have been issued for the arrest of the defendants. As for the Bail Reform Act, the D.C. Code, Section 1321, discusses release prior to trial. It goes through the conditions of release to ensure appearance at trial, such as third-party custody by parents or an organization, or placing restrictions on travel, or requiring an appearance bond or a surety bond. But here's the main point. The judge may not set financial conditions on release merely to ensure the safety of the community. He may only do that if the prosecutor shows likelihood of flight by the accused."

"Merely" to ensure the safety of the community? Could that be right?

"Here's the wording," Lee Cross said, showing me the D.C. Code. *"No financial condition may be imposed to assure the safety of any other person or the community."*

That seemed odd, I thought.

"To hold them, you have to use preventive detention," Lee Cross went on, "and you will recall the screaming that went on among liberals when that was passed by Congress."

I hadn't realized that "preventive detention" meant holding suspects charged with such crimes as murder and rape prior to trial. I had been under the impression that it was some sort of repressive scheme to lock up radicals—devised by President Nixon, no doubt.

"But preventive detention is so hard to apply it's not used very often," Lee Cross continued. "The government has to reveal practically its whole case to show probable cause to the judge; the defendant has to be brought to trial within 60 days, he has to have been convicted of a violent crime within the past ten years; and the government has to show that no other condition will reasonably assure the safety of the community." According to one figure I had read, preventive detention has been applied only 50 times since it went into effect in 1971.

"How often do defendants released without bail not show up for trial?" I asked Lee Cross.

"It's disturbingly frequent," she said. "To get the exact figures you should talk to Peter Chapin, who is in charge of the Felony Bench Warrant section, and John Hume, chief of the Felony Trial section. If you had more intelligent criminals, a lot fewer would show up, I can tell you that. Fortunately for us, most of them aren't too bright. It isn't easy to track these people. Under the provisions of the Social Security Act, they can go and get a job as a plumber, say, in Seattle, Washington, use their social security numbers, and Social Security won't give that information to the FBI, even though they're wanted for armed robbery."

That seemed odd, too.

'YOUR FIRST ROBBERY IS FREE'

"Often the defendant is back on the street before the victim leaves the hospital," Cross said. "A defense attorney just told me that two clients told him: 'Your first robbery is free.' Routinely they get probation for armed robbery. God only knows why." She lit a cigarette and considered the question before continuing: "So many judges look at it from a middle-class perspective. For a professional person a felony conviction is a serious matter: it's on his record, he loses the right to vote, loses the right to get certain government jobs, various trades won't take convicted felons, you can't practice law, and so on. But for most of the people we get, these considerations don't bother them at all. The *only* thing they worry about is getting time. The rest they couldn't care less about. I had a defense attorney tell me about a case the other day, a client who pleaded guilty to forgery in return for a likely probation sentence. 'I tried to tell the girl what she did was wrong,' the lawyer told me, 'but she thinks I'm crazy. She got 1,500 bucks out of it passing bad checks, and she isn't going to jail. That's all she cares about.' She beat the system, in other words."

Lee Cross ran a finger through her hair and absently glanced at a strand for a second. "I'm convinced that the big unanswered question in all this is witness intimidation," she said. "We have two or three good cases a day dismissed because we can't get the witnesses to come down here. In some cases it's overt intimidation—a phone call from the defendant—but more often just a feeling because they saw the guy back on the street. The Sally Ann Morris case you are referring to—we have much worse ones than that, where the witness and suspect live together on the same block and know one another.

"In such cases as these, the concept of 'innocent until proven guilty' is a pure legal abstraction, you have to remember. You can't expect the victim to believe it when he knows the person who robbed him. Or take the case of the person who is arrested right at the scene of the crime. Again, you can't expect the victim to believe his attacker is innocent until he's been brought to trial."

According to one study, as many as 1,000 cases in D.C. are dropped each year because of witness intimidation. "And here are some statistics we don't have," said Cross. "How many people are deterred from reporting crime because of probation and bail? How many people go to police line-ups and don't identify the person because they know he's already made bail? Many of them refuse to come down here to the Grand Jury and testify. Sometimes they disappear completely. The police can't find them. Or they come down here and say things that just aren't so, like, 'I saw him standing by the truck, but I didn't see him getting out of the truck.' Or they'll say: 'No, that isn't the guy who robbed me. That was the guy who *didn't* rob me.' Just like that, when earlier they have told us who it was. Witnesses may come down here four, five, or six times. And what do they get out of it? They'll say to me: 'But he'll be out in no time,' or 'he was already out on pretrial release.' So I have a standard little speech I give them. I say we have a very good case. If it's suddenly dropped, he'll know why. He'll know you refused to identify him. That's just like writing 'pigeon' right on your forehead. Anyone want to rob someone, come and rob me."

She lit another cigarette and went on: "The citizens don't understand, either, especially the ones who are poor but honest. I had a case once, a victim in an armed robbery. A blue-collar worker. By the time of trial he had been laid off his job. The defendant was convicted, but he had no prior convictions. Then, pending sentence, he was released by the judge on condition that he take a certain job which the judge had arranged for him. Of course, the victim would have liked a job, too. The defense attorney later told me that the kid quit the job a few days later—it was hard work. But he still got probation. So what does the victim think? He had to come down here a number of times, no job. . . ."

"You know, if a Martian were to come down here, he wouldn't believe it," Lee Cross went on. "A crime is committed, right? What happens? In some cases, the witnesses are locked up for their own protection, the alleged criminal goes free. There are now such things as 'witness protection units,' used primarily for organized crime cases, but sometimes with street crime. Then the case goes to trial, and you lock up the jury. Then he's convicted, let's say. At last he goes to prison—maybe.

"But to answer your question about the Sally Ann Morris case, if the defense lawyer can persuade the judge that there is no danger of flight, then there is no reason for not releasing the defendant on his personal recognizance. If they've lived for years in the District, the judges tend to be impressed that they have ties to the community. I've heard lawyers defending multiple offenders tell the judge with a perfectly straight face, 'Your Honor, my client has been charged 35 times, and he has shown up in court every time.' Their long record is used as an argument to release them.

"One more point before you go," she said "Catch-22 for prosecutors. Say a man is convicted of armed robbery. He's a first offender, and he gets probation. Out on probation, he's arrested again for armed robbery. What happens? We keep him on five-day hold and ask the judge to revoke his probation for the first offense. But often the judge doesn't. He'll say, 'Let's see what happens in this case first.' He's not been proven guilty yet, you see. So that's what they mean when they say the first robbery is free.

"Meanwhile the judge in the new case will release him again, so that he may be on the streets for seven or eight months pending trial, because to set a bond you have to show likelihood of flight, not danger to the community.

"Now you should talk to John Hume. I'll tell you a story about him. He was trying a first-degree murder case also involving a rape. Bond was $10,000, but the defendant had made bond. In most cases you only have to put up one tenth of the amount, so the figure is meaningless, but it makes the judges look good because it seems as though they are setting high bonds. The day before the trial Hume's wife had to leave, so they had a baby-sitter come over. Her boyfriend came to see her during his lunch hour, and he brought a friend with him. The friend turned out to be the man charged with murder. While he was in the house, he looked around and saw that he was in the house of the man who would be trying him the next day, in the house with his one-year-old son. The suspect was convicted a few days later. He was a refrigerator repairman, who had gone into a woman's house and had found her there alone. He raped and murdered her. He later gave a detailed confession."

Before seeing Hume the next day, I went to the Bench Warrant section and requested to see the "jacket" on cases 48406 and 48407, for James A. Weeks and Roy Wade Weeks, the male suspects in the Sally Ann Morris case. Roy Weeks was listed as living on 10th Street, N.W., and as having resided there for "three months, with girl friend." James Weeks had been living on A Street, S.E., "for one month." Eunice Walker, an alleged accomplice was listed as living on A Street, S.E., for "three weeks." How could such brief residences be construed as evidence of "ties to the community," I wondered. And who was the unnamed "girl friend"? I recalled Lee Cross' response on this point: "What kills me," she said, "is when the person listed as 'friend' is the co-defendant in the crime." Police have been searching for Roy and James Weeks, as well as Eunice Walker and Terry Ann Stewart, since July 11.

I spoke to John Hume next, on the third floor of the Pension Building. For the past six months Hume has been head of the Felony Trial section in the U.S. Attorney's office.

"Of the felony cases that we have indicted," he said, "we have 500 fugitives right now. That is 25 per cent of the cases. There is a variety of reasons. The defendants don't get proper notice, or they say they never received it. Many of them come to arraignment, learn about the strength of the case, and don't come back. Of those arrested on felonies, I would guess that 65 to 85 per cent are back on the street before trial. When I was in Arraignment Court two years ago, we did not get money bond in as many as 25 per cent of the cases. When you consider that we convict 75 per cent of those indicted, and that about 75 per cent of those indicted are on the streets before trial, you've got a lot of dangerous people on the streets of D.C."

About 3,000 defendants are free on bond on any given day in D.C., about 2,250 of whom are statistically likely to be found guilty.

"With a stick-up in D.C.," Hume went on, "if the person is 18 to 22, he can commit two or three or four felonies and keep going down to Lorton for a hand-slapping under the Youth Corrections Act—six months to a year for even the most heinous crime. Then the Supreme Court finally ruled that the judge can use his discretion about applying the Youth Act in sentencing. Since then, adult sentences have been occasionally imposed on youthful offenders. But there is still a widespread tendency to sentence under the Youth Act."

'IT IS THE AMERICAN WAY'

Hume continued briefly on the subject of lenient sentencing—a defect in the present system of criminal justice as pervasive as the pretrial release of suspects who may reasonably be presumed to be dangerous. He mentioned one case which was publicized in the spring of 1975—*U.S. v. Olen Lebby*—which is a case study in lenient justice. First of all, Lebby was convicted of assault with a dangerous weapon. He was out on parole on this conviction when he was rearrested and charged, once again, with assault with a dangerous weapon. Once again he was convicted, but once again was out on parole, this time to await sentencing on the second conviction. At large again, he shot and killed a policeman. He was then picked up and sentenced on the second dangerous-weapon count, for which he got 30 to 90 months. He was then convicted of the murder charge and was sentenced to 9 to 27 years, the sentence to run concurrently with the earlier sentence. This means that he will be eligible for parole once again after nine years.

"But it is the American way," Hume concluded. "Instead of making the hard decision, we lower the standards for all. So my criticism of the system is that it tries to do too much for too many. Most of them just aren't going to be turned into law-abiding citizens, but after six months most of them are right back in the community. What you read about in the *Post* and the *Star* is just the tip of the iceberg. There's a lot of human misery all over this city, and mainly because there are people out on the street who shouldn't be."

I asked Hume to tell me how he felt about the accused murderer having come over to his house that day.

"Well, it upset me," Hume said. "I realized for the first time how the witness feels when he sees that the person who attacked him is back out on the street before the trial."

Hume then introduced me to Peter Chapin, a curly-haired man whose office was across the hall and who was in charge of the "felony fugitive program—designed to keep track of felony fugitives," he explained, adding that there was a "backlog of approximately 530 felony bench warrants ranging from unauthorized use of a vehicle up to first-degree murder." This, he said, was 25 to 30 per cent of all felony indictments.

Chapin lit a pipe and reached for a file. "Okay, some egregious cases," he said, "but bear in mind that these are not typical cases. I prepared a memo for Earl Silbert, the U.S. Attorney, in April of 1975. Here's one: *U.S. v. Raymond Boswell.* Boswell had several cases pending. Originally he was arrested for second-degree burglary. Personal recognizance was not recommended by the Bail Agency. He had several prior convictions, including rape, unauthorized use of a vehicle, rape reduced to simple assault, and an escape in 1971. The court ordered a $2,000 surety bond, which meant he had to pay $200. Okay, in July 1974 he was rearrested on first-degree burglary. On that date the Bail Agency indicated he had been booked under a different name for a third first-degree burglary. Since he had no previous record under the fake name, he was released on his personal recognizance in that case. The parole board meanwhile required his arrest for violations of his earlier parole. And the Bail Agency could not verify his address. But the court released the defendant on $1,000 surety, which meant he had to pay $100, and he then failed to appear for all three charges."

Chapin read out about ten such cases, and I then went down to the Bench Warrant section and requested to see the jackets on these cases. Now I was told I wasn't allowed to see them, according to chief deputy clerk Frederick Beane, because I was a reporter, not a lawyer. (This denial of access to what is supposedly a public record was later repudiated by a spokesman for Chief Judge Harold H. Greene.) But in another office I found out that Raymond Boswell had been caught, once again, and his case was now available for study in Judge Charles Halleck's chambers, where it was soon coming up for a hearing (although Halleck had not been responsible for the earlier disposition of the case).

'TOO MANY CASES'

I approached Judge Halleck's chambers with curiosity. There had been publicity about him in recent weeks, since a judicial review commission had held hearings to determine whether he was qualified as a judge. Finally they had agreed that he was "qualified," but not "well qualified," and President Ford had reappointed him. He now awaited Senate confirmation.

In *The Washington Post* I had read that "Halleck underwent a radical change in philosophy and lifestyle—but not his colorful courtroom manner—in the early 1970s. He divorced his first wife and married a probation worker, grew a beard and moderately long hair, and became, in the eyes of some, as pro-defendant as he once had been pro-prosecution."

Although there had been a lot of implied criticism of judges in what the prosecutors had told me, they had carefully avoided mentioning names. But it seemed clear that Halleck was someone they had in mind. One person I spoke to would say only that, from the prosecutor's point of view, the black judges tend to be better than the white ones, because they have more "street sense." About 80 percent of the D.C. judges are white—as is Halleck.

I asked the law clerk if I could see the Boswell case. Suspicion, barely concealed hostility, was the response.

Why did I want to see it? Who did I work for? What was the article about? Why this particular case? Were all the cases I wanted to see in Halleck's court? She went to ask the judge's permission, returned, and said it was okay.

I looked through the file, but it was hard to unravel the legal jargon. Then Judge Halleck himself swept into his chambers—during a recess in a trial—and unbuttoned his long black robe.

"It's no use your looking through those cases," he told me. "All you're doing is fueling public sentiment against judges. You should be up there on the Hill talking to congressmen if you want to change the system. The problem is we have too many cases. 160 indictments in my court in eight weeks. If we could cut down on the cases and bring the remaining ones to trial within 30 to 60 days, the crimes by those on pretrial release would be cut way down. Studies have shown that. If the trial is speedy, the suspect on pretrial release is less likely to be rearrested within the first month after his initial arrest."

What about the violent offenders, I asked.

"You can't predict lethality," he said. "I'm going to co-author an article with a psychiatrist. If a psychiatrist can't tell, how can I? There is no way a judge can predict what a man will do. We have no psychiatric training, all it is is a guess. The problem lies here," he said, taking his glasses off and shaking them at me. "We have too many cases, and so the backlog is too great. We ought to be trying felonies. But with one third of our misdemeanor calendar we're talking about prostitution—not dangerous; or selling half-a-pint out of your back door—not dangerous; nickel bags of marijuana—not dangerous. Let's put a stop to that foolishness. Here I'm doing for society what the Baptist minister is supposed to do.

"And they keep indicting them," Halleck went on, his voice rising. "They keep flooding the court system. You know what they could do to cut down on the backlog?" he asked me suddenly. "*Shut* the courthouse doors. . . ." He made a sweeping motion with his hands. "But the Logan Circle liberals who are fixing up the old houses are upset because of the prostitutes and. . . ." An aide tugged at his sleeve, but the judge seemed not to notice.

"We can't talk here," he said, ". . . go out and have lunch and talk it over. All right. What's the public upset about? Two things. Crime in the street. And too much tax money going out. So there's a freeze on. No more judges, fewer staff people. We judges are the ones that get dumped on. I'm here till seven at night, trying to get caught up." Again an aide tugged, but again he paid no heed.

"Here, let me get you a book," he said, darting off to an inner room. He came back with two: Norval Morris and Gordon Hawkins' *The Honest Politician's Guide to Crime Control,* in which the judge had underlined a proposal to de-criminalize a number of "victimless" crimes (drunkenness, gambling, drug abuse, abortion by a qualified medical practitioner, sexual behavior between consenting adults), and *Alice In Wonderland.* He pointed out a passage he had marked in this classic, and finally, reluctantly, allowed himself to be dragged back into court, declaring as he went that 40 to 50 per cent of the arrests in the U.S. were for drunkenness.

LIBERAL ASPIRATIONS

I set off for the library, to find out about the circumstances surrounding the passage of the Bail Reform Act. It was debated in Congress in 1965, at a time when the aspirations of liberalism in America were perhaps at an all-time high. There were many problems in need of a solution—the poor to be treated with greater consideration, the blacks to be given equal treatment, the hungry to be fed—but no problem, surely, was so intractable that it could not be dealt with by a judicious admixture of goodwill, money, and kindly government programs. And just as the blacks had been mistreated, so had many criminals, in the view of a good number of repentant and self-accusing Americans. This was the time when it became a tiny bit fashionable (although a touch risky) for northerners from wealthy backgrounds to spend a long, hot summer in Mississippi and, by the same token, equally fashionable (although not at all risky) for liberal lawyers, often working for firms with a healthy corporate practice, to take up the cause of defendants' rights.

Abe Fortas, who was then with the Washington law firm of Arnold, Fortas and Porter, had set the pace, having championed the cause of an indigent convict in Florida named Clarence Earl Gideon, who was a harmless repeater, of the type that in England is known as an "old lag." Gideon had been convicted of burglary without benefit of defense counsel and was fighting a lonely battle, so it seemed, to have the U.S. Constitution applied fairly and equally, for the benefit of the poor as well as the rich. A perfect cause to champion! The case was influential. It was easy, from the example of *Gideon,* to form the impression that criminals in America were in many instances true-life versions of characters in Dickens—wonderful people, really, but sorely mistreated by society and, more often than not, sent off to prison or the workhouse for nothing more serious than stealing a loaf of bread.

And so, in the early and mid-1960s, there was a build-up of such sentiments in America, although they had appeared earlier, in the 1930s, and were familiar, of course, to readers of Dickens and Victor Hugo. In many cases, these sentiments of optimism and good will were tinged with guilt, because have we not all come close to committing a crime, or actually committed one, at some point? Were we not merely the lucky ones who didn't get caught? Or if caught, the ones who could afford to pay a lawyer and thus buy our way out of trouble? And so the criminal became, for many people of at least moderate means and liberal disposition, largely sentimentalized. And the rising liberal sympathy for the criminal became a tide.

Gideon's case became, in the hands of *New York Times* correspondent Anthony Lewis, not merely a fascinating legal case study but literature as well, and was praised in print by a Supreme Court Justice, Truman Capote, David Brinkley, Edward Bennett Williams, and Paul Freund of the Harvard Law School. It was but a small step from this to the Miranda and Escobedo decisions, to the Supreme Court that saw itself more and more as an institution of crusading reform, and to the Bail Reform Act of 1965.

THE BAIL REFORM DEBATE

The perception of the criminal as a poor and downtrodden victim of society seemed to underlie almost every comment made during the congressional debate on bail reform, although there wasn't much debate. The bill was heralded and trumpeted by Senator Sam Ervin so successfully that there is no evidence, in the Congressional *Record,* of any demurring senator speaking up at all. Ervin sponsored the bill, Senator Roman Hruska co-sponsored it. Ervin's technique was to make oratorical statements so preeminently reasonable that no one with a speck of human decency could disagree.

"When government maintains peace and order," Ervin said in the Senate on January 22, 1965, using an argument that would be repeated perhaps a hundred times, "it must exclude irrelevant factors—such as the financial status of the accused—in determining his guilt or innocence." Grotesque tales were told of wicked bail bondsmen crossing state lines and kidnapping their fugitive charges. "The only objection to the measure came from bail bondsmen," Ervin later reminded the Senate. Extreme cases of injustice were quoted, for instance that of a man who spent 54 days in jail awaiting trial on a traffic violation for which the maximum penalty was five days. Senator Tydings said: "Such unfortunate cases mock the presumption of innocence and threaten the democratic values which that presumption protects."

After the bill had passed the Senate, without any record of a dissenting vote, Ervin (rather late in the day, one might think) brought before his colleagues an ominous matter: "This bill does not deal at all with one serious ancillary problem studied by the subcommittee," he said, "—the concept of the 'preventive detention' of an accused person on the grounds that his liberty might endanger the public welfare because of his predisposition to commit further crimes, intimidate witnesses or destroy evidence." Ervin stressed the "serious constitutional problems," the "grave difficulties" in such a measure, and it was therefore deemed "premature at the time the bail reform bill was drafted." The problem was left for the Nixon Administration to deal with—and be blamed for.

Meanwhile *The New York Times* and many other newspapers took up the cudgels on behalf of bail reform. "The bail system, as it has operated in federal and state courts for generations, is fundamentally undemocratic and unjust," said the *Times.* "Why should the man who can afford to post a bond be permitted to go free between arrest and conviction . . . while the poor man must remain in jail?"

The Manhattan Bail Project, financed by the Vera Foundation, was cited time and time again, both in Congress and out. Vera Foundation personnel had been allowed to interview arrested suspects in Manhattan over a three-year period. As a result of these interviews, a total of 3,500 suspects had been released on recognizance by judges, who in those cases were following the Vera Foundation's recommendation.

The all-important resulting statistic was that only about one per cent of those released on their own recognizance had failed to appear in court for trial, as against a normal three-percent forfeiture of bail bonds.

Herbert Sturz, the executive director of Vera, was quoted as saying: "I don't know of any serious crimes committed by people released in the bail or summons projects. There were only 30 persons rearrested of the 3,500 released on recognizance in the Manhattan Bail Project."

This bail project was undoubtedly highly influential in persuading Congress to vote for the Bail Reform Act. Yet the statistics cited by Vera Foundation personnel are grotesquely at odds with what was later found to be the case in the District of Columbia, where, according to the D.C Bail Agency, nine per cent of the total number of suspects released on recognizance fail to appear later, and among those with felonies it is between 25 to 30 per cent; 14 per cent are rearrested and charged with other crimes.

The explanation for this discrepancy is that, in making recommendations for release, the Vera Foundation excluded first of all the most serious categories of crime from consideration: homicides, sex crimes, and drug addiction cases. In the remaining cases Vera workers interviewed suspects at length, and in some cases recommended release on recognizance. Of the cases that were then recommended for release on recognizance, a further one third were not released by the judges—undoubtedly the most serious remaining cases. The Vera report on the bail project does not specifically list what offenses its 3,500 released suspects had been charged with, but there is some doubt as to whether anything other than misdemeanor cases were involved. Misdemeanor offenders, of course, are not likely to get themselves into the more serious trouble of violating parole conditions. But now, in Washington, D.C., as a result of the Bail Reform Act—whose major statistical support was provided by the Vera study—accused murderers and rapists with a very good motive for not showing up in court are routinely released on recognizance.

"What you have to realize about Vera," said former Justice Department official Donald Santarelli, "is that they set out to prove a point even before they had any statistics, and they subsequently proved it. And then they did a very good job of selling it to their liberal friends in Congress." One person who worked on the Vera project, incidentally, was Judge Halleck's wife.

Following its passage in the Senate, the bill was debated in the House of Representatives in 1966. Here, at last, one or two cogent objections were raised; one, for example, was by Rep. Waggonner of Louisiana, who had the foresight to ask: "Could the gentleman from New York [Emmanuel Celler] tell me what the situation would be should capital punishment be outlawed, and with what we would then be faced?" He received no substantive answer, and *The Washington Post,* of course, was asking essentially the same question nine years later.

The following colloquy suggests that the Bail Reform Act, as it has worked out in practice, at least in D.C., went way beyond the intent of Congress.

"Mr. Jonas: Is it fair to say that we are dealing here with a body of law almost outside crimes of violence?

"Mr. McCulloch: I would say that is a reasonably accurate generalization."

The bill finally passed in the House by a record lopsided vote—yeas, 319; nays, 14.

By 1970 the problem that Senator Ervin had belatedly commented on —the absence of preventive detention—was becoming painfully obvious in the District of Columbia. There was, according to a strict interpretation of the law, no way of holding dangerous suspects in many cases. So the Nixon Administration proposed the D.C. Crime Bill, with a preventive detention clause.

The cries of horror that went up from certain columnists and editorial writers now seem immoderate and, in fact, extremist in nature. Anthony Lewis, for example, who in 1964 had written the admirable study of the Gideon case, would have this to say six years later about preventive detention: "And so the majority wearies of the effort to work out the difficult problems of race and poverty. It is tempted to take care of itself, to build a white middle-class enclave protected by police measures. That sounds fanciful, but that is precisely what the District of Columbia crime bill symbolizes to black critics: a model for state and national legislation to make the country 'safe' by putting dangerous people, mostly blacks, in jail without trial."

Another columnist who cast the issue in conveniently racial terms, thus making his plea for the defeat of the bill seem like a plea to end racial discrimination, was Tom Wicker. "What they hope to do," he wrote, "is chilling—preventive detention of those who *might* commit a crime if released on bail. . . . Preventive detention is class legislation, particularly in the District, where its burden will fall with precision on black people. As the foremost victims of a discriminatory social system the blacks provide the heft of the street criminals who are most likely to be jailed preventively.' "

The New York Times delivered itself of frequent editorials on the subject, the words "repression" or "repressive" occurring almost every time. Parts of these editorials today have an irony all their own: "The District of Columbia crime bill is political legislation with a vengeance. It would inspire new disrespect for the law and seriously interfere with the major function of the courts, which is the administration of justice."

(*The Washington Post*, be it said, did not join in the chorus. A year before the bill passed in Congress, Ronald Goldfarb, a frequent contributor on criminal matters to the *Post*'s editorial page, had written an article for the *Post* in which he perceived the necessity for preventive detention. Today, Goldfarb says he has almost given up trying to persuade the "civil libertarians" on this point. Although in other respects Goldfarb's liberal credentials are in perfect order, his advocacy of preventive detention is seen as a sign of incipient fascism. A major problem, as he points out, is that most people don't understand what the term means; "pretrial detention" would be an improvement.)

By 1972, with the abolition of capital offenses, the Bail Reform Act became even more untenable. And by 1975, as James Q. Wilson and others were beginning to say, the problems of crime were looking insoluble. As for the preventive detention statute, the most frequently heard complaint about it has become that it is not used often enough.

By this time, however, a good deal of damage had been done by the "liberal" rhetoric of the previous decade. The liberal usually spoke as the reasonable man who merely opposed unfairness and inequality. As a result, whoever called for harsher treatment of violent offenders was often subtly painted as a racist; whoever called for less lenient judges was viewed as a primitive lacking in higher education; whoever demanded longer sentences was surely insensitive to the social roots of crime; whoever argued that prisons were primarily for punishment and only secondarily "correctional facilities," as they are often today officially dubbed, was surely an anachronism from the Stone Age; whoever urged that suspects charged with violent crimes be locked up before trial was alleged to hold the Constitution in low esteem, if indeed he had ever heard of it.

Nevertheless, from whatever vantage point you observed the spreading evil of crime ("problem" seems too mild a word), it was becoming clear by the mid-1970s that the liberal solutions of the past decade had not worked. And this was *not* just because the prisons were rotten, or because the programs weren't "innovative" enough, or because too many hookers and drunkards were being arrested, or because there weren't enough judges or clerical workers, or because not enough money was being spent. These were only practical shortcomings; the major defect was conceptual, not practical.

The problem is that built into the optimistic rhetoric of the past decade is a "liberal" view of man which seems to be unrealistic in the extreme. It is also extremely modern; certainly it is at odds with the traditional conception of man.

According to the modern view, man is an almost infinitely malleable entity, plastic in his make-up, capable of being warped, bent, distorted, but capable also of being straightened out again. According to this view, he is born naturally into a state of innocence, but made of a soft and fragile substance, so that an evil society can easily twist him away from goodness. By the same token, however, he can be restored to this original virtue by programs, re-educated by educators, corrected through the good offices of a panoply of contemporary social sciences, manipulated, if need be, by the most modern techniques.

According to the traditional view, however, man is to a very large extent "born" the way he is. He is born, moreover, in a state of sin, not primal innocence. And after a very few years the soft clay hardens, his nature is "set"; perhaps society can "bend" him, but only within narrow limits. And if he goes wrong, then there is usually little hope of redemption—at least outside a church. Redemption should be no concern of the state.

This, I feel, is the more realistic view. But even those who regard it as excessively bleak, who believe in the possibility of rehabilitation, must concede that society has not yet found the way to change a violent criminal into a peaceful citizen. At least until this discovery is made, all of us should be able to agree that the criminal justice system must be changed to make it protect society; to make what John Hume called the "hard decision"; to realize that a man who has pleaded guilty to between 500 and 1,000 rapes should not be offered a "deal" of total immunity from prosecution, an actual case that was recently reported in Prince George's County, Maryland; to appreciate finally that a system where such things happen has become intolerably wicked and corrupt.

As for pretrial release, the "hard decision" is, surely, quite simple: the preventive detention statute needs to be dis-encumbered; that is, made easier to apply. With one exception, the suspect charged with a crime of violence—rape, armed assault, murder—should not be released at all before trial. The exception is the crime resulting from a domestic quarrel, where the accused may be assumed not to repeat a similar act. Also, there is clearly no need to lock up the defendant charged with non-violent crimes: Oliver Twist gets paroled, to quell liberal fears on that point. Similarly, the decriminalizing reforms urged by Judge Halleck have plenty to recommend them, especially the shorter interval between arrest and trial that would result because of the smaller caseload, and the savings in police man-hours. But the armed robber does not get probation, and the man charged with armed robbery should be held "preventively."

This, in fact, would bring the American system more into line with the British system, which was on several occasions held up as a paragon during the congressional debate of the Bail Reform Act. While working on this article, I was given two comments on the British system. First by Lee Cross, who spent some time in the Old Bailey courts during a vacation in London. She was surprised to see that the judges routinely denied any form of bail to suspects who, in D.C., would routinely be released on recognizance. The second comment came from David Austern, a defense lawyer in Ronald Goldfarb's Washington law firm. Austern accompanied a British magistrate to a preventive detention hearing for a D.C. defendant charged with a violent crime. The magistrate found it hard to believe that all this complex procedure had to be gone through merely to decide whether the man should be detained before trial. "In England, we'd have just held him in jail," the magistrate remarked.

Following conviction, the violent offender should be put in prison, and, if he has a prior criminal record, kept there. And this is so *especially* if he is a "youthful offender"; not for "life," but until the burning adrenalin of youth has stopped flowing so hotly. These are the highwaymen of our time. In his *Life of Johnson,* Boswell reports dinner conversation in London about whether it is right to shoot a highwayman on sight or to hang him later. Today, a comparable conversation at a Washington dinner party would no doubt focus on his underprivileged upbringing. But the fantasy of social workers notwithstanding, a multiple armed robber is not just some put-upon victim of society, but a very likely incorrigible menace to society who should be dealt with accordingly.

Very soon we must come to our senses and realize that there is something very wrong with a society in which, in the name of the presumption of innocence, the suspect is freed and the witness must then be protected; in which the convicted robber is given a job by the judge instead of a sentence, and his victim is allowed to go jobless; in which a girl who has been shot in the back must hide from her attackers because the suspects were freed after being caught; in which convicted armed robbers immediately roam the streets after they have been sentenced; in which the concept of punishment has been almost entirely discredited; in which "your first robbery is free"; in which the rights of accused criminals are thought of as having to balance the rights of the rest of society.

If we do not, then the society which *The New York Times* feared was approaching, in which there will be a "new disrespect for the law," will very soon come to pass, if indeed it has not already arrived.

Now You're Thinking Like a Lawyer

Michael Kinsley and Charles Peters

It is "Interview Season" at what is known in Cambridge as "The" Harvard Law School. This highly stylized mating ritual for law students and law firms begins September 30, lasts until Thanksgiving, and is run by a computer. Each second- and third-year student receives a print-out, listing by city and by date the hundreds of firms coming to Cambridge to interview, and a set of computer cards with his or her name punched onto them.

To obtain an interview with a particular firm, you merely wait until the appointed time three weeks before the firm's representative is scheduled to appear, then file one of your computer cards in a special file behind the computer card of the firm you wish to interview. The computer, which knows your class schedule, sends you a postcard listing the time and place of your interview, and assigns you a number. Two days before the interview, you write your number on your resume and drop it in the appropriate slot in a bank of such slots at the Placement Office. Then you put on your grey "interview suit" and go "interview."

Like a stacked deck of Tarot cards, the computer cards predict a future that is uniformly bright. Pick a card, any card, and the next thing you know you are a leader of the community earning top dollars in the city of your choice.

The popularity of legal careers requires no elaborate explanation. Lawyers run the country. Nothing could sound more antiquated than that

Michael Kinsley is a contributing editor of *The Washington Monthly* and managing editor of *The New Republic.* Charles Peters is editor-in-chief of *The Washington Monthly.* Both are also lawyers.

famous comment by Commodore Cornelius Vanderbilt, the 19th-century robber baron: "Law? What do I care about the law. Hain't I got the power?" At most, a modern corporate baron could boast, "Law? What do I care about the law. Hain't I got the lawyers?" And the lawyers he "got" would not come cheap.

This very popularity, however, is threatening to destroy the law's appeal to the thousands of bright college graduates who pour into it every year. The profession is facing a crisis of over-supply and under-demand. This is a problem medicine managed to avoid by artificially limiting the number and size of medical schools. The lawyers were not so far-sighted. In the decade between 1964 and 1974, enrollment in ABA-approved law schools jumped from 54,265 to 110,713. During approximately the same period, the number of new admissions to the bar each year almost tripled, from 10,788 annually to 30,707.

> "... anthropologists of the next century will look back in amazement at an arrangement whereby the most ambitious and brightest members of each generation were siphoned off the productive work force, trained to think like a lawyer, and put to work chasing one another around in circles...."

Aggravating the problem is the impact of no-fault automobile insurance and the probable spread of the no-fault concept to other areas of tort law such as medical malpractice. Already, many law schools report that some of their graduates cannot get legal jobs at all; and even at Harvard, the students entering those interviews—if mountains can be measured in millimeters—are not quite as confident as they once were. Some of the lawyer glut may be blamed on the sick state of the economy, but not all of it. There is a wonderful resilience about the legal profession: in good times there are mergers to arrange, prospectuses to write, construction contracts to negotiate; in bad times there are lots of bankruptcies and divorces. One beauty of the adversary system is that every lawyer who finds a job for himself creates work for another lawyer to represent the other side. But this Newtonian effect is not working fast enough to provide lawyer-like incomes for the increasing thousands of young people choosing to devote their lives to the practice of law.

It's interesting to examine several currently popular schemes for legal "reform" in the context of the lawyer glut. Many of these come from Senator John Tunney, who has staked out the issue as his own and talked the Senate leadership into creating a special subcommittee for him to use as a platform on the subject. Tunney has made the connection explicit. "It's no secret that the lawyer population is exploding; if present trends continue, it will double in ten years," Tunney wrote in a recent issue of *Juris Doctor,* a "Magazine for the New Lawyer." He continued, "According to Department of Labor statistics, half of each year's law graduates from now through 1980 will not be able to find jobs in traditional areas of law. Surely these people could profitably join pre-paid panels or legal clinics, or create even newer forms of legal services programs. They will undoubtedly exert pressure on the organized bar to force down barriers to new markets for their services."

As a matter of fact, almost every major political reform of the past decade—with the significant exception of no-fault auto insurance—has had the important side effect of increasing business for lawyers. The Tax Reform Act of 1969 is known in professional circles as the "lawyers and accountants relief act," because of the wide areas of complicated litigation it opened up. The same could be said of the Freedom of Information Act, the campaign spending reform act, and the acts creating new regulatory commissions, such as the Environmental Protection Agency.

It would be absurd to suspect that this common feature of such disparate reforms—all associated with what has come to be called the "public interest law movement"—is the result of a conspiracy led by Ralph Nader and Senator Tunney, secretly financed by the American Bar Association. But it would be equally absurd to write it off as a coincidence. It is actually the result, not of any overt conspiracy, but of a process taught at all law schools across the country and known as "thinking like a lawyer." Thinking like a lawyer means believing that legal tools—primarily the adversary system—are ideally suited to solving all problems that come along. If there is an area of life outside the legal system in which things are not going as they should, the solution is to expand the legal system in order to bring that area within it. Properly recognizing that the legal system often fails because the "bad guys" have lawyers and the "good guys" don't, reformist lawyers set about supplying lawyers to the good guys.

Over the past decade the public interest law movement, by using the instruments of the legal profession in novel ways, has become this country's most successful force for beneficial social change. Its most important contribution has been to break the bureaucratic hold on the governmental process, slicing through red tape with legal tools sharp as surgical steel. Ten years after the emergence of Ralph Nader, however, the movement is entering a second phase. Funded primarily by foundation grants, it has learned how best to use these tools. Now it wishes to use them not just selectively, but as part of the everyday functioning of government. Unfortunately, the grants are running out, and the movement needs a permanent source of funds for its activities. The most permanent source around, of course, is the federal government. So it is no surprise to find that public interest lawyers are seeking, through various devices, to tap the federal treasury. These efforts ought to provide the occasion for a bit of soulsearching on the part of the public interest law movement. As is usually the case, however, access to tax dollars has instead made it easier to push such questions aside. But whether or not the public interest lawyers wish to face it themselves, their claim for subsidy poses the question of whether the hiring of more lawyers is the most promising avenue to beneficial social change.

REGULATORY INTERVENTION

The area of public life where public interest law probably has had its greatest impact is the world of the federal regulatory agencies. These agencies are run according to the elaborate adversary-proceeding rules set forth in the Administrative Procedures Act. The theory is that the public interest will emerge from the give-and-take of the private interests which choose to enter various policy disputes. Too often, as everybody knows, the debate covers only that narrow part of the spectrum representing the interest of the corporations which the agency was supposed to regulate. By intervening in favor of the "public" interest, Ralph Nader and others like him achieved some important reversals of policy and generally put the agencies back on their guard. But this kind of intervention is expensive, and the public interest groups lack the resources of the private corporations they are fighting. So they can intervene in only a very few disputes.

The request for a government handout follows naturally and with seeming logic: if public interest intervention serves the public by improving the quality of decisions turned out by regulatory agencies, the public should help pay for such intervention and make it a routine part of the regulatory system. Congress recently authorized the Federal Trade Commission to set up a $1-million fund for underwriting intervention by citizen groups in FTC rule-making procedures. The new Nuclear Regulatory.Commission, successor to the duties of the Atomic Energy Commission, hired a public interest law firm to study the possibility of creating a similar arrangement for atomic energy controversies. (According to an "Executive Summary" wisely supplied with the firm's report, "The Report suggested that one must balance the arguments in favor of intervenor financing with those against it.")

The problem with these plans is that the outside intervention was necessary only because the agencies themselves were not doing their jobs properly. It hardly makes sense to institutionalize this intervention as part of a major "reform." These agencies were, after all, set up to determine what the public interest is, and to make their decisions accordingly. For reasons best known to lawyers, it was decided that elaborate and expensive adversary proceedings were the best way to arrive at this result. If, however, there is some easy and inexpensive way by which someone who is charged with intervening on behalf of the "public" interest can independently determine what that interest is, the proper arrangement would be to put that someone in charge and dispense with the whole expensive regulatory apparatus. Probably there is no such easy and inexpensive way. We can look forward, it is safe to predict, to much complicated and costly litigation about who is entitled to use these "public interest intervention" funds in each case, *followed* of course by the costly and complicated traditional regulatory process.

The public interest lawyers are not through with the regulatory agencies at this point. In his well-received 1974 book about public interest lawyers, *The Genteel Populists,* a former public interest lawyer named Simon Lazarus (now with the firm of Arnold and Porter) staked an elegant claim for the title of chief dialectician and theorist of the public interest law movement. After placing the movement in the perspective of history and legal theory, he concluded that the real hope for reform lies in making regulatory-agency decisions more easily appealable to the courts. You have to be a true believer in the adversary system to believe that a three-level sandwich of procedures, with the government paying for the judge and one side of the dispute at each level, is really the most effective method of government decision-making.

The answer is not to add levels of adversary proceedings, but to strip them away. In many areas, complete deregulation will restore the competitive rigors of the marketplace, for which adversary proceedings before a regulatory agency are only a pale and ineffectual metaphor. In areas (such as health and safety) where government regulation must continue, expedited proceedings should depend less on the lawyers and more on the reservoir of expertise and good sense available to well-chosen commissioners.

What the adversary system does is pit two sides against one another, with self-interest motivating their lawyers less toward the pursuit of truth and justice than toward the pursuit of victory. Between the lawyers stands a judge, who in the dominant tradition of American law is not a seeker after truth, or justice either, but rather a neutral referee seeking only to ensure that the combatants obey the rules of fair play.

It is possible for disputes to be handled otherwise—by judges who do seek justice and truth (as they do in England in at least some cases), who keep lawyers out of their courtrooms and take responsibility themselves for protecting each party's rights (as they do in a few American small claims courts). It is also possible for disputes to be handled by mediators who seek solutions that are fair to both sides and that will enable the disputants to go forward as friends rather than enemies.

But as Laura Nader and Linda Singer pointed out in a recent paper, "Dispute Resolution in the Future: What Are the Choices?", lawyers are doing very little to encourage any solution of disputes outside the adversary system. When the Los Angeles County Bar Association attempted to provide arbitration of disputes between attorneys and their clients, the lawyers refused arbitration more than half the time.

FEE SHIFTING

Another major reform being advanced by the public interest law movement appears at first to address itself to a broader slice of American legal life than the regulatory agency subculture. This reform involves the controversial principle of "fee shifting."

The long-standing "American Rule" holds that each side of a civil suit must bear its own legal fees, no matter who started it in the first place, and no matter who ends up winning. In England the court usually is free to force a losing party to pay the winner the legal costs generated in vindicating his or her rights.

The American exceptions to the "American Rule" always have been very limited, but one of them has been expanding in recent years. This is the so-called "private attorney general" exception, which holds that when a suit is brought which not only benefits the individual plaintiff, but furthers an important and clearly established government policy, the court can force the defendant to pay the plaintiff's legal fees on the grounds that the plaintiff is acting not for himself but as a "private attorney general" on behalf of all the people.

Most of the expansion of the fee-shifting principle has occurred in the area of the civil rights laws. Hopes that it might be extended to other areas were thwarted by the Supreme Court last May. In the *Alyeska Pipeline* case, the Court refused to make the oil company consortium which was building the Alaska pipeline pay the legal costs of a challenge by Friends of the Earth and other ecology groups. It did, however, explicitly invite legislation to clarify the fee-shifting issue.

Following *Alyeska,* Senator Tunney introduced a bill authorizing fee shifting in civil rights cases. Moreover, as chairman of the Constitutional Rights Subcommittee of the House Judiciary Committee, Tunney is on record as favoring the expansion of this principle to other areas of "public interest" litigation.

Under the "American Rule," some stranger may descend upon you out of the blue, sue you for a variety of fabricated reasons, lose, then disappear leaving you with a mountain of legal bills and no recourse. This is one of the absurdities which first-year law students struggle against in their hopeless battle against the legal mind-set. The reason most frequently given in defense of the rule is that we don't want to discourage people from exercising their right to sue other people by placing too great a burden on the risk of losing (the fear of discouraging litigation being an important part of thinking like a lawyer). On the face of it, a change in the American Rule seems eminently reasonable.

But it is clear from the exceptions already made, and from the line-up of forces urging more, that the reforms now being pushed by public interest lawyers are intended to help not unwitting defendants but plaintiffs. In particular, they are intended to pay the fees of public interest lawyers who want to sue the United States government. Lurking behind the fee-shifting proposals is the same theory of government decision-making by adversary proceeding that has provoked the public interest intervenor proposals. When public interest groups see a regulatory agency, or the antitrust division of the Justice Department, or the HEW Office of Civil Rights failing to perform its legal duty, they will be able to dig up a plaintiff, sue the government on his or her behalf and have the government pay for it.

So far so good—if they win and the government loses. But suppose the government wins. Should it still pay the fees? A lot of public interest lawyers think so. And there are already cases holding that such fees may be awarded if the court feels that important policy questions were raised, whatever the ultimate outcome. Thus a reform which could be profound —if the losing party had to pay the fees, those in the right would be encouraged to use the courts and those in the wrong would be encouraged not to use the court—is perverted into a method of getting the government to finance the public interest law movement.

LAW FOR THE MASSES

Most far-reaching of all are the various schemes to expand the availability of legal services to the masses of American citizens for use in the struggles of their daily lives. Once again Senator John Tunney is in the forefront. Tunney spearheaded the bill creating the Legal Services Corporation, a government organization providing legal services to the poor, a job abandoned during the dismantling of the Office of Economic Opportunity.

Tunney also has held hearings on what the government can do to encourage creation of pre-paid legal services plans, in effect legal insurance, under which individual members of unions and other groups would pay a set annual fee, which would entitle them to whatever legal care they might need each year. Under some such plans, the legal services are provided by members of a particular law "clinic" ("closed" plans); under others, the plan pays the bill of any private lawyer the member wishes to retain ("open" plans).

Tunney believes that millions of Americans suffer every year because they do not have access to, or cannot afford, decent legal services. In support of this proposition he advances an oft-cited statistic first published in 1974 by the American Bar Association: two thirds of the people in the United States have consulted a lawyer only once or twice in their lives, and one third have never consulted a lawyer at all.

Undoubtedly millions of average Americans get screwed because they do not have access to a lawyer. But this statistic alone does not prove it. The vast majority of Americans has never had the occasion to call upon the services of an accountant or a glass cutter or a flower arranger. And, however much of this fact may pain the members of these professions, it is not likely, let alone obvious, that the vast majority has suffered as a result of this deprivation. Inherent in the use of such statistics as the ABA'S, and in the whole notion of pre-paid legal services, is a hidden analogy to medicine. The fact that millions of Americans go through a year without seeing a doctor may indeed be a scandal. It is possible, however, to lead a happy and healthy life which is nonetheless litigation-free.

Death brings out what would seem to be an inevitable need for lawyers. You need a lawyer when you make a will and your family may need a lawyer when you die. But even these real needs are not as great as the legal profession would have you believe. Most wills, for example, are almost all "boiler plate"—chunks of colorful but standardized verbiage required, where simple declarative sentences might otherwise do, to satisfy the voodooistic needs of the legal profession. Determining which chunks of boiler plate you need is usually a simple process which could be done quite cheaply by walk-in clinics. As for probate, Wisconsin is the first state in the country with a do-it-yourself probate law. It permits you to settle your parents' or your spouse's estate without paying thousands of dollars to lawyers as you do in most states. Naturally it was opposed by the state bar.

The other occasions when every man needs a lawyer are divorce and auto accidents. Both can be solved by the no-fault concept. Under the adversary concept in divorce cases, every Othello not only must suffer an Iago, but must pay him for his services. Desdemona must do the same. Under no-fault, simple forms are filed with the court and a divorce may be obtained without involving the parties in life-long hatred of each other.

The auto accident is the most absurd situation of all for adversary proceedings. Remember the word is "accident." No one did it deliberately or recklessly—if someone did, there would be criminal prosecution. In the typical "accident" case, each party is trying to prove the other was at fault when no one was really at fault. This involves both parties in lying, which in turn makes them hate the other guy even more. In no case does our righteous anger against the lies of another mount to such heights as when we are lying, too.

This particular charm of the adversary system was well illustrated in a recent Corporations class at "The" Harvard Law School. The professor proposed a "hypothetical": Two men want to buy a photography business owned by a third man. Although they have not settled on the exact price, all three are amicably agreed on the general contours of the deal. They come to you to write up a contract for them. What's the first thing you should do? The answer: send either the buyers or the seller out to get another lawyer because for one lawyer to represent all of them would be a "conflict of interest." The class was divided down the middle aisle, with each half of the room assigned to represent one party to the deal. By near the end of the hour, several promising areas of discord had developed. The last few minutes were spent discussing whether the two buyers shouldn't really have separate lawyers as well.

It used to be that only the rich needed lawyers. As the law infiltrates more and more aspects of daily life, it is increasingly necessary for poor and middle-class people to have legal advice available to them. If you are a group, such as a union, representing a large number of middle-class people, it is quite reasonable to arrange to provide the legal services your members need at a reasonable cost. But if you are the government, making social policy, you might more profitably concentrate on eliminating the various problems that drive people to lawyers. Tunney and others have attempted to delegalize various aspects of modern life and to reduce the cost of lawyers when they are needed. But if lawyers are available to all at what appears to the client to be no cost for any individual visit or service, it's hard to see how the trend can be anything but the exact opposite.

When pre-paid legal services become universal, this country will become a nightmare of litigation. As we put it in *The Washington Monthly* of February 1974, "If paranoia is the major mental disorder of America, lawyers are its Typhoid Marys." People worry about medical insurance causing over-use of medical resources by people who don't really need them. This is why most medical insurance plans do not cover basic office visits. Obviously the potential for this kind of abuse is infinitely greater in the legal area.

The American Bar Association is slowly coming to support most of the schemes to increase public "access to" (read: dependence upon) legal services. The big news coming out of the ABA convention last summer in Montreal (front page, Sunday *New York Times*) was that—"belatedly, according to some critics"—the legal profession was beginning to realize "that millions of Americans do not get the legal services they need."

At this convention, the ABA officially recognized the public interest law movement with a resolution stating "that it is a basic professional responsibility of each lawyer engaged in the practice of law to provide public interest legal services." This resolution had been amended at the last minute, with lawyer-like precision in the use of ambiguity, from an earlier version referring to "the professional duty" rather than "a professional responsibility."

In 1972 the ABA House of Delegates officially acknowledged the existence of pre-paid legal services plans. The Bar Association even funded two experimental "open panel" plans, in which the clients were free to choose their own lawyers from any member of the local bar. In 1974 the ABA helped Senator Tunney lobby through the bill creating the Legal Services Corporation.

The reasons for the change of heart on the part of the legal establishment are not hard to fathom. The evolution in the ABA's attitude closely parallels that of the American Medical Association toward Medicare and other government-funded medical programs. First comes total opposition —fear of the unknown. Next, we have attempts at co-option. The ABA's "open plan" pre-paid experiments come under this heading. While endorsing those plans which merely added the element of insurance to the present unregulated private law industry, the Bar Association was busy placing obstacles in the way of attempts to create "closed panel" plans which would replace private practice with legal clinic-type arrangements. Anyone who has studied the AMA's answer to the calls for national health insurance will notice the similarities.

When the doctors discovered that Medicare and similar plans could, if kept properly out of control, double or triple their incomes, their attitude underwent a final change from reluctance to wary embrace. We predict that the lawyers, always a bit quicker on the uptake than the stethoscope set, are on the verge of a similar revelation. It is clear after ten years that Medicare and Medicaid are the best things that ever happened to the medical profession. They have increased the doctors' business, eliminated the need to charge any patient less than the highest normal fee, and together with Blue Shield, made the average patient totally indifferent to rises in charges for medical services.

HUMAN CAPITAL SHORTAGE

Recall Senator Tunney's image of thousands of bright young men and women fanning out from law school, using their tightly rolled diplomas as battering rams to break down the barriers to new markets for legal services so they can put their degrees and intelligence and energy to some use. This image suggests that the greatest waste is not simply that of government money. Few of those thousands of bright young men and women coming out of law school were naturally attracted to legal careers. Rather, they have sat—bored out of their minds—through three years of Civil Procedure, Corporate Tax, and Commercial Transactions, captive to a social incentive structure in which lawyers reap the greatest rewards of money and power.

To most bright people, lawyering is a boring and demeaning way to make a living. If society really needs thousands of new lawyers every year in order to function properly, this incentive structure would make a good deal of sense. But if, as it is moderately popular to suppose, the United States has passed its zenith and entered a long period of decline, anthropologists of the next century will look back in amazement at an arrangement whereby the most ambitious and brightest members of each generation were siphoned off the productive work force, trained to think like a lawyer, and put to work chasing one another around in circles; where, as things got worse and worse, social reformers, cured by the Republicans of the habit of trying to solve all problems by throwing money at them, took to throwing lawyers at them instead; and where the portion of the population that went through a typical year happily oblivious of the legal profession slipped from two thirds to one half, to a quarter, to none at all.

Afterword

Senator John Tunney was upset in his 1976 reelection campaign by S. I. Hayakawa, now the junior senator from California. But the public-interest law movement is still very much alive.

We've been following with great enthusiasm the *U.S. v. IBM* antitrust case, which keeps hundreds of lawyers terribly busy filing memoranda and documents and taking testimony that will cover every conceivable point of antitrust law. The case should be with us at least into the 1980s, and lately the judge has been wondering out loud if he'll survive it.

Computer Decisions captured some of the lively flavor of the case when it reprinted some testimony from a similar, earlier marathon lawsuit, *Telex v. IBM.* In the passage here, Mr. Walker is a Telex lawyer, Mr. Shelton is an IBM employee being cross-examined, and Mr. Goodfriend is an IBM lawyer. Read and weep:

Mr. Walker: During the period that you were an Associate Financial Analyst, will you tell us and describe to us the nature and extent of your job responsibilities?

Mr. Shelton: At that point I didn't do a lot.

W: Okay. Did you work under the supervision of other people to a large extent during that first eight to 10 months?

S: Yes.

W: Did you receive any kind of specialized training during that eight to 10 months, any schooling or training at IBM?

S: I don't quite understand the question.

W: Well, you know what schooling is.

S: Yes.

W: All right. Did you receive any schooling at IBM during the first eight to 10 months you were there?

S: Again, I—could you explain that just a little bit more?

W: Mr. Shelton, after your first eight to 10 months on the job at IBM as an Associate Financial Analyst, did you receive another job title?

S: Yes.

W: What was that?

S: Senior Associate.

W: Senior Associate Financial Analyst. Is that correct?

S: Yes.

W: How long did you remain a Senior Associate Financial Analyst? Do you have any judgment at all, your best estimate?

S: Two years.

W: Will you describe the nature and extent of your job responsibilities during the approximate two-year period that you were a Senior Associate Financial Analyst on the Group Staff at Data Processing Headquarters in Harrison?

Mr. Goodfriend: I object to the form of the question. You may answer if you can. (Attorneys for both parties agreed that only objections to the form of a question could be made.)

S: Well, I don't understand the question.

W: Well, during the period that you were a Senior Associate Financial Analyst, were you still on the Data Processing Group Staff?

S: Yes.

W: Did you still work at Harrison?

S: I don't fully understand that.

W: I'm sorry. I cannot hear you.

S: I don't fully understand that one.

W: Would you describe the nature of your job responsibilities and the things that you did during that period of time?

G: I object to the form of the question. You may answer. Off the record. (Discussion off the record.)

S: Would you read the question? (Pending question read.)

S: I did financial analysis.

part 5
PRESSURE GROUPS

Every year the federal government grows in complexity and power, and as it does the desire and the ability of organized groups to influence the government to act in their interest grows too. The *desire* to influence is growing because more and more people see the government as having a great effect on their lives, so understandably they want a say in what that effect will be. The *ability* to influence is growing because most powerful government officials (especially congressmen) are involved in so much at one time that a strong or well-reasoned position on any issue is usually enough to persuade them.

This persuasion, called lobbying, goes on in all sorts of ways in Washington. Thousands of opponents of the Panama Canal treaties flood their senators' offices with postcards stating their views. A well-connected lawyer makes a discreet phone call to an official of an agency to straighten out a problem for a client. President Carter has a dozen congressmen to breakfast to tell them why they should support his energy plan. Tongsun Park slips officials envelopes of cash.

The only one of those lobbying techniques that's uncommon today is the last. Lobbying has become honest and respectable. Many lobbyists have as their most useful tool an impressive technical expertise in their field, so that they know more than the official they're trying to influence does and can help him put together a reasoned position on the issue at hand. Another powerful weapon of lobbyists is connections, which means access for your client's views; that's why so many Washington lobbyists are former high government officials. Another is votes—the ability to deliver them in return for support, or, more important, to cut them off in return for opposition. And the smartest lobbyists continue to offer their prey rewards —not envelopes of cash, but perhaps the chance to live glamorous lives, or the promise of future employment. As Walter Shapiro points out in "What Politicians Really Want," many members of Congress ran in the first place so they could live like important people, and lobbyists can help them fulfill that dream without any money changing hands.

The most powerful lobbies do a great deal. They can, for instance, control congressional policy-making on broadcasting matters, as is detailed in Thomas Redburn's article about the broadcasting interests and the counsel to the Senate subcommittee that regulates broadcasting, Nick Zapple. They can keep the pay and benefits of government employees high and ensure that new programs will be enacted, as Leonard Reed shows in "The Bureaucracy: The Cleverest Lobby of Them All." Lobbyists, you see, aren't just working for big businesses—they can be government workers, Presidents, even college professors. In "The Harvard Brain Trust: Eating Lunch at Henry's," Michael Kinsley tells the story of a group of Henry Kissinger's former colleagues who came to Washington to convince him to pull out of Cambodia. It was an example of the rare lobbying effort that has no effect whatsoever on the operations of the government.

What Politicians Really Want

Walter Shapiro

It started with a disappearance. Marvin Mandel, Spiro Agnew's successor as governor of Maryland, left Annapolis on Thursday, January 8, without announcing his destination. Within a few days, *The Washington Post* discovered that Mandel and his wife had gone on a Jamaican vacation aboard a corporate jet provided by Steuart Petroleum—an oil company which just happens to be trying to build a controversial refinery on the Eastern Shore of the Chesapeake Bay. The efforts by the governor's office to cover up the story were breath-taking in their ineptness. First they claimed that the Governor had won the vacation in a raffle, and then they changed the story to read that Mandel and several others, including a Steuart vice president, had put up $1,200 at a charity auction and won the use of a cottage in Jamaica.

This was just the beginning of a series of disclosures which prompted the Baltimore *Sun* to publish an editorial cartoon with the caption, "I'm Marvin, Fly Me." By early February it had been confirmed that since he became governor Mandel had accepted at least ten other trips on corporate jets. Some of the flights were unabashed luxury vacations such as a one-day trip to Wyoming in 1973 for an antelope-hunting contest held primarily for celebrities and business executives. Throughout the entire furor, Mandel stoutly maintained that "I haven't done anything wrong," although he did acknowledge that the trip to Jamaica might have been "a public relations mistake."

Walter Shapiro is a special assistant to Ray Marshall, the Secretary of Labor.

Compared to the conduct of his predecessor, Spiro Agnew, Mandel's behavior seems tame. As one Maryland politician put it, "If this becomes a major scandal, it will be like a champion swimmer drowning in the bathtub." Mandel's free plane flights are important, however, because they are typical of the ways lobbyists influence the majority of government officials—those who are neither explicitly corrupt, nor inflexibly wedded to the public interest.

Not consumed by anything resembling ideological passion, Mandel is emblematic of many in public life in that he seems more interested in the pleasures of being governor than in accomplishing anything specific in office. It is not surprising that several of his free flights were to the National Governors' Conference. Held at beautiful resorts like Lake Tahoe, these conferences accomplish little substantive business, but they do provide the governors with the elevated lifestyle which many believe is their automatic due. This attitude is not reserved to governors. Despite press criticism, congressmen continue to take junkets to Europe and Asia for much the same reason. Since there is a limit to how many trips and full-dress dinners can be charged to the public, a passion for living on this level leads public officials such as Mandel straight into the hands of the lobbyists.

Despite the intensity of our current national crusade against corruption, the number of public officials who are actively for sale is relatively small —and, one suspects, they tend to be expensive. But the shrewder lobbyists know that the friendship of even uncorruptible officeholders can be won with such blandishments as luxury vacations, elaborate dinners, introductions to celebrities, and the other perquisites of the American upper class.

Status in this country is based primarily on two factors—prominence and wealth. A governor like Mandel may be better known than almost all corporate executives, but he is forced to live on the maddeningly middle-class salary of $25,000. A senator may regularly appear before 50 million Americans on the evening news, but he must make ends meet on a salary of $57,500. For an elected official without personal wealth, this discrepancy between prominence and salary often rankles.

Some politicians overcome this problem by becoming so oblivious to reality that they actually live as if they were supported by accumulated capital rather than by their government salary. An extreme example is former New York Congressman Seymour Halpern. *The Wall Street Journal* revealed in 1969 that Halpern, who was then third-ranking Republican on the House Banking Committee, had more than $100,000 in bank loans that were either seriously overdue or totally unsecured by collateral. Halpern's indebtedness—which eventually helped hasten his retirement —stemmed from his insistence on living in a manner that may have fitted his prominence, but certainly not his income. As Jerry Landauer put it in the *Journal,* Halpern is a "man of extravagant habits—reaching impetuously for dinner checks at fine restaurants, sending his attractive wife to costly vacation spas, collecting valuable manuscripts. . . ." Not only was Halpern overdrawn at the bank, but he owed sizable sums to expensive French restaurants and hotels such as the Plaza in New York and the Fountainbleu in Miami Beach.

THE STATUS SEEKERS

The phrase "living beyond one's means" has a dated ring, yet this expression often fits congressmen as closely as it fits the proverbial Westport advertising executive mortgaged to his eyebrows. Sometimes legislators find themselves in serious trouble, as did recently retired Illinois Congressman Ken Gray, who, according to *The Washington Star,* used left-over campaign funds to help buy his $40,000 houseboat, Rollcall. Gray justified the complicated transactions which paid for the craft by arguing that it helped him entertain visitors from back home: "I thought the best way to entertain constituents was to let them see the beautiful Capitol from the Potomac." Even the more dedicated members of Congress feel a conflict between their lifestyles and their income. In a forthcoming book, *Inside the House,* Daniel Rapoport provides this glimpse of a prominent House liberal: "Ben and Leila Rosenthal do not live opulently. But they do live nicely. They enjoy the familiar comforts of an expensive country club and two vacations a year. . . . The Rosenthals readily concede that they live well. But in 1973 they said they were approaching the point where they would be living beyond their means." Similarly, many senators are feeling the financial pinch caused by a recent $15,000-a-year limit on the amount of speaking fees they can collect to supplement their salaries. Kandy Stroud recently reported in *New York* that a number of Senate wives are being forced to go to work to help make ends meet. The wives of both Mark Hatfield and John Tower, for example, are selling real estate.

Obviously, some of these salary problems are caused by expenses unique to Congress, such as maintaining two homes and frequent travel back to the home district. But many more stem from the exigencies of maintaining a suitably elevated life-style. Antoinette Hatfield, for example, explained that her clothing costs tended to be high because "Senate wives are expected to look better than the average person."

Recently, Alaska Senator Mike Gravel was described by columnist Jack Anderson as "living beyond his means" to support a $200,000 dream house. . . . in the fashionable Maryland countryside." In response to questioning about the column, Gravel, who was originally a real estate promoter in Alaska, justified his home ("it's actually worth $250,000") both in terms of his work ("in my business entertaining is *de rigueur*") and its investment possibilities. According to Gravel, this last idea came from none other than Lyndon Johnson, who, on the verge of leaving office, took some freshmen senators aside and gave them this secret of success in Washington—"invest in local real estate." More than any other recent figure in public life, Richard Nixon illustrates the degree to which elected officials can come to believe that their prominence should permit them to live on a par with millionaires. Ever since Nixon journeyed to Wall Street after losing the 1962 California gubernatorial race, he has been devoured by his passion to accumulate enough capital to guarantee an upper-class lifestyle. It is this passion which explains his curious real estate transactions with Bebe Rebozo and Robert Abplanalp. Early this March, Jack Anderson reported that the former President "is deeply depressed over his finances." With a $60,000 pension, Nixon is in no real financial danger. But Anderson pinpoints the source of Nixon's anxiety: "He lacks the income to sustain his lifestyle. He is desperately looking for ways to increase his cash flow."

'I'M CALLING FROM MY CAR'

I am not making a case for asceticism. Obviously, public officials should not be required to live like Ralph Nader. Neither should we overly praise Jerry Brown for deciding to live in a scantily furnished one-bedroom apartment instead of the California governor's mansion. But the financial problems of many in government explain why so often they become entranced with the trappings of office, with chauffeured limousines and elaborately equipped offices. George Reedy has written about the seductions of life in the White House. On a less exalted level, the chairman of the Equal Employment Opportunity Commission is known, when driving around Washington, to call his staffers merely for the pleasure of saying: "I'm calling you from the phone in my car." For some, these luxuries can serve as tangible reminders that they have arrived, that they actually are high government officials.

For those (and there are many) who have gone into public service in quest of a certain lifestyle, there is a limit to how much satisfaction can be derived from having a refrigerator and a shower in your office. This explains why the most astute lobbyists can often win the friendship of congressmen and governors through little favors. For Marvin Mandel, the favor was a vacation in Jamaica. For someone else, it might be a chance to meet movie stars or to be accepted in the homes of aristocratic families. There are undoubtedly senators in Washington who are more likely to be swayed by a $30 lunch at an exclusive club which they don't belong to than by a $300 campaign contribution.

The shrewd lobbyist need not spend vast sums of money to provide a public official with what he wants. All he need do is follow the maxim that the perfect gift is something the recipient wants but would never buy for himself. (In contrast, even if a senator with a middle-class income took a bribe, he probably would feel obligated to do something sensible with it, like putting it aside for his children's college education.)

In December, 1974, Tongsun Park, a somewhat mysterious Korean with a host of interests ranging from oil supertankers to the international rice trade, gave a birthday party for House Majority Leader "Tip" O'Neill. It was neither the kind of party that O'Neill, said to be a man of relatively modest habits, would have given for himself, nor just a mechanical tribute like a testimonial dinner. No, this party was elegant rather than political. The 100 invited guests were served wild goose at Washington's prestigious and genteelly subdued Madison Hotel.

If Park had been asked his motive for giving the party, he probably would have smiled and answered "friendship." Henry Mitchell of *The Washington Post* wrote that Park "was once a Georgetown student and roomed in those days with Rep. John Brademas and was interested in student politics and got to be friends of many congressmen. As the years passed, some of these friendships ripened and hence his fondness for O'Neill. . . . " If Mitchell was serious, this is an unbelievably saccharine view of the cosmos. Yet, one should not take too cynical a view and automatically assume that this party was given in return for a favor from O'Neill; for lobbyists like Park are often more subtle than that. Take, for example, the exquisite indirection of Park's going-away party for outgoing Attorney General William Saxbe. In the cutthroat world of Washington society, there are few gestures so seemingly selfless as giving a party for someone about to leave office. But parties like this cement ties of friendship with those in public life. There is no need for explicit *quid pro quos.* What Park has done is increase the likelihood that leading public officials will deal with him on a personal rather than a bureaucratic level the next time he wants something from the United States government.

Such subtle courting by lobbyists is one of the major problems of American political life. It would not disappear with tougher restrictions on campaign spending or with raising congressional and gubernatorial salaries to $80,000 a year. For as long as there are men who dream, not of the work they will do in office but of the life they will lead, there are going to be lobbyists who know how to get what they want by exploiting those dreams.

Afterword

Marvin Mandel was convicted of mail fraud in 1977 and left the Maryland governorship. Tongsun Park, in exchange for immunity, told a special Congressional committee about his illegal cash gifts to congressmen. In 1977, Congress raised the salaries of its members to $57,500 a year.

Wedding Presents, Cigars, and Deference

Thomas Redburn

It's a Washington party. The details are unimportant. Perhaps it is part of the convention of the National Association of Broadcasters (NAB); or perhaps it is the annual gathering of the Federal Communications Commission Bar Association; or a celebration to kick off a new television program. There are probably two or three genuine celebrities present, but most of the people are broadcasting network executives, owners of television stations, lobbyists for the industry, communications lawyers, and a few government officials involved in broadcast regulation.

A broadcast lobbyist is wandering through the crowd. He spots a familiar face. Almost automatically he reaches into his coat pocket to find the cigar he is in the habit of offering to this man. This time, however, he discovers that he has run out. Oh well, he thinks, the man will never notice. But he's wrong. "Where's my cigar?" demands Nick Zapple.

Nick Zapple has come to expect such favors as a matter of course. In his mind, they go with his job. A cigar may not seem like much, but on the face of it, neither does his job. Zapple is one of the more anonymous holders of power in Washington. The *Congressional Staff Directory* lists him merely as one of 21 staff counsels for the Senate Commerce Committee. And while the guide contains nearly 2,000 brief biographies of important Capitol Hill staff assistants, there is none on Zapple. To the people engaged in the politics of broadcast regulation, this is a startling omission, for, to them, Zapple is a central figure. Almost *the* central figure. As one

Thomas Redburn is a contributing editor of *The Washington Monthly* and a reporter for *The Los Angeles Times*.

communications lawyer told me, "For those of us who work in this world, from the way we talk and act, you'd think there was no one more important than Nick Zapple. It must seem a little unreal to an outsider, but we can't help it."

Zapple's importance derives from his position as chief counsel (and virtually the only professional staff) of the Senate Commerce Committee's Subcommittee on Communications. He can be seen at any public hearing of the subcommittee, sitting next to the subcommittee chairman, Senator John Pastore. There are seven senators on the subcommittee, but at most hearings the other six wander in and out, asking only an occasional question. Whenever the senators appear they make a point of remembering to put up their name cards—in case anyone forgets who they are. There's no need for a name card for Zapple; everyone in the room already knows who he is. It is a small world, of which Zapple is a central part, that revolves around the Federal Communications Commission (FCC). More than a hundred people are in the room whenever the subcommittee meets, and they may be practically the only ones in the world who find the testimony and questions absorbing; to anyone else, the session would seem boring and irrelevant. But this insularity of interest is exactly what gives the comparative handful their influence.

Nothing makes this clearer than witnessing a typical subcommittee hearing. For instance, at the annual FCC oversight hearings in April, Richard Wiley, the FCC chairman, read a 31-page summary of all the Commission's activities over the past year. None of it was noteworthy enough to make the daily newspapers, yet within the audience, carefully following copies of the testimony, were many of the people who comprise the subgovernment within which broadcasting policy is set: the seven FCC commissioners, the Commission staff, the communications lawyers who make up the FCC Bar Association, the representatives of the television networks, the lobbyists for the NAB and the Association of Maximum Service Telecasters. You could also see reporters for the trade magazines like *Broadcasting, Television Digest,* and *Variety.*

EVERYBODY KNOWS MY NAME

Nick Zapple is the man who brought all these people together. He sits next to Pastore, occupying one of those high-backed, overstuffed, leather chairs normally reserved for elected legislators. No small wooden chair set against the back wall for him. From his prominent position, he surveys the crowd with a knowing half-smile on his face. He still has a flat-top out of the 1950s, like H. R. Haldeman before he grew his hair. He is clearly content with where he is and what he is, and with reason. Zapple claims he has been asked to become FCC chairman, but he's turned it down because he finds his present position more important and more interesting.

Zapple's reluctance to go to the Commission doesn't come from the fear that the FCC is unimportant or ineffectual. He, more than most people, is aware of the crucial part the FCC can play in regulating the television and radio industries. But although it is the FCC which draws most of the attention from the public, it is Zapple, not the FCC commissioners, who is spoken of with a mixture of fear and respect by broadcast lobbyists. One indication of this is that just one person I interviewed, a former reporter for *Broadcasting*, was willing to speak on-the-record about Zapple.

'YOU BELONG TO US'

By now it is a truism that the FCC is not the independent commission the law says it is. The FCC has often been pointed to as a prime example of a regulatory agency "captured" by the industry it is supposed to oversee. While there is a good deal of validity to the charge, it also oversimplifies the process. What is often forgotten is that occasionally the FCC breaks out of its lethargy and does something unexpected, creating an uproar among all those broadcasters who depend on a docile Commission. When the smoke clears, the true pecking order is revealed, as the FCC is quickly reminded that it isn't allowed to just wander off on its own, doing whatever it feels like.

This is where Congress enters the picture. Newton Minow, FCC chairman from 1961 to 1963, tells the story of an encounter with House Speaker Sam Rayburn soon after being appointed. Rayburn, exuding friendship, put his arm around Minow and said, "Just remember one thing, son. Your agency is an arm of Congress, you belong to us. Remember that and you'll be all right." Rayburn then warned Minow to expect a lot of pressure from outsiders. In retrospect, Minow said that "what he didn't tell me was that most of the pressure would come from Congress itself."

But what is wrong with that? Isn't that just democracy in action? Not exactly. Congress' relationship with the FCC is complicated by the awareness on the part of each legislator that he is dependent on local broadcasters for his access to the voters. A majority of congressmen regularly use free time offered by these local broadcasters to report to their constituents. Congressmen also know that broadcasters have a great deal of latitude when it comes to how politicians are presented on news programs. It may be only a simple matter like a post office opening. The local newscaster can say just as easily, "The Postal Service announced the opening of ..." as "Congressman X announced the opening of a new post office...."

At the same time, broadcasters are dependent on the FCC to retain

their licenses, the government charters which assign them broadcast fre-
quencies. Such a permit may be an entirely artificial product, but it has
very aptly been called a license to print money. In any major city a
television station can probably be sold for about $50 million. Since the
value of the station's tangible assets probably do not exceed $3 million, the
$47 million remaining is the real value of the government franchise, the
broadcasting license. What drives fear into the soul of a broadcaster is the
realization that periodically these licenses must be renewed by the FCC.
Theoretically, the Commission has the right to assign these valuable com-
modities elsewhere.

With their sway over elected legislators, however, broadcasters have
found an effective way to guarantee that the bonanza does not end. Paul
Comstock, former vice president of the NAB, has said: "Most of our work
is done with congressional committees. We concentrate on Congress. We
firmly believe that the FCC will do whatever Congress tells it to do, and
will not do anything Congress tells it not to do." Thus both Congress and
the industry, united by a mutual fear of each other, coexist warily, like two
boxers just sparring for a few rounds. They circle each other uneasily, both
afraid to strike a serious blow.

Imagine what can happen, then, when this delicate equilibrium is disturbed. In January 1969, for example, the FCC voted to take away the
license of TV station WHDH in Boston and award it to a competing
applicant. The reasons for the decision were complex, the circumstances
unusual, but the decision touched off a firestorm since this was the first
time ever that the FCC had failed to renew the license of a television
station.

Although the Communications Act explicitly holds that stations are
granted no legal property right to their licenses, the unwritten code of the
FCC was that licenses would only be revoked for high crimes and misde-
meanors. But in the minds of the broadcasters, the WHDH decision destroyed this delicate understanding. *Broadcasting* set the tone of the
ensuing debate, charging that the FCC was out to "jeopardize broadcast
holdings that, in the top 50 markets alone, are valued at more than $3
billion. . . . The shock waves of the losses would be felt by thousands of big
and small stockholders alike, threatening the financial underpinnings of
the broadcast industry and possibly swamping many small broadcast
groups."

The only hope of stemming the tide of anarchy seemed to be Congress.
After enjoying being the object of an almost indecently intensive lobbying
effort, Senator Pastore vowed at the NAB convention to protect the precious licenses: "It is my deep-seated conviction that public service is not
encouraged or promoted by placing the sword of Damocles over the heads
of broadcasters at renewal time."

When Pastore and dozens of other legislators introduced bills to change the Communications Act to prevent a recurrence of the WHDH decision, the FCC got the message. It adopted a policy statement which had approximately the same effect as the proposed congressional legislation. Although the FCC policy statement was voided for a number of intricate reasons by the Federal Court of Appeals, the crisis was over. Broadcasters became confident that the FCC had learned its lesson and had no further interest in threatening the sanctity of broadcast licenses. Still, license renewal hearings around the country began to attract competing applicants with annoying frequency, so the NAB continued to push for congressional protection. In 1974, with congressional elections near, the House passed a new license renewal bill providing broadcasters with a number of protections against challenges. The Senate followed suit with a slightly different bill. It appeared that the broadcasters had finally gotten what they wanted. But Rep. Harley Staggers, chairman of the House Interstate and Foreign Commerce Committee, was angry at the broadcasting lobby for forcing through a provision extending the license period from three to five years. Peevishly, he refused to appoint conferees and the bill died at the end of the session.

ZAPPLE DAYS ARE HERE AGAIN

The license renewal issue is the most important recent example of the lengths to which the broadcast industry will go to protect itself from outsiders. What has Zapple's role been in these efforts? Zapple served as a quarterback for the industry lobbyists during the 1974 attempt to push through the bill. He met with broadcasting representatives frequently to plan approaches to individual senators. This went on behind the scenes, usually at lunch or dinner, because Pastore, for reasons of his own, tried to avoid being too closely identified with the proposed legislation.

But in this case, Zapple tried to use his position to go beyond the legislative intent of the Senate. The 1974 bill was not a complete sell-out to the broadcasters. Yet Zapple was able to undermine the bill's more public-spirited provisions. He did this through his position as chief counsel of the subcommittee, which gave him responsibility for writing the committee report on the bill. These committee reports, which are long and detailed documents written by the staff and almost never read by the senators, are important because they help the courts and administrative agencies interpret the legislative intent of Congress. Normally they adhere as closely as possible to the language of the bill and the oral discussions in committee. In mark-up sessions, Zapple surprised some observers by taking "a public interest line." But when it came time to write the report, Zapple, who had the actual writing done by someone else, attempted to have the report phrased in such a way that it, in the words of one observer, "changed the meaning of some sections 180 degrees."

License renewal protection is not the only issue in which broadcasters have used congressional committees to alter the actions of the FCC. Another example involves cable television, which the broadcasters see as a threat to the preservation of their markets. The FCC has, under the prodding of Pastore, generally worked to delay the development of cable systems because of this fear. Pastore was also angry at cable television because back in 1960 the industry at the last minute failed to fully support a bill he introduced to regulate them. Originally assured of the support of the industry, Pastore discovered that one faction of cable system owners was working against him and they managed to defeat the bill on the Senate floor by one vote. Pastore has yet to forgive them.

The dispute between cable and conventional broadcasting is complicated and the issues are generally not clear-cut. But here again Zapple has been able to help the far more powerful broadcasting industry against competitive efforts. For example, consider what happened when the FCC, under the chairmanship of Dean Burch, attempted to institute regulations governing the infant pay cable television industry. Over a year's time the FCC went through the long administrative procedures leading to the writing of new rules. The Commission, after holding hearings, oral arguments, and the like, was finally prepared to issue the rules in early 1974. Burch pledged to finish the job before he left the FCC to join the sinking White House. But only a few days before Burch was to depart, with rumors flying in the trade press, Gordon Rule and Leonard Goldenson of ABC went to Zapple and demanded that something be done to prevent the FCC from acting. Zapple persuaded Senator Magnuson, chairman of the full Commerce Committee, to talk to Howard Kitzmiller, the FCC's mild legislative liaison. Kitzmiller, who spends more time in Zapple's office than in his own, dutifully warned Burch that Zapple and Magnuson were displeased. Burch was surprised and angry that this was happening at such a late date. Burch asked for a meeting with Pastore, but Zapple, performing his role of buffer for the Senator, tried to put Burch off. Much of Zapple's importance derives simply from his control over access to Pastore on communications issues. Finally Burch managed to see Pastore by going directly to the Senate without an appointment. Pastore, sources say, "yelled and screamed" that the FCC was trying to ruin the public's right to free programming. Burch tried to persuade him that the rules were not a serious threat to free broadcasting at all. Yet when Burch left the FCC soon thereafter, nothing had been said or done about the new rules for pay cable TV.

Zapple seems to relish such opportunities to wield his power and to keep those who must deal with him on edge. During the most recent congressional effort to provide appropriations for public broadcasting, he could not resist playing games. What Zapple did was to create the impression that Pastore was wavering in his support for the money the public broadcasting system was asking for. Although the evidence suggests that Pastore never had any doubts about supporting the funding request, Zapple's maneuvers created such furor among the public broadcasting executives that they courted Zapple shamelessly. Earlier the Public Broadcasting Service had given prime time coverage to the subcommittee's hearings about public broadcasting, an event lacking most of the elements of drama of, say, the Watergate hearings. Nonetheless, while somewhat incestuous, the whole episode isn't particularly surprising. What is odd about the whole affair is that even in the one instance where he was on the right side, Zapple could not help acting in his traditional fashion and promoting his own importance.

A GROSS MISTAKE

Another way in which Zapple uses his position is to make constant, petty demands of the people he deals with. For instance, Zapple once asked Doug Anello, then general counsel for the NAB, to send a dozen steaks to him at his home on Cape Cod. It seems that you can't get good meat on Cape Cod. The steaks were ordered from Bolton and Smart, a meat company in Boston, but by mistake Zapple was sent 12 boxes of 12 steaks each. The NAB picked up the tab and Zapple never even said thank you.

Over the years, Zapple has demanded that industry lobbyists take him to lunch, pay for his liquor, and generally supply him with what Zapple sees as all the appropriate perquisites of an important position. In nearly all cases these gifts have been minor. Zapple was once caught by Jack Anderson accepting a number of gifts, including a $1,000 silver service set, from Don Burden, a broadcaster in trouble with the FCC, but that seems almost an exception to his general pattern. What seems to motivate Zapple is not the value of the gifts, but the recognition of importance and power they represent.

For instance, in the summer of 1968, one of Zapple's daughters was married. It was important to him, naturally, that his daughter have a fine wedding appropriate to his station in the world. He solicited presents from a number of broadcasters and lobbyists for the event. Among other things he asked one group to supply the champagne, another to bring a turkey. A Seattle television station sent his daughter a color television set.

The pattern of relationships between lobbyists and public officials is often smoothed, of course, by free meals and other perqs. What is strange about Zapple is how he has come to expect such things as his due. You can be sure the lobbyist mentioned earlier did not again forget to bring Zapple a cigar. To many of those who know him, Zapple seems to keep a mental ledger, with each token of friendship neatly catalogued in place. One former member of the White House staff says that it is his impression, "Zapple has never picked up a tab in his life."

At times he can carry things too far. It isn't enough that he be given just one cigar, I've been told. There are times when he's reached into the box, as it is being passed around the dinner table, to take four or more. Such behavior leads some lobbyists to disdain Zapple for his boorish habits. It's as if Zapple wanted to be sure that the important people he deals with cut him in on the good things, yet doesn't know quite how to respond when they do.

This sets up a tension in the relationship between Zapple and the lobbyists. *Broadcasting,* the mouthpiece of the industry, even felt called upon once to mention Zapple's outstanding ability for sponging: "He is generally conceded to be the most knowledgeable man on Capitol Hill when it comes to broadcast regulations. He has acquired a store of information by assiduous research. At almost any accessible gathering of broadcasters, especially if the wines are vintage and the cuisine dependable, Mr. Zapple is to be found collecting expertise and often disseminating it."

What strikes one about so much of this is the overwhelming pettiness of his demands. It all appears far more important for its ritual content than for the gifts themselves.

PRESENT AT THE CREATION

Zapple has been connected with the rise of television almost from the beginning. From his position he has been a part of practically every important piece of broadcasting legislation or congressional study of the last 25 years. His service on the committee predates Pastore, who became subcommittee chairman in 1955, by almost five years.

He has been a constant disappointment to those trying to push Congress in a more liberal direction: "At first I thought Pastore was just a servant of the broadcasters and that Zapple was venal, even corrupt," says one source who's tried to influence legislation in the Senate. "But I don't think so anymore. Pastore has divided impulses between a populist streak and his softness toward business interests. The frustrating thing is that time and time again Zapple has missed the opportunity to push Pastore in the direction of serving the public."

Such idealism seems incongruous when talking about Zapple, for he is clearly a man without idealistic impulses of his own. While it is certainly true that a staff assistant can be an important force for good, Zapple is in an entirely separate category. But it is undeniable that he has power, even if it is primarily only the power to promote the interests of an already rich and important group.

This may help explain Zapple's reluctance to assume the post of FCC chairman. Zapple himself knows the advantages of relative anonymity— he does not need or crave the limelight. You only need contrast the publicity Nick Johnson received when he was a relatively ineffectual FCC commissioner, with Zapple, who rarely emerges from the shadows. Johnson's power to enlist the press was important, but ethereal, quickly fading away like the smoke from a gun. Yet Zapple continues to be courted with a deference which borders on sycophancy.

Despite an occasional success by outsiders in pushing the broadcasting subgovernment in a more liberal direction, it is still true that most of the questions concerning industry policy are decided by a small and close-knit group. Against this backdrop, it is particularly disturbing when journalists from the trade press do little to overcome the closed nature of the subgovernment. A number of trade reporters are aware of the practices which have been described here, but they are never written about. Partly there is the sense that such matters aren't really news, for they simply describe the way things are. More important, though, is the manner in which reporters are frequently drawn into the net by their dependence on people like Zapple. One former reporter told me: "Zapple was a good source. When he said, 'This is what we're going to do,' it happened. He was nearly infallible. Consequently I could go in and talk to him on a not-for-attribution basis for 20 minutes and emerge with one or two good stories. I didn't have the time to chase all over town."

It is difficult to say how different television would be if these arrangements were transformed. Practically all domestic politics is organized along essentially the same line, with each congressional fiefdom supporting its own world of executive branch bureaucrats, lobbyists for the affected interests, and assorted lawyers, consultants, and trade reporters. Perhaps these institutional arrangements arise from what the public really does want, or at least will tolerate. Still, you don't have to be a Marshall McLuhan devotee to realize that television has had some fairly profound effects on our lives and that the question of control of such a medium deserves to be considered among a far wider public than it is now.

Afterword

Shortly after this article appeared in The Washington Monthly in 1975, Nick Zapple announced his early retirement from the Senate Commerce Committee's broadcasting subcommittee staff. In 1976 John Pastore retired from the Senate, and the subcommittee's present chairman is Ernest Hollings of South Carolina.

The Bureaucracy: The Cleverest Lobby of Them All

Leonard Reed

There are two kinds of lobbying that government employees do. The first, and most familiar, involves working through unions to get increased pay and benefits. It is a problem, but it is at least one that the public can recognize and, perhaps, confront. The second is less well known, more important, and potentially more dangerous. It is more difficult to deal with because it is submerged from public view. It consists of the bureaucracy obeying its most basic impulses—the deep desire of the eager bureaucrat to do much more for the public than the public need requires. It is effective because the bureaucracy is familiar with the levers of power and good at manipulating them.

POLITICAL APPOINTEES

The executive branch of the federal government has been described as two-and-one-half million people of whom one (two if you count the vice president separately) has been elected. The rest consists of the bureaucracy and the political appointees, who except for those on the White House staff, soon find themselves absorbed into it. To assume, as the textbooks tell us, that the executive branch is an arm of the President is to face away from reality.

In anticipation of power struggles with each new administration, the bureaucracy's first order of business is the taming and gradual absorption

Leonard Reed is a contributing editor of *The Washington Monthly*.

of political appointees. The process by which appointees, right up to the Secretary of the Department, are gradually integrated into the bureaucratic camp is a familiar one to any federal manager. The new chief comes in feisty, convinced that he is going to cut the bureaucrats down to size and bring them under control (although, tongue in cheek, he tells them that *they* are the experts; they listen, outwardly rapt, inwardly yawning at this formula speech). His patron is the President, with whom, he is certain, he will have an intimate relationship.

Somehow, the President turns out to be a busy man. The chief finds that his day is spent with his subordinates, the senior bureaucrats. He discovers that they are a surprisingly capable and intelligent group of people; whatever their flaws, senior bureaucrats don't get there by being dopes. These top aides know their field, they understand federal budget jargon, they know how to get things done, and they have what appear to be workable programs to suggest. New initiatives are what the chief needs if he is ever going to get the President's attention. Indeed, unless he is the rare Cabinet member who comes with his own agenda, when he does see the President his ideas will be those of his subordinates. As his relationship with the senior career servants grows more respectful, intimate, and dependent— as he begins to feel a genuine need to be liked and respected by them— the appointee's identification with their expansionist drive begins to place him in a somewhat different role vis-a-vis the President.

OPEN CONFLICT

Through such identification, for example, Patricia Roberts Harris, Secretary of the Department of Housing and Urban Development, has gradually come into a position of more or or less open conflict with the President who appointed her. Part of the conflict centers about the spending programs Harris wants. All Cabinet officers had been under presidential instruction to avoid expensive new initiatives. Harris proposed and adamantly insisted upon programs for 1979 that would cost about 40 per cent more than the White House's Office of Management and Budget had allowed for. If that irritated the President, one of *his* notions set the Secretary's teeth on edge. His desire to have the states take over an increasing share of the responsibilities for their cities runs into one of the bogeys of bureaucracy: the transfer of power to other jurisdictions.

Joseph Califano, Secretary of Health, Education, and Welfare, did not throw his hat very high into the air at Carter's proposal for a separate Department of Education. The American Legion and the Veterans of Foreign Wars, aided by the House Veterans Affairs Committee, and urged on, one can assume, by the Veterans Administration, have successfully lifted veterans' educational programs out of the proposed department.

The Washinton Post reported the unkind rumor that Califano publicly raised the prospect of taking over those programs "in order to covertly stir up veterans' opposition that could block the creation of the new department.... Califano has repeatedly denied this. However, he has brought up the idea of including the veterans' program in the new department on several occasions in the past few weeks." HEW bureaucrats opposed to the idea will not be alone as they conduct a sub rosa battle to scuttle the plan. They will be joined by bureaucrats from the Departments of Agriculture and Defense, which have big education programs they don't want lifted out, and from the Department of Labor, which has its own training programs.

Each bureaucracy has its own constituency that it helps support and upon whose support it relies in its battles—battles in which the enemy is often the administration. The example too obvious to dwell on is the Defense Department, with the huge contracts it holds out to an eager and powerful clientele. But *every* bureaucracy has alliances with special interest groups (and congressional committees, about which more later). The interest groups have motivations ranging from a simple and ravenous appetite for the buck to the relative altruism of the Sierra Club in its patronage of the Environmental Protection Agency or the work on behalf of the foreign aid bureaucracy done by the League of Women Voters and the American Association of University Women.

Just as the Labor Department maintains a cozy relationship with the AFL-CIO, HUD has a whole battery of client organizations, such as the National Housing Conference, the U.S. Conference of Mayors, the National League of Cities, and a host of associations representing homebuilders, mortgage bankers, and savings and loans as well as a shifting pattern of coalitions with a big stake in urban spending. Add to these the "think tanks" like the Brookings Institution, the Harvard-MIT Center for Joint Studies, and various university centers that receive study grants from HUD, on the basis of which they develop reports often suggesting new programs. Relationships are likely to be personal and intimate, with officials of HUD frequently being chosen from these organizations or leaving HUD to take posts in them.

A former HUD assistant secretary, now with an interest group, told me that the bureaucracy will often take the idea for a new program to its contacts in the "support" groups before turning it into a legislative proposal. "It's important to tell them what's in it for them and to get them on board while you're developing legislation," he said. "And it has to be attractive to as many of these groups as are needed for the formation of what we call a critical mass—large enough to swing the necessary bloc of votes in Congress." The President is then confronted with a powerful bloc supporting an expensive program proposal in which he may have little interest and that was generated entirely by the bureaucracy.

A LITTLE GIVE AND TAKE

The support lobbies are particularly valuable to the bureaucracies at budget time (which, considering that agencies regard budget preparation and requests for supplemental appropriations as their first priority, is virtually all year round). The budget process is supposed to work something like this: The Office of Management and Budget lets the agencies know roughly how big the whole pie is this year, what the President's priorities are, and about how much less or more than its current appropriation the agency should base its proposals on. Within the agency, then, the call goes out for program proposals from the bureaucracy, with emphasis on proposals that support presidential priorities; the bureaucracy is also encouraged, however, to propose additional programs. According to the plan, the agency brings its proposed legislative program back to OMB, a little give and take occurs, and then, like good soldiers, the agency officials accept the decision. Their lawyers draft the agreed-upon legislation, which the White House then sends to Congress.

In real life what happens is quite different. As soon as the OMB gives the agency its preliminary guidelines, those bureaucratic fiefdoms within the agency who stand to get less than they hoped for crank up the lobbying machinery. Almost before the agency officials leave the OMB office, the press is alerted to any proposed cut; newspapers like *The New York Times* and *The Washington Post* has contacts—some high, some low—within the bureaucracy of every agency, who supply them a wealth of detail on the damage the cuts will cause. (David Broder, as the President was preparing to present his 1979 budget, reported: "*Washington Post* reporters have been called in the past week by agency officials or leaders of allied interest groups to warn of possible budgecide all across the government, affecting everything from foreign aid to assorted minor programs run by the Energy and HEW Departments.")

The bureaucrats are not interested in the publicity for its own sake but for its power to mobilize the interest groups to take action aimed at influencing the President. When the HUD bureaucracy leaked Secretary Harris's conflict with the White House to the press, statements from such groups as the U.S. Conference of Mayors began to appear in newspapers and on television, and other groups obtained audiences with the President to impress upon him their support of some of Harris's proposed programs. The bureaucrats, strictly speaking, don't lobby the President—they get someone else to do it. We have come to an uncomfortable acceptance of the tremendous influence interest groups have on the legislative process. We are less cognizant that the collusion that takes place between these groups and the bureaucracy makes the latter a legislative power in its own right.

THE GAIN OR LOSS OF POWER

Reorganization is always an area of sharp conflict between a President and the various bureaucracies. What is involved for the bureaucracies is the gain or loss of power, prestige, and funds. With or without the acquiescence of its chief, a threatened bureaucracy will muster the support of its allies to protect its interests.

The bureaucracy, of course, is not a monolith. Perhaps fortunately, much of its energy is dissipated in intramural squabbles—both within the same department, like, for example, the Thirty-Year War between the FBI and the Justice Department and the Voice of America vs. the U.S. Information Agency, or between contending jurisdictions reaching out for the same prize.

Responsibility for the Carter administration's plan for civil rights reorganization was given to an OMB task force, which came up with a blueprint that centralized various antidiscrimination functions in the Equal Employment Opportunity Commission. Among these were responsibilities for administering the provisions of the Equal Pay Act and the Age Discrimination in Employment Act that are currently held by the Department of Labor. The bureaucracy of the department was not amused and, according to a congressional committee staff member, lobbied extensively with organized labor, women's groups, and senior citizens' organizations to have them take a position against the plan and launch mail campaigns to Congress and the White House. According to the same source, the following sequence of events took place (our camera isolating just one part of the action):

The OMB task force discussed its plan with the American Association of Retired People and came away convinced that the group would support the reorganization. Some Labor Department officials then talked with the AARP, which shortly thereafter drafted a letter to the White House opposing the plan. Eleanor Homes Norton, director of the EEOC, got wind of the letter. She went to talk with the AARP. The AARP decided not to send the letter and to support the reorganization.

Lauren Selden, a spokesman for the AARP and the National Retired Teachers will say only that the associations changed their position because of Mrs. Norton's strong promise of commitment of resources to the age discrimination aspect of the proposal and her promise to appoint an advisory committee from the senior citizens' groups to help administer the program. Selden denies being lobbied by the Labor Department, saying only that the Labor Department "solicited our views." It should be noted that no competent spokesman for interest groups can afford to make public his dealings with bureaucrats—especially if those bureaucrats are conducting a sub rosa compaign against an administration proposal.

THE NATURAL ALLY

Suspicion of the bureaucracy is so deep-seated in the grass roots of the country that running against the bureaucracy is one of the traditional rites of electioneering. And Congress would seem to be almost the last bastion of defense the public has against the expanding size and power of the bureaucracy.

In fact, Congress is the natural ally of the bureaucracy in its expansionism and in its subterranean war with the President. For every bureaucracy there is either a congressional subcommittee to "oversee" it or one whose legislative work meshes with it. An almost complete coincidence of interests exists between these committees and the bureaucracies they monitor. The power structure of Congress is built on the committee system and the bureaucracies constitute the raison d'etre of the subcommittees. The loss of a bureaucracy's power or influence through a cutting of its budget or a threatened reorganization translates into a similar loss for the key members of the subcommittee. Throw in, too, the fact that each subcommittee has exactly the same constituency as its counterpart bureaucracy: the urban coalitions, for example, which have a mutually supportive liaison with HUD, maintain a similar relationship with the House Subcommittee on Housing and Community Development. So while candidates talk economy, incumbents know that the votes lie in spending. As the aide of one senator who has a record of unfailing backing for the programs of "his" bureaucracy told me, "My senator gets elected for what he supports on behalf of organized groups, not for what he dismantles on the public's behalf."

It's not that the organized groups control the voters—for the most part, they don't. But they do have the money to finance an opposing candidate, and a well-heeled opponent is what an incumbent fears the most.

LONG STANDING RELATIONSHIPS

Congressmen and their committee staffs deal on a daily basis with representatives of the bureaucracy. Typically, a ranking political appointee will bring with him to the congressman's office a senior bureaucrat who has at his fingertips the facts about a proposed piece of legislation. For committee staff members, dealing directly with senior civil servants with whom they have long-standing relationships is an important part of their work. They will call on civil servants for their off-the-record views on administration proposals, for advice, and for advance warning of any conflicts between the career bureaucrats and the political leadership of the agency.

Career bureaucrats know how to protect their flanks while, nevertheless, getting their message across. "Well, the agency position is that the legislation should be drafted *this* way," the bureaucrat may say, "and the rationale is thus and so. Some people here, however, think it would be more effective with a slight switch in emphasis. . . ." Frequently, the alternate approach then suggested is one the senior bureaucrat fought for and lost in discussions with his political superiors; as often as not, however, the political leadership of the agency so thoroughly identifies with the top stratum of civil servants that the bootlegged modification of the administration's legislation represents a common position.

Each successive adminstation, while recognizing the necessity and inevitability of the bureaucracy's contacts with Congress, as well as with the interest groups, tries—with uniform lack of success—to place constraints on the bureaucracy's use of these exchanges for its own purposes.

What the administration fears is illustrated by the account Senator Charles Mathias gives of a session that Carl Vinson, when he was chairman of the House Armed Services Committee, held in his office with a high-ranking Navy officer. The officer had just testified in House hearings in support of a rather modest defense budget proposed by the administration. Vinson ushered him into his office, sat him down and said, "And, now, Admiral, take off your muzzle. . . ."

Inevitably, the most loyal administration appointee loosens his muzzle when speaking into receptive congressional ears. "The budget? Well, the President has problems holding it down all across the line, and I'm with him all the way. But, I have to admit I'm disappointed in what he's come up with for us. I had hoped. . . ."

The Harvard Brain Trust: Eating Lunch at Henry's

Michael E. Kinsley

Perhaps the most remarkable of antiwar activities involving Harvard people was an odyssey to Washington in May, 1970, by thirteen senior Harvard faculty members, most with long-established ties to the government, to lobby for the first time against the war and particularly against the invasion of Cambodia.

At their rooms in the Hay-Adams, on Lafayette Park directly across from the White House, the early arrivals spent Thursday evening, May 7, planning strategy for the following day, mainly for their meeting with "Henry" —Henry Kissinger, who used to be at Harvard himself. It was a highly intense discussion among some of the most noted intellects of the country, and they consumed two bottles of Cutty Sark Scotch in the process.

The group included Thomas Schelling (professor of economics; author of *The Strategy of Conflict,* and organizer of the group), Richard Neustadt (author of *Presidential Power*), Francis Bator (formerly Deputy Special Assistant to President Johnson for National Security Affairs), Ernest May (professor of history and former military historian for the Department of Defense), Seymour Martin Lipset (professor of government and social relations), George Kistiakowsky (professor of chemistry and chief science advisor to President Eisenhower), William Capron (associate dean of the Kennedy School of Public Affairs, former assistant director of the Bureau of the Budget), Adam Yarmolinsky (professor of law, adviser to Presidents Kennedy and Johnson), Paul Doty (biochemistry), Konrad Bloch (biochem-

Michael E. Kinsley is a contributing editor of *The Washington Monthly* and managing editor of *The New Republic.*

istry, Nobel laureate), Frank Westheimer (chemistry), Gerald Holton (physics), and Michael Walzer (government).

THE MONSTER SPEECH

According to the participants, the meeting with Kissinger turned out to be one of intense emotions painfully suppressed. "We made it clear to Henry from the beginning," Schelling said, "that we weren't here lunching with him as old friends, but were talking to him solely in his capacity to communicate to the president that we regard the invasion of Cambodia as a disastrously bad foreign policy decision, even on its own terms."

As reported by one member of the group, "Ernest May told Henry, 'You're tearing the country apart domestically.' " May said this would have long-time consequences for foreign policy, as tomorrow's foreign policy is based on today's domestic situation.

"Then Bator and Westheimer chimed in with an explanation of how difficult it was for us to have Henry read in the newspapers beforehand of our coming. Bator said it was especially painful for him since he had held part of the same portfolio Kissinger now handles. But we felt that the only way we could shock him into realizing how we felt was not to just give him marginal advice. We wanted to shock him into realizing that in the short run this latest decision was appallingly bad foreign policy.

"At this point Henry got called out to see the president. He asked to have someone explain to him when he returned what short-term mistake the Nixon policy made. We decided to let Tom do it, as he was the one who organized us and he was Henry's closest academic colleague in the group. So when Henry returned after a few minutes, Schelling gave him the Monster Speech."

Schelling's Monster Speech was one he used frequently during that day. It's a metaphorical analysis similar to those he used frequently in his undergraduate course on game theory and decision-making. The speech went something like this: "It's one of those problems where you look out the window, and you see a monster. And you turn to the guy standing next to you at the very same window, and say, 'Look, there's a monster.' He then looks out the window—and doesn't see a monster at all. How do you explain to him that there really is a monster?"

Then Schelling continued, "As we see it, there are two possibilities: Either, one, the president didn't understand when he went into Cambodia that he was invading another country; or, two, he did understand. We just don't know which one is scarier. And he seems to have done this without consultations with the Secretary of Defense or the Secretary of State, or with leaders of the Senate and House. We are deeply worried about the scale of the operation, as compared with the process of decision."

Richard Neustadt then added, "What this is going to signal to American senior military officers—and the Saigon government—is that, if you put enough pressure on Nixon by emphasizing that 'American boys are dying,' you can get the president to do very discontinuous things. And this makes his whole promise of withdrawal open to question."

"Each of us spoke to Henry at least once," a participant reported. "Michael Walzer told him that, as an old dove, he was impressed by the intensity of the concern of us old government boys. Gerry Holton talked generally about the lack of restraint in Nixon's policies.

"When we were all through, Henry asked if he could go off the record. We said no. Schelling said one reason we had brought non-ex-government types like Walzer was to keep us honest. Henry replied that the nature of his job as an adviser to the president was such that he never spoke on the record."

Kissinger did tell his former colleagues three things.

"First," Schelling reported, "he told us that he understood what we were saying, and the gravity of our concern. Second, he said that if he could go off the record he could explain the president's action to our satisfaction. And third, he said that since we wouldn't let him go off the record, all he could do was assure us that the president had not lost sight of his original objective or gone off his timetable for withdrawal.

"Bator muttered something about the interaction of means and ends and how he doubted whether with even the best of intentions Nixon and Kissinger could control the process when Johnson and Bundy couldn't. Schelling told him to be quiet and let Henry go on. But there wasn't much else to say.

"So afterwards we all got up and shook hands, with a sense of sadness. It was painful for us, but it wasn't a personal thing. It was an impersonal visit—to try to save the country. I think Henry fully understood the gravity of what we were talking about."

"NOBODY CAN CALL US RADICALS"

Back in their headquarters at the Hay-Adams, the professors discussed their confrontation lunch with Kissinger. Holten said, "It was not exactly what I would call a love feast. He said that he was moved by our visit, that he felt that it's all a tragic situation. But he refused to speak on the record, and we refused to go off, so we had an hour and a half of presenting views."

Bloch said, "Kissinger told us 'When you come back a year from now, you will find your concerns were unwarranted.' But he doesn't understand that the end-justifies-the-means philosophy is exactly the problem and what is antagonizing the large part of the population. Kissinger just did not realize that we'd crossed the threshold." Schelling said, "We had a very painful hour and a half with Henry, persuading him we were all horrified not just about the Cambodia decision, but what it implied about the way the president makes up his mind. It was a small gain to be had at enormous political risk. He refused to reply on the record, therefore he had our sentiments heaped upon him, sat in pained silence, and just listened." Lipset said, "I think we have a very unhappy colleague-on-leave." Schelling added, "I hope so." Then, the professors swirled out of the room to catch cabs for the Pentagon and a meeting with Undersecretary of Defense David Packard. Schelling turned back into the room and perspired, "You know, this is hard work."

The professors returned to the Hay-Adams from their meeting with Packard—barely an hour after they'd left—in a highly agitated state. William Capron complained, "He gave us the straightforward party line—he sounded just like John Foster Dulles. It was nothing like Henry in terms of emotional content. We gave it to him very hard and he said to please wait six weeks and we'd see that everything will turn out all right. He said he understood our concern, but asked for our *forebearance!* In six weeks, he said, we'll be out and it will be a great victory! We were just talking past each other."

Neustadt agreed: "Mr. Packard heard us out, then responded in a perfectly canned way that we should be patient. His explanation was irrelevant to our concern. It was a matter of our reporting our feelings to him and hearing no attempt to exchange. Perhaps we underestimated the credibility gap. Ghastly. The president's credibility is hopeless. And nobody can call us radicals, either. The purpose of giving our views was precisely that. We're not voicing our concern because of Harvard or the domestic impact. We were offering our professional judgment as former advisers to presidents that it was a horrendous act of foreign policy.

"We said to Henry, and we said to Mr. Packard, that the military-civilian imbalance today is the greatest threat to the presidency since MacArthur's challenge to Truman. I myself don't see anything that can restore the military's credibility."

Bator said, "From Packard we got a canned speech—a casual pat speech about his Administration and Vietnamization and wiping out a few bases. He said it would all please us in just about six weeks. He seemed very aware of our campus origins. We reacted quite strongly."

Konrad Bloch said, "It was the straightforward drivel. He coldly misinterpreted what we had to say. It was hard to know how to explain our position, although Schelling put on a great performance with his Monster Speech when Packard was finally through. Later Packard started talking about Stanford—he said it is infiltrated by a hard core that will have to be eliminated. He said tension in this country will have to come to a head some day, and it might as well be now."

"THAT WAS AVERELL"

A bellhop brought Pepsi and Michelob for the overheated professors. The phone rang. Bator answered it.

"Hello, Averell!" He smiled. "Well, hello, Governor! Yes, Governor, I'm here. This is Francis." As Bator talked to Harriman, Yarmolinsky dashed to the extension phone in the bathroom to listen. "Yes, Governor, well, Scotty said . . ." When Bator finished, Yarmolinsky started talking on the bathroom extension. Neustadt quickly established possession of the bedroom phone. Alarmed to discover the conversation wasn't over, Bator scurried to the bathroom to listen in when Yarmolinsky was finished. Finally they all said good-by and hung up. "That was Averell," Bator explained.

After a long but uninspiring meeting with then Undersecretary of State Elliott Richardson, the professors reassembled in the dining room of the Hay-Adams. Over double martinis and Caesar salads, they evaluated the day.

Bator summarized, "In the Executive branch we've shot the bolt today. From now on we have to work with Congress. If these guys get us all out of Vietnam in ninety days, we'll have the biggest crow dinner in our lives —and we'll vote for Richard Nixon in 1972." There was nervous laughter around the table; for if the professors disliked anything more than cutting themselves off from their councils of government, it was the prospect of looking foolish—of the war ending routinely with their making unbecomingly alarmist statements on the outside.

Bator flew out the door with a cheery "Good-by, gentlemen." Others followed, including Schelling, who instructed Neustadt to take care of the bill, saying they would straighten out the finances back at Cambridge.

Neustadt and Lipset relaxed briefly over strawberries and cream. "You know," Neustadt said, "this is the first time in years that I've come to Washington and stayed at the Hay-Adams and had to pay for it out of my own pocket. Many of us will now have to decide whether we will resign from all our consulting positions with the government. It's sort of silly. I have some contracts on which I haven't been consulted for years. But it's hard after a thing like today to keep operating in the Executive branch. People whose advice was being asked on a number of issues have now cut themselves off by announcing that they're going to the Hill to lobby. But there's so much disaffection within government that us academics resigning will be no big deal. That's why we put so much emphasis today on those of us who were ex-officials of government. We were trying to distinguish ourselves—today at least—from those who are merely professors."

"Packard today dismissed us as 'professors' and 'liberals'—same thing," Lipset shrugged.

The professors filtered back to Harvard over the weekend having reluctantly and, they hoped temporarily, exiled themselves from power. They would have much preferred to stay in or near the government, hanging on like everyone else.

part 6
THE
BUREAUCRACY

In this book, bureaucracy has two meanings. In the narrow sense, we're talking about the civil service, that vast system that staffs the executive branch and makes up most of the population of the federal government. More broadly, to understand practically anything about American society today it's necessary to understand the dynamics and incentives that exist in the large institutions that dominate our lives. In government and out, bureaucratic behavior strongly influences the way the country works.

Lately the country has woken up to this fact, at least as it applies to government. Nobody likes the bureaucrats in Washington any more. Everybody has a favorite story of governmental delays and incompetence, of paperwork and unresponsiveness. And as it is in government (though this isn't fully realized yet), so it is in schools and hospitals and corporations. In none of these settings do people do bad jobs out of spite. They just lack any sense of a purpose as to what they are doing or of responsibility to the people they serve. They care more about what life inside the organization is like than about what the organization produces. The articles in this section concentrate on the government bureaucracy, but the phenomena they describe exist everywhere.

The federal civil service was set up nearly a century ago by reformers who hoped to replace the political hacks who then populated the government with professionals of proven competence. In hindsight, it's clear that those reforms were a classic case of overdoing it; as a result of them, the civil service today is so apolitical, so protected, and so devoid of any standards of performance that it has become a refuge for cautious people who want a secure lifetime income. The first article in this section is a description of how one of them—a high-ranking one—spends his time, as told by his own press agent.

Applicants flood the civil service and many tests precede hiring, though it helps a lot to be a veteran or to have friends already on board. But once you're in, you're in for good, as Leonard Reed's article in this section shows. Raises and promotions are fairly easy to come by, and the pay is generous. Federal employees supposedly earn wages comparable to those paid in private industry, but in fact the government workers are often paid more than their brethren in business. The reason is that wages are a function of job description, and the job descriptions of many federal employees have been wildly inflated in order to justify promotions. So a clerk in the government might, from his job description, sound like a manager, and will be paid a comparable salary.

Now that government bureaucrats are unpopular, attempts to unseat them (like Proposition 12 in California) have begun. Whether these attempts will succeed remains to be seen; the bureaucrats are well entrenched. They're spread out all over the country—since World War II the size of the federal civil service has remained relatively constant while the states' employee rolls have grown enormously. Also, bureaucrats have weapons to fight off budget cuts, one of the most potent of which Charles Peters describes in "The Firemen First Principle": when threatened, bureaucrats usually say that any cut in their budgets will mean cuts in essential services.

Besides wasting everyone's money, bureaucracies have many other bad effects. The most important of them is the tendency to lose sight of what's really important in favor of petty in-house concerns. Sometimes this can have deadly results, as in James Fallows' "Murder by the Book," the story of how State Department employees, in their eagerness to keep up on one another's careers, published information that essentially told foreign terrorists the names and addresses of CIA agents.

A Day in the Life
of a Government Executive

"A Day in the life of a Government Executive" was written for OASIS, a publication of the Social Security Administration. Its ironies may be unconscious, but they are devastating nonetheless—and provide the truest picture of life in the upper levels of bureaucracy we have ever encountered.

As Commissioner of Social Security, James Bruce Cardwell administers a program that touches the life of virtually every American and handles one out of every $4 spent in the government.

What follows is a typical day.

Rockville, Maryland

The Commissioner's day begins at 5:45 a.m., more than an hour before his chauffeur will arrive to take him into the District. In suburban Maryland there is near-quiet at this time of day. The Commissioner takes advantage of the silence to enjoy a leisurely cup of coffee with his wife and to scan the morning papers.

At 6:50 the Commissioner's chauffeur, Willie Falcon, arrives in a small government sedan. Commissioner Cardwell climbs into the car with a pair of worn leather briefcases at his side. Each briefcase is stuffed with the inevitable governmental memoranda which have been a part of his life for the last 30 years.

As the sedan edges onto Interstate 70 and heads toward the Washington Beltway, Commissioner Cardwell's workday has already begun. He uses the half- to three-quarter-hour travel time for reading Social Security Administration staff reports and memoranda submitted the previous day.

7:30 a.m.

The Commissioner arrives at HEW, North. He will spend the morning here before going on to the Woodlawn Social Security complex near Baltimore. The Washington office maintains liaison with other HEW components and congressional committees. While Woodlawn is only 30-some miles distant, it is nevertheless too far from the seat of government.

He takes the elevator to his fourth floor space and greets Mary Grabarek, the office secretary.

The Commissioner's private office at HEW is attractive but utilitarian —a massive walnut desk, beige carpet, a few pieces of darkwood furniture with vinyl upholstery. Opening off the Commissioner's office is a small library. Handsomely bound government volumes line bookshelves along the wall, and a conference table sits in the center of the room.

In his office, Commissioner Cardwell begins work by scanning press reports on items of interest to Social Security. He then turns his attention to the more time-consuming task of reading and signing correspondence prepared by his staff.

8:00 a.m.

Deputy Commissioner Arthur Hess arrives. The previous day was the Deputy Commissioner's birthday and the Commissioner asks about his evening dinner party in Annapolis. They then turn their attention to an item in the morning press reports about a Dartmouth University student who has had his social security benefits terminated on a legal technicality. It is decided that the Office of the General Counsel should look into the case. Another item discussed is a call the Commissioner made to the Office of Management and Budget to check on the status of SSA's request to build two new headquarters buildings—one at the present complex in Woodlawn and the other in downtown Baltimore.

8:15 a.m.

Commissioner Cardwell briefly outlined for *OASIS* an upcoming presentation in the Secretary's Chart Room. "Usually I'll meet with the Secretary . . . well, every morning that he's in town. His staff and the agency heads are always present at those sessions. Wednesdays are a little different, however. These meetings are opened up—more staffers—and there is usually a presentation of some sort. For instance, the HEW Comptroller recently gave a presentation on cash flow analysis. Today, the Secretary has requested that we give a general presentation on the status of the social security program."

8:20 a.m.

Commissioner Cardwell and Deputy Commissioner Hess leave the Commissioner's office for the Secretary's Chart Room. They meet SSA's Deputy Chief Actuary, Francisco Bayo, on the way. Bayo has just arrived at HEW, North, and will be available for a long-range actuarial projections, if needed, during the morning's presentation.

8:30 a.m.

Secretary Caspar Weinberger, Under Secretary Frank Carlucci, and 20 to 25 other top Department executives enter the Chart Room and take designated seats around the room's long oval table. Five minutes elapse while coffee is served from an adjoining anteroom and materials related to the SSA presentation are sent around the table.

Secretary Weinberger than opens the meeting and immediately gives the floor to Commissioner Cardwell. The Commissioner outlines the morning's program, saying that the presentation would be in three parts: 1) a review of basic social security program data; 2) a report on current problems confronting Social Security; and 3) a period for questions and answers.

Deputy Commissioner Hess gives a comprehensive, 20-minute chart presentation of basic social security data—extent of coverage, number of people receiving benefits, benefit amounts related to average monthly earnings, etc.

Commissioner Cardwell then outlines the problem areas. He says throughout its history there has been tugging and pulling about the basic purpose of social security. Originally designed as a means of replacing part of family income lost due to age or death, social security has grown to include other programs, other benefits. The growth has been accompanied by a public uncertainty about what social security now promises —and about its ability to deliver on those promises.

The Commissioner cited a series of articles on social security which were printed in *Chicago Today* and distributed nationwide via *The New York Times* News Service. The articles are very critical; they charge that social security is a rip-off and assert that retirement plans available through private companies would yield bigger dividends for smaller investments.

"The press tends to focus on sensational aspects of the program," the Commissioner says. "And while there are legitimate issues raised in these articles there are also serious misstatements."

The Commissioner then reviews what he considers legitimate issues regarding social security. Is social security adequate? Are social security contributions regressive? Does social security treat men and women, rich and poor, minority and majority, equally? Will low population growth and an increasing number of retirees mean an unfair financial burden for future workers? Is there a necessity for the social security retirement test?

The Commissioner says these questions, together with proposals for general fund financing and negative income tax, are being studied by the Social Security Board of Trustees and the Advisory Council on Social Security.

"The Advisory Council began work on May 3 and will finish by the end of the year. The Council seems especially capable of dealing with these issues," the Commissioner says, "and we can expect some proposals from them deserving of consideration."

During the question-and-answer period, the Secretary focuses on what is being done—on what can be done—about the bad publicity.

Commissioner Cardwell replies that a response to the *Chicago Today* series has been written by Professor Richard E. Johnson of the University of Georgia. Dr. Johnson is a nationally recognized authority on insurance and is a former executive of two leading private insurance firms. SSA's Office of Public Affairs is negotiating with the *New York Times* News Service, the Commissioner says, to distribute the Johnson article. The Commissioner also notes that former HEW Secretary Wilbur Cohen is writing a rebuttal which will be available later in the month.

9:40 a.m.

Meeting adjourned, Commissioner Cardwell speaks privately with the Secretary for a few minutes before leaving the Chart Room.

9:45 a.m.

Commissioner Cardwell and Deputy Commissioner Hess meet briefly in the hallway outside the Chart Room with Lew Helm, Assistant Secretary for Public Affairs. Helm tells the Commissioner that his office would be available to lend assistance to SSA in rebutting the *Chicago Today* series of articles criticizing the Social Security program.

9:50 a.m.

Stanley Thomas, Assistant Secretary for Human Development, catches the Commissioner just as he is preparing to leave the building and requests a brief meeting. Commissioner Cardwell, Deputy Commissioner Hess, and Thomas duck into a small anteroom nearby. Thomas says he met the day before with the National Council on Children and Youth and that this organization would like SSA to undertake a program to locate an estimated 200,000 to 400,000 disabled children who are eligible for, but not enrolled in, the SSI program.

"You're saying a ... well, a sort of SSI alert for children. Right?" the Commissioner asks Thomas.

"Yeah, it would be something like that."

Commissioner Cardwell asks how they want to proceed. Thomas replies that, tentatively, a feasibility study for a pilot program would be conducted first. Maybe five states. The Commissioner says he will have his people look into it and get back to Thomas.

"They want a rush on this," Thomas says.

"So what else is new?"

10:05 a.m.

Commissioner Cardwell and Deputy Commissioner Hess leave HEW, North, for SSA headquarters in suburban Baltimore. During the hour-long journey, the discussion covers the morning's session with the Secretary, the remainder of the day's agenda, and an upcoming meeting with Mayor Donald Schaefer of Baltimore on the new downtown building.

11:20 a.m.

Arrival at SSA headquarters.

The Commissioner's Woodlawn office on the ninth floor of the Altmeyer Building is a near replica of the one he has just left in Washington but has a few more personal touches.

11:30 a.m.

A closed luncheon meeting with several members of the executive staff is held and runs until 12:50.

Doris Conley, the Commissioner's secretary at Woodlawn, told *OASIS* that working luncheons are more often the rule than the exception. "The travel time between Washington and Baltimore breaks up the rhythm of the work day," Doris explained. "With the Commissioner's tight schedule, that hour lost in travel is very important. We often find it necessary to schedule meetings through the lunch hour."

1:00 p.m.

This is the Commissioner's regular Wednesday meeting with all bureau directors and assistant commissioners.

Commissioner Cardwell opens the meeting by briefly reporting items of interest discussed in his meetings with Secretary Weinberger and other HEW officials during the past week.

One item the Commissioner talks about is a growing consensus among HEW staffers to lobby for restricting the use of the social security number as a general identification number. Their thinking, the Commissioner reports, is that such restriction would help protect public privacy and prevent a monolithic computer filing of citizens' records and activities.

"I think the privacy issue is one of legitimate concern," the Commissioner says, "but I'm not sure we want to support this particular move. I think the emphasis is wrong. It should be on the proliferation of the data itself—on the actual need for this or that institution to have information and not on their means of . . . well, filing or classifying it. They can always adopt their own numbering systems.

"What I'm saying is this. By concentrating on restricting the use of a social security number as an identification number, we sidestep more basic issues of individual privacy. [Pause] Am I right on this?"

After a brief discussion, the bureau and office heads are asked to prepare memos on their positions.

The Commissioner also reports Secretary Weinberger's concern about the recent "bad press" given social security and outlines the steps taken to rebut printed misstatements.

Another item reported is an agreement reached with the Treasury Department to issue SSI replacement checks without waiting to see if the original check was negotiated.

"A small victory—but a victory," the Commissioner says.

He then turns the discussion to the new Federal Labor Standards Act and its effect on SSA operations. The new Act *requires* that clerical and many technical employees be paid for any overtime work rather than be given the option of compensatory time off. There is a general consensus that the Act could detrimentally affect SSA operations.

A quick around-the-table check with each bureau and office follows. Are there any problems? Is there anything to report? Any comments?

Input is sparse this week. Within 10 minutes, everyone present has either spoken or declined to speak and the last half hour is turned over to an Office of Research and Statistics committee studying proposed changes in the disability program.

2:45 p.m.

Bureau of District Office Operations Director Robert Bynum has asked for a brief meeting with the Commissioner. The schedule does not indicate what will be discussed.

Commissioner Cardwell and Bynum seat themselves at a small office sidetable over coffee. After a few comments on the weather, the Commissioner says he is planning a meeting sometime later with bureau directors and assistant commissioners to frankly discuss problems and accomplishments of the past year. The meeting, like an earlier one in May, would be held informally, outside SSA, and probably last two days.

"I think that's a good idea," Bynum says. "It's . . . it's a good way to open communications channels among our offices."

"Yes, we can look at what we've done thus far, look at any problems, look at any mistakes we've made," the Commissioner said. "The kind of organizations which worry me the most are those that close ranks and are not ready to admit mistakes."

Bynum and the Commissioner then turn to a discussion of administrative entanglements plaguing the SSI leads program and to the rationale for a zero-base analysis of BDOO operations.

The latter topic is of special concern. It involves a far-reaching analysis of the present work force and operating systems within BDOO. Such an analysis begins at a "zero-base" with no assumptions and proceeds to evaluate what resources and operations are necessary to achieve organizational goals. Bynum expresses concern that the analysis will interfere with processing of field office workloads. The Commissioner says the task force for the analysis will be as unobtrusive as possible and that other bureaus are also slated to undergo the same thing.

They then discuss an invitation from the National Council of Social Security Management Associations to speak at their convention in San Francisco this October. Bynum says he will accept the invitation to speak and Commissioner Cardwell says he can make no commitment at this time but will note it on his calendar as a possibility.

3:30 p.m.

A meeting with Texas business executive Mitchell Hart has been scheduled and *OASIS* given permission to sit in. However, Hart requests a private session with Commissioner Cardwell to talk about his data processing firm's problems in obtaining subcontracts from carriers which process Medicare claims.

4:30 p.m.

Commissioner Cardwell is slated to meet with BHI Director Thomas Tierney and Tierney's committee on National Health Insurance. However, the meeting with Hart runs longer than expected. At 5 o'clock, with the Hart meeting still in session, Commissioner Cardwell asks Deputy Commissioner Hess to chair the National Health Insurance meeting.

"It isn't uncommon for the Deputy Commissioner to take over for me when there are schedule conflicts," Commissioner Cardwell says. "He is an exceptional administrator . . . a fine person. I believe Art Hess reflects the kind of leadership we want to develop here."

Hess apologizes to the committee for the delay, says he realizes the time is inadequate but that another meeting can be arranged later. He then asks for a report on committee problem areas and asks if any assistance from the Commissioner's office is needed.

Deputy Commissioner Hess has the same directness, the same decisiveness in these sessions as the Commissioner. Yet there is a difference in their manner, which may be traced to their professional backgrounds. Hess approaches a problem with the probing exactness of a lawyer (which he is), and the Commissioner brings to a problem the analytical detachment of an ex-budget officer (which he is).

5:10 p.m.

The Commissioner's meeting with Mitchell Hart ends; since Deputy Commissioner Hess has taken the meeting with the NHI committee, the Commissioner decides to squeeze another meeting into the day's calendar.

On any given day, there are more people waiting to see the Commissioner than can be scheduled. Many appointments must be postponed or fitted into breaks in the schedule. Doris Conley earlier notified an inter-bureau committee studying SSI provisions for drug addicts and alcoholics that they would be "on hold" that afternoon. She now calls them in.

During the few minutes it takes the committee members to make their way through the maze of corridors and up the elevator to the ninth floor of the Altmeyer Building, Commissioner Cardwell calls his wife. He assures her that he will be on time for his son's birthday celebration at seven.

The major thrust of the discussion with the new committee is toward resolution of a misunderstanding between SSA and New York City officials. NYC officials erroneously believed that SSI would pick up drug addicts and alcoholics disabled by their addiction alone.

Deputy Commissioner Art Hess spoke with *OASIS* earlier about the demands made upon the Commissioner by the schedule he keeps. "As you can see, one meeting often runs into another. And the day's itinerary is subject to change at a moment's notice. Handling this sort of workload calls for a quick transition of thought and a refocusing of attention upon a completely different—but equally complex—set of data. It's a helluva job."

6:10 p.m.

Meeting ends; Commissioner Cardwell asks that Doris have Willie bring the car around to begin the 45-mile drive home.

Because today is his son's birthday, he is able to gracefully bow out of a Washington engagement he would otherwise be expected to attend. The missed engagement is a dinner at the Washington Sheraton-Carlton Hotel where Wilbur Cohen, former HEW Secretary and an old friend of the Commissioner's, will be the evening speaker.

"I do regret not attending the dinner this evening. But not that much, I guess. One of the toughest parts of this job is separating family obligations from work obligations. I don't like to take the work home ... to have it intrude on all facets of my life. I like a few hours of leisure away from it all."

At home, the Commissioner usually sequesters himself in his den with a new best-seller or joins Mary Louise for a few hands of bridge with neighborhood friends. During the fall and winter months, he follows the fate of the Capital city's football team, the Washington Redskins.

Much of his free time is spent with his family. Two of his four sons—David Bryan, 18, and John Richard, 10—live at home and the two elder sons, James, Jr., 26, and Mark Edward, 24, are married and live in other areas. Vacations for the Commissioner and his family are rare and therefore highly valued. Recently the Cardwell family managed to break away for a four-day vacation.

Afterword

James Cardwell has retired from the Social Security Administration and is now vice president for financing and administration of the Corporation for Public Broadcasting.

Firing a Federal Employee: The Impossible Dream

Leonard Reed

Among the more curious notions in contemporary America is that the way to dispose of an irksome charge is to label it a myth. Myth is the intellectual's substitute for "abracadabra," a mantra for driving out intrusive thoughts. So it is not surprising that at the United States Civil Service Commission the question of why it is so difficult to fire an incompetent government employee is greeted with an indulgent smile and the reply, "That's one of those myths."

Smile or not, the difficulty of dismissal for incompetence is an uneasy subject at the Commission. Officials would rather talk about what civil servants *can* be fired for. They call your attention to the Internal Revenue Service where, they say, people found guilty of wrongdoing are quickly dismissed. (Actually, they aren't dismissed. Faced with the alternative of jail, they resign. In 1976, of 71,000 tenured employees at the IRS, only six were dismissed for inefficiency.) If pressed on the problem of firing incompetents, the Commission's officials fall back on another formula: "Any unproductive employee can be fired if his supervisor has balls."

"That's where the problem is," Raymond Jacobson, executive director of the Commission, insists. "It's not the system."

But the statistics either belie Jacobson's contention or prove that federal managers are the world's largest collection of eunuchs. In 1976, out of two-and-one-half million federal employees, 21,710 were discharged, according to the Commission's method of bookkeeping (which includes in

Leonard Reed is a writer who after graduate studies in public administration worked in the civil and foreign services for 24 years.

the total some strange categories, such as voluntary early retirements). Even at face value that amounts to an incredibly low discharge rate, slightly more than three fourths of one per cent. (In the Washington headquarters of the Civil Service Commission, home of the Balls Theory and 3,300 employees, the discharge rate was less than half the federal average.) But closer examination of the books reveals that, if limited to tenured civil servants who were actually fired for innefficiency or "cause," the number is less than 3,500, for a discharge rate of one seventh of one per cent—and, of those, a substantial number were reinstated in their jobs after appeal to the Commission. At that rate, a small business employing ten people would fire one person for inefficiency every 70 years.

The figures are so striking—it is so difficult to believe any work force could be so spectacularly efficient as to justify such a low dismissal rate— that one is led to suspect that what makes federal managers impotent is, in fact, the system itself.

The Civil Service Commission and the system over which it presides had their origins in the Pendleton Act of 1883. The system was conceived as a way of giving some stability to a career service and of freeing the President from the incessant pressure of office seekers by making competitive examinations the basis for hiring. The Act does not mention firing, and farthest from the minds of its sponsors was any idea of making it difficult to fire civil servants for poor performance. The only firings it meant to stop were mass *political* ones aimed at providing more jobs for loyalists.

Limitations on firing civil servants were first established in the Lloyd-LaFollette Act of 1912, and the Civil Service Commission has since then prescribed a maze of regulations regarding those limitations. The Commission has sole responsibility for amending firing procedures, and, in the words of a Commission attorney, "the admendments have almost invariably resulted in greater employee protection."

The movement away from the flexibility that any organization needs if it is to operate efficiently took on added impetus when the courts weighed in. Until the late 1950s the courts rejected attempts by dismissed civil servants to get judicial redress. Then a significant change took place: the Supreme Court held that under the Lloyd-LaFollette Act a federal employee's job was, in effect, property, and that he therfore could not be deprived of it without "due process of law." This interpretation has given the federal worker a special privilege granted to few other people in our society.

WONDERLAND

In one part of the Civil Service Commission's literature appears the sentence: "The Commission also established a Division of Efficiency to set up a system of uniform efficiency ratings for the departmental service, for use as a basis of promotions, demotions, and dismissals."

So much for Wonderland. In real life, efficiency ratings perform no such function, and as instruments in the firing process they are worse than worthless. Customarily the ratings of an incompetent worker consist of platitudes designed to make it easier for his supervisor to live with a situation he can't cure. Any criticism is veiled—instead of saying that Bledsoe has an infinite capacity for bollixing up schedules, one says, "As Mr. Bledsoe acquires managerial skills, his value to the agency will increase accordingly."

"Top management tells us to get tough in our efficiency ratings," one executive remarked. "But if you put in a critical sentence and the employee threatens a grievance action, they 'suggest' that you delete or tone down the offending sentence."

So year after year the unproductive employee accumulates ratings that make him out to be a Renaissance Man. When, indeed, matters reach the point of crying out for an employee's dismissal, the supervisor who contemplates the action is in a vulnerable position: the record shows a succession of satisfactory evaluations by previous supervisors, and he seems to be the only one who couldn't get any decent work out of the man or woman.

A LONG, LONG PROCESS

For other reasons having to do with the instinct for self-preservation, the federal manager is strongly motivated not to fire the incompetent. He knows, for one thing, that it will be a long, long process once he embarks upon it. S. John Byington, former chairman of the Consumer Product Safety Commission, once wrote to Senator Charles Percy:

"A manager in the executive branch of the federal government who finds it necessary to terminate an unproductive or non-contributing employee—or even an obstructing employee—must be prepared to spend 25 to 50 per cent of his time for a period that literally may run from six to 18 months."

One such manager related his frustration in trying to get rid of an incompetent who had been the despair of several supervisors before him: "When I came to the conclusion that he'd have to go, I went to the Agency Executive Officer, a man who was well aware of the problems this employee had been causing for years.

" 'Keep a book on him,' he told me. 'Keep a diary of when he comes in, when he leaves, how many times he is out of the office, how many times he goes to the john and for how long. Give him assignments and keep track of how many he flubs. Make sure you don't softpedal his failings when you write his performance ratings.' O.K., I kept a book. I felt like a fink. After several months of this I showed the Exec what I had.

" 'You can do better than that,' he said. 'I want an ironclad case.'

"This kind of thing went on for a while," said the executive, "and then I began to realize something: *I* was becoming the problem. This fellow had a lawyer. He was a member of the union. He had complained to his congressman that he wasn't being given fair consideration for *promotion*! And the agency just didn't want to get into a tangle. It was easier for them to adopt the attitude that I wasn't compiling a convincing case, that I was a lousy manager."

. The executive shrugged. "There are lots of people around here who are misfits or incompetents," he said. "You get used to them and you learn to put up with it, like you learn to live with a toothache or a sore toe."

The federal manager who refuses to put up with it soon finds that his own reputation is beginning to suffer. He is creating friction, and at the higher levels of government, harmony is valued well above function. In writing *his* performance rating, *his* boss may well remark upon the unfortunate "personality conflict" with Bledsoe. Where the incompetent employee can "grieve" (personnel shorthand for filing a grievance claim) that he is being discriminated against—and it is an unimaginative clod who can't find *some* ground for so charging—the executive literally finds himself on trial; even if he is exonerated the charge becomes part of his own file.

Further weakening any determination to fire Bledsoe is the inflated condition of government agencies. Over the years most agencies have attained a degree of featherbedding that means underwork or makework for substantial numbers of employees. But since anyone who suggests that his section or division is overstaffed is considered treasonable, tolerance for non-productive work becomes the ambient culture. In this laissez-faire atmosphere, Bledsoe's supervisor doesn't aspire to be the lone tilter against windmills. It makes more sense to work around Bledsoe than to fire him.

And, if patience is finally exhausted, Bledsoe can probably be transferred to another part of the agency. In a large agency there are many such "floaters"—people who live a nomadic existence, foisted on each successive supervisor when it is recognized that the previous one has suffered enough.

THE DEAN OF THE DEFENDERS

"Why do you want to fire anyone?" Donald Dalton asked, parrying my query about whether it has become virtually impossible to fire a federal employee.

Donald Dalton is the dean of a group of Washington lawyers who specialize in defending civil servants whose jobs are threatened. Chairman of the Civil Service Law Committee of the Bar Association of the District of

The Myth of the Probationary Year

Defenders of the system of protection that surrounds civil servants point to employees' initial probationary period of one year, during which time they have no tenure. That is the time, the argument goes, to get rid of the incompetent or the goof-off. That's when it is simple.

As the summer of 1977 began, an observer in a federal courtroom in Washington would have received a different impression.

The plaintiff, a contract specialist, whom we can call Parouk, had been fired by his agency in June 1974, near the end of his probationary period. His dismissal notice included three charges of inefficiency, supported by 40 specifications. Parouk appealed the dismissal to the Civil Service Commission, claiming he had been discriminated against because of his "country of origin." Although it found no proof of discrimination, the Commission ruled that the agency had not offered sufficient proof of non-discrimination and ordered Parouk restored to his job. Some time later, still within the probationary period, the agency fired Parouk again. This time the Commission sustained the dismissal.

Then Parouk sued the U.S. government for restoration of his job and back pay. Represented in the court by two lawyers provided at no cost to him by a federal employees' union, Parouk charged that the Civil Service Commission had not fully recognized "the nature of the interest involved," that is, the legally guaranteed right of a federal employee to continued employment. He also charged that the second firing constituted a reprisal against him for having charged discrimination in the first firing. In the course of the presentation to the judge, it was mentioned that a U.S. senator had intervened with the Civil Service Commission on Parouk's behalf.

After an hour or so, the judge, trying to delineate the legal issues involved in the mass of charges and counter-charges, asked the lawyers for both sides to come back in two months with additional arguments on a specific point of law.

Almost three years had gone by since the original action and the end was not yet in sight.

As the various participants filed out of the courtroom, I spotted one of the two agency lawyers heading toward the elevators. He was pushing a supermarket-type shopping cart filled to the top with documents.

"Are all those about this one case?" I asked him.

The lawyer nodded. "Yes, that's the administrative record."

Columbia, Dalton says he has taken "hundreds and hundreds of such cases."

He and the other lawyers who handle these cases are part of the system of job protection for federal employees, and, not surprisingly, Dalton sees the federal government as the oppressor of those employees who take their cases to him. Because under the law as now constituted his client always has a case, in Dalton's eyes the employee is always a victim of injustice—whether or not he is competent at his job.

"Government isn't like business," Dalton said. "People who work for the government have certain property rights in their job. There are laws you have to follow before you can fire somebody. The government wrote those laws, I didn't. The fellow who works for government has a right to see that they follow their own laws, and he comes to me for help to see that they do."

Dalton is undoubtedly right. If in the conflict between a federal employee's right to absolute job security and the public's need for a manageable bureaucracy, the Civil Service Commission, the Congress, and the courts continue to favor the former, the substandard federal employee can hardly be blamed for hanging in there.

HOW STURDY A BULWARK

Except for an office on the fifth floor occupied by its architect, a modern, seven-story building on Washington's Massachusetts Avenue is occupied exclusively by the national officers of the American Federation of Government Employees, who, from here, preside over the union's 1,500 locals.

As unions go, the AFGE, lacking for all practical purpose the ultimate weapon of the stike, is something of a marshmallow. Its bargaining power for higher wages is limited to lobbying Congress. This limitation hampers the union's ability to attract members from the federal work force. That it has succeeded so well (it has about 300,000 members) results from its having become another bulwark of the government worker's job security. Should a worker fail to receive a promotion he alone feels he is entitled to, the union takes up the cudgel for him. And if a worker's job is threatened, the union becomes a tiger, providing legal counsel. In 50 per cent of the cases of dismissals that are appealed to the Civil Service Commission's Federal Employees Appeals Authority, the employee is represented by a labor union.

The AFGE is fortunate in having an unusually capable general counsel, in the person of Leo Pellerzi, a man who knows the working and nonworking of government from inside and out. His inside experience came as general counsel for the U.S. Civil Service Commission from 1965 to 1968 and as the Department of Justice's Assistant Attorney General for

The Strange Case of Norval Perkins

Because of the quagmire a federal executive sinks into when he attempts to fire an incompetent, impatient souls sometimes try shortcuts—but these attempts to cut through the prescribed procedures invariably end in disaster. Of the "adverse actions" that employees successfully appeal, the Federal Employees Appeals Authority reverses two thirds on the basis of procedural errors.

On March 8, 1976, for example, *The Washington Star* said that the executive director of the District of Columbia's Board of Elections and Ethics had reportedly (the report proved premature) been removed from his job "in a general restructuring of function. . . . In the last few elections, the Board has come under criticism for its handling of various contests. . . ."

The executive director was a man named Norval Perkins, and the story was, for a Washington newspaper, an uncommon deviation into understatement. Norval Perkins presided over a series of election capers compared with which a Laurel and Hardy shin-kicking episode is an exercise in human dignity. The kind of election legerdemain that big-city machine bosses strenuously contrive happened effortlessly and mindlessly in Washington. In the 1974 primaries it took the Board's staff 12 days to count the votes. On another occasion, filled ballot boxes were temporarily lost (it turned out that they had fallen off a truck). Computers were so thoroughly mismanaged that ballots had to be counted by hand, and at one point a well-known computer manufacturer contemplated suit against the city for what was happening to its reputation.

Because of these and other irregularities, the Board, at the end of July, voted to fire Perkins. But, as a District of Columbia employee, Perkins was covered by the Civil Service Commission's provisions for federal employees. So, since another election was coming up in November, the Board changed its mind about undertaking the interminable process of firing Perkins "for cause" and decided on a shortcut: it reorganized the Board's staff and abolished the job of executive director.

Perkins took his case to the Federal Employees Appeals Authority, which ruled that he had been improperly organized out of a job. The Authority noted that the Board had chosen this route to avoid *proving* Perkins' incompetence. After a few back-and-forths between the Board and the Civil Service Commission, *The Washington Post* noted on March 22, "Perkins will report for duty Thursday and start getting his former pay (about $35,000 a year). But the Board maintains that his former position no longer exists, so what he'll do remains uncertain."

Since then a compromise has been struck under which Perkins withdrew the suit he had instituted against the city claiming $125,000 in damages and was in return appointed executive director of the newly formed D.C. Citizens' Gambling Study Commission.

Whether Perkins mismanaged his job, as the Board claims, or whether he was more victim than perpetrator in the sequence of election buffooneries is beside the point. The fact is that the Board *considered* him incompetent. It recognized the virtual impossibility of removing him on that basis and resorted to the reorganization gambit, a thrust the Appeals Authority parried. The eventual compromise resolves the problem for the Election Board but puts in charge of another presumably important city function a manager the Board could not fire.

Administration—the highest civil service level in government—during the next four years.

Like the Civil Service Commission itself, and like private lawyers who make their living by fighting dismissals of federal employees, Pellerzi sees as relatively inconsequential the unfireability of the incompetent civil servant. Like the Commission, whose philosophy he absorbed during his service there, Pellerzi takes the view that a dismissal action usually stems from the incompetence of the supervisor rather than the employee.

"Generally," he says, "you will find that a dismissal action is a failure of discipline, a result of falling out between the supervisor and the employee rather than any change in the employee's performance. And you can't just fire someone arbitrarily, I don't care what business you're in—as long as it's unionized."

Does the union concern itself at all with the question of incompetence when defending an employee against a dismissal action? That is a question that makes Pellerzi somewhat uncomfortable.

"The union," he says, "owes the duty of representation to *all* of its members."

BURDENING THE SYSTEM

The notion that dismissal actions are taken capriciously doesn't stand up under examination. The evidence all points in the opposite direction: that federal managers will put up with incompetence, laziness, and outrageous behavior far longer than the public has a right to expect. The Civil Service is weighed down with unproductive employees against whom no action is ever taken because of the frustrations involved in bucking the system of protection.

A federal executive, a woman, describes what is involved in trying to dismiss a typist who has become impossible to work with:

"She had been unsatisfactory for close to a year. . . . She was extremely moody and temperamental. Her attendance was terribly spotty. She did not take criticism of any sort. You never knew when she was going to blow.

And during a long period when I took no notes—it was not yet even in my mind to start an adverse action—she would come into my office and ream me up one side and down the other. She would make the most outlandish accusations about my relations with other people in the division. It would happen, usually, when I called her in to discuss her attendance. She was hot-tempered, she had a foul mouth, and you could hear her all the way down the corridor when she laced off.

"The straw that broke the camel's back was her rather sudden refusal to carry out one clerical function which was a necessary part of her duties. She flatly refused. She just stopped doing it. When I realized that other people on the staff were having to do this girl's job I knew I had to take a hand. I went in and told her that I expected her to perform that function and complete it by four o'clock that afternoon. She was typing and she didn't reply. She went on typing and I asked her if she'd heard me. Without looking up, she said, 'I heard you.' And I said, 'Are you going to do it?' She said, 'We'll see.'

"She went home that day without having done it. I believe that was when I realized that drastic measures would have to be taken. I consulted with a great number of people in the administrative area of our agency. I got all the books and received verbal advice on how you initiate an adverse action. And I carried everything out to the letter. I spent a good part of the next two months documenting the girl's performance on the

---

It's Just as Bad in the Schools

The government is far from the only place where firing is impossible. Another example is in the public schools, as this report by Gloria Borger in *The Washington Star* shows:

"In Pennsylvania, a recent study of teacher hiring and firing trends between 1940 and 1970 revealed that only 65 tenured teachers had been dismissed during those 30 years. With more than 100,000 teachers in 505 school systems throughout the state, the report concludes, slightly more than two tenured teachers are dismissed per year.

"In the District, which has about 6,800 teachers, there have been about 21 tenured teachers dismissed formally after hearings because of unsatisfactory ratings over the past eight years. There were 56 cases in all, leaving an average of about two to three teachers dismissed after hearings each year.

"In Montgomery County [Maryland], one tenured teacher has been dismissed for incompetence over the past four years. In Fairfax County [Virginia], four cases charging incompetence have reached the board in the last several years."

job. I wrote an extensive evaluation of her work, which I gave to her, and followed this with a memo to her requesting improvement in the deficient areas. She wrote a memo to me asking for 'specifics.' I asked her supervisor to reply by memo, giving more specifics. You would be astonished at the number of memos which flowed back and forth between me and various elements of the agency on this one case. Finally I was in a position to write the girl a formal letter telling her that I was initiating action to have her dismissed. I had the letter looked at by the people who know about this kind of thing and, on their instruction, gave it to her in the presence of a witness.

"The girl asked for a formal agency hearing on the charges, which is her right, and she got the union to represent her. The agency appointed a lawyer to represent me. More months went by and lots more paperwork. A hearing examiner was assigned. He wrote telling us the requirements for the hearings—you have to set the room up exactly the way they want it. The tables have to be set up in certain ways, you have to rent a tape recorder and hire two operators to take down the proceedings—that alone, and the subsequent transcriptions, ended up costing the agency something like $2,000.

"When the hearings finally did take place, six months had elapsed since I had decided to take action. The hearings lasted three days. By the rules of the game, the girl was there the whole time. I was only permitted in while actually giving my own testimony; I couldn't even be there when witnesses on my own side were testifying.

"Anyway, another month or so elapsed while the recordings of the proceedings were transcribed and relevant portions sent to all concerned parties for their comments or corrections. Then, after the transcripts were returned to the examiner and he was pondering his recommendation, the girl found another job and quit. Otherwise, it might still be going on.

"The system is actually geared, in my mind, to the incompetent. You really have to do something heinous for your supervisor to take any action because it's so damn much trouble. And it *is* a lot of trouble. I was warned it was a lot of trouble. And I found it occupying, and I'm not kidding, five eighths of my day toward the end. And 110 per cent of my mind. The system and the rule book are geared to making you think 50 times before you start. The system assumes a supervisor has nothing else to do; the paperwork is unbelievable. My assistant, call her the office manager for this particular episode, and my secretary, the two of them were spending 50 per cent of their time—that's one person, 100 per cent—typing up reports with umpteen copies. A copy of everything, incidentally, had to go to the girl's representative. We couldn't hold a meeting to discuss the case and what we were going to do without either her or her representative being present. That's all in the rules and regulations."

MISSIONARY ZEAL

There are a few agencies that perform finite, measurable tasks and that are small enough to offer strong motivation for firing incompetents. In a small agency the word gets around about the person who's deadweight, and it isn't so easy to palm him off. And budgetary limitations militate against hiring an additional person to do his work. Under these circumstances—which sometimes exist when an agency is young, still imbued with missionary zeal, and led by people not yet anesthetized by apathy—dismissal actions become somewhat more plausible. In the Edward Lafferty case, all of the above factors were present and the case was energetically and successfully prosecuted. Nevertheless, the task was a formidable one.

Lafferty, an economist who had been in the federal service since 1968, came to the agency in 1973. His job centered about plotting statistical charts in a very limited sphere, and it soon became apparent to his supervisor that Lafferty didn't measure up to even this relatively simple chore.

In light of Lafferty's having served in the government since 1968, the personnel people at the agency thought the problem might be less a question of competence than of a personality conflict with the supervisor. Adjustments were made in Lafferty's work arrangements and a series of specific assignments were given him. The results confirmed the supervisor's judgment that Lafferty had neither the economics background for the job nor any willingness to acquire it.

In March 1976 Lafferty's supervisor handed him a letter of intent to terminate his employment in 30 days. Signed by a top agency official, the letter cited incompetence, insubordination, and generally abusive conduct as the causes of dismissal. The charges were documented with specific instances, testified to by memoranda from a variety of people who had dealt with Lafferty, and by an account that his supervisor had kept over a period of several months detailing the results of assignments given to Lafferty. The letter plus the exhibits ran to 60 pages.

The accounts of the assignments were technical, but the descriptions of Lafferty's behavior are understandable to the layman. On one occasion, the letter said, his supervisor came to Lafferty's office to check on the status of the project Lafferty had been assigned. Lafferty became enraged, charged the supervisor with "harassment," and, threatening physical violence, ordered him out of the office. On another occasion, when the supervisor asked for additional data on work Lafferty had turned in, Lafferty told him, "You can take it the way it is or stuff it...." On meeting the director of personnel in the cafeteria on one occasion, Lafferty said, "So you're the son of a bitch who's got it in for me. Maybe you'd like to step outside and settle it." The personnel director stared embarrassedly at his mashed potatoes as Lafferty let forth with a two-word description of him

Tenure: Riding the Eurailpass

What is the effect of the tenure system on the civil servants themselves? Suzannah Lessard addressed this question in a *Washington Monthly* article called "The Case Against Tenure":

"The crunch of the tenure system is that people in it find it very hard to leave. Tenure is like a Eurailpass. Having bought the pass, you are perfectly free to stop riding the train, but if you come upon a town that promises an unprecedented good time if you would only stop over, chances are you will be simply incapable of staying there, or if you do stay, you will dance on thorns, knowing your pass is expiring unused. Likewise, a tenured person is theoretically no more prevented from seeking new work than his untenured neighbor, but the plain truth seems to be that somehow job guarantees intimidate people into staying when they would otherwise go. This makes about as much sense as refusing to trade in a toaster that clanks and smokes for a better model because noxious and irritating as it is, it is guaranteed to go on working.

"In order to work well, particularly at something that demands imagination, intellectual energy, and dedication—in other words, something other than plain labor—people have to feel free to leave: they stay only because they choose to stay, not because they are afraid to leave. It's rather like a troubled marriage in which the wife can't decide whether she really wants to leave or stay, but because she is so terrified of being alone, stays, never discovering that in the absence of terror she would have decided for positive reasons to stay. Such a marriage would limp along, slowly wearing down the partners. But if she felt ready to leave if necessary, and felt able, then having decided to stay, she could face the problems with confidence and work fearlessly to make something constructive out of the relationship. Paradoxically, by being willing to dump the marriage, she would make it worth saving. The same applies to a job. If, unafraid of being fired, you work courageously, with conscience and commitment, then the job is far more rewarding—worth staying in—than if cowed by the fear of dismissal, you yielded to all pressures in the effort to keep it."

as the south end of a northbound horse. That any one of these incidents could be tolerated without causing Lafferty's dismissal is itself a measure of how job security affects discipline in the federal service.

Lafferty had 15 days to reply to the charges and two days of official time off. On April 25 the agency's highest administrative officer wrote Lafferty that his reply had been considered and the decision made to terminate his employment on May 12. The letter told him he had 15 days to appeal the decision to the Federal Employees Appeals Authority.

Lafferty did appeal the case and hired a private lawyer to represent him.

The agency then had to provide the Civil Service Commission with his entire file, now 103 pages long. The file, which contained a memorandum on every meeting at which the case had been discussed, was also available to Lafferty to help him prepare his defense. The appeal hearings, which took place in September 1976, lasted two days and resulted in two volumes of transcripts. The following month, the Appeals Authority issued a decision affirming the agency's dismissal action.

But more than two years had elapsed since Lafferty's incompetence had first been recognized. During most of that time he continued to receive his $20,000 salary. For about a year, various highly paid administrators at the agency had been spending a significant amount of their time on the case. And Lafferty still has recourse to the courts. How realistic is it to expect the people involved to continue to tackle such prosecutions? And this agency will one day become old, fat, tired, and cynical.

NOTHING OF VALUE

"Why do you want to fire anyone?" Lawyer Dalton asks.

There are two reasons.

The first is a coal miner in West Virginia who rarely sees the sun. He spends his days in a black hole, sometimes working in a tunnel too low to stand up in and breathing in dust that blackens his lungs and shortens his life. The money he earns from all this is taxed to pay for the upkeep of the federal establishment, and it is simply not fair to this man to make him contribute part of his wages to pay the salary of another man who is doing nothing of value.

The other reason is the need to make government perform better, a goal to which President Carter (like many of his predecessors) has pledged himself. For many fine and capable civil servants, the acceptance of the incompetent and the slacker affects their own attitudes and performance. For federal executives, the invulnerability of the unproductive worker makes a mockery of the whole concept of efficient management. While a general thinning out of the least productive people in the government would be desirable, what is needed is not necessarily the mass exercise of fire power but rather the realistic capability. A great many of the marginally competent people would radically improve their performances if the safety of their jobs was not so absolute. The overprotection of the civil servant is not only destructive of an efficient government service; it encourages too many federal employees to make the least of themselves and ends by destroying them, too.

Firemen First
or
How to Beat a Budget Cut
Charles Peters

Since parsimony is becoming almost as fashionable among politicians today as patriotism was in the 1940s, a wave of budget-cutting seems likely at all levels of government. The results could be salutary, but might be disastrous. To avoid the latter possibility, it is essential to understand how the Clever Bureaucrat reacts to the threat of fiscal deprivation.

The very first thing C.B. does, when threatened with a budget reduction, is to translate it into specific bad news for congressmen powerful enough to restore his budget to its usual plenitude.

Thus Amtrak, recently threatened with a budget cut, immediately announced, according to Stephen Aug of *The Washington Star,* that it would be compelled to drop the following routes:

San Francisco-Bakersfield, running through Stockton, the home town of Rep. John J. McFall, chairman of the House Appropriations transportation subcommittee.

St. Louis-Laredo, running through Little Rock, Arkansas, the home of Senator John McClellan, chairman of the Senate Appropriations Committee.

Chicago-Seattle, running through the homes of Senator Mike Mansfield, Senate Majority Leader, and Senator Warren Magnuson, chairman of the Senate Commerce Committee.

And in a triumphant stroke that netted four birds with one roadbed, Norfolk-Chicago, running through the home states of Senator Birch Bayh, chairman of the Senate Appropriations Transportation subcommittee,

Charles Peters is editor-in-chief of *The Washington Monthly.*

Senator Vance Hartke, chairman of the Commerce Surface Transportation Subcommittee, Rep. Harley Staggers, chairman of the House Commerce Committee, and Senator Robert Byrd, Senate Majority Whip.

The effectiveness of this device is suggested by a story that appeared in the *Charleston* (West Virginia) *Gazette* a few days after Amtrak's announcement:

Continued Rail Service Byrd's Aim

"Senator Robert C. Byrd, D-WVa, has announced that he intends to make an effort today to assure continued rail passenger service for West Virginia.

"Byrd, a member of the Senate Appropriations Committee, said he will 'either introduce an amendment providing sufficient funds to continue the West Virginia route or try to get language adopted which would guarantee funding for the route for Amtrak.' "

In the Amtrak case, C.B.'s budget-cutting enemy was President Ford. Sometimes it is a frugal superior in his own department. C.B.'s initial response is much the same. If, for example, a Secretary of Defense from Massachusetts insists upon eliminating useless and outmoded bases, the Navy's C.B. will promptly respond with a list of recommended base-closings, led by the Boston Navy Yard.

ANOTHER BAY OF PIGS

An irate constituency is, of course, a threat to all elected officials and to every other official who dreams of converting his appointive status into one blessed by the voting public. Even a small irritation can suffice. Thus, Mike Causey of *The Washington Post* tells of a National Park Service C.B. who, confronted with a budget cut, quickly restored congressmen to their senses by eliminating elevator service to the top of the Washington Monument. Every constituent whose children insisted on his walking all the way up was sure to place an outraged call to his congressman's office. Similarly, a Social Security Administration C.B. faced with a budget cut is certain to announce that the result will be substantial delays in the mailing of social security checks.

Whenever possible, a C.B. will assert that the budget cut is certain to result in the loss of jobs. The threatened employees are sure to write emotional protests to their congressmen. And, as the National Rifle Association has proven, even a tiny minority, if sufficiently vigorous in its expression of opinion—vigorous meaning that they make clear they will vote against you if you fail to help them—can move a legislator to take the desired action in the absence of an equally energetic lobby on the other side.

C.B.'s concern about loss of others' jobs is a deeply personal one. He knows that you can't be a commander unless you have troops to command.

Not long ago Jack Anderson discovered that the Navy, trying to adjust to less money than it had requested, was depriving the fleet of essential maintenance, while continuing to waste billions on useless supercarriers and transforming small Polaris submarines into giant Tridents. The reason of course is that the more big ships with big crews we have, the more admirals we need. Rank in the civil service is also determined in part by the number of employees one supervises. Thus a threat to reduce the number of one's employees is a threat not merely to one's ego but to one's income as well.

In its first flush of victory after the 1960 election, the Kennedy Administration embarked on two ill-fated missions. One was the Bay of Pigs. The other was an effort to fire 150 AID employees, all of whom wrote their congressman, as did their fathers, mothers, brothers, sisters, and in all probability their creditors and the creditors' relatives. The 150 were, of course, reinstated. If a Jimmy Carter or Ronald Reagan does become President, he might also ponder the lesson of Gail Parker, who found that to keep Bennington College afloat she would have to deprive teachers of tenure and rehire them each year on the basis of their merit and of what the college could afford. The threatened faculty stirred up such a storm that the Board of Trustees, which had originally backed Gail Parker, deserted her and she had to resign.

The tenured employee can even go to court. A recent decision by the U.S. Court of Appeals for the District of Columbia held that a college that fires a tenured professor because too few students are taking his course to pay for it must find another job for the professor, even if it requires dismissing other more competent but untenured professors.

FIREMEN FIRST

On the other hand, there are the teachers we don't want to fire—those in the public schools, for example, where teacher-pupil ratios of 1 to 40 are common. These are the ones C.B. always says he will have to fire when he is menaced with a budget cut. This tactic is based on the principle that the public will support C.B.'s valiant fight against the budget reduction only if essential services are endangered. Thus, C.B. always picks on teachers, policemen, firemen first. In the headquarters bureaucracy of the New York City and the Washington, D.C. school systems there are concentrated some of the most prodigious, do-nothing, time-servers of the modern era. No administrator threatens to fire them. If they are "the fat," and if he is to fight the budget cut, it would of course damage his cause to admit their existence. He must concentrate on threatening a loss of muscle.

Similarly, the Army, when faced with a budget cut, never points the finger at desk-bound lieutenant colonels. The victims are invariably combat troops. This is particularly unfortunate, since in government, as in human beings, fat tends to concentrate at the middle levels, where planning analysts and deputy assistant administrators spend their days attending meetings, writing memoranda, and reading newspapers.

Sometimes, however, the C.B. will be deliberately non-specific about the jobs that might be cut. When the City Council of the District of Columbia recently proposed a $67.2-million cut in the city's budget, Mayor Washington responded with an announcement that he would have to fire 4,000 city employees, but with no indication of exactly where the axe would fall. This tactic is designed to arouse all city employees who don't want to be among the 4,000—which of course means *all* city employees—to write the City Council protesting the outrageous cuts.

Another approach, which might be called "How Can You Guys Be Such Scrooges," was tried on the Council by Joseph Yeldell, the director of the city's Human Resources Administration, who proclaimed that yes, he knew exactly what the budget cut would do to his department, it would mean the cancellation of the foster parents program for 2,000 orphans.

But such appeals are guaranteed to work only during the Christmas season. The more reliable year-round tactic is to threaten the loss of essential services that affect almost all voters.

John Lindsay was a master of this technique. Confronted, for example, with a 1971–72 budget of only $8.6 billion, he said he would have to fire 10,000 policemen, 2,500 firemen, 3,600 garbage workers, 12,000 hospital workers, and 10,800 teachers.

In the end, he didn't have to fire anyone. Abe Beame was not so lucky. He threatened to fire 67,000 similarly essential employees, and—when the bastards actually cut his budget—found that he really had to drop 35,000.

There's the rub. If we really cut the budget of the C.B. who has bluffed by saying that he will have to fire essential employees, he may—to preserve his credibility—actually have to fire them, instead of the middle-level newspaper-readers who are the real fat. We could end up with a government of planning analysts, friends of congressmen, and trains running to Bakersfield via Stockton.

Murder by the Book

James Fallows

A worthy enough sentiment, but it does seem to miss the point of what's been going on. During the laments and eulogies for Richard Welch, the CIA station chief who was murdered in Athens, the authorities had great fun blaming the press—especially the previously unheralded *Counter-Spy* magazine—for sending Welch to his doom by publishing his name. The underlying idea seemed to be that a group of Greek leftists had been sitting at home, frustrated in their desire to assassinate an agent, until *Counter-Spy* gave them the necessary and otherwise-unavailable clue.

It must have been difficult to deliver these admonitions with a straight face, since no one knew better than the CIA men themselves that *Counter-Spy* added very little to the perils of their trade. As the agency has known for years, anyone bent on killing an agent—or merely blowing his cover in an American embassy—need hardly resort to such exotic publications as *Counter-Spy,* but can instead rely on documents provided by the U.S. government itself. As long as the State Department keeps publishing its Diplomatic List and Biographic Register, enemies of the CIA will have quick and authoritative means of identifying our agents overseas.

As John Marks explained in The Washington Monthly in November 1974, the system works this way: The Diplomatic List tells you who's working in each overseas embassy, with their rank (FSO-3, for example, or FSR-4) and job title (secretary, deputy chief of mission, etc.). The Biographic Register provides a career history of the people mentioned in the Diplomatic List. For bona fide members of the Foreign Service, certain familiar patterns emerge. There is often a first consular assignment in Juarez or Lahore, then a spell back with the African desk in Washington,

James Fallows is a contributing editor of *The Washington Monthly* and Washington editor of *The Atlantic.*

and next a step up the ladder as a deputy political officer in Quito or Bonn. Along with the assignments, ranks are listed, from the starting level of FSO-8 on up to the top, FSO-1.

Amidst these capsule biographies are alien entries for diplomats who are not FSOs but FSRs, or Reserve officers. Not all these Reserve officers are camouflaged spooks, but a good many are. When the CIA wants to hide a man in, say, Athens, it may designate him a "political officer" in the embassy and assign him an FSR rank. But the sophisticated observer will know that the only true political officers are FSOs. This is one clue. Another is Washington assignments such as "analyst" for the Army or Navy or Air Force. With such clues, the CIA man's listing in the Register might just as well say "Spy." To anyone who cares to look, the message will be clear.

The signposts provided by the Biographic Register are so plain that the CIA has on at least one occasion pleaded with the State Department to stop publishing it, or failing that, at least to make it a classified document. "I believe it was in 1968 that the Agency asked State to stop putting it out," says Ray S. Cline, who worked many years for the CIA before moving to the State Department as head of the Bureau of Intelligence and Research. (He has since joined Georgetown University's Center for Strategic Studies.) "It had always been a problem that the CIA was concerned about. After two or three tours as an FSR, you really began to stand out in the Register. The fact that you falsely contaminated a few other people, who happened to be Reserve officers but didn't work for the Agency, didn't give a great deal of satisfaction, either."

The State Department turned the CIA down. When Cline moved over to State, he tried once again. His position within the Department was an influential one, but on this issue he could not make the Foreign Service budge. Finally, he says, "I tried to get Richard Helms [then the director of the CIA] to go to bat on this. I told him that I would be his advocate inside State. But Helms was never much of a scrapper."

And so the beleaguered agents were left to fend for themselves, knowing that the hand that lifted their cover came not from their foes of the committed left but from their brethren in Foggy Bottom.

What is so fascinating about all this is the State Department's intractability. Part of it, of course, results from the absence of fraternal affection between the two departments. In its own version of utopia, the CIA would give its agents much-improved cover by making them full-fledged members of the Foreign Service, complete with FSO rankings. The State Department, of course, will have none of that. On its scale of values, protecting its members from "contamination" by spies vastly outranks protecting the CIA. But the Foreign Service could still preserve its own integrity without actively torpedoing the CIA if it simply refrained from publishing the Register. Why does it continue to do so? The answer leads us into the thickets of organizational life.

"It's a kind of stud book," says Cline. "When you run into someone, you can look him up and say, 'Oh yes, he was in Kuala Lampur when I was in Hong Kong.'" Like the alumni directory for a high-powered school, the Register enables Foreign Service officers to keep track of their colleagues, especially on matters of advancement and decline. Has old Bill made Three yet? Who got that posting to Paris? Am I gaining or am I falling behind? The Register provides another service as well, for, like a Blue Book or Social Register, it indicates the appropriate degree of respect due any given visitor. The military has solved this problem by letting its members wear their ranks on their uniforms. When a general comes calling, you only have to count his stars. Rank is nearly as important for an FSO, but the Foreign Service has not yet developed a tasteful means of putting stars on pin-striped suits. The solution is the Register. "It was miraculous the way people started treating me better after I became a One," says a former official at State.

There is one grand, solemn moral to this story, which is that the CIA has been pointing the finger at the wrong culprit. There is a more whimsical moral as well, which, in the days when Richard Welch and Philip Agee are long forgotten, may be the more important. It is that the necessities of organizational life—wanting to know how the competition is doing, needing a quick guide to protocol—can sometimes have as great an impact as the most fervent ideology. *Counter-Spy* wants to rub out the CIA; the State Department merely wants to keep score on the climb up the greasy pole. From which does the CIA have more to fear?

Afterword

As a result of the outcry that followed the death of Richard Welch, the State Department has made its Biographic Register a classified document.

part 7
THE WATCHERS

Nowadays it's standard practice to regard those who watch government —academics, columnists, book and magazine writers, pollsters, and, mainly, people in daily journalism—as another branch of government. Not only do these people greatly influence the government, and see themselves as quasi-governmental officials, but enlightened opinion considers these watchers the best part of the world of public affairs. The press is now widely credited with bringing the Vietnam War to its end, with exposing Watergate and deposing President Nixon, and with other happy developments of the last ten years.

The danger of treating the press as another branch of government is that it isn't subject to any checks and balances, but can act as an overriding mechanism on everyone else—deciding, for instance, what to make public and what to keep secret. A press with that power is in danger of repeating the sins of the other branches of government. It's also susceptible to the legal but nonetheless grave sin of arrogance.

The Washington press corps is big and varied. Its members range from the lowliest hacks to the loftiest grandees. But most of them aspire to either a prestigious beat like the White House, Congress, or the State Department, or to a job as a tough, roving investigator. The Achilles Heel of the investigative reporters is that they often look for illegality (which is relatively rare in the federal government) and ignore deeper and more important problems that don't involve lawbreaking. On the other hand, the beat reporters, as Charles Peters points out in "Why the White House Press Didn't Get the Watergate Story," usually live on the steady diet of news their sources provide for them and seldom try to talk to unofficial, middle-level officials to find out what's really going on.

A step up the Great Media Chain of Being are the columnists, who are supposed to bring seasoning and perspective to the day's news and thus detect the important themes that the reporters ignore. Joseph Kraft is an example of a columnist (a very good one) who is imprisoned by his sources —very subtly, but nonetheless imprisoned. Kraft genuinely sees the world as the important men who are his friends see it, and that means he has the same failings of vision that they have.

A further step up the chain ought to be the political scientists—well-trained thinkers with years to puzzle out what it all means. Instead of doing that, though, or helping people understand how to deal with the government, they study trivia, write it up in jargon, and are listened to by practically nobody but each other. Which leaves the task of reporting on the government and suggesting improvements in its operations practically wide open.

Poll-takers are the fastest-growing class of watchers. They watch for newspaper readers, for politicians, and for private businesses, and increasingly they're thought to be endowed with magical powers of divination. A large measure of the credit for President Carter's amazing victory in 1976 is commonly given to his pollster, Pat Caddell, who knew what pitch would work on which voters. Now a major politician won't make a move without taking a poll, and the stock of Presidents and Senators is measured not by their accomplishments but by how they fare in the Harris and Gallup surveys. In the article that closes this section, Michael Wheeler shows that it's a mistake to take polls as seriously as they're now taken. Because their information can be distorted by biased questions and sloppy questioning, most pollsters practice a science that's as inexact as the journalists'.

Why the White House Press Didn't Get the Watergate Story

Charles Peters

One of the great remaining mysteries of the Watergate affair is why the White House press corps failed to get the story. From the time of the break-in, the investigatory momentum was not with the White House correspondents, even those of *The Washington Post*, but with two of the *Post's* metropolitan reporters, Bob Woodward and Carl Bernstein. As the story developed [in 1972], the big names from CBS, NBC, *The New York Times, Newsweek, Time,* etc. were reduced to reporting the *Post's* accusations and Ron Ziegler's denials.

The Watergate plans were conceived, carried out, and covered up in the White House offices only yards away from the press lobby where at least a score of correspondents wait each day. The number of reporters triple for major presidential trips and soars into the hundreds for press conferences. Why didn't they give us any idea of what was going on in the offices of H. R. Haldeman and John Ehrlichman?

The word "prisoner" may soon replace "conspirator" in describing former members of the presidential staff. It is already an accurate description of some members of the White House press corps, for the constraints they work under make them captives not only of Richard Nixon, but of whoever holds the office.

"Your time is taken up by the large, regular flow of presidential news announcements, the campaign, summit meetings," says Robert Donovan, who became Washington bureau chief for the *Los Angeles Times* after serving as White House correspondent for the *New York Herald Tribune.* "There's almost always something going on that deprives one of the time to dig underneath." Donovan's successor at the *Herald Tribune,* David

Charles Peters is editor-in-chief of *The Washington Monthly.*

Wise, remembers that his editors put pressure on him to do those regular stories better than the AP, instead of looking for the story AP was missing.

As the 1973 Iceland summit meeting between Nixon and President Pompidou retreats into the past, a reasonable man can conclude that nothing happened there that couldn't easily have been covered in dispatches from the Reykjavik wire bureaus or from Paris and Washington a few days after the meeting. But because the president was traveling, an entire press entourage accompanied him. The energy devoted to local-color stories about Iceland and TV shots of diplomats entering buildings might have been enough to break the whole Watergate case if it had been directed at the White House.

Since presidential election campaigns amount to a long series of Iceland summits, reporters are left exhausted and stupefied by the interminable string of staged events. When asked to explain their attentiveness to these ceremonial functions, reporters often mention the "assassination mentality"—the fear that, if the president were killed, their paper might have to pick up the story from the wire services.

The assassination mentality is evident in the importance accorded the press secretary's daily briefings. Reporters religiously attend the sessions because no one wants to miss the meeting at which a Ziegler produces some big news. The correspondents are like a herd of seals waiting for the fish that are reliably tossed their way instead of looking elsewhere for sustenance. Russell Baker, who once covered the White House for *The New York Times,* says, "I was always fed enough information by [Eisenhower's press secretary] Jim Hagerty to take care of page one. I wasn't encouraged by my paper to get anything else." Such behavior allows the White House virtually to choose the main story for the next day's front pages by setting off for Iceland, importing Leonid Brezhnev, or announcing major appointments on the day that a scandal is breaking. As Bill Moyers, press secretary to Lyndon Johnson put it, "The White House press corps is more stenographic than entrepreneurial in its approach to news gathering. Too many of them are sheep. Sheep with short attention spans. They move on to tomorrow's story without pausing to investigate yesterday's."

Moyers also notes that it is not so much that the press is kept too busy, but that they're kept waiting all day in one room. "They sit and sit and shift a leg and sit some more." It all seems to be very much like the "hurry up and wait" of the Army and jury duty.

PRISONER OF THE SOURCE

Rare is the reporter who has not at some time or other felt himself bound by his news sources. The most difficult story to write is not the one that angers editors or officials but the one that dries up sources.

In 1971, *Newsday,* the Long Island newspaper, ran a series of exposés on the financial affairs of Bebe Rebozo, concluding with the editorial comment, "Let's face it, the deals made by Bebe Rebozo and the Smathers gang have tainted the presidency." Ron Ziegler would not speak to *Newsday's* White House correspondent, Martin Schram, for three months afterwards and excluded Schram from the China trip. This was also enough to put *Newsday* on the White House "enemies" list; IRS agents audited the editor's tax records and those of the paper.

Bill Moyers recalls that Lyndon Johnson once forbade him to give any White House exclusives to the *St. Louis Post-Dispatch's* James Deakin, simply because Johnson thought Deakin's questions at press briefings were too tough.

A journalist will hesitate to write tough criticism of Henry Kissinger because in the future Kissinger might give him that extra bit of information on our policy toward Cambodia. Peter Lisagor, White House correspondent for *The Chicago Daily News,* calls this a "psychological undertow that can obscure and minimize things that the public generally ought to be hearing about."

Even the president's press secretary can become a protected source. According to Bill Moyers, the White House reporters are reluctant to criticize the press secretary "because they are dependent on his benificence for whom they see and where they travel—even for favors like getting their publishers a private luncheon invitation from the president. Some publishers cared more about that than any exclusive their White House correspondent could get."

The judgment of how long to coddle a source can place a reporter midway between a grand jury and God, as he calculates whether avoiding Kissinger's anger is more important than revealing what he has learned about the Vietnam "peace" deal. If the reporter writes the story, his sources will dry up and the public will be denied any further information. The question is, when does the reporter decide that the information he has is so important that he must jeopardize information he hopes to get in the future. "We will give immunity to a very good source as long as the information he offers us is better than what we've got on him," columnist Jack Anderson has said.

PRISONER OF OBJECTIVITY

Throughout the fall of 1972, *The Washington Post's* stories made serious accusations and then attributed them only to unnamed sources. Although it is easily forgotten, now that the *Post* has been proven right, the White House was not alone in labeling the paper's coverage unfair, biased, irresponsible.

Behind these criticisms is a peculiar distortion of the notion of "responsi-

bility." For many reporters the goal in preparing a story is finding someone they can quote, someone who will say that the president has been
deceptive or that a policy is not working. When White House statements
represent a total contradiction of what has gone before, reporters often
hesitate to say so, preferring instead to quote Senator Muskie.

This is the very opposite of real responsibility. The *Post* was far more
responsible in ascertaining the truth for itself, and then putting its own
name behind the charges, than were the papers who waited until they
could say "John Dean alleges" and "Ron Ziegler denies." Responsibility is
a different concept from objectivity and fairness, which the press should
also maintain. But none of these standards should require a reporter to
withhold what he knows to be true merely because he cannot find anyone
to say it for attribution. How would the press have reported the Emperor's
new clothes?

Why can't reporters and papers establish their own reputation for reli-
ability? I would trust *The Washington Post*'s David Broder as much as any
source he could name. In fact, if he says he stands behind a story, I'm more
likely to believe it is true than if he simply quotes a source for the story
and says the source "alleges" it is true.

Another ball and chain for the prisoners of objectivity is their reluctance
to draw obvious inferences and to supply known background facts that will
make the significance of a story clear.

By the end of October 1972, the press knew that:

1. Dwight Chapin, the president's appointments secretary, had clearly
been connected with campaign saboteur Donald Segretti. Chapin was
Haldeman's protégé in the White House, and insiders knew he wouldn't
turn around without orders from Haldeman. If Chapin's relationship with
Haldeman had been reported to the public, the people would have had
some idea how high the scandal went. But to our knowledge, only a
gossip-type story in the Style section of the *Post* pointed out this key fact
before the election.

2. A California judge had found that Haldeman, Nixon, and friends had
engaged in similar dirty campaign practices in California in 1962. Although the *Post*'s Sanford Ungar reported this before the election, it was
pushed aside in the *Post* by "Peace is at Hand" and was buried in the other
papers (*The New York Times* ran it far inside). From then until June 1973,
this crucial information seems to have appeared only a few places, including a series by *The St. Louis Post-Dispatch*'s James Deakin, a story by
Adam Clymer in *The Baltimore Sun*, a *New York Times Sunday Magazine*
piece by R. W. Apple, and a story in *The Boston Globe*.

The point is not that the press should have launched smear campaigns,
especially right before the election when false charges would be hard to
refute. For the kind of "responsible" journalism we have described,
meticulous fidelity to fact is even more important than when merely

quoting. David Wise recalls that, shortly before the 1960 election, he got a tip about the Howard Hughes loan to Nixon's brother; he wasn't able to use the story because he could not confirm its accuracy in time. Wise's hesitation was justified, but it was in a different category from judgments such as the one Walter Rugaber provided in a pre-'72 election Watergate wrap-up for *The New York Times:* "There has been no public indication that either the president or any of his close advisors played roles in or had advance knowledge of an illegal assault upon the opposition party."

Another element in the journalists' Watergate failure is the trepidation which the presidency creates even in veteran reporters. "They get goose pimples when they hear 'Hail to the Chief,' " says Douglas Kiker of NBC. "They tend to believe a man with a big title and a big car. They very much want to believe the president of their country," which implies that they don't want to call him a liar.

James Reston cites another reason to explain why the press failed on Watergate:

Some reporters found that their trusted sources lacked the courage to speak out on Watergate. This happened to Reston, whose knowledge of what the CIA was up to had included before-the-event awareness of the U-2 incident and the Bay of Pigs. I asked him why he thought his sources failed him on the White House attempt to use the CIA to cover up Watergate. His reply was that fewer and fewer government officials facing the possibility of losing office agree with Joseph Kennedy's "Home holds no terrors for me." In other words, the seductions of office keep them from resigning and letting the public know what is going on. Reston described a lunch he had with former CIA director Richard Helms in January, where he asked if Helms had been bounced from the CIA and if so, why. "Helms was obviously angry at the White House clique, but not one thing did he say about the Watergate connection. He took the easy way out, a job overseas (ambassador to Iran), and didn't seem to feel he had any obligation to disclose."

While anyone who had ever observed a pack of reporters in a press lounge questioning each other to make sure no one had a special angle might think that their professional camaraderie dominated their inter-paper jealousy, petty rivalry among the newspapers also influenced the Watergate coverage. Conformity did, of course, play a role: "Because you all gather together in one place, because you all focus on one man, because all of you travel together, there is a herd instinct to report the same things the other guys are reporting," says R. W. Apple.

Apple notes, "There is a tendency, if you can't confirm it independently, not to run a story that begins, '*The Washington Post* said today....' My impression is that there is an effort to hold that sort of thing to a minimum.... I think a case can be made that the *Times* did not devote the resources it should have to Watergate until the second month of this year [1973].

WHAT CAN BE DONE

Remedying the press' defects is important not simply in terms of preventing another Watergate. As Apple observes, "Watergate is but one example of the kind of story that's missed by the White House press corps."

The *Post* and the *Times* now cover the White House with two-man teams. One is supposed to watch the trees, the other the forest. But both Clifton Daniel of the *Times* and Benjamin Bradlee, managing editor of the *Post,* say that these efforts need to be supplemented.

Everyone agrees there is a need for more investigative reporters. But most think it would be futile to assign them to the White House. Hugh Sidey of *Time* can't imagine a Seymour Hersh being welcomed by Ron Ziegler. Mel Elfin of *Newsweek* says the lesson of Watergate to him has been to beef up *Newsweek's* coverage of the Department of Justice, particularly the FBI, where *Time's* Sandy Smith had been beating *Newsweek* —and of the lobbyist-trade association-superlawyers group where so much of the town's hanky-panky originates.

Certainly many of the best reporters are convinced that you can't find out the truth about the White House from the president's staff. Bob Donovan says, "The White House staff is a perfect source for letting you know how great the Administration is. I got most of my good White House stories from the Hill. The congressional staffs are full of bright people, each of whom has a piece of what's going on and is freer to talk about it than the White House staff."

James Reston says, "I worked in this town for 20 years as a scoop artist. The way you did it was to work the periphery. If you knew the president was going to bring out a tax bill, you knew there would be consultation with Wilbur Mills and other leaders to see if the Congress would go along. Again, in foreign policy, you knew Acheson would try out ideas with the British and French ambassadors, so you would call up Wilbur Mills and the ambassadors. I knew Acheson went to drink whiskey with Senator Arthur Vandenberg every night so I went to see Vandenberg in the morning."

"It is in the narrow space between the formulation of policy and the announcement of policy that scoops are to be mined," says Reston.

Russell Baker translated this into: "When I was covering the State Department, I always looked for the sorehead, the guy who was coming out of the meeting defeated and angry and ready to talk. . . . I didn't look for soreheads at the White House because I assumed there weren't any. They were all on the team."

But there are always soreheads in the White House and the press should look for them. Doug Kiker recalls the Marvin Watson-Bill Moyers rivalry under Lyndon Johnson, which meant that you could get almost anything out of one if you mentioned some threat from the other. Only in April, 1973, did Christopher Lydon of the *Times* begin uncovering the various cliques in the Nixon White House that had existed from the beginning and which could have been used to find out the truth about Watergate.

R. W. Apple says, "The press doesn't demand to see the White House staff members often enough. I think there's a certain accountability they should fulfill. We have to demand that they be open to questioning. After all, they work for the country."

This doesn't mean there has to be some legal requirement that government employees see the press. It does mean that civil servants should accept some reasonable availability to the press as part of their responsibility to the public they are supposed to be serving. Of course, Henry Kissinger shouldn't have to give every interview requested—if he did, he wouldn't have time for anything else. But there is no excuse for the H. R. Haldemans who refuse to be interviewed at all.

LOOK FOR THE SHREDDER-MAN

Another version of "looking for the sorehead" is "going down the line." Sy Hersh says, "The little guy who runs the xerox machine may only be able to give you an extra copy, but that may be all you need." And the guy who runs the Xerox machine is not an intimate friend of the president, will not lose a $42,000-a-year job if he talks to you, and just might put the interests of the country above the interest of the current incumbent in the White House.

Hugh Sloan, while not a Xerox operator, was a guy down the line who was known to have resigned because of Watergate. We now know he was deeply disturbed, disturbed enough to take his concerns to Stans, Chapin, and Ehrlichman in July, 1972. Who was the reporter who called him up in July? Who found out that Magruder advised Sloan to commit perjury? Only Woodward and Bernstein.

Bill Moyers says that when he was press secretary, the reporters he most feared were those who followed the agency head out the White House door and back to his office where he would immediately tell his assistant what had happened at the White House. As the assistant told *his* assistant and so on, the story would soon reach someone of sufficiently modest loyalty to the Administration that the reporter could get him to talk. Moyers also feared the correspondent who went down the line at the White House to talk to unknown middle- or lower-level assistants who were doing important work but who had every reason to believe that the public, not to mention their friends back home, didn't know it. The temptation to reveal the inside knowledge that proved their importance was often overwhelming.

One of the most important things the reporters could have done to prevent Watergate was to have alerted the public about their inability to report the presidency. Mel Elfin, Washington Bureau Chief of *Newsweek*, told us he had never been able to get an interview with H. R. Haldeman. But he never told *Newsweek* readers. James Reston has not been able to interview Nixon, Haldeman, or Ehrlichman since 1968, but he had never reported this fact in his column. R. W. Apple one day in March called 17 different White House officials without getting an answer. But he, too, has not reported these rebuffs.

Reston says, "Turner Catledge [former managing editor of the *Times*] had a strong feeling that we should not seem to be whining and complaining about lack of access. It was our job to get the news no matter what barriers they put in the way." Apple adds, "It seems awfully self-pitying and self-serving to write about how mean those fellows are because they won't return your phone calls."

In addition, one suspects that while it may not have been true of men so secure in their jobs as Elfin, Apple, and Reston, many reporters were afraid to admit their lack of access because it might reflect on their competence to do the job.

Another way newspapers could have made their readers aware of how the story was being hidden is suggested by James Deakin: "I'm convinced that if the press had regularly printed the transcripts of Ziegler's press briefings from last June on, the public would have become aware much earlier of the pattern of evasion and deception. But only one or two papers printed even one of these transcripts." This would also protect the public from those reporters who heard the contents of the transcript first-hand but failed to report the legitimate inferences.

THOU SHALT NOT LIE

Congressman Paul N. McCloskey has proposed that it be made a crime for a government employee to willfully lie to a committee of Congress. Because of the failure of past attempts to legislate openness in government —witness the marvelous skill of the federal bureaucracy in evading requests for documents under the Freedom of Information Act—little attention has been paid to McCloskey's proposal. We think it should be revived and expanded to forbid officials to lie to reporters—or to any other citizens. It has become justifiable and the accepted thing for public officials to lie. This does not mean that they always have to be forthcoming. There may be some things they can't or won't talk about. In such cases, as Clifton

Daniel notes of his father-in-law, Harry Truman, they can say, "It's none of your damn business." But they don't have to lie. The government can fine or imprison the taxpayer who lies. It seems only fair that the taxpayer have some remedy against the government official who lies.

Finally, the press has to deny the president deniability. Its reports of what his subordinates are doing must be searching—not simply to inform the public as we have already argued, but to make sure the president cannot plead ignorance of their behavior and thereby escape responsibility for it.

General Abrams was praised by congressional committees and his promotion approved because he said he didn't know that General Lavelle was bombing the hell out of North Vietnam. It seemed to be the view of everyone that President Nixon should escape liability if actual knowledge of Watergate can't be pinned on him.

In an important new book with an unfortunate title, *Administrative Feedback*, Herbert Kaufman points out that leaders "may resort to a strategy discouraging feedback about administrative behavior because they privately approve of the behavior they know they should, according to law and morality, prevent."

Remember Colson to Hunt, "Don't tell me," and Ehrlichman to Sloan, "I don't want to know."

Kaufman continues. "The temptations to establish claims of ignorance are as great when one is truly an accomplice as when one is truly a victim." He goes on to suggest that "one approach would be to abandon the fiction that leaders are by virtue of ignorance untouched" by responsibility for the actions of their subordinates.

But to pin the leader to the wall, the press must zero in on the subordinate. Too often they do not. Instead, in Kaufman's words, "The journalists focus on programs, the high politics of forming policies, or the sparring footwork of political maneuvering. There is hardly ever an examination of subordinate behavior that would instruct leaders."

FACING THE REALITIES

One thing is clear, the "periphery" of sources must be expanded beyond the senators and ambassadors that gave Reston his scoops. Sy Hersh got the My Lai story from a bunch of guys you never heard of, which is, of course, the way the *Post*'s Watergate story began. *The Washington Monthly*'s greatest scoop, how the Army was spying on civilian politics, came not from the Secretary of Defense but from a captain in the Army Reserve named Christopher Pyle.

Reston looked for his scoops in the gap between the formulation of a policy and its announcement. Another place to look is the place where the policy is being executed. I used to work for the Peace Corps. My job was to evaluate Peace Corps programs overseas. I felt my main mission was to rub Washington's nose in the realities of the field. My best sources were not the top bureaucrats but the volunteers out there doing the job. Increasingly, I think the reporters will find their best sources closer to the cutting edge of policy. The Air Force press office can tell you what the policy is, but you have to go to Indochina to find out what General Lavelle's bombers are doing. There is one story in the political intrigue between the White House and the Congress and the lobbies in, say, the formulation of educational policy. A more important story may be out in the schools where that policy is being carried out.

On January 9, 1972, *The New York Times* published a story saying that some months earlier the White House had decided to do something about all those leaks and that a group devoted to plugging them had been formed under the leadership of Egil Krogh and David Young. The press might well have looked into how that policy was executed.

The Most Famous Journalist in America
James Fallows

"I think I'm good," said Joseph Kraft, and paused to pick up the phone. He was sitting in the basement office of his home in Washington's Georgetown on election day 1974. Upstairs there were *Paris Review* posters on the wall and *objets d'art* from China on the coffee tables. Here in his office, his secretary typed quietly behind him while Kraft took the call from Gerald Warren at the White House. Kraft was leaving for Greece in a few days, on assignment for *The New Yorker,* and before he left he wanted to arrange a rendezvous with President Ford's party in Japan.

"Look, Jerry, I just want to be sure we have things straight. I am one of the very few people with a serious interest in both the domestic and

James Fallows is a contributing editor of *The Washington Monthly* and Washington editor of *The Atlantic.*

foreign implications, and. . . ." he stopped for a moment to listen. "Look, I think my case is very strong."

He hung up and came back to the question under discussion, the changing fortunes of the newspaper column as an institution, with special emphasis on the columns of Joseph Kraft.

"I think I'm good, and I think the reason I'm good is that I think hard and I work hard. I'm the hardest-working columnist I know."

He had been speaking very quickly, leaning forward in his chair and looking his visitor in the eye. Now he tilted back and said more reflectively, "I've had a very successful career as a columnist. I like my job. I get up in the morning, and, you know, I really do like what I do all day. It's gone very well for me."

Indeed it has, and Kraft is not the only one to say so. Since he took his first job 25 years ago as an editorial writer for *The Washington Post,* Kraft has risen to the top of political journalism. He spent a total of seven years at the *Post* and the Week in Review section of *The New York Times.* In 1957 he began free-lancing. One year later he won the Overseas Press Club's award for "Best Magazine Reporting" for coverage of the Algerian civil war. In 1960 Kraft signed on as a speechwriter with John Kennedy's presidential campaign. He was apparently good at that, too, for in the first of his "Making of the President" books, Theodore White described Kraft as one of the two "ablest writers in America"—the other, in White's view, being John Barlow Martin. After the campaign Kraft succeeded William S. White as Washington correspondent for *Harper's,* a position he held until 1963, when, at the age of 39, he began writing his thrice-weekly syndicated column. Almost as soon as it appeared the column met acclaim. The British writer, Henry Fairlie, never renowned for his flattery, expressed a widely accepted view when he said that Kraft was "Lippmann's only visible successor." Walter Lippmann himself, Kraft's predecessor in the upper-left-hand corner of the *Post's* op-ed page, called him "the most promising commentator of his generation," a judgment *Newsweek* reiterated in a story about Kraft in 1965. Anthony Lewis is one old friend who admires and respects him. Stanley Karnow is another. Even David Halberstam, whose personal distaste for Kraft is scarcely contained, wrote in *The Best and the Brightest* that Kraft was "one of the best political writers in America."

Kraft is intelligent: valedictorian of his class at Columbia in 1947, he spent a year at Princeton's Institute for Advanced Study after graduation.

Kraft is well-connected: On his frequent travels abroad he consorts with the likes of Brandt and Brezhnev, Yevtushenko and Malraux, King Hussein, King Faisal, and Premier Chou En-lai. Back home, he and his wife Polly winter in Georgetown and summer in the Hamptons on Long Island, next door to Clay Felker, the editor of *New York.*

Kraft's column is widely read: *The Washington Post* gives him better placement than any other columnist, and outside Washington he appears in some 180 newspapers. He is denied the major outlet only in New York, where he is not in the *Times* but the *Post.*

Despite all this, Joseph Kraft's career illustrates all too clearly the limitations of his form of political commentary. In the columns and magazine articles he has written over the last 12 years, Kraft has treated political personalities in a distorted and misleading way. In his analysis of domestic affairs he has too often been blind to the most fundamental sources of change. In his coverage from abroad he has been uninformative and thin. These and his other shortcomings are significant because they are not unique to Kraft. Most of the other columnists are simply less successful versions of Joseph Kraft, sharing the same values and techniques and subject to the same constraints. By examining the way those constraints have affected Kraft, we may help explain the pallor and predictability of our columnists in general.

THE LIPPMANN LEGACY

First, some distinctions. Several different styles of column-writing have evolved during the last 50 years, but one has clearly predominated. That is the heavy-weight, "analytical" style, of which Lippmann was an early representative and Kraft is the current standard-bearer. The characteristic of these "analysts" is that they provide ideas, not information; they digest and reflect upon the news reported on the front page, rather than breaking the news themselves. The extent to which the "analytical" style has dominated the column is made clear by a list of the analysts: Lippmann, Kraft, Arthur Krock, James Reston, Tom Wicker, and Anthony Lewis (these last four all of *The New York Times*), Marquis Childs, the brothers Alsop, George F. Will, Charles Bartlett, William S. White, Carl Rowan, James F. Kilpatrick, and many others.

The "analysts," as this list suggests, are by no means homogeneous. To cite the main sub-group, there are the "conservative" analysts as opposed to the "liberals" like Wicker and Kraft. Every decade or so a promising conservative voice appears—William Buckley in the 1950s, James Kilpatrick in the 60s, now George Will in the 70s—and is hailed by onlookers hoping desperately to find the new Burke. But there is an overriding similarity between these conservatives and the liberals in their non-reportorial approach to the news. To see just how similar the analysts are, we need only consider the handful of columnists who tried to do something besides pure "analysis" with their daily 800 words. There are really only three such alternate ideas about what a column should be.

The first alternate tradition is one that has recently fallen on hard times. During the 1950s and 1960s, Murray Kempton of the *New York Post* wrote a column that was different from any of its predecessors. Unlike the Lipp-mann-style columnists, Kempton would observe events first-hand and re-port on them in his column; but unlike the straight-news reporters who were also on the scene of breaking news, Kempton felt free to include in his column all the human nuance and political implication of the event. More recently, Jimmy Breslin has written in this vein, and Mary McGrory does it even now. What has changed since Kempton's days is the unique-ness of the product; with the coming of the "new journalism," the front page now contains the kind of "color stories" and news analysis previously left to Kempton and McGrory.

The second kind of non-analytical column is still going strong. It is the muckraking column pioneered by Drew Pearson and Robert Allen and now carried forward by Jack Anderson. What distinguishes Anderson's "Washington Merry-Go-Round" from the other categories of columns is its reliance on facts. Curiously, this column appears on *The Washington Post's* comic page.

The third and newest category is that created by Rowland Evans and Robert Novak in the early 1960s. Like Pearson and Anderson, Evans and Novak provide facts; but unlike the "Washington Merry-Go-Round," the Evans and Novak column does not confine itself to muckraking. It is easy to make fun of the column's ludicrous bias in favor of Scoop Jackson and Melvin Laird; and serious charges of conflict-of-interest have been raised against Evans and Novak by Stephen Nordlinger in a issue of *[MORE]*. Still, these two men did have a new idea when they started the column, and on the days when their sources are in power, they can come up with stories no one else has.

With these three exceptions, the rest of the op-ed page is given over to the analysts, the Krafts and Restons who puff on their pipes and deliver their views of the world. On those mornings when the "analysis" consists of virtually identical views about the Future of the Democratic Party or the Meaning of Impeachment, it is tempting to conclude that everyone but the working reporters should be thrown off the paper. Never was this temptation stronger than during the year and a half of Watergate, when the contrast between the engrossing detail of the newspage and the col-umnists' stale opinions made one feel that the analysts could be dropped without loss. There is, however, a genuine need the analysts can fill, and that is to provide a sort of detachment and perspective one finds nowhere else in the press.

Perhaps the best illustration is the series of columns Walter Lippmann wrote during the fall of 1950 (and then recycled over the next few years to prove that he had been right). The question at the time was how far MacArthur could or should go with his North Korean invasion, and Lipp-mann argued that he should be pulled back fast. Lippmann based his position on an examination of the *pattern* of U.S.-Soviet relationships, which gave the invasion a different meaning than was immediately apparent. Since World War II, Lippmann said, the United States and Russia had reached a kind of gentlemen's agreement about incursions on one another's territory. When the Russians acted to upset the "status quo" in some portion of the world—in Berlin, in Greece, in Iran—we would act to restore the status quo, but no more. We would start the Berlin airlift, but we would not bomb the daylights out of East Germany. According to this pattern, we would respond in Korea by pushing the Communists back across the 38th parallel, thus restoring the status quo. By doing more than that, Lippmann said, we would run the risk of upsetting the gentlemen's agreement and enlarging the war—and of course he was right. MacArthur recklessly advanced to the Yalu river, the Chinese entered the war, and all sides were involved in three years of bloody and unnecessary conflict.

This example does not prove that columnists are always effective, but only that they have the potential of developing standards which will persuade some people and help others see how the govenment should act. No columnist can be expected to fulfill this potential every time; rather, the test is whether, in the long run, the columnist provides the perspective that the rest of the press lacks.

It must be said straightaway that Kraft has provided the best kind of analysis on several crucial occasions. He was one of the first columnists to declare that the war in Vietnam was not going to work, a judgment he attributes to his experience with the guerrillas in Algeria. During the 1960's, Kraft also understood the limitations of the Great Society programs far better than most others who were writing at the time. In his first column after the Watergate burglary, Kraft noted that it defied logic or evidence to believe that Richard Nixon was not deeply involved. And, to give him credit for the most attractive aspect of his current performance, he continues to address the central question of public affairs at the moment, the question of the country's economic survival. While most other columnists stay away from the topic, perhaps from apprehension about their lack of expertise, only Kraft and Nicholas von Hoffman, so unalike in every other way, give consistent attention to our economic emergencies.

Yet to read back over 12 years of Kraft's output, as I have done, is to be struck not by his insight and perspective but by the opposite: by his inability to perceive some of the most significant kinds of change in the country, and his failure to detach his own critical standards from those of the people he is writing about.

MISSING THE HUMAN DIMENSION

As the first illustration of Kraft's failed perspective, there is his treatment of the major political personalities of the last few years. A balanced portrayal of public figures is not easy to achieve. Both Washington, with its tendency to lionize whoever is in power, and New York, with its tendency to classify all politicians as charlatans and crooks, project one-sided views of political and human reality, overlooking the fact that most public figures are neither heroes nor villains but normal humans, with both good and bad sides. One of the services a columnist might provide would be to help correct this imbalance. Yet this is a service they neglect, and none more flagrantly than Joseph Kraft.

In 1963, Kraft wrote an article for *The Saturday Evening Post* about Oklahoma's Senator Robert Kerr. There could hardly be a richer subject for analysis, or one better suited for developing the human complexity. Kerr was an extremely smart man, one of the great masters of manipulation in the Senate. At the same time, he was Bobby Baker's dark angel—less because he wanted to enrich himself than because he seemed to be one of those people who takes deep pleasure in bringing others to corruption, as some men are sexually satisfied merely to witness the corruption of a woman. Such was the press corps' respect for technical proficiency, however, that almost no one wrote about the several sides of Robert Kerr —just as they avoided writing about Wilbur Mills until his pathetic downfall was thrust under their noses. Kraft, too, celebrated Kerr's technical skills and brushed aside questions about motivation, insisting that "the truer measure of his purpose" was his book on water conservation.

Kraft's problem is endemic to the press as a whole, and is more fully illustrated by his treatment of three other recent figures: McGeorge Bundy, John Connally, and Wilbur Mills. These men are textbook cases of the one-sided view of public personalities. All three were made heroes by the press—Bundy for his brains, Mills for his relentless mastery of the tax code, Connally for his charm and force. All three were vilified in the end by that same press, apparently astonished to find a dark side to their knights. Far from correcting this excessive flattery, Kraft was one of the most rhapsodic members of the claque.

Consider, for example, his portrait of McGeorge Bundy, written as a magazine article in 1965 and republished the following year in Kraft's book, *Profiles in Power*. It concluded with these words: "The central fact, what I most want to say, is that Bundy is the leading candidate, perhaps the only candidate for the stateman's mantle to emerge in the generation that is coming to power—the generation which reached maturity in the war and post-war period. His capacity to read the riddle of multiple confusion, to consider a wide variety of possibilities, develop lines of action, to articulate and execute public purposes, to impart quickened energies to men of the highest abilities, seems to me unmatched. To me, anyhow, he seems almost alone among contemporaries, a figure of true consequence, a fit subject for Milton's words:

A Pillar of State; deep on his
  Front engraven
Deliberation sat, and publick care;
  And princely counsel in his face. . . ."

One reads these lines with wonder. What could have prompted Kraft to write them? The evident sincerity of the admiration is not in question. For the moment, the significant point is the lack of balance of this passage: the "good" side of Bundy, his intelligence and ability, is given here without any suggestion of his limitations or fallibility (for example, his role as one of the architects of the Vietnam war).

Kraft's treatment of Wilbur Mills was less extreme. Like most of the press, and his fellow columnists, Kraft emphasized Mills' technical virtuosity to the exclusion of all else. Within a relatively brief period in 1971 —just before Mills decided to run for president—Kraft wrote half a dozen items about Mills in the following view:

■He wrote at one point that Mills' "four-cushion shot," involving legislation on trade reform, social security benefits, national health insurance, and revenue sharing, "is an achievement on the grand scale. No other man in the country has the mix of talent, outlook, and power to bring it off. And he emerges as a major national figure, sure to dominate the shaping of new health legislation that lies at the center of political action for the next few years."

■"As Congress returns from its summer recess," he wrote on another occasion, "the man to watch is more than ever Chairman Wilbur Mills. . . ."

■"By far the most consequental boomlet in progress," he continued as Mills' presidential campaign got under way, "is the scarcely visible one going for Chairman Wilbur Mills."

Small wonder that Mills believed he was the man with the "mix of talent, outlook, and power to bring it off" at the Democratic convention.

Kraft, now, is astonished that Mills should have drawn such a conclusion: "I would have thought his talents were distinctly congressional talents," he said in our interview. Poor Mills must have missed the distinction, and must have been equally mystified and angry when, in June of 1972, Kraft finally dismissed the Mills-for-President campaign as "one more reminder of a fact of Washington life that is especially painful for those of us who have admired the Congressman from Arkansas. The fact is that even the most sagacious of Washington leaders lose their sense of proportion when bitten by the Presidential bug."

In the Connally story, as with Mills', what was missing was any counterweight to the prevailing mood of adulation—specifically, to the hoopla being put out by the White House about the new wonder-worker from

Texas. Much later, after Connally had a few economic-policy mistakes to his discredit, Kraft came down harder on him than most other columnists did. But that was not before he had welcomed him to town with this cloying praise:

"It must be understood that Connally is one of the most able and intelligent men in American politics," Kraft wrote shortly after Connally's appointment as Secretary of the Treasury. "He is a born leader, intelligent in the analysis of problems, sensitive to surroundings, full of poise and public presence, and with great force." For balance, Kraft touched on Connally's bad points: "He is also a local patriot, not to say Texas firster. And he is not free of ambition, even vanity. . . . He is in close touch with the impressive young man sure to lead the Texas delegation to the convention in 1972, Lieutenant Governor Ben Barnes."

Kraft had no way of knowing that Barnes would leave office in disgrace after the Sharpstown bank scandal, or that Connally would soon be on trial. But if his function was that of analyst rather than tout, he should have told us more. Connally's immediate background, after all, was big business in Texas, and the unmistakable motif of that background was money. From his dirt-poor upbringing in central Texas, through his $750,000 fee as executor of the Sid Richardson estate, to his service as a partner in the Houston law firm, Vinson, Elkins, Connally's career had revolved around the two poles of power and money—and Kraft mentioned only the first. When he finally got around to looking at Connally's other side, in a *New York* article published in May 1973, Kraft emphasized the money, and concluded that Connally "is a wheeler-dealer, and nothing can make him look like Caesar's wife." But how much of that cautionary advice had we previously heard from Joseph Kraft? Not a bit. Even late in 1972 he was writing about Connally in terms of unmeasured praise: "Mr. Connally, judging by a chat in Washington last week, likes action at the highest level of government. He is not unaware of the historic things he has done in his short term of service as Secretary of the Treasury. He mightily believes he can do more in the same vein—perhaps as Secretary of State. But he does not expect to hold office again. Indeed, he wants to to take himself out of the partisan zone, the better to continue distinguished service in the foremost appointive offices."

Apart from simple gullibility, which is hardly the case with Kraft, there are two explanations for his misjudgment. One has to do with technique —the challenge of turning out decent material at the columnist's grueling pace. The other concerns values—the things toward which Kraft is reverent, and those he holds in contempt. At the risk of repetition, Kraft's difficulties in these two areas are typical of his fellow columnists, and that is why they deserve close examination.

MORE DEADLINES THAN IDEAS

The first problem, that of technique, boils down to the question of how any writer can produce a fresh and thorough column three times a week. "I've considered doing a column," says Richard Reeves of *New York*. "I finally realized that a good column is essentially *an idea,* as a good magazine piece is an idea. Now, you know that most of us are lucky if we can come up with a dozen ideas a year, and that leaves a lot of columns to write."

Reeves is on to half the problem, for the time pressure causes more than a shortage of ideas. It is also responsible for the shortage of facts, since the 48 hours that separate one deadline from the next allow little time for serious research.

Over the years columnists have had one classic response to the idea shortage, and that is simple recycling. Kraft returns every few columns to his Message about the Economy (that we need a variety of remedies rather than a single quick fix), as Joseph Alsop used to return to the Decline of the West. In general, this is far less objectionable than the consequences of the fact shortage, which leaves the familiar ideas resting on thin air.

Given the unrelenting time pressure, can any writer prevent these shortages? Two "analytical columnists" have tried. Nicholas von Hoffman and William Raspberry, both based at *The Washington Post,* have been the genre's real innovators in means of gathering material. Raspberry's trick is to turn the traditional analyst's approach on its head: instead of reaching up to the secretary of state or president for a shred of evidence on which to hang a column—as Kraft and Reston do—Raspberry reaches down, to the readers in suburban Maryland who complain about police brutality or lousy schools. Von Hoffman's approach is to read, read, read, ripping through the *Monthly Review* and *Bulletin* of the Federal Reserve Bank of St. Louis in search of the fresh idea.

Sometimes von Hoffman's receptivity to unconventional ideas leads him right over the brink, and sometimes Raspberry's grass-roots columns grow as repetitious and thin as the high-level analysis of the conventional columnist. But at least these two have tried to find a way around the time constraints of the column—which is the very opposite of what one can say about Joseph Kraft. Instead of concentrating his limited resources on the column, Kraft has spread himself so unbelievably thin that he can only fail.

Apart from those three columns every single week, Kraft produces in a typical year the following: three or four substantial articles for *The New Yorker,* three or four shorter pieces for *New York,* and a handful of articles for the *Atlantic, The New York Review of Books,* and *The New York Times Magazine. The New Yorker* articles alone would be a full-time job for most writers; that Kraft can also write the column is evidence of his extraordinary productivity.

William McPherson, editor of *The Washington Post*'s Book World section, took a trip through the Middle East last fall in the wake of Kraft's tour and found that Kraft had made a great impression. One of McPherson's early stops was Beirut. There, with the *Post*'s correspondent, Jim Hoagland, he looked for an English-speaking driver to take them around the town and found one who specialized in serving visiting Americans. As they struck up a conversation, the driver was interested to learn that they were journalists. "Do you know," he said, "that the most famous journalist in America was in my car?" McPherson and Hoagland looked at each other, then asked the driver who he meant. He thought but could not remember the name. He could only remember the sound "K—" "K—." McPherson and Hoagland considered the possibilities. "Hodding Carter?" one of them asked. No, it was not Hodding Carter. They thought a moment more. "Joseph Kraft?" "Ah yes, it was Joseph Kraft. He told me himself he was the most famous journalist in America."

Shortly thereafter McPherson was in Petra, Jordan, again looking for a guide. While negotiating with one man, McPherson mentioned again that he worked for a newspaper. The man's eyes lit up. "Do you know," he said, "the most famous journalist in America was here...." This time, as it turned out, Kraft had not actually dealt with McPherson's guide. He hadn't needed a guide because he'd arrived by helicopter with King Hussein and left the same way.

A comparison of Kraft's work from these different media makes clear how he allocates his efforts. His best work invariably appears in *The New Yorker;* those who know him only from his columns would be astonished at the difference. Kraft's specialty for *The New Yorker* is foreign affairs. His recent contributions have included dispatches from both sides of the Middle East from Greece and Russia, and from the OPEC minister's meeting in Vienna. These articles do have their drawbacks; like another of *The New Yorker's* foreign correspondents, Robert Shaplen, Kraft often projects a high-road chatting-yesterday-with-the-prime-minister view of foreign affairs. Nonetheless, the articles are usually well-written, informative, and demonstrably the result of careful work.

Next down the scale are Kraft's pieces for *New York*. "Nobody at the magazine thinks the pieces are any good," says Richard Reeves. "Are they considered thin?" he was asked. "Thin is hardly the word for them. Sometimes you can tell that Kraft is making up the copy as he dictates over the phone, because he'll stumble and take a long time over the words. If someone asks him to repeat a line, he'll come up with something entirely different from what he said the first time." A more charitable view comes from editor Clay Felker, who is a devoted friend of Kraft. He too was asked

From Alexander Cockburn's "Press Clips" column in the *Village Voice:*
Under the heading "Lead of the Week," Cockburn quotes the following from Kraft: " 'Not far from the vast imperial palaces built by the Hapsburgs; hard by the Burgtheater, where the purest of all German was once supposed to be spoken; facing the ancient university where Freud once taught; diagonally across from the perfect Gothic-style twin-steepled Votivkirche, built to celebrate the Emperor Franz Josef's escape from an assassination attempt, there stands, at No. 10 Dr. Karl Lueger-Ring, an ordinary modern building of concrete and glass.'
"Who could this be but our old friend Joe Kraft again," Cockburn continues, "writing in *The New Yorker* about OPEC. Kraft is awfully above himself in this article. He meets the Secretary-General of OPEC, Dr. Khene. 'When I greeted him in French,' reports Kraft, 'he was visibly pleased.' I should say so. If a fellow said to you, 'Bonjour, Monsieur, je suis Joseph Kraft, meilleur ecrivain, homme le plus intelligent parmi tous les columnistes du monde,' you might be pleased too."

about the "thin" pieces, and replied, "I couldn't disagree more. You have to understand that many of the stories are very, very quick responses to immediate assignments—two or three days, maybe, reacting to an event. Joe Kraft has a body of information and contacts that no one else has, and so in even that amount of time he can say something no one else can."

Felker mentioned a few of the stories he considered successes—the 1973 piece debunking John Connally, another about the "real reason" behind the firing of Archibald Cox—and concluded, "I feel very strongly that what he does for us is better than his columns." With that judgment, unfortunately, we must agree.

One can sympathize with the predicament that leads him to slight his column. If Kraft has power and prominence these days, he has earned them by himself, for he is a purely independent entrepreneur, without even the institutional security of a columnist on the staff of the *Times* or the *Post.* He has earned something rarer as well—the privilege of a personal platform; and if, to preserve that privilege, he feels he must visit the editors of small-town papers or pay court to big-city publishers, it would be hard to fault him for it. His outside articles are sensible for him not only because they are lucrative (Kraft says that his income from all sources is "in six figures," but his expenses are also high), but also because, by adding to his celebrity, they help him sell the column.

But sympathy only goes so far, when it becomes clear that Kraft's efforts to protect his column have destroyed its very quality. The contrast between Kraft's magazine articles and his columns is not quite as dramatic as in the case of Gary Wills, who writes brilliant long essays while turning out one of the sloppiest columns in the business. But the efforts Kraft would be embarrassed to show William Shawn or even Clay Felker are served up readily on the op-ed page. As proof, I invite any reader to compare the series of columns Kraft wrote on his long foreign tour last fall with the two recent *New Yorker* pieces that grew out of the same trip. *The New Yorker* articles are informative, if idiosyncratic: "Even the wily Odysseus, with the help of the prototypical trio—the faithful wife, Penelope; the dutiful son, Telemachus; and the original Jeeves, Eumaeus—did not manage his return to power more smoothly than has the veteran Democratic politician Konstantine Karamanlis," was the lead of his Greek piece. Cf. Kraft's 1974 column on Cyprus beginning, "Odysseus at his wiliest couldn't have put together a more clever ending than the outcome which now emerges from the Cyprus conflict."

The columns, on the other hand, included some of Kraft's thinnest efforts in recent memory. Most notable was his account of a dinner party with Melina Mercouri.

The Mercouri column is significant, for it illustrates one classic time-saving device columnists so often fall back on. Lacking the time for genuine inquiry and analysis, especially when traveling abroad, Kraft and his fellow columnists often "report" by arranging cameo appearances—interviews with famous personages whose simple presence justifies the column even though no new information is transferred. Most of Kraft's subjects are more plausibly significant than Mercouri—King Hussein, the Shah, etc. —and so the ploy is less readily apparent.

This and the columnists' other time-saving devices have serious consequences, one of which is illustrated by a scene from Kraft's latest foreign tour. Kraft was in the anteroom of the Greek prime minister's office awaiting his interview. The prime minister was delayed, and as the time went by it became clear that Kraft was not the only one waiting for the promised interview. Another journalist was there as well, and in an effort to provide the greatest good for the greatest number, the prime minister's aide finally said, "Well, gentlemen, I'm afraid you'll have to see the prime minister together." At that Kraft leaped up and said, "I'm Joseph Kraft, and I'm accustomed to seeing people on time! And when I see them, I'm accustomed to seeing them alone!"

OLD FAITHFUL

The scene in the prime minister's office is a grotesque parable for one consequence of the all-star system of column-writing. Because Kraft and his colleagues are counting so heavily on the cameo appearance by the political star, they become desperate if these contacts are threatened. In the long run, they learn to avoid situations where any remote threat exists —where their phone calls would be ignored and their access cut off. The result is what the economists would call a "risk averse" philosophy among the columnists.

If a reporter like Seymour Hersh is the wildcat driller of the journalism business, willing to risk (at the *Times'* expense) 20 dry holes in search of one gusher, then columnists like Kraft are Mobil Oil. Their success depends not on the high-quality surprise find, but on a steady, predictable flow. More than other journalists, they must be able to expect that their calls will be returned, their lunches productive. This necessity can affect not only the topics they select but also the way they choose to write about them.

The point was never more bluntly expressed than by Kraft himself, in his *New York* article about Connally. "As I had known John Connally," he said, "and written favorably of him as Governor of Texas and Secretary of the Treasury, I thought there would be little difficulty in arranging an appointment." Kraft is not saying he deliberately flattered Connally in order to get an appointment, but the connection between writing "favorably" about a public figure and having easy access to him, cannot be lost on men as perceptive as John Connally or Joseph Kraft.

The ill harvest of this time-saving device, the concentration on governmental all-stars, involves something more than overly charitable treatment for types like Connally. The danger, more simply, is that so much attention, charitable or otherwise, lies in focusing on the Connallys of the world and so little on the subtler, or more fundamental forces which shape public affairs. Drawn by their time constraints toward the easily visible public figures, the columnists become the printed press' version of the TV news. The world they present is one of Fords, Kissingers, and Connallys, an ascendant one in which bureaucratic, economic, even historic forces play little part. Some columnists may actually believe this is the way the world works. Nicholas von Hoffman is an exception and has put it: "If you really believe that it makes a difference whether Mr. Simon is in or out at the White House, then you spend a lot of time talking to him and his friends. A lot of people do seem to believe that Mr. Simon makes a difference. But if it is your profound conviction that when Mr. Simon goes, he will be replaced by another Mr. Simon, then you look someplace else for ideas about the economy."

Kraft's problem is not any such a naive belief in appearances; Kraft knows that there is more to government than the whims of the political all-stars. In his book, *Profiles in Power,* he takes great pains to describe the complexities of public life and the constraints on apparent power. But all too rarely do these distinctions appear in his column, and the most obvious explanation is the pressure of space and time. Specifically, by neglecting to tell his readers about the hidden dimension in public affairs—the part which depends on rules of bureaucratic behavior, and which often contradicts the superficial logic of a situation—Kraft has overlooked three of the most important developments of recent years.

1. Amid his reports from the war zone and his ceaseless broadsides against Lyndon Johnson's war policies, Kraft in no way indicated how great the struggle was within the Administration, especially during the time between the Tet offensive of 1968 and the beginning of the Nixon presidency. Temporarily, at least, Clark Clifford and his allies turned the war policy around, and the story of their successes and failures might have helped explain the part of the war neither the hard-liners nor the antiwar forces seemed to understand—the non-ideological, bureaucratic forces that sustained it. Kraft's omission is the more tragic because he *did* understand. He revealed just how well he understood that bureaucratic culture when, in the summer of 1971, he began arguing that the Pentagon Papers were misleading and inconsequential. To judge by the Papers, Kraft said, one would conclude that Robert McNamara's assistant, John McNaughton, was the intransigent hawk, whereas anyone who knew McNaughton understood that he was playing a delicate bureaucratic game. His personal conviction had turned against the war, but he saved those arguments for McNamara alone, meanwhile protecting his bureaucratic position by sounding like a tough, determined member of the team whenever he had to commit his views to paper. Kraft was exactly right about McNaughton —but had never mentioned it before, not even after McNaughton's death in a plane crash in 1967, when the need to protect his confidence presumably ended.

2. Neither during Nixon's four years of the war did Kraft explore one of the most troubling questions of all. Why those wonderful dove senators never got around to voting for a strong antiwar bill. He made no attempt to understand what their fears were and how those fears might be set to rest.

3. While his first column after the Watergate burglary was more perceptive than most, up until that time, Kraft, with all his high-level contacts, had provided no insight about the palace guard structure of the Nixon White House. In this, unfortunately, he was typical not only of other columnists, but of the press in general.

By this over-commitment, then, Kraft has painted himself into a corner where only a limited number of topics are within reach and from which he must project a view of politics he himself knows to be false. He is not alone in his corner, but that is small consolation to the reader as he scans the op-ed page.

CULT OF RESPONSIBILITY

Yet there is something more than haste at the root of Joseph Kraft's difficulties, something sure to affect his least hurried work. To explore what it is we must enter the realm of speculation and examine the beliefs which undergird Kraft's writing. One word will emerge as the key to his attitudes and to those of his peers. The word is "responsibility," and it requires careful definition.

One way to begin the definition is to consider the words other than "responsibility" that come to an outsider's mind when thinking about Kraft, Reston, Alsop and the rest. The first word might be "reverence"—reverence for the established institutions of government and society, and for the people who control them. Nicholas von Hoffman clarifies by contrast, for he is utterly irreverent of leaders and organizations. A second word might be "loyalty"—the sense so many columnists project that they will be dealing with the same cast of governmental characters tomorrow and next year, and that they will not carelessly abuse the privilege. A third word, connected to the previous two, is "elitism": the understanding that a certain class of people is better equipped than most to deal with the problems of the world, and that—happy fortune—most men who have power deserve it. A final word is "respectability"—the columnists' reluctance to take either the outrageous or the embarrassing position, and their consequent overcaution. Again, von Hoffman is the illuminating exception, for he is the one columnist willing to embarrass himself in his search for new ideas.

Following the example of Walter Lippmann, Joseph Kraft does not hesitate to apply the term "elitist" to himself; but probably neither he nor his colleagues would accept the foregoing outsider's description of them as accurate. If forced to choose a single word to describe themselves, the word would most likely be "responsible." As Kraft put it during our interview, "I think the column is distinguished from the rest of the press by its sense of intellectual responsibility. You know, the press as a whole suffers terribly from intellectual irresponsibility, perhaps because it's always part of the opposition. You can say of a few columnists—not all of them, but a few, such as Joseph Alsop, with whom I have profound disagreements—you can say that at least they are willing to take responsibility for the consequences of their ideas."

To people like Kraft, this kind of "responsibility" implies a hard-headed acceptance of the complexity of things, a mature understanding that the easy answers are almost never the right ones. Their outlook is akin to that "responsibility" of the young lawyer who decides, after four years of talk about "the public interest," to join the large private firm. He knows all too well that his friends will over-simplify his motives. He is sadly aware that their condemnation will be automatic and facile. He wishes he could communicate to his friends the excitement and importance of playing hardball on the inside of an immensely complex and powerful world, of being tested against the best. But he is resigned, finally and tragically, to the impossibility of such communication and the necessity of living with misguided censure. In that resignation he makes it easier for himself to avoid the more serious questions about his new life.

There is a secret shared between that lawyer, the "responsible" columnist, and the men who make the tough decisions in the White House and the Senate. They all know that the public will call for unbroken eggs and omelets too, that it will not be grateful to those who shoulder its burdens. They understand *Coriolanus* too well.

Living within this world, the responsible columnist comes to respect its noblemen, the class of public servant exemplified by Acheson, McCloy, Bundy, and Kissinger. Respecting them, he seeks their respect in return. Reston and Alsop sit in the Metropolitan Club, sipping drinks and exchanging views with the leaders, placed among heavyweights as equals. This physical contact is only the most obvious manifestation of the quest for mutual respect. Similar feelings affect the spirit of those columnists who consider the Metropolitan Club a waste of time but who aim their most important work not at the public but at these, their responsible peers in government. These responsible leaders would be disappointed and shocked if Joe Kraft or Scotty Reston leaked a document which rudely upset the policymakers' applecart—as Jack Anderson and Seymour Hersh have several times done. They would be disappointed, too, if Kraft or Reston publicly attacked a Kissinger or a Bundy, knowing he was doing his best. As Kraft explained about Kissinger in the fall of 1974, "Anybody who attacked him was running the risk of playing into the hands of hardliners. A good many of us accepted that line and pulled punches."

As this quote suggests, a large element of "responsibility" is trust—the deep-seated confidence that the Kissingers and Bundys will do the right thing. This is a significant element, because it helps explain the difference between several of the most skilled analytical columnists. In terms of ability and energy, five analysts are a clear cut above their peers: Kraft, Reston, George Will, Wicker, and Lewis—but only the first three are "responsible" in the sense just described. The simplest way to state the difference is that Wicker and Lewis have lost their sense of trust. Ten years ago, most of them were fully as reverent, fully as "responsible" as the Kraft-Reston mainstream; Lewis' treatment of Abe Fortas and the justices of the Supreme Court in *Gideon's Trumpet* is a reminder of that fact. The trust is there no longer because of what happened in the intervening years —Wicker's experience at Attica and Lewis' with the war. A core of bitterness and mistrust has crept in and dissolved the strands of responsibility that still bind their peers.

This "responsibility" has a good side, and that is its resistance to the mushy thinking of the left. "There is a certain kind of liberal," George Will has said, "who thinks that because Richard Nixon was guilty, Alger Hiss must have been innocent." Joseph Kraft would never be that kind of liberal. He was raised in a generation acutely aware of the dangers of mindless, emotional leftism. During those post-war years at Columbia, Kraft and his contemporaries needed only to look back to the 1930s, to

Clifford Odets and the rhapsodic, *Mission to Moscow*-type visions of kindly Uncle Joe Stalin, to realize how large a dose of intellectual rigor the nation's liberal needed. Kraft took courses under Lionel Trilling during those years, and one of the highest accolades Trilling could give was "tough." In the preface to *The Liberal Imagination,* Trilling elaborated on the kind of toughness he called for: "It has for some time seemed to me that a criticism which has at heart the interest of liberalism might find its most useful work not in confirming liberalism in its sense of general righteousness but rather in putting under some degree of pressure the liberal ideas and assumptions of the times."

SUCKERED BY THE RIGHT

This is the credo under which Kraft operates, and it is the best thing about his "responsible" generation. Kraft did put the Great Society "under some degree of pressure" when others did not; he did understand the terrifying implications of the Weathermen and the Black Panthers; he has seen, within the last few months, that the reaction provoked by the CIA scandals is often too simplistic. He has seen that it's wrong to condemn all forms of secrecy and every request for foreign intelligence, because he knows that in certain cases secrecy and intelligence may be essential.

But even to mention these CIA columns immediately shifts our attention to the bad side of "responsibility"—that it can turn intelligent men into uncritical suckers for the mushy thinking of the respectable center and right.

It is disappointing, but no great surprise, when a "conservative" like George Will falls for the right's old slogans—as Will has done, for example, in saying that liberals shouldn't complain about corporate tax loopholes because they were originally enacted by Democratic Congresses. It is surprising, and equally disappointing, when it happens to Kraft. Its most recent occurence has been his columns on the CIA; for while picking the proper holes in the emotional case against the agency, Kraft has bought every bit of the mindless conventional "security" pitch coming from the other side. He has been absolutely insensitive to the valid complaints about duplicity and secrecy in our foreign relations, as he was the last time these issues came to the fore. That was late in 1971, when Jack Anderson published the "India-Pakistan Papers." These, the edited transcripts of a National Security Council meeting, showed that Henry Kissinger had been lying about American policy on the subcontinent war. Their significance was that foreign policy was being made in the dark. Neither the Congress nor the public knew that we were deciding to support one side over the other, so neither had a chance to advise, acquiesce, or complain. Kraft seemed incapable of understanding this point, directing his outrage instead at the tastelessness of the leak. His comments are worth quoting at some length for the insight they provide into the "responsible" frame of mind:

"Seen thus starkly, Kissinger told a flat lie . . . But so what? Does the new evidence do more than confirm a universal judgment? After the U-2 and the Bay of Pigs and the credibility gap, is there anybody not impossibly naive or ill-informed who doesn't know that the government lies? Is one more bit of evidence a noble act? Or is it just a pebble added to the Alps? . . .

"There is every reason to figure bureaucratic rivalry as the key element in the background of the Anderson papers. There is no case for lionizing or even protecting the sources of the leak. On the contrary, for once there is a case for a presidential crackdown. Mr. Nixon's interest—and that of the country as a whole—is to find the sources of the leak and fire them fast."

In these columns, Kraft understood a partial truth—that the breach of security would drive the Nixon Administation deeper into its shell of secrecy—but he let that blind him to the larger issues. He even let it force him to the gracelessness of his "pebble added to the Alps" line, which implied that readers of his own column had been informed about government lying.

LOVES AND HATES

In his "responsible" myopia, Kraft embodies in particularly dramatic form an attitude which has spread into so many corners of our national culture. That attitude is the reverence for tough, skillful, professionalism, without regard to its results. Its most pronounced traits are its celebration of the proficient, unemotional, professional, be he lawyer, soldier, or diplomat and its corresponding contempt for the fuzzy-headed amateur, even when this sloppy fellow has something more important to say. Its effect on Kraft may be most clearly demonstrated by comparing the three objects of his most sincere respect—McGeorge Bundy, Henry Kissinger, and William Rehnquist—with three whom he utterly disdains—Daniel Ellsberg, Jack Anderson, and Allen Ginsberg.

Kraft's attitude toward Rehnquist was summed up in a column entitled, "Rehnquist: Top Mind," which endorsed him for the Supreme Court: "What the court needs is more brains. Mr. Rehnquist has them—more abundantly, perhaps, than any present member. And by uplifting the quality of the court in general, he will do far more than any particular decisions in any particular cases can do to enhance the values thoughtful men hold dear." His feelings about Bundy are already on the record. While he has not written about Kissinger in the same Miltonesque terms, one suspects that he would have, had he not already used them on Bundy.

Personal motivation is always more complicated than the outsider can readily apprehend, and so one hesitates to step onto this uncertain ground. Yet as one tries to understand how so many able men have been led down the same path, it is hard not to be struck by the apparent connection between "responsible" professionalism and the writer's social standing.

This is not a question of "social climbing," in its crass sense, but rather of elevation to a higher social plane, a more distinguished cast of associates. Tom Wicker provides one example in his new book, *A Time to Die:*

"The luncheon of the Bill Fay Club on Friday, September 10, 1971, was a gregarious affair as usual. The scene of the feast was the executive dining room of the National Geographic Society, in the Society's elegant building on Seventeenth Street Northwest, a few blocks from Lafayette Square and the White House. Members had sipped sherry in the office of Franc Shor, a Geographic editor, then moved into the dining room for lamb chops and an excellent wine. . . .

"Around Shor at the long table high above Seventeenth Street were Ambassador Frank Corner of New Zealand; Ambassador Egidio Ortona of Italy; A. Doak Barnett, the China specialist (a visitor that day); J. Carter Brown, the director of the National Gallery of Art; John Walker, Brown's immediate predecessor; William McChesney Martin, the former chairman of the Federal Reserve Board; Herman Wouk, the novelist; Richard Scammon, the political analyst and statistician; Edward P. Morgan, the radio and television commentator; and Tom Wicker, political columnist and associate editor of *The New York Times.* Former Secretary of Defense Clark Clifford and Herbert Block—*The Washington Post*'s famous Herblock, as gentle in person as ascerbic in ink—were frequently at the club table, but were not present that day.

"These were erudite men, in everything from art to politics, as Tom Wicker had come to know. He always studied Franc Shor's wine choices with care, and was perennially surprised to find himself able to hold up his end of the conversation, and even on occasion to bring the table to his own point of view. But much of his life had been a surprise to him; and it was not only in the executive dining room of the Geographic that he sometimes had a vivid sense of having come a long, long way."

To take Kraft as another example, he is undeniably aware of the minute gradations of the social hierarchy. According to acquaintances, when Kraft and his wife hold a Christmas party, they hold two—one for the true elite and another for the rest of the people Kraft has worked with during the year. It is said that the first time Kraft met the British writer, Godfrey Hodgson, he told him, "You remind me of one of those English boys who wishes he had gone to Winchester and Magdalen"—

which was exactly where Hodgson had gone. And there is the house in the Hamptons.

With antennae this acute, can Kraft have overlooked the class implications of his own story: raised on Central Park West, the son of a reasonably affluent Jewish textile manufacturer, sent first to the Fieldston School, then to Columbia, then to Princeton, then on to the most WASP-ish sort of social respectability on the circuits of Washington, New York, and abroad. Talent undoubtedly played a large part in this rise, and Kraft himself may consider the social element to be insignificantly small, but when stacked up against the similar rises of so many other columnists, it may help provide one insight into the origins of responsibility.

Whatever superficial differences may separate them, these three men are the quintessence of hard-minded professionalism—and that is what Kraft has so enthusiastically celebrated. In doing so he has been blind to the dark side of professionalism—Bundy's role in the war, for example, or Rehnquist's decisions at the Justice Department. Only in Kissinger's case, in the critical columns he began writing after he found out he had been bugged, has Kraft shown the slightest awareness that men as intelligent as these might make mistakes. The complaint against Kraft is not that he failed to denounce these men, for each of them has his good side, but that his uncritical respect for position and power has deprived him of his critical standards.

Under opposite circumstances, when dealing with those he detests, Kraft is similarly blind—this time, to the good his enemies can do. When Ellsberg leaked the Pentagon Papers, Kraft's hatred of the act made him ridicule the man: "To a divorced man living in the semi-bohemian atmosphere of a Malibu beach house with a flashy sports car and an off-again on-again romance that eventually culminated in marriage, the themes of duty and guilt were heavy stuff." He contemptuously dismissed Anderson as a low-brow, unfit for the nuance of foreign policy: "He is not deeply versed in foreign affairs. No one who aims to change a line of international policy would single out Mr. Anderson for deflecting that result through the leak of secret information." To friends he has denounced Ginsberg as a "charlatan."

No doubt there is a bit of truth in what he says, for none of these three men is perfect. But it is equally beyond doubt that the three of them have seen things Kraft has failed to see. These contributions, Kraft refuses to acknowledge. In Ellsberg's case, Kraft wrote off the Pentagon Papers as "the non-event of the year." They were wholly uninformative, he said, since everyone had heard the same stories years ago. But of course they were informative, enormously so, for a reason no man as intelligent as

Kraft could fail to understand—that it is one thing to speculate about how the government reaches its decisions, and something altogether different to have the evidence laid out on paper. Similarly, with Anderson Kraft could not bring himself to admit that there was a shred of value to the India-Pakistan disclosure.

The third pariah, Ginsberg, was even farther from the frontier of "responsibility" than Anderson, or Ellsberg; but as the intellectual father of the counter-culture, he was perhaps more far-sighted than the others in helping us glimpse fundamental truths about our society. These same truths the "responsible" analysts chose to ignore. To give only the most obvious illustration, Kraft and his colleagues utterly failed to understand the role that machismo has played in this nation's affairs, especially in the shaping of the Vietnam war. Nor have they grasped that the sexual revolution has helped unseat that mystique. Because ideas like this sounded loony when coming from Ginsberg, Kraft refused to touch them.

In one of his own analyses of the Washington press, published in 1966, Kraft concluded that "the central requirement is that the press and TV find and promote more intelligent and better-trained people.... We need, as Meredith once put it, 'More brain, O Lord, more brain.'" As applied to the columnists, this prescription is flawed. Kraft does have the brains; that is not his problem, or the columnists' in general. What he lacks is the time to devote himself properly to his columns, without cutting corners and without driving himself at the same frantic pace that gave him his first heart attack long before he was 50. While Kraft's overcommitment is unusual, nearly all of his colleagues are prisoners of the same time trap. The best way to free them might be to follow the example of *The New York Times'* op-ed page, which prints outside contributions only when the writer has something to say. None of these outsiders is expected to produce three times a week, and neither should the columnists. If the columnists were cut back to writing on a once-a-week basis, both they and their readers would benefit by the change.

Rather than extra brains, Kraft needs to give his intelligence free rein by removing the blinders of "responsibility" which now so restrict his view. In this, too, Kraft is the symbol of his colleagues' predicament. By his ability and his drive, Kraft has made himself probably the best of the columnists' whole bunch, but that is primarily an indication of how much more they all have to do.

What's Wrong
With Political Science

Michael Nelson

I don't know how many times I've had this conversation.

"I'm a grad student in political science," I'd tell people foolish enough to ask.

"Oh, mm-hmm. That must be very interesting. What does one do with a degree in, uh, political science?"

"I plan to hang out a shingle. You know: 'Michael Nelson. Political Scientist. By Appointment Only.'"

"Hang out a—? Oh, I get it, very funny. No really, what does one do with a—"

"One teaches."

That is about the extent of what a political scientist can do with all his years of advanced and specialized training: teach undergraduates who are, I suppose, hoping to learn how to read the newspaper a bit more intelligently, and teach the graduate students who will someday take his place. The "real world" places almost no value, financial or aesthetic, on the training we political scientists receive. And the academic well is about dry: by the early 1980s, the American Political Science Association (APSA) reports, there will be no new faculty positions in political science.

"If a political scientist comes to Washington and waves his sheepskin," says Thomas Mann of APSA, "he'll get his ass kicked. People in government, in business, in the media, and so on have no expectations of us at all. In fact, some employers have to be convinced that a political scientist isn't overly handicapped by what he learned in graduate school."

Michael Nelson is a contributing editor of *The Washington Monthly* and teaches political science at Vanderbilt University.

Maybe I'm crazy, but this bothers me. You would think, wouldn't you, that newspapers (which report on government), businesses (which are vitally affected by what government does to and for them), and the government itself would have some interest in the services of highly educated people who study government for a living. You would think, to be crassly material, that the market would be willing to pay such people for their services.

After all, other social sciences are valued in the marketplace. Nearly half of America's psychologists and economists actually practice their professions. A psychologist can hang out a shingle and reasonably expect that people will come knocking at his door. *Psychology Today* sells half a million copies every month; "pop" psychology books like *I'm OK, You're OK* frequently crowd the best-seller lists. The bearer of a Ph.D. in economics may not get on the Council of Economic Advisers or *Time's* Board of Economists, but he can take some comfort in knowing that these things exist as he chooses from a range of high-paying careers in business and government.

Even sociologists and anthropologists do better. While we in the political science department at Johns Hopkins walked around on linoleum floors and sat in creaky chairs supplied by the university, the sociologists upstairs enjoyed wall-to-wall carpeting and plush conference rooms, paid for out of the grants they were continually receiving to study this or that. Sociologists get six times per capita what political scientists get in research money from the federal government; anthropologists four times; economists eleven times.

I won't belabor the comparison. Suffice it to say that there is no *Political Science Today* magazine, no Council of Political Science Advisers. When Watergate (a purely political crisis if there ever was one) exploded the world turned not to us but to lawyers and historians to find out what had gone wrong. The National Science Foundation "had to be bludgeoned into accepting political science as a legitimate social science," according to an APSA report. The Civil Service Commission recognizes anthropologists, economists, et al. as distinct occupational categories, but—you guessed it —not political scientists. Thomas Mann reports that "even when political scientists get jobs outside the classroom, they turn their backs on us. They say 'political science doesn't tell me anything; it's obscure, it's outdated, it's unintelligible.' In fact, they would be no more inclined to hire a political scientist than anybody else."

But economists, psychologists, and the rest actually seem to thrive on the incomprehensibility of what they say and do. People who look at our journals and sneer at the jargon and statistics look at an equally baffling economics journal, slacken their jaws, and hire an economist to translate for them. "It's like the scene in Moliere," a fellow-sufferer told me, "where the guy asks the doctor why opium makes you sleep and the doctor says it's because of opium's soporific power. If a political scientist said something like that they'd laugh; if an economist or a psychologist said it they'd give him a grant."

FORWARD THROUGH THE CENTURIES

None of this brings us any closer to an answer. In truth, the only place we are likely to find out why political science is so little valued is in this history I am about to tell.

You may well suppose that you are about to be taken back to the ancient Greece of Aristotle and Plato, guided about, and led triumphantly forward through centuries of Augustine, Locke, Rousseau, Jefferson, and the other distinguished political thinkers of history. You are not. Modern political scientists don't claim kin with the likes of them. When Albert Somit and Joseph Tanenhaus wrote their semi-official history, *The Development of Political Science,* they said, "We deliberately limited our attention to those aspects of the past which bear directly on the present 'state of discipline.' " That took them back not to Plato's cave but to New York in 1880.

This may seem strange (in the same way that not claiming legitimate royal ancestry would seem strange), but it provides a handy excuse when you ask a political scientist why nobody is buying or listening to what his profession has to say. "You've got to remember," Austin Ranney, a political scientist with a Washington think tank, the American Enterprise Institute (and thus a bit of an exception himself) told me, "that we're a very young discipline, less than a hundred years old. Modern economics and the others go back a century or more before that. They had a head start."

The story begins, then, just before the turn of the century, at a time when there was hardly any "modern" political science worth talking about. But this was the heyday of the professional, and every trade from barbers on up was caught up in the rush to organize itself. By 1903, the historians, economists, and sociologists had formed associations, so those few scholars who were chiefly interested in the goings-on of governments figured they had better get on the bandwagon too. The American Political Science Association was created, its rather vague purpose being to "do for political science what the American Economic and American Historical Associations are doing for economics and history," according to one of its founding fathers.

There was just one problem: because political scientists abandoned their own philosophical heritage for the sake of aping their colleagues, it was now hard to find two of them who agreed on what their newly professionalized discipline was. Was it contemporary history, as some argued, or political economy, or political sociology, or law, or what? An English historian named Morse Stephens complained that after two frustrating years in the United States, he had been unable to find anyone who could explain to him what this political science was supposed to be.

Unfortunately, things went downhill from there. If, as Shaw said in *The Doctor's Dilemma,* "all professions are conspiracies against the laity," political science at the age of 21 was clearly a failed one. Though APSA had tried to establish all the trappings of a profession—journal, conventions, and so on—by 1924, only a handful of colleges recognized political science as meriting a department of its own; the rest lumped it in with history or something. Further, political science was becoming an intellectual desert; the typical scholarly *oeuvre* consisted of sleep-inducing, legalistic descriptions of the formal institutions of government.

'MAKE X HAPPEN'

What made political science's failure even worse was the success that its sister social sciences were enjoying. They advanced because they *built* on their philosophical foundations rather than abandoning them. After a century or more of Adam Smith, David Ricardo, Karl Marx, and several others—people who had thought about the great economic questions at their most profound, theoretical level—economics produced its Keynes, a doer who could take this knowledge and show how the economy could be not only understood, but directed. At about the same time, psychology turned up its Freud and sociology its own somewhat lesser lights, Weber and Durkheim. What distinguished the theories of this new generation was that when people outside academics came to the professors who had mastered them and said, "Make X happen," the social scientists could tell them which knobs to turn—and sometimes X happened.

They weren't always right, of course, but they were right just often enough so that people began to believe that theirs were true sciences. At that point, they were free to get as statistical and obscure to the layman as they wanted. Which they did, cognizant perhaps that the hooey just made them seem all the more scientific. In fact, as the mental, social, and economic health of the nation worsened, one could always count on an increase in the number of psychologists, sociologists, and economists hired. That's success.

But this didn't help political science any as it sat home on APSA's 21st birthday, all dressed up and no place to go. Having rushed to imitate its fellows by professionalizing, it now found itself a profession without a clientele. The feeling was strong that something had to be done to make the rest of the world sit up and take notice; not surprisingly, two very different schools of thought emerged on what that something ought to be.

Professor Thomas Reed led one of them. It was Reed's ambition to transform political science from an enterprise of dry and largely unread description to an instrument of "education for democratic citizenship:" political science would see to it that both citizens and public officials were thoroughly trained to exercise their powers and meet their responsibilities. Reed briefly managed to grab control of APSA; he also turned up $75,000 in Carnegie Corporation money, which financed a lot of conferences and the like.

But Reed's vision was not nearly so bold, nor his foundation resources so vast, as those of Professor Charles Merriam of the University of Chicago. In 1924, Merriam was 50 years old, a vibrant, articulate scholar-politician. Seeing how well the other social sciences were doing with their jargon and models, he trumpeted a new, "behavioral" approach to the study of politics that would be as scientific as the rest of them. Its methods would be statistical and technical, its avowed purpose to discover the basic laws of political behavior. So eager were many of the political scientists of that and succeeding generations to get once again on the economists' and psychologists' bandwagons—to follow their colleagues in hope of sharing in their prestige—that they rallied enthusiastically to Merriam's call. But in their eagerness they ignored a central point: scientific methods enable one only to test theories, not to create them; theories are born of those long years of "unscientific" stewing and pondering that political science, unlike the other social sciences, had never gone through.

Still, Merriam had another selling point that was, if anything, even more compelling than his vision: millions of dollars in Laura Spelman Rockefeller Fund money for his newly created Social Science Research Council (SSRC). Beardsley Ruml, the Fund's director, was a young alumnus of the University of Chicago who had admired Merriam greatly and later became his close personal friend.

To political scientists, particularly during the depression years that followed, those dollars were virtually all the research money there was to be had. Scholars who hoped to receive grants soon saw the advantages in doing behavioral studies; universities found that by setting up independent political science departments they could lure some of the money their way. Clearly the Merriam wing was holding all the cards: status, professional envy, and money.

'CONVERSIONS TO THE FAITH'

Propelled by the proliferation of computing devices, European intellectual currents, and the general ascendancy of science, the behavioral tide surged even stronger after World War II. Soon the Ford Foundation was pouring in all sorts of money to fund behavioral research in the social sciences; "[w]idespread knowledge of this situation," Somit and Tanenhaus note in their history, "did not adversely affect conversions to the faith."

Merriam's intellectual heirs eventually began to think him a bit antiquated, for Merriam had been personally active in politics outside the classroom and saw no conflict between his avocation and his scientific studies of the subject. But the new behavioralists eschewed personal value judgments on the grounds that morals clouded understanding; through their logic, politics took a back seat to science. It got to the point where one could pick up the current issue of the *American Political Science Review* and come away blissfully ignorant of all the burning political questions of the day. When Hubert Humphrey, a one-time doctoral candidate in political science, among other things, let it be known in 1969 that he might like to teach at the University of Minnesota, the highly behavioral department there rebelled—after all, what did Hubert Humphrey know about modern political science?

Perhaps nothing illustrates the barrenness of the behavioral movement —its sacrifice of concern for learning how the system really works for the sake of intricate statistical models—better than the University of Michigan's Center for Political Studies. As wealthy Midwesterners once sent their daughters East for finishing, so graduate departments now pack off their progeny to Michigan each summer to learn the latest in statistics and modeling. In a sense, it is the mecca of modern political science.

Michigan's flagship has been its election studies series. Back in the dark, pre-behavioral days, students of politics used to approach elections primitively, by exploring questions like these: What is their role in a democracy? What effects do they have on what the government does? Are elections a good or bad thing? The first contribution of the Michigan people was to take the most trivial of all these questions—How do people decide who to vote for?—and study the hell out of it. Why concentrate on that? Because once one has decided to quantify, one can study only that which is quantifiable.

From election to election, ever more powerful statistical techniques were brought to bear by the Michiganders, awesome and complex models developed and refined to recreate the voter's psyche. This produced the remarkable insight that voters make up their minds through some blend of their party affiliation, their opinions on the issues, and their appraisals of the candidates—the nature of the blend is still hotly contested.

One is impressed, in reading the collected works of three decades of Michigan and other behavioral researchers, with both the dullness of their questions and the poverty of their answers. Herbert Kaufman, a political scientist at the Brookings Institution who *is* listened to by many people outside academe, concedes that "what I know directly from modern political science you could write on the back of a matchbook cover. And what's worse is that we've got a Gresham's Law of our own: for the sake of keeping up with all this current stuff that has little or nothing to say, our students stop reading the ancient political philosophers, who had plenty to say."

WE'LL GO KNOCKING ON THEIRS

The latest fad to sweep political science is equally unpromising. Variously called "policy studies," "policy analysis," and "policy science," and a host of other names, it rests on the premise that if business and government will not beat a path to our door, we will just have to go knocking on theirs with an offer to, uh, analyze their policies for them. (It's about that vague. Kaufman describes policy analysis as "plain old public administration with a couple of economics courses thrown in.") Thus the cover of the new *Policy Studies Journal* shows two little boxes, one each for "Academic Political Science" and "Government Practitioners." Thick arrows go back and forth from one box to the other—"we need them," the drawing suggests, "but they need us just as much," a notion that will undoubtedly come as news to "government practitioners." Apparently it is not enough to look silly; now, like camp followers whose idols keep forgetting their names, we are to be pathetic as well.

There are, of course, exceptions—political scientists who have managed to reach out to a larger audience. Jimmy Carter said James David Barber's *The Presidential Character* was the best book on the presidency he had read; Doris Kearns wrote a best-selling psychohistory of Lyndon Johnson; James MacGregor Burns writes widely read biographies and essays, as did the late Clinton Rossiter. These are exceptions, however, that prove the rule: Barber and Kearns rooted their research not in the methods of political science but in the substance of psychology; Burns and Rossiter based theirs in history.

There is also an entire wing of the political science profession that is listened to: Henry Kissinger and Zbigniew Brzezinski are ample proof of the influence of international relations scholars. But they too are exceptions that affirm the rule, for their historical, non-quantitative research methods leave them in a quite different field from their behavioral brethren. When I asked Evron Kirkpatrick, executive director of APSA, whether anyone listens to political scientists, he thought about it for a couple of days, then triumphantly showed me a half-dozen dusty old reports that his colleagues had had some hand in writing. He never thought to mention Kissinger or Brzezinski.

RUSHING TO IMITATE

So here we are after almost a century of trying to keep up with the Joneses, as ignored and unvalued as ever. In light of political science's history, the problem seems clear enough: over the years we have spent most of our energy rushing to imitate our sister social sciences' methods of finding answers, conveniently fooling ourselves into forgetting that they have something we lack—a rich legacy of provocative questions, born of long years of purposeful thinking. As a result, says George F. Will, the political scientist-turned-journalist, "other social sciences deal with matters of substance. When they look at a question, it's more likely to be a question whose answer a layman might want to hear. When political scientists look at questions, I'm struck by the synthetic nature of their concerns. They shape the questions to fit their models and methods, not the other way around, and they get answers that either no one is interested in or that are perfectly obvious."

Will, who took his doctorate at Princeton and then taught for a while, went on to suggest that "we should take all the political philosophers and send them off to the philosophy departments, send the political sociologists to sociology, the political historians to history, and so on. Then turn the abandoned political science offices into squash courts."

Fortunately, things have not gotten that bad: in fact, we still have our best option left. It is not, however, an easy option, for it requires us to go back several decades to the prebehavioral days, bury our mistakes, and take the fork in the road we bypassed then.

That fork, of course, leads to a political science dedicated to education for democratic citizenship, to "better minds for better government" in Thomas Reed's phrase. People on all rungs of the social ladder are more intimately affected by government today than ever before; in my research, I have found that they sense, and resent, the weight of bureaucratic regulation bearing down heavily on them in their personal lives. They still believe in the basic goodness of the system, but feel powerless to make unelected bureaucrats and distant legislators respond to their needs instead of the other way around. The pollyanna-like civics training most people got in school, which probably did not even mention bureaucracy, political parties, pressure groups, mass media, and other components of real-world politics, left them no better informed.

Political science's contribution to the American people could be to help them remedy this frustration, to teach them how their system really works and how they can make it work for them. Clearly our first task, though, is to find out these things for ourselves. This means changing not just our purpose, but our methods of discovery.

We ought to begin by recognizing that wisdom is the result of equal parts of philosophy and experience, of thinking and doing. It is no coincidence that our last generation of great political thinkers—the framers of the Constitution—was also intensely involved in politics. In fact, *The Federalist Papers,* thought by many to be America's one enduring contribution to political theory, was first published as a series of campaign tracts by James Madison, Alexander Hamilton, and John Jay.

Personal experience in politics will quickly disabuse political scientists of the notion that the most important factors in making the system work can be fitted into equations. They will learn from being in or around government, as much by feel as by analysis, the subtle interaction of personalities, values, pressures, and uncertainties that are involved in the way things really work. Of course, the great danger of getting inside the system is that one can get co-opted or, more innocently, simply lose sight of the forest for the trees. That is why the study of philosophy, history, and literature remains vital both to keep us mindful of our duty to the people and to enable us to place the insights of experience into a perspective broad enough to yield understanding.

This curriculum of thought and action will surely improve our work in the classroom. But it will mean that we can also work outside of the classroom, helping people fend for themselves against their grossly overgrown government.

In short, we can hang out shingles. There is a market for political scientists, a set of ears willing to listen. For some reason we have chosen to ignore the people up until now—in fact, to write and speak in a language they could not understand. But now, by lowering our sights, we can elevate our purpose. And, who knows, maybe we will earn the pleasure of seeing the next generation of economists, sociologists, psychologists, and anthropologists jump on our bandwagon.

Political Polling:
The German Shepherd Factor

Michael Wheeler

Pollsters have been able to insulate themselves from criticism by constructing a barricade of statistical and scientific jargon. "Cross-tabulations," "area random sampling," "flow-coding"—the language sounds so technical, so formidable that most of us are intimidated into believing we are not qualified to judge whether public opinion polling is a legitimate science.

To the same end, many pollsters affect the same pretensions assumed by faith healers, astrologers, and other quacks: it does not escape our notice that we are dealing with *Dr.* Gallup's American *Institute* of Public Opinion in *Princeton,* New Jersey. New polling firms spring up right and left, and each one seems to be called Survey Research Associates or some such name which conjures up images of white-jacketed computer technicians poring over print-outs.

If polling is a science, it is at best a crude one. Polling theory in fact is not complicated, and to understand it is to know just what polls can and cannot do. Even a public opinion poll with a perfect sample and unbiased questions has inherent limitations. When the theoretical precepts are not scrupulously applied—and they seldom are—the results become all the more shaky.

Diane Bentley* does interviewing for both Louis Harris and Pat Caddell. To follow her as she makes her rounds is to peer behind the wizard's

---

Michael Wheeler teaches at the New England School of Law. This article is adapted from his book, *Lies, Damn Lies and Statistics,* with the permission of Liveright Publishing Corporation. Copyright © 1976 by Michael Wheeler.

*Diane's real name is not used here. A few identifying details have been changed to protect her anonymity.

curtain and see polling as it really is. The practice is a far cry from what the pollsters would have us believe.

Diane began working as a poll-taker several years ago. Originally, she did it principally to get out of the house, since her children were both well along in school. Now, however, with family money tight, the pay is an important incentive, so she takes on any polling assignment she can get. Most pollsters imply they have their own special force of field workers, but in fact many interviewers like Diane work for two or more polling firms.

On a Tuesday morning in June, Diane went to a working-class section of New Haven, Connecticut, where she had to complete ten interviews. Some firms tell their interviewers to start at a certain house and work in a particular direction, but this day she was simply given a map of the neighborhood and told to begin wherever she wanted.

"If I get to choose, I like to drive around the area a bit. I look for parked cars, toys in the yard. That means that it's more likely people are around and I don't have to waste time at empty houses."

Judged by Diane's standards, none of the neighborhood looked very promising, but she managed to find a street where there were a few cars. The first house she tried was surrounded by a chain link fence. The door had two locks on it and a small decal which said the premises were protected by Lectronic Alarm Systems. The occupants, one guessed, were conservative in their politics, but no one answered the door, so whatever their views, they went unrecorded.

Next door was a rather run-down, two-family house. No one was home on one side. An older man answered Diane's knock on the other, and she was pleased, as it is harder to find men at home during the day. Her pleasure was brief, however, for the man spoke so little English that an interview was impossible. Diane tried to explain what she wanted, but her attempt left him confused and Diane embarrassed.

Diane crossed the street to talk with a woman who was hanging up her wash. Diane introduced herself, though with the over-sized button she wore on her blouse, that was hardly necessary. Diane's manner is naturally friendly, and three years of work as a poll-taker has polished her ability to put people at ease. Nevertheless the woman refused to be interviewed; she said she had too much house work to do before her daughter came home from kindergarten. Diane persisted, saying it was important to express one's opinion and the whole thing was strictly confidential, but the woman still said no.

In theory every person in the United States must have an equal chance of being selected in a sample if the survey is to be reasonably representative. In practice, however, certain types of people are much easier to find than others. Housewives, retired people, and the unemployed may be found at any hour, but young working people are hard to track down; and on many issues homebodies tend to have different opinions than those who are on the move.

BIG DOGS AND BLACKS

One after-the-fact explanation for the pollsters' blunder in predicting that Dewey would win the election in 1948 was that many of their interviewers stayed out of the black neighborhoods in the Northern cities, where the vote went heavily to Truman. Most pollsters try to hire people who will feel comfortable in various kinds of neighborhoods, but problems still persist. Gallup is concerned that some urban people may become inaccessible. "As the crime situation actually gets worse in some cities, it becomes more and more a problem to send interviewers into areas where the crime rate is high. We are reluctant to do it, and so are our interviewers."

Another group that may be underrepresented is owners of German shepherd dogs. Diane's sample included one. She took one look at the dog and without hesitating walked to the next house on her list.

Many pollsters are reluctant to reveal the trouble they have getting to talk to people. When questioned on this they generally say that "people are most cooperative." If pressed, however, Louis Harris admits that upwards of 20 per cent of the people his interviewers contact refuse to talk, and this figure does not include those who are not at home.

The rate of refusal has gone up in recent years, a fact that leads some to speculate that Watergate and all its fall-out have caused people to be suspicious of anyone asking questions. Someone who says she is a pollster may actually be with the FBI or the Internal Revenue Service. Also, there are door-to-door salesmen who introduce themselves as poll-takers; people who have been taken in by this pitch may be wary of others who make the same claim. Whatever the reason, the kind of people who do not feel comfortable talking to strangers probably have different attitudes about themselves and the world they live in, yet their opinions are under-represented in public opinion polls.

Pollsters try to control the problem by hiring interviewers who will have the greatest chance of winning people's trust. The major pollsters agree the most important criterion is sex. George Gallup states, "Almost all our interviewers are women. And the same is true for other firms all over the world. Women have always been better interviewers. People are really less reluctant to talk with a woman, and women are much more conscientious."

Burns Roper says that perhaps 98 per cent of his firm's interviewers are female. "Access is the big thing. Women are superior at getting cooperation from either sex. Chivalry isn't dead—men will be more responsive to a woman than they will be to a man. And women aren't afraid of another woman, as they might be of a man coming to the door." Lou Harris similarly reports that over 90 per cent of his house-to-house interviewers are women.

There are other criteria for interviewers. The late Oliver Quayle candidly stated that the best ones are "not *too* intelligent so they will not get too curious and involve themselves in survey analysis." Other pollsters are more guarded on this point, for they understandably do not want to slander their own employees, but it is clear that you can be considered "overqualified" for public opinion research.

Diane Bentley approached a woman returning from the supermarket with two large bags of groceries, who said she would be willing to talk for a little while. Diane did not mention that the survey would take more than an hour. If she had, the woman would probably have declined, as would most people.

The house-to-house surveys taken by the major pollsters are getting longer and longer. A typical Harris interview takes more than an hour. Those done by Cambridge Survey Research, Pat Caddell's firm, often last an hour and a half. Caddell's polls are usually commissioned by a single political client, but most of the other pollsters use one interview to ask questions for a number of subscribers. The Gallup surveys commonly start with questions which will be used for his newspaper column, and then go to matters which are being probed for one or more private businesses.

This practice of piggy-backing allows the pollsters to spread the costs of interviewing among several clients, but it also means that the interviews are long and ponderous. Harris questionnaires can run up to 30 pages with perhaps 200 questions. Other pollsters who do personal interviewing follow similar practices. People who are willing to be interviewed get nothing but the satisfaction of knowing their responses will fractionally affect the totals spewed out by the pollster's computer.

Diane did not know who was the principal client for the survey she was conducting, but most of the questions dealt with energy problems, which made her guess that the client was either an oil company or a public utility.

Diane followed the woman into the kitchen and sat down with her clipboard to conduct the interview while the woman put away her groceries. She said she just wanted "your reaction to these questions—it doesn't have to be something you would stand by." The first questions asked whether there was an energy shortage, either locally or nationally, and whether there would be one in the future. The woman hesitated. "Well, I think the gas crisis was manufactured by the companies." Diane checked the boxes that said there was no energy shortage.

Diane moved crisply through the questionnaire, politely but firmly insisting on specific answers to the questions she put. As the interview went on, however, the woman got increasingly impatient. "Everything you're asking me is yes or no, black or white. I just don't think that way." She felt trapped by a question which asked her to agree or disagree with the statement, "Since Henry Kissinger failed to make peace between Egypt and Israel, it looks as though he is losing his touch as a peacemaker."

She said she had never liked Kissinger. Were she to take the question literally, she must answer no, for she believed he never had a touch as a peacemaker. But that answer, as she could plainly see, would be taken as an endorsement of Kissinger. On the other hand, she could not bring herself to say "yes," as that implied she had until recently supported him.

Diane was pleasant but persistent. "Just answer the question as best you can. Choose whichever is the lesser of two evils." The woman still could not subscribe to either of the two offered alternatives. Diane eventually put her down as "not sure," when in fact the woman had a clear and strong opinion about Kissinger.

The question, typical of many on that survey, illustrates a serious problem common to much of public opinion polling: complex attitudes are artificially forced into neat little boxes—agree/disagree or favor/oppose. No analyst, no matter how sophisticated, could divine the woman's real views from the "not sure" recorded by Diane.

The pigeon-hole effect is the result of the polling mechanism. If the pollster sets out to report public opinion in some unified and comprehensible fashion, he must get answers which fit into categories which can be easily tallied. Open-ended questions which ask people to state their views in their own words allow each individual to express himself accurately, but the very diversity of expression which is produced necessarily means that it cannot be tabulated into neat "for" and "against" columns.

AGREE/DISAGREE

This pigeon-holing is a fundamental weakness of public opinion polls. Even if a poll is based on perfectly constructed samples and even if the results are scrutinized by a sophisticated analyst, the results will be meaningless if the questions were simplistic.

Peter Hart, a young Washington, D.C. political pollster, is one of the few in his profession to even acknowledge the problem. "Look at the newspaper polls. All the questions are 'agree/disagree.' Well, life isn't that simple. It isn't just 'excellent, good, fair or poor.' It makes cleaner newspaper copy to make everything 'agree/disagree' but that's an awfully simple way of looking at public attitudes."

To the extent that other pollsters have felt this sort of criticism, their usual response has been simply to ask more questions, not better ones. Each individual agree/disagree question is flawed, but most pollsters think that the total value of a survey can somehow be more than the sum of its parts. Pat Caddell, for example, prides himself on the depth of his interpretation of his surveys, but his analysis can be no better than the questions he asks. If anything, Caddell's questions tend to be even more restrictive than those of his major rivals.

Caddell is hardly alone, however, in forcing people to choose between two positions, neither one of which they support. Consider some of the questions Diane Bentley was asking. "Would you like to see the U.S. become *totally* independent of all foreign sources of energy, or not?" You must answer yes or no. You cannot say that you are more concerned with dependence on Middle Eastern oil than with Canadian sources. Nor can you qualify your answer by saying your support of energy independence depends on how much more energy will cost when it is produced solely from domestic sources. Both those considerations would seem to be essential to any intelligent response to the question, yet the pollsters demand a simple yes or no.

A simple test for determining the meaningfulness of poll results is to read the questions to see if you would be comfortable giving agree/disagree answers. If you would not, then you must discount the results of the poll, no matter how conclusive the statistics seem.

THE ONTOLOGY OF THE FACT

The Gallup Poll is careful to include the wording of all questions in the releases. Gallup himself says, "We regard ourselves simply as fact-finders. We publish the questions, tell how they were collected, and let the reader draw his own conclusions from the facts."

Unfortunately, not all pollsters follow this procedure. Harris usually does not supply the wording of the questions which are asked for his syndicated column, and he is sensitive about criticism that he should. "This is the big argument I have with Burns Roper and others in our field. He says that we shouldn't report a question unless we also report the wording and the tabular results. Well, all our columns are based on eight or ten questions and there is no way to get all that information in with a word limit of 800 or 850."

Harris notes that complete information about his published surveys is on file with the University of North Carolina and that his firm has always made it a practice to disclose wording or questions and other information to anybody who requests it. As helpful as that may be to serious scholars, it does little good for the average reader, who is left in the position of having to trust Harris' judgment in interpreting the meaning of his surveys.

In zeroing in on simple agree/disagree questions, the pollsters often ignore other indicators of opinion which may be much more revealing. The way a person lives may tell much about his attitudes.

The woman interviewed by Diane Bentley was unemployed. The man with whom she lived (the poll had categories only for "married" or "single") was a truck driver. There were four posters taped on her kitchen walls. Three were of pop music and television stars. The fourth poster said more about her attitude toward the energy crisis than her answers to any of the questions which Diane asked her. It showed a half-dozen greedy and bloated figures, each one representing a major oil company. Underneath, there was a caption: "Don't blame the truckers, it's these motherfuckers."

This kind of background never finds its way into polls, and as a result, the full texture and shape of public opinion goes unreported. Pollsters behave as though opinion can only be located through asking questions, often artificially narrow ones, but in fact we express ourselves in many ways. Unfortunately, these clues to our attitudes and opinions are almost always lost on the pollsters.

Diane faithfully carried out her assignment. Though the woman's interest flagged after 45 minutes, Diane kept firing off questions, carefully recording a response for each one. Not all interviewers are so diligent. The problem pollsters are least inclined to acknowledge is cheating by their interviewers, but it occurs fairly often.

PHONY INTERVIEWS

The pollsters claim they are very careful about whom they hire and that they summarily fire anyone who fabricates data, yet the very nature of personal interviewing means the pollsters have little control over their employees in the field. Most pollsters say they routinely double-check a portion of all their interviews to be sure they were really conducted, but incidents involving both the Gallup Poll and the Harris Survey indicate this validation process is not nearly so rigorous or effective as the pollsters would like us to believe.

In 1968 *The New York Times* commissioned Gallup to do an intensive survey of attitudes of Harlem residents. The information was collected, tabulated, and submitted to the *Times* for publication. An editor was so pleased with the poll he decided to play it up by sending a reporter and a photographer to get a story about some of those who had supposedly been interviewed. At seven of the 23 addresses Gallup had given them, the newsmen could not even find a dwelling. Moreover, five other people who had allegedly been polled could not be traced—the addresses existed but apparently the people did not. Not even all the remaining interviews were legitimate. In one case the *Times* reporter learned the interviewer had talked to four people playing cards and incorporated all their answers into one interview.

When the *Times* confronted him with this fakery, Gallup ducked the responsibility for the phony interviews. He pointed out the interviews in question had been submitted by two Columbia law students who had been specially hired for the project. There was no explanation, however, why the Gallup organization had not discovered the fakes themselves.

Both before and after the incident, Gallup has repeatedly made the claim that his firm validates every interview made by new interviewers and every fourth or fifth interview done by one of their experienced employees. Obviously that was not done in this case. It was accidental that the *Times* uncovered the specious poll. Only sheer luck prevented them from printing it. Newspapers almost never doublecheck polls they print, but the Gallup incident suggests that perhaps they should.

The *Times* tracked down one of the special interviewers whom Gallup had tried to make a scapegoat. He claimed he had actually talked to people "in the streets," but admitted he had made up the names and addresses because he was under pressure from the Gallup organization to complete his assignment—"I was uptight to get it in."

A year later Gallup's rival Lou Harris had exactly the same problem, but Harris was more fortunate in being able to keep his client from knowing it. Harris conducted a private survey in which several questions which had been contracted for were inadvertently left out. The client insisted on getting the information it had paid for, so Harris' firm sent out a special questionnaire by mail to those people who had supposedly been interviewed. According to a person who worked for Harris at the time, 25 per cent of the questionnaires were returned as undeliverable: there were no such people or addresses. If Harris' firm had not erred by leaving several questions out of the original poll, the fabricated interviews would have slipped through.

Even the most conscientious pollsters are limited in how much they can do to check the validity of interviews. They usually only call back people to see if they were interviewed. Checking their responses is simply too difficult when 100 or more questions have been asked, and after all, the pollster may not really care if the responses are legitimate as long as they are plausible.

Albert Sindlinger is a self-styled maverick within the polling profession. He has all his interviewing done by telephone so that he can monitor his employees' work. He simply does not trust interviews done without supervision. "Ask the other pollsters if they ever listen to their interviewers," he says. "They can't. I have an asset, I can listen to every damn interview we make. I know that it was really done and that the questions were asked the way they were supposed to be."

ASK ME NO QUESTIONS

Sindlinger says that he has occasionally hired Gallup and Harris inter-viewers to do his telephone canvassing, and from this experience he has a very low opinion of them. "They play the expert, but that's wrong. To do objective research, the interviewer has to be the dummy, not the other way around."

Sindlinger believes that there is a paradox which undermines personal interviewing. "If you hire somebody with any intelligence, after the tenth interview they're going to sit down and make up the other 25. If you have somebody who is too dumb to do that, they're too dumb to record people's answers." Given Gallup's experience with the Columbia Law School students in Harlem, Sindlinger may be right.

Another successful pollster, who asked not to be identified, says he knows several former Gallup and Harris interviewers who have admitted to him that they faked interviews regularly and were never caught. Like Sindlinger, he, too, now relies principally on telephone interviewing.

Most of the polling establishment, including Gallup and Harris, regards the use of the telephone as the sign of a minor-league operation, claiming it has many built-in drawbacks which make it unreliable.

It is true, for example, that in the past the rate of refusal was higher for telephone interviewing than for that done in person. Recently, however, personal interviewers have encountered an increasing number of locked doors, so now the telephone produces an equivalent level of cooperation. In large part the hostility to the telephone seems to be a legacy of the *Literary Digest* prediction that Landon would defeat Roosevelt in 1936. The *Digest's* sample was based in part on telephone books, which at the time made the sample heavily biased toward Republicans. That is no longer a real problem today. More than 90 per cent of the households in the country have listed phone numbers.

Were it not for their desire to do long interviews, more pollsters would probably use the telephone. The surveys which Harris, Caddell, and others conduct often take well over an hour to administer. It would be very difficult to get people to stay on the telephone that length of time. It is much easier to hang up a phone than to get someone out of your living room, particularly when they have been trained how to stay long after they have worn out their welcome.

Irwin Harrison, of Decision Research in Massachusetts, thinks that this is an illusory advantage. "You just don't need surveys that long. Whether it's a commercial client or a political client, they use only a fraction of the data you give them." A more limited study, he believes, can help the client understand what the real issues are instead of being overwhelmed with page after page of computer printout.

Harrison has found that in a 15-minute telephone interview, he can ask 35 or 40 questions, which will produce more than enough information for most clients. He is also justifiably suspicious of the information which personal interviewers elicit toward the end of interviews. "People get tired talking; all they're thinking about is how they can get the interviewer out of the house without being rude."

No matter how polling is conducted, in person, by telephone or by mail, the pollsters have to take on faith that people are being honest with them. That faith may often be misplaced. A revealing statement recently appeared buried deep within an instruction circular the Harris firm prepared for its interviewers: "It's been brought to our attention that almost all of our surveys are showing the population to be more educated than what the census says it actually is. Nothing seems to be wrong with our samples, and there is no indication of error in recording or processing. Therefore, we feel respondents are exaggerating the amount of schooling they've had."

The language is blandly bureaucratic, but the fundamental meaning is nothing less than startling: The Harris organization admits that "in almost all" of their surveys, people have been lying to them. Other studies have confirmed that, when asked, most people will say they are somewhat better paid and more highly educated than they really are. The pollsters have responded by making minor changes in their method of asking those demographic questions. For example, Harris interviewers now hand people a card on which different levels of education are placed in numbered categories. People are apparently somewhat more honest in assigning themselves to a category than they are in stating their education outright.

TELL ME NO LIES

There is other evidence that people do not always tell the truth to poll-takers. In 1964 Elmo Roper discovered that a significant portion of people would not say outright they intended to vote for Barry Goldwater. When he told people to mark an ostensibly secret ballot, Goldwater invariably did four percentage points better than when they were asked directly for their preference. Goldwater ultimately did somewhat better than the pollsters had reported, even those using secret ballots, which indicates that even more people were refusing to disclose their actual feelings to the pollsters.

In a number of recent surveys for various Democrats, Pat Caddell has regularly asked people for whom they voted in 1972, Nixon or McGovern. In some states which Nixon actually won, a majority now say they voted for McGovern. Caddell says, "California was the first state in which we found this. McGovern won by an eight-point margin. We sent him a telegram saying, 'Demand a recount!' "

If people do not always tell pollsters the truth about how they voted in the past, then we must suspect what they say they are going to do in the future. In primary polls, George Wallace's strength has almost always been underestimated. People either say that they are undecided or that they are going to vote for someone else. According to Pat Caddell, the post-election studies which Yankelovich did in 1972 for *The New York Times* were unsuccessful in locating the full extent of Wallace's support. Even as people walked out of the voting booth, they still were reluctant to admit they had voted for Wallace.

If people lie to pollsters about how much money they make and are not always truthful about whom they will—or did—vote for, they also are likely to be coy about giving their true feelings on controversial issues.

Ordinarily it is difficult to measure the extent of lying that goes on in issue polling. Only the person who is answering the poll knows whether the opinion he expresses is truly his own. That people feel the need to be deceptive is of interest in and of itself, but unfortunately from the bare statistics of a public opinion poll, there is no way to tell who really believes what. The liars are lumped together with the truth-tellers.

In sum, though the theory of polling is scientifically sound, the actual practice is not. The next time you read what purports to be a scientific survey of public opinion, recall what really goes on as interviewers like Diane Bentley move from door to door.

part 8
OUTSIDE
THE SYSTEM

Previous chapters of this book have been concerned mainly with how Washington works; the following chapters are concerned with how Washington affects the rest of the country. Just as the Congress, the bureaucracy, and the courts don't work as they were intended to, neither do specific programs work out there in the hinterlands the way the planners in Washington thought they would. As a result, most Americans feel they're not getting from the federal government what they're paying for in taxes.

Nicholas Lemann's "The View From a Small Town" shows that even in a tiny, remote country hamlet the federal government has an enormous effect, both through taxes and restrictions and through subsidies and benefits. The government's problem in trying to help a small town is that its giveaway programs are usually designed to be taken advantage of by New Yorks and Chicagos, cities with huge staffs of paperwork-processors. For a town with a one-man government, federal loans and subsidies can be too complicated to get.

Besides their complexity, a common problem of government giveaway programs is that they attract people who aren't supposed to benefit from them. Lenny Marx, for instance, lived the good life for more than a year, courtesy of the taxpayers, by pretending to look for work so that he could receive tax-free unemployment benefits.

The cumulative effect of stories like these two, as Michael Nelson points out in "The Bureaucracy Crisis," is deep distrust of government. Nelson interviewed groups of randomly selected people in three towns, and found they were interested not in politics, but in bureaucracy. Their anger over the government's bungling of its attempts to serve them was growing steadily, and the anger of people all over the country about that continues to grow. The people Nelson spoke to didn't want to do away with big government and its services; they just wanted it to work. If it continues not to work—and if Washington seems not to care whether it does or not—the rest of the country may try to bring about a radical change in the size and scope of its government.

The View from a Small Town

Nicholas Lemann

Early on in the new Washington novel by Ben Wattenberg, who became famous as a man attuned to the hearts and minds of average Midwestern Americans, a White House speechwriter has lunch at Sans Souci with a savvy *New York Times* reporter, the kind of character who's obviously there to say what's on the author's mind. The reporter is just back from several weeks of traveling around the nation to sample the simple folks' attitudes, and the speechwriter straightaway asks her, "How are things in the country?" Which elicits the following response:

" 'Strange.' Her brow furrowed. 'I'm always amazed at how different the rest of the country is from Washington. In this town, you'd think politics was at the heart of the universe. Out there'—she waved her hand—'people manage to hold jobs, have babies, and wash their cars without thinking about Congress or the President or Washington for days—hell, years—on end.' "

It is doubtless true that the daily concerns of the people out there are not those of Joseph Kraft and James Reston, but it's hard for anyone to live in complete blissful ignorance of the federal government. The long arm of Washington touches almost everybody in one way or another.

At President Carter's town meetings, people were too busy asking about federal programs that touched their own lives to worry about the burning issues of the big-think set. In Washington state, farmers are furious at the government for having encouraged them to plow under their crops in anticipation of a drought that never arrived. In Louisiana, towns live and

Nicholas Lemann is a contributing editor of *The Washington Monthly*.

die according to two-cent fluctuations in federal sugar supports and import taxes. In Indiana, a town is closing down because of federal water-treatment requirements it can't meet. In California, the cancellation of the B-1 bomber threw thousands out of work.

And in La Plata, Maryland, population 1,800, the town manager says the federal government "is involved in every facet of life that we have." La Plata is the county seat of Charles County, Maryland, population 50,000, which sits astride the Potomac south of Washington and west of the Chesapeake Bay. Charles County is an old farming area, and La Plata is the kind of town that serves most agricultural regions. Everybody knows everybody. A couple of old families (the Diggeses and the Bowlings) run most major enterprises. There is a main street, a high school, and a few stores and offices, all of which make up a commercial district about five blocks long. For half a mile on either side of the main street there are single-family houses and a few apartment buildings, which give way to miles of farms—tobacco (the county's original economic base) and corn and soybeans.

La Plata is the kind of place that's usually written about these days in sepia-tinted prose that is meant to indicate a quaint, remote, placid, and dying way of life; it's well known, after all, that America is now 75-percent urban. But that's a misleading statistic; a full 40 per cent of the population still lives outside cities of more than 50,000 and their suburbs. To people in Washington there's a certain mystery enveloping these areas. They are known to vote against Washington—they formed the solid backbone of the Nixon-Ford constituency—but that's usually chalked up to a general pastoral conservatism. The possibility that it might be the government's fault is left unexamined.

$2,000 A PERSON

The first striking aspect of the federal presence in a small, mind-its-own-business county like Charles is how large it is. These may be proud and independent people, but in the 1976 fiscal year the government spent $97.2 million in Charles County, which works out to about $2,000 a person. In addition, it lent out $26.3 million. All this is considerably more than the county pays the government: nationwide, federal taxes in 1976 were $1,328 per capita, and in Charles County, which is fairly low-income, they were probably less.

The government's largesse to Charles County has come gradually over the last 50 years; there have been three major waves of federal domestic spending in this century, and a county like Charles is in a position to have profited from all three.

The first wave was the New Deal, under which Social Security ($10 million a year in Charles County) and various relief programs began. The New Deal's social programs were aimed first and foremost at building a firm economic floor under agricultural America, which they did quite effectively. The Department of Agriculture is today the most visible federal presence in Charles County, with a brand-new office building in La Plata, and it guarantees decent housing and a farm to every citizen who makes less than $15,600 a year. The chief agency of this generosity is the Farmers Home Administration (called, for some reason, the FmHA, which, its genial county director, Thomas Potter, says, can "do just about anything in a rural area as far as financing."

As long as they've first been turned down by a bank, anyone under the income ceiling, even single people, can get from the FmHA a loan to buy or rent a house or farm, at low interest and long terms, that can cost as much as $45,000 (which still does buy something in Charles County). Loans are also available to cover farm operating costs, start businesses in town, and build community facilities like sewage and water treatment plants, roads, and drainage systems. Through its price-support system, the Agriculture Department also guarantees the county's corn and soybean farmers that they'll never have a bad year. Should drought or heavy rain destroy the crops altogether, the government will step in with disaster relief—in fact, there are two programs, the FmHA's and the Small Business Administration's, that provide identical disaster loans to the same people, the only restriction being that nobody can be on both agencies' caseloads simultaneously. In 1976, the SBA lent farmers in Charles County $28,000 in disaster loans after heavy spring rains, the FmHA (which seems to be winning the bureaucratic battle on this front) $187,000. The FmHA also lent out $300,000 to cover farm operating costs; $64,000 to buy farms; and, to farmers and townspeople, $2.5 million to buy houses.

The second and third waves of government spending—military, starting with World War II and continuing apace in the years thereafter, and social-services, taking off during Lyndon Johnson's presidency—have bestowed their gifts on Charles County too. The Defense Department spends $50 million a year there, most of it in pay for the 2,500 employees of a Naval Ordnance Station in the town of Indian Head, and the Department of Health, Education, and Welfare chips in nearly $25 million, the biggest single chunk of which goes to Medicare ($2 million) and Medicaid ($6 million). Another $2 million in social-services programs—mainly food stamps and school lunches—comes through the Agriculture Department. Rural areas get more than their share from the federal government because it's hard to build military installations in cities; and social-services grants, usually thought of as aimed at big cities, do a lot for the low-income country as well.

Otherwise, federal spending in Charles County is a miscellany—$6 million in insurance for low-income homeowners from the Department of

Housing and Urban Development, $329,000 in unemployment compensation, $824,000 in highway construction grants. Two-and-a-half million dollars comes in from the Veterans Administration for pensions and training; $1.2 million from the Treasury in revenue sharing; $6.1 million from the Civil Service Commission in pensions on federal salaries. All eleven Cabinet-level departments and ten independent agencies put some money into Charles County.

Overall, the federal government's spending in Charles County breaks out like this: $35 million in salaries, mostly to Defense employees (who average about $16,000 a year); $20 million in pensions; and $25 million in loans, most of which help low- and moderate-income people buy houses. In other words, the government primarily helps its own (which in turn helps the local economy, but also leads to resentment and inflation), the retired, and the housing industry. By comparison, only $6 million a year is for the kind of payments to poor people that could conceivably be called the dole—Medicaid, food stamps, welfare, and the like.

THE SHORT END OF THE STICK

For all this government generosity, Charles County does not send its gratitude back toward Washington. In fact, both by their votes (conservative Republican) and in conversation, the county's residents make it clear that they think they're coming out on the short end of the federal stick. Most don't realize that the government spends more on the county than the county gives it, but even if they did, it's a fair bet that they'd insist the relationship isn't worth it. The people of La Plata are glad to enumerate their theories about the federal government: that it pays people to sit around and do nothing, and that the money it puts into the county is less than what the county has contributed because bureaucrats skim a large percentage off the top for themselves before giving it back. They resent the high salaries paid the county's federal employees. The government "is to Charles County what Con Ed is to New York," says Daniel Kennedy, editor of the *La Plata Times-Crescent.* "Everybody blames them even when they're right."

All these are general complaints, often arising out of no more specific a burden than paying taxes; but they certainly show that the government has a public-relations problem even if they don't explain why. More particularly, people in La Plata, especially businessmen, complain that they are overburdened with federal regulations that were designed for giant corporations, crush the small ones, and make it impossible to earn a profit. That kind of griping goes on all over the country (the giant corporations that the rules were designed for complain the loudest) and probably always has. Recently the small-town businessman has even obtained a spokesman, in the person of Billy Carter, whose complaints about OSHA inspectors, hiring regulations, the minimum wage, unemployment compensation, and, generally, federal "paperwork" are echoed by businessmen in La Plata.

There's no doubt that the state of bureaucratic affairs small businessmen allude to can come about; in France, reports Alain Peyrefitte in his book *Le Mal Francais*, the federal government closed down a small town's only store, a cafe-grocery-general store, because it is illegal to serve liquor less than 200 meters from a school and the store was ten meters too close. But while that kind of horror story is worth keeping in mind for its cautionary value, in America the government's oppression of the small businessman seems to be exaggerated. Its truth is mostly symbolic; to an entrepreneur who is accustomed to answering to nobody at all, even the slightest intrusion takes on an importance that those of us who are accustomed to drawing a paycheck would find hard to understand. And small-town life is a mixture of two strains, the independence glorified in *Our Town* and the xenophobia condemned in *Babbitt* and *Main Street;* sometimes the two work in opposition, but whenever government regulation is involved, they gang up and damn it.

A case in point is James Hancock, a weather-beaten, articulate man who runs La Plata's shoe repair shop out of a tiny, cinder-block building on the main street. Hancock started his shop in 1949 and, he says, has made less money every year since then—mainly because the government has swamped him in regulations and paperwork. He says he'd expand his business except that, with all the regulations involved, it just isn't worth it.

But asked to produce some of the paperwork that plagues him, Hancock can only shrug his shoulders—all he does at the government's behest is keep books, "just like I was Ford Motor," for income-tax purposes, something he wouldn't otherwise do. The rest of the paperwork is more in the realm of threat than reality. It is worth noting, though, that for a really small businessman—not Billy Carter, but Hancock—the minimum wage is a genuine hindrance. He and his assistant are both below the poverty level, and the assistant has to be hired as a subcontractor rather than an employee because he can't be paid the minimum wage.

A LITTLE MORE COMPLICATED

Hancock's perceptions are shared by most people around La Plata. A defender of the government would say life has to be a little more complicated in order to bring about a better society—for instance, aren't OSHA inspectors worth it if they'll stop industrial accidents? But in Charles County there's no perception of a reason behind the complication, and it's seen as better just to avoid it, to keep life simple. A local lawyer told me he gave up his real-estate practice rather than comply with the "paperwork and nuisance" of the truth-in-lending act, and reported with great umbrage that the government "sent a man around with a tape measure to measure my damn farm." The manager of the La Plata Chamber of Commerce says solemnly that there are "government agencies created just for the purpose of making more rules." Being brought into a complex society of guarantees and strictures and subsidies designed to bring the greatest good to the greatest number is not what the people of Charles County have in mind.

The question this raises is, are perceptions of overwhelming paperwork and government interference a valid cause for concern if in fact they're only perceptions? (In those specific cases when they're real, as Marjorie Boyd's article in this issue shows, they're well worth worrying about.) Surely government officials shouldn't spend their time trying to keep imaginary dragons away from small businessmen. More broadly, is Charles County, despite its sentiments to the contrary, really getting a good deal from the federal government when everything is taken into account?

Despite all the money that flows in, the answer is not a sanguine one for the government. What it takes out, it takes with impressive efficiency from one and all, but what it puts back, other than salaries and pensions, it does in a way that leaves much to be desired. The money that is spent to help the people in the county who need help, while generous in theory, is often bungled in practice. The fact is that when the government is bestowing its direct gifts on the citizenry, there really *are* a lot of rules to follow and forms to fill out—enough of them to make people shy away from the gifts, acting against their economic interest. In cases like that, the sincerity of sentiments against the government can't be doubted, and something must be wrong.

The two major giveaway organizations in the county—the FmHA and the county department of social services (which is largely federally funded) both have caseloads that are far smaller than they should be. At the social services agency, a supervisor named Sarah Mitchell says, the forms that must be filled out to get on welfare and other public assistance programs, designed in Washington, are "quite detailed—people have difficulty filling them out, and they're bothered by the requirement of a personal interview with a caseworker." Welfare recipients have to submit proof of income, and forms having to do with their housing and children. "Any time you have outside forces dealing with your life in that way," she says, "you'll resent it."

At the FmHA the caseload is only 650, just one of which is a loan to a local business. In 1976, Thomas Potter handed out 700 loan applications, but only 112 came back for processing, and at least part of the reason is that the applications must have held the promise of some future pain. For a housing loan to go through, for instance, the house must conform with a detailed code that specifies the kind of beams that must be used and requires a smoke detector in every room. The Agriculture Department's farm storage loan program, which provides funding for the storage of crops, has had no applications so far—"a lot of people don't understand it and don't want to be bothered with the government," the program's director says. HUD's block grants program is far under-utilized because, the people who run it in the county say, there is so much paperwork involved—every application has to have at least 12 forms, six statistical reports, and three copies of lease agreements, just for a grant for one house.

THE GOOD THE GOVERNMENT CAN DO

The largest-scale case of a government program not helping people as it should in Charles County is the new sewage treatment plant in La Plata. A sewage plant project in a rural area—improving the environment, providing jobs, a big capital investment—is the kind of project liberals are accustomed to pointing to proudly as an exemplar of the good the federal government can do, and indeed there is a whole range of programs through which a town like La Plata can fund such a plant. But the plant, now under construction, is being financed locally—not out of ignorance of the government programs available or blind mistrust of outsiders, but because local financing is faster and almost as cheap for the town as federal funding.

The story of the sewage treatment plant begins in 1970, when the town of La Plata hired an intense young man from Utah, John Newman, for the one full-time administrative job in its government, town manager. At that time La Plata was short of drinking water, so Newman set out to get a new water treatment plant built—with federal money. The plant was originally estimated to cost $380,000, of which the Department of Housing and Urban Development would fund 90 per cent, leaving the town with a cost of only $38,000. Five years later, the plant was built, at a cost of $1,150,000, of which the town paid $347,500.

The huge increase in cost was due in large part to inflation, although government building requirements also played a large part. Of course, the requirements and the inflation are intimately connected; every requirement means paperwork, every piece of paperwork means delays, and every delay, in inflationary times, means the cost of a project goes up. Newman has the paperwork for the plant in a cardboard box in his office; the box is four feet long and is filled with the most detailed sort of requirements, preapplications, applications, impact assessments, engineering reports, promises of nondiscrimination. Newman says for four years he "practically lived" in the HUD regional office in Baltimore.

So in 1973, when La Plata started having sewer problems, Newman was already not kindly disposed toward the federal government. But since the town was low on money, and the plant would cost more than half a million dollars, he decided to give it another try.

First Newman took his project to the Environmental Protection Agency, which had a program that would pay directly for 75 per cent of the cost of the plant and arrange for the state to contribute another 12½ per cent. EPA decided that perhaps a sewage plant for all of southern Charles County, rather than just La Plata, might be a good idea, so it had the County Sanitary Commission look into it. The commission contracted for a $106,000 study, which turned out to take three years to complete and to conclude that a county-wide plant *wasn't* needed. In the middle of this, with annual inflation well over ten per cent, Newman decided he couldn't wait any longer and pulled out.

He next looked into getting an HUD community facility grant, although with extreme trepidation, because from his experience with the HUD-funded water plant he knew all his plans, bids, and pay vouchers would have to be federally approved at great additional time and cost. But in the midst of the application process HUD replaced its community facility grants with block grants, which were billed as a streamlining of the bureaucracy. To get a block grant, a small community had to have a certain level of unemployment, which La Plata, though above the national average, then did not meet (it now does). Newman had to go elsewhere.

Having given up on the idea of a grant, he went to the FmHA for a loan —the terms were good (40 years at five-percent interest) and he imagined that a loan would be simpler in the processing than a grant. In April 1976 he approached Tom Potter about applying.

Here came a rude awakening for Newman, for he found that the instructions for filling out the loan application ran to 50 single-spaced pages. Among other forms, he had to fill out a pre-application, a full application, a balance sheet, an engineering contract, an operating budget, contracts for professional services, evidence of compliance with various rules, preliminary reports, and a project summary—quite a load on a one-man government. All plans had to be reviewed by FmHA architects and engineers. Every step of the process took time. For example: Newman had to send all his plans for approval to a state clearinghouse, which in turn sent them to five separate state agencies for *their* approval. Everybody approved in the end, but the process took months.

Finally, in April 1977, the FmHA sent the town a request for form FmHA 442–46, Letter of Intent to Meet Conditions; this was a final step to make sure the town understood it had to submit to the FmHA details like all construction contracts, an accountant agreement, monthly progress reports for each contractor, and non-discrimination reports. (Bear in mind, this is a program only for towns of less than 5,500 people, a group in which La Plata is a rarity for having any full-time administrative staff. In most places, all these forms would have to be filled out after hours by someone with a full-time job.) A month later, the grant was approved.

'FOR *OUR* APPROVAL'

In the meantime, however, as Newman grew impatient, he had been talking to a local financial firm about floating a bond issue. He found the terms wouldn't be quite as good—20 years at 5.85 per cent—but that the bonds could be out on the market by July 1. He submitted a short report on the financial condition of the town, which the firm used to write a bond issue report. That was the only information La Plata had to submit. When the bond issue papers were ready, Newman says, "*They* brought it down for *our* approval"—and he decided to forget about the FmHA. On June 3, he wrote Tom Potter that he was going on the open market. "I'm appalled," Newman wrote, "at the amount of paperwork that is required by the United States Government through the FmHA for a loan . . . levels and levels of bureaucrats seem to feed on themselves as make-work projects to justify their own existence."

Potter says now that the processing of the La Plata loan application was among the fastest he's seen. As for the plant, construction should be finished by the first of this year.

The forms and regulations in which the government enshrouds its gifts are not without some logic, of course: the theory is that if Washington is going to pay for something, it is its duty to make sure the project conforms to various noble social goals. Would it be right, the planners think, to fund a building on which there's discrimination by the contractor, or faulty construction, or an incompetent architect, or unsafe working conditions? But what this attitude does is effectively take federal programs out of the reach of small-scale America—there are few small towns whose governments can keep up with all the paperwork for every federal program they're eligible for. By not being able just to grit its teeth and give away money, Washington is short-changing small-town America on a major category of its benefits.

A good example of the problem is the impoverished shoemaker, James Hancock, who complains that the government is biased against a small businessman like him. To be sure, Hancock suffers a little under the burden of taxes and the minimum wage law—but that ought to be countervailed by a helping hand from the government when he can't make ends meet. Poor as he is, he's eligible for a number of federal loans and perhaps even subsidies to finance the expansion and operation of his business—and personally, he could get food stamps and housing subsidies. The government should buoy him up far more than it grinds him down.

But Hancock participates in none of these programs designed to help people like him. "I haven't looked into it," he says. "I think it's wrong. If the government robs you so you have to go beg 'em for something to eat, that's wrong. You don't take anything free without controls." Maybe that's an emotional view, but the evidence in Charles County shows that there's a lot of truth to it.

Confessions
of an Unemployment Cheat
Lenny Marx

The envelope looked like all the others. It contained the latest unemployment check from the bountiful Kansas Division of Employment, and I ripped it open with a trembling, eager greed. It was a weekly ritual I had grown to love in the year since I had lost my job. In that time I'd become a familiar sight to my mailman, greeting him in my pajamas and bathrobe at two in the afternoon. But as I pocketed the check and headed back to the kitchen for a snack, I noticed another card in the envelope: the State of Kansas was cutting off my benefits. In April 1976 my free ride would be over.

The news came as a shock, and I felt a queasy sensation in the pit of my stomach. I might be forced to . . . *get a job*. It was all terribly unfair.

By losing my job and then studiously avoiding work for over a year, I had managed to become eligible for 65 weeks of regular, extended, and emergency benefits. Better yet, the law graciously delayed paying benefits for each week that I earned money. Thus, I'd once imagined, by making enough magazine or book sales, I could stretch out the benefits until I was 65 years old, at which time I'd become eligible for social security. I often

Lenny Marx is a writer. Aleta Kaufman provided research assistance.

imagined the scene as I returned to file another request for an extension: I am 55 years old, with 8,524 rejection slips behind me. Looking over my records, the sympathetic clerk has a striking resemblance to her mother, with whom I filed 30 years before.

"Still no work, Mr. Marx?"

"You know how it is," I say. "There just aren't any openings in the newspaper business."

And now it was all about to end. A lifetime subsidy, my carefree exist-ance—all of it would vanish. It seemed that the state had to end its partici-pation in the federal emergency benefits program, which was passed by Congress in 1974 and expired in 1977. Under the law, a state was cut off when its insured unemployment rate dipped below five per cent. So, in Kansas, enough of my fellow jobless were willing to give up the good life and find work, thus selling me out. Perhaps I shouldn't have complained: I had already gotten 26 weeks of unemployment under the earliest unem-ployment law, passed in 1935; 13 additional weeks had been brought to me courtesy of a 1970 law; and I was well into the 26 more weeks that the federal emergency benefits program provided when the spigot was cut off. To get all this bounty, all I'd had to do was work six months, and get fired. For this I was paid a comfortable majority of my previous salary, tax free. And nationwide, there were roughly 12 million other grateful people accepting unemployment benefits each year. A surprisingly large number of them were just like me—men and women, who, for one reason or another, had no intention of finding work. Many others simply didn't bother to report the income they were earning.

A BIT CRAZY

Like other well-meaning programs, unemployment insurance has gone a bit crazy, draining government treasuries, harassing businesses, and adding to unemployment. Its purpose is admirable enough—helping the unemployed through a temporary financial crisis—but it has now joined the crazy-quilt of government direct and in-kind subsidies to individuals that are shot through with waste, duplication, fraud, and incompetence. Nearly half of the federal budget is being spent on direct payments like welfare, veterans' benefits, social security, workmen's compensation, and unemployment insurance. Add to that private pensions and union em-ployment benefits and in-kind services like Medicaid and food stamps, and you have a rather unpleasant picture of a nation of hustlers, grabbing for what they can, the cost to others be damned.

And who can blame them? Or me, for that matter? We want food, clothing, a place to live, a little cash, and, in some publicized cases, Florida vacations and Cadillacs. We are ambling in a kind of instinctive tropism towards a makeshift guaranteed annual income, taking our checks here and there from whichever agency is handiest. Meanwhile the government is wasting millions in spreading around cash to people who don't really need it, and ignoring others who do. It's an ass-backwards approach that will eventually bankrupt us all. The real solution has been obvious for years—a simple income maintenance program—but each succeeding administration remains content only to tinker with the mechanics of its spending programs.

CONTRITE THOUGHTS

In the meantime, my friends and I took our unemployment checks and stayed at home, sleeping late and smoking dope. I suppose, if pressed, I'd have to admit that contrite thoughts crossed my mind occasionally. Although there was considerable glee in my reaction to finding out what a good deal I'd stumbled on to, I did realize that I was taking money from government treasuries that wasn't intended for people like me. Sure, that money might otherwise have gone to worthier causes, but more likely it would have paid for aircraft carriers or bureaucrats' salaries; and besides, I was living a fairly modest and virtuous life to which I saw no satisfying alternative.

In my case, the unemployment checks were my personal instrument of liberation. I had been fired from a Topeka newspaper and was living in a commune in Wichita. After years of newspaper journalism, I had a chance to try fiction, magazine work, and poetry. I became a gentleman of leisure, a member of the idle rich. With my $72-a-week tax-free income, I felt that most work was beneath me. With aristocratic disdain, I could do only that work which was interesting—no dreary reporting or research jobs for me.

It could not be said, however, that I had no interest in holding down a regular job. This is a rather common slur against the unemployed. In fact, there were several promising jobs I would have been glad to have. One post that appealed to me, for example, was that of Associate Editor of *The New York Times*. Write a few editorials, do a column now and then, lunch with the Mayor—all these tasks could be admirably handled by a person with my skills. I would also have been willing to work as a staff poet on *The New Yorker* or writer-in-residence at the University of Honolulu. But these jobs, unfortunately, weren't available at the time I applied.

Not that I didn't try. Under the law, I had to fill out a card each week that asked several questions, including, "Were you ready, willing, and able to work during the week shown on reverse side?" and "Did you actively look for work during the week shown on reverse side [If yes, list two contacts in space provided]." Naturally, under such insistent prodding, I desperately scoured the land for work. Each week, I began my search with fresh hope, only to be rebuffed.

Fortunately, because of my training and experience, I was required to look for work only in the field of newspaper reporting. To claim benefits, all workers are required to accept only offers of "suitable work," based on their prior experience, earnings, or training. The higher up the career scale you are, the more rarified is the concept of suitable work. Thus the proles have to accept virtually anything the state employment service might offer, but professionals like myself are shielded from such discomforts. I was dismayed to learn that my local employment office, after requesting that I register for work, had no listings from newspapers seeking reporters. I was on my own.

I started by calling the newspapers near my home and then moved on to other publications. At first, I actually placed the calls myself. After all, it was a criminal offense to make false statements on my weekly card. I wasn't eager to bring down the wrath of the state by not at least *seeming* to be looking for work. At one time, I sincerely believed that there was some kind of Archangel of Unemployment who was watching over me at all times, ready to pounce if I made a false move.

Thus, fearful of arrest, I began my long job search. My day would start bright and early at noon, when I'd rush downstairs to get the classified section of the newspaper. I'd flip through the want ads until I found what I needed: the comics at the back. After reading "Peanuts" and "Doonesbury," I'd fold the section carefully into neat squares and drop it in the wastebasket. Pencil in hand, I then wandered over to the Yellow Pages to find a newspaper to call. The routine was invariably the same.

Lying on the couch, I picked up the phone.

"Editor-in-chief, please."

After a while, a busy, gruff man came on the line. "What can I do for you?"

"Well, Mr. Editor, I'd sure like to work as a reporter on your newspaper," I said, my voice cracking in an adolescent whine. "Are there any openings?"

"No. Try again some other time."

The news came as a sharp disappointment. No jobs in journalism! How could that be? I was so upset that I often found it impossible to make any more calls for the next few days. I was also so exhausted by the effort of lifting the phone and turning pages that I was forced to lie outside in the sun, taking along a transistor radio to calm my shattered nerves. Afterwards, rested and refreshed, I managed to summon the courage to place still another call. The results, I'm sad to say, were the same. I took some comfort, however, in the knowledge that I had discharged my obligation under the law.

As time wore on, I refined my job-hunting techniques. The clumsy hit-and-miss method I was using was clearly getting me nowhere. My valuable time was being wasted, and my energy sapped, by all the fruitless phone-calling. As a time-saving device, I took to opening up the Yellow Pages at random and writing down the names of any businesses I found. At the end of the week, I sent this information to the state, and then merely waited for my next check to arrive. I was surprised at how easy this was. And by skipping the tiresome process of actually contacting employers, I spared myself the embarrassing prospect that someone might offer me a job.

But this method posed more dangers than the direct-dial approach. So, on one Sunday night in the fall, I came perilously close to a fine, or imprisonment, or both.

A CLOSE CALL

Sundays between 11:30 p.m. and 11:35 p.m. were traditionally set aside for my arduous weekly job hunt. Sitting in front of the TV, I balanced the Yellow Pages on one knee while writing down on the unemployment form the employers I'd purportedly contacted. The card was supposed to be mailed on Sunday for the previous week. On that night, I wrote down the names of two local newspapers, while consulting my pocket calendar to search for appropriate application dates to use. Then, with the satisfaction of one who has completed a job well done, I licked the envelope and headed towards my mailbox with a confident swagger.

When I got back, I took a second glance at the newspapers I listed. Even to an untrained eye, it looked awfully suspicious. They were both on the same street, with similar titles. To reassure myself, I dialed one of the numbers.

"I'm sorry, the number you have dialed is not a working number."

The tape-recorded voice of the operator came as a shock. With hands trembling, I quickly phoned the other paper. It, too, was out of business. They'd probably been part of a small chain. Obscure weekly papers fold constantly, and I'd been foolish enough to use an outdated Yellow pages in my job search. I started sweating heavily at the thought of what I had done. This time I'd gone too far: this fraud could be easily spotted.

I envisioned the headlines following my arrest: STATE NABS 'WRITER' IN JOB SCAM. The short AP story would no doubt be seen in newspapers around the country, including those read by my mother:

"State prosecutors today announced the indictment of Lenny Marx, 28, an unemployed Wichita resident, on 14 counts of defrauding the government and 'illegal laziness.' Marx, a self-styled 'writer,' was charged with falsely claiming unemployment insurance benefits, although he has made no attempt to find work in the last ten months.

" 'This was easy to crack,' said one investigator, 'because he wrote down the names of two defunct newspapers located on the same street. It stuck out like a sore thumb.'

"Marx, who faces up to three years in jail and a $1,000 fine, had no comment."

With that scenario in mind, I thought about my unemployment form lying placidly at the bottom of the metal mailbox, waiting to spirit me away to my doom. I had no choice; I had to retrieve that envelope. But how? It was now 12:30 a.m. By noon, the mailman would come, open up the box, and my fate would be sealed.

A slight, misty rain was falling outside. Running to my closet, I put on my raincoat and took out a wire hanger. Bending it into shape, I forged a tool that I hoped could do the job. With luck, the aluminum hood could scoop up the letter. I went out to make my rendezvous with destiny.

If anyone caught me, I would surely go to prison or at least Allenwood, for this was a crime. On the front of the box, it clearly stated, "It is a crime to tamper in any fashion with this property of the U.S. Governement. Anyone caught doing so will face up to a $1,000 fine or three years in prison, or both." It was a risk I had to take. I unfurled the coat hanger from underneath my raincoat and got to work.

Looking around casually, like just another neighbor mailing a letter, I quickly rammed the wire down the opening of the mailbox. I could feel it rustling and scraping down there, but I sensed that my envelope was having a good laugh at my expense. I thrashed the wire against the sides of the box, as if that could stir up a response. All the while, I kept a watch out for any patrol cars.

Looking over my shoulder, I soon saw the beams of approaching headlights against the overhanging trees. I froze in panic: I was about to be caught red-handed. Soon the whole neighborhood would be surrounded with squad cars, SWAT teams, megaphones, sirens, flashing red lights. The jig was up.

I grabbed my coat hanger and jumped into some nearby bushes and watched the car move slowly by. Although it turned out not to be a police car, I realized that it had been a very close call. I got up, badly shaken and wet, too, and made a few more desperate lunges with the wire. Then I headed back to my house, a defeated man. My only hope lay with the mailman.

UGLY POSSIBILITIES

It would be unseemly, of course, but I had no choice but to beg him to return the letter. The pick-up was scheduled for noon. I took no chances: at 11:30 a.m. I was out there in my car, ominously parked across from the site, waiting for him to show up. Passers-by stared at me, as I did my best to look non-criminal. Time passed, noon came and went, and still the mailman hadn't arrived. The confining atmosphere of the car was slowly driving me mad. All sorts of ugly possibilities crossed my mind: I had missed the pick-up, or the FBI was waiting for me to blow up the mailbox, or the mailman had been replaced by an undercover agent. One thought that never occurred to me was that I should be out looking for work. Finally, the mailman arrived.

"Please, sir, I need a letter in there." My eyes glazed over with a look of soft yearning. "I made a mistake and I need to get it back. Is that okay?"

"I'm sorry, man, I can't do that," he responded with Superfly ease. "You'll have to fill out a letter retrieval form at the post office."

"But by then it could be too late!" I waited. "Can't you just give it to me now? I won't tell anybody."

"No, man. Rules are rules. Dig?"

So it was that I found myself down at the local post office, filling out the proper forms. I felt distinctly uncomfortable, as if the clerks there suspected that I was up to no good. I was using one agency of the government to help outwit another, and I expected at any moment that the postmaster might swoop down on me:

"What's this? Another free-lance writer trying to retrieve a fake unemployment form? We can spot your kind a mile away. Hold him, boys, while I call Washington."

But on the surface, I did my best to act calm. And late in the afternoon, I came by to claim my long-lost letter. I had been saved. More importantly, I had learned a vital lesson: next time, I would be more careful in pretending to look for work.

Thus imbued with the fear of God, I decided to make sure my efforts could be well documented in case the government investigators came calling. This did not, however, put me in any danger of finding work; in fact, I was able to cut down my job-hunting to a mere three minutes a week. With a nationwide newspaper directory and a *Writer's Market* as my guides, I was assured of an endless stream of publications that would never consider hiring me. To comply with the law, I actually wrote letters to employers—but they were guaranteed to alienate even the most sympathetic boss.

Of course, the first step in this nationwide job hunt was to pick publications that looked like they were run out of somebody's basement. This was called hedging your bets. Thus, I favored the poetry section of *Writer's Market,* where I'd look for entries like this: *"The Paisley Rainbow,* Free Thinker Press. Editor: L. B. Davis. Established in 1972. Bianual. Circulation: 400. Acquires all rights. Pays in contributor copies." Inevitably, they had no openings for reporters.

I did, however, try to balance my search by applying to heftier specialty magazines, like *Stock Car Review* of Tupelo, Mississippi. For them, I'd concoct letters aimed at, shall we say, attracting attention. Hand-written on yellow-lined paper, the letters went like this:

"Dear Sir:

"I would like to be the editor of your magazine. Although I know very little about stock cars, I am willing to learn. I have some writing experience and have attended an accredited college. I am in good health, except for occasional attacks of *grand mal* epilepsy. In addition, I am no longer addicted to heroin. I am interested in a salary range of $250 to $500 a week. If there are any openings, please don't hesitate to get in touch with me.

"Sincerely,

"Lenny Marx"

In response, I'd get back amazingly cordial letters informing me that while there were no vacancies at the moment, they were keeping my application on file. The sad part was that I received the exact same response when I really *was* interested in a job, sending off newspaper clips and a fancy resume to papers around the country.

HEIGHTENED SELF-WORTH

All this futile job-hunting had a marked impact on my personality. Most articles in the press focus on the deterioration that follows prolonged joblessness: lowered self-worth, marital problems, increased alcoholism and suicide rates. There is supposed to be some kind of stigma attached to unemployment, but for increasingly large segments of the population that just isn't so. For a middle-aged aerospace worker, say, with a family to support, losing your job is indeed a major crisis. But for young people, singles, artists, it's a great chance to fulfill yourself—at government expense. Listen now to the agony of America's unemployed, as reported in *The Washington Post:*

Stuart Waters, 21: "Everybody is looking forward to retirement at 65. I figure I might as well retire now. I mean, if I'm going to work, why shouldn't I work later instead of now? . . . And there's no such thing as not being able to work, either. I could walk out of here tomorrow morning and get a job doing something."

Pat O'Connor, 40: "It gives you and your mind a time to be much more creative than you ever were. . . . To think that I've done Russian novels, that I've tackled Dostoevski on my own, without even taking a course. I've used the time so fruitfully, whereas before I'd be caught up in all this trivia. . . .

"I would never have quit. I would have been an unhappy person. I knew it, but who leaves a $20,000-a-year job? I was afraid to quit because I thought it was terribly essential that I get another $20,000-a-year job, because I couldn't live. Can you believe it? Incredible! And this is the horror of so many job situations."

Edward Kostin, auto worker: "I think being unemployed was the happiest six months of my life."

Let me add my own voice to this chorus of misery. While on unemployment, I blossomed as a writer, my emotional and physical health improved, and my love life picked up dramatically. There was a new bounce in my step, a ruddy glow of good health on my cheeks. "Hey, Lenny," friends asked me, "what's your secret?"

"Unemployment insurance," I smiled back.

At parties, on the street, in unemployment offices, wherever my friends and I gathered, there was nothing but kind words for this magical program that was transforming all our lives, "I couldn't live without it," one freelance director told me. In preparing for a play, he collected unemployment for several weeks prior to opening night, then only reported the income paid to him for the two-week run of the play. That way, he recalled fondly, he only missed two checks. Another friend, a sculptor, collected thousands of dollars in unreported income as a bartender while devoting himself to his art. I was a bit more honest, dutifully reporting my income from an occasional short-story or article sale.

Still, I had a sense of luxury, of freedom, that I had never had before. Better yet, unemployment, far from being a stigma, was actually something of a status symbol. It helped me lure women. I had become a man of independent means, almost as if I had inherited wealth. Moreover, while the typical writer was paid five or ten cents a word, I was pulling in an average of three dollars for each word I wrote down on my unemployment form. It was terse, economical prose, and it brought me a steady income.

For me, and people like me, unemployment insurance had become that long-cherished liberal dream: government funding of the arts. While the National Endowment for the Arts and Humanities spent about 10 per cent of its budget in 1976 on indivivudial artists and writers, the state and federal governments were doling out millions more to virtually every struggling artist in the country. Unemployment is far more democratic than the usual grant program: anyone can apply, without the benefit of big-shot connections or a university affiliation. There are no cumbersome proposals to submit, and no petty bureaucrats to oversee works-in-progress. My own project, "The elevation of Lenny Marx into a Rich and Famous Writer by 1978," would hardly qualify for government or foundation support, but was tailor-made for the unemployment program.

THE REAL WORLD

For others with no artistic bent, the unemployment program is allowing them to live out the fantasies of their undergraduate days. Back-packing across the country, setting up communes, sleeping on beaches, America's young are learning that all the parental horror stories about the "real world" are just so many fairy tales designed to scare them into regular work. "Work for six months and go on unemployment" is their new motto, and it's working out just fine, thank you. Unemployment offices are beginning to resemble youth hostels, with nomadic college grads checking in for their weekly out-of-state employment reports.

The old-fashioned desire to work to the top of a given career is being replaced by other sets of values. Bright young people are approaching their work like illiterate slum dwellers, taking odd jobs and menial labor as a way to earn money, then moving on when the mood hits them. Or they are landing high-paying jobs, then getting themselves fired so they can collect unemployment. And in nearly half the states, they can simply quit and collect their checks after a slight delay. Meanwhile, to cover the costs of the program, their employers are paying taxes into state and federal treasuries, and throwing up their hands in despair at the rapid turnover of workers.

Employers have a right to feel resentful. They are paying about $6 billion a year in unemployment taxes. They are hit with an average of nearly three per cent in state and federal taxes on the "wage base," or taxable payroll, defined as each employee's wages up to $4,200. And *then* they are penalized with higher taxes up to a state maximum if there is a big worker turnover. These penalties have a polite liberal logic, but it means that in some cases industries are being dunned extra for each rip-off artist who breezes through a plant and leaves six months later. Or they have to endure incompetents in order to keep down their taxes. On the other hand, conservative economists like the Public Research Institute's Kathleen Classen charge that the maximum turnover tax rule is too low, allowing stable companies to in effect subsidize the frequent layoffs of seasonal or cyclical industries like agriculture, construction, and mining, many of which exceed the maximum. Along with Harvard economist Martin Feldstein, she also argues that the availability of tax-free unemployment benefits only encourages businesses to lay off workers. Feldstein estimates that it contributes to half the temporary layoffs in the country. It has become part of an unofficial wage package offered to workers in high-turnover industries.

One sign of the lure of unemployment benefits is the "inverse seniority" provisions in the contracts of several industries. These provisions give workers with more seniority the privilege of being laid off *earlier* than other workers and being rehired *later.* Without unemployment compensation, Feldstein contends, there would be fewer unstable jobs in the economy. Some economic studies have also found that increasing the tax rate on the wage base would lead to more firings.

And the taxes are not as small as they seem. In large industries, they can make a dent in profits, and many corporations look to consulting firms or their own legal departments for ways to reduce unemployment taxes. And one obvious way is to fire workers.

All in all, unemployment taxes seem to have been designed by Lewis Carroll, with amendments by Joseph Heller. A system that was originally supposed to have been self-financing has, under the pressure of a recession and expansive legislation, turned into an overgrown idiot child, devouring general revenues needed elsewhere. Raising unemployment taxes can add to unemployment, thus further draining government treasuries and causing still higher taxes, again costing more jobs. But raising taxes seems to be the only funding alternative for a literally bankrupt system.

Total costs for unemployment jumped from $7 billion in 1974 to $20 billion in 1976, while revenues increased only $1 billion to $7.5 billion. Obviously, something has to give. By the end of 1976, 21 states had depleted their unemployment funds and had to turn to the federal government for $3 billion in loans. And the federal government in turn had exhausted its trust fund and had to borrow $11 billion from general revenues for federal and state payments. Naturally, that borrowing cut into monies available for other programs. Things will only get worse, because benefits increase automatically with pay raises, while the wage base has a flat ceiling.

We thus have created the seeds of a system that could turn every state government into another New York City, but few people seem to notice. Congress goes on raising taxes and expanding coverage, without giving much throught to who will pay the final bill. Those who do complain are merely traditional conservatives and businessmen, and we all know how heartless *they* are. One reason there are few other protests is that no one is willing to jeopardize his own personal security. Unemployment insurance has as its potential constituency every wage earner in the United States. Unlike most other government subsidy programs, it is broadly available to the middle class, so it is less vulnerable to attack. Over half the benefits go to families with incomes over $10,000

Although workers are generally satisfied, businessmen are starting to protest the unemployment system. Even so, they speak cautiously, as if pointing out some of the more obvious flaws could only get them tagged as Neanderthals out to starve the masses. In 1976, for example, the National Association of Manufacturers asked for an end to duplicate benefits for former federal employees, who may, at the same time, receive unemployment, pension and social security benefits. The group estimated the savings at $3 billion a year. Its suggestion had no impact, and nothing at all has been done to cut back on the range of duplicate payments available to both government and private workers.

Now and then, a businessman's group issues a report denouncing fraud and waste in the unemployment system. In 1975, the Washington Board of Trade chimed in with its call for a crackdown, and its proposals disappeared without a trace. Obviously, Washington, D.C. is not the most receptive home for a stirring cry on behalf of the work ethic. The nation's capital is in fact, something of a Freeloader's Paradise, boasting both the federal bureaucracy and a welfare and unemployment system that supports a relatively large portion of the city's population. The unemployment program is especially generous, with benefit levels up to $148 a week, and only a one-week wait after quitting your job to collect benefits. The area is a magnet to unemployed people around the country, some who come for less than noble reasons.

In addition to groups, individual businessmen also make their own, less restrained attacks on the system. At a Maryland legislative hearing, for example, one suburban auto parts dealer complained that he was tired of paying benefits for "drunken, thieving, drug-addicted" people who lose their jobs. Another critic, Robert D. Snelling, chairman of the board of the nation's largest employment agency, said, "Open-ended unemployment benefits are the primary reason why our greatest problem this year has been not locating jobs but finding people to fill them."

The workers feel otherwise, and small wonder. They have available to them a pleasant range of unemployment benefits. The regular 26-week program originated with the Social Security Act of 1935. Because of high unemployment, Congress in 1970 passed an extended benefits program that added 13 weeks of payments. This was followed in 1974 by Federal Supplementary Benefits (FSB), which expired in March. This plan added up to 26 more weeks, courtesy of the federal treasury. Both the extended and FSB programs are triggered by high unemployment rates. I took advantage of all of them.

But unemployment benefits are not the only subsidies available to the jobless. According to one study, fully *half* of those receiving unemployment benefits are getting other payments. The study, by the Mathematica Policy Research Project, found that the most common additional sources of unearned income were social security and railroad retirement payments, followed closely by all manner of pensions. Social Security and railroad retirement payments may rank so high because unemployment payments do not affect them, so the recipients lack much incentive for going back to work. Welfare and food stamps recipients who go on unemployment, on the other hand, have their benefits cut.

Of course, government largesse isn't the only laziness incentive. Among the better deals available to the unemployed are union supplemental benefits programs. For auto workers, this amounts to nearly 95 per cent of their take-home pay for up to a year, when combined with government unemployment checks. Layoffs are little more than tax-free holidays. Unfortunately, only a fraction of those receiving unemployment insurance are so blessed, and few states pay benefits to strikers. Still, even *without* any other subsidies, government unemployment benefits usually replace two thirds of a worker's net income.

Recent analyses of unemployment statistics have produced some startling findings. The Brueau of Labor Statistics generally classifies people as unemployed if they are not now working, but have looked for work in the past four weeks. But its surveys also count those who are on temporary layoff and those who will be starting work in a month. All these categories, incidentally, are based on the assumption that the respondents aren't lying. When I was getting unemployment checks, any government pollster interviewing me would have been loudly told how hard I was looking for work. "I'm out pounding the pavement every day, sir," I would have said with an earnest look.

In February 1977, the unemployment rate was 7.5 per cent—that's 7,183,000 people. Only about a third of them, 33.5 per cent, were fired outright or had jobs that collapsed. Even those fired and those laid off together amounted to less than half of the unemployed; the rest were people who had left their jobs voluntarily (11.9 per cent), people who were just returning to the job market after a voluntary absence (27.5 per cent), and new entrants into the market (13.1 per cent).

And Martin Feldstein found that among men aged 25 to 64, prime members of work force, nearly half of them, classified as "job losers," were only on a temporary layoff. Using 1974 figures, he also discovered that 38 per cent of all job losers—the biggest category of unemployed—were waiting to be recalled to their jobs. This is hardly the picture of unemployment that Jimmy Carter paints.

In addition, most people find work quickly after losing jobs. More than half the unemployed go back to work in four weeks or less, and only one-eighth of the jobless have been looking for over six months. Moreover, the American people seem to treat jobs as revolving doors: over 20 per cent of the work force is at least temporarily unemployed during the course of a year—three times the monthly figures.

Understandably, the job search becomes more successful once unemployment benefits run out. One study found that two thirds of those who exhausted their benefits then found jobs or withdrew from the labor force. Generally, about a fifth of all those eligible for unemployment benefits collect the maximum allowable amount.

The heart of the question, of course, is to what extent unemployment benefits actually promote unemployment. Unfortunately, in this area there are wildly contradictory findings, often based on inexact data. Some of these studies are also an affront to common sense. One is Stephen Marston's influential Brookings Institution research, which concluded unemployment benefits only add .3 per cent to the unemployment rate. That's still roughly 288,000 more unemployed people. Marston's work, however, has been criticized by some in the Congressional Budget Office and Labor Department for using fancy computations to cover up a weak data base.

Kathleen Classen's 1974 work for the Labor Department is thought to have more reliable data, because she examined the effect of a rise in benefits on job searches in a single state. She concluded that a $10 rise in benefits leads to an extra week of joblessness, and that the overall impact at that time was a .9-percent jump in the unemployment rate. Later estimates have gone as high as 1.2 million more people unemployed because of benefits, or 1.25 per cent. Interestingly enough, Classen also undercut one of the social justifications for the long delays in finding work: the search for a better job. She found that longer spells of unemployment didn't lead workers to either better-paying or more permanent, satisfying jobs.

Two of Classen's colleagues at the Public Research Institute, Arlene Holen and Stanley Horowitz, have made additional findings that underscore the role of benefits in adding to unemployment. The two researchers found that increasing the rate at which people are denied benefits—either because they quit or didn't look for work—decreases the unemployment rate. They concluded that doubling the denial rate might lead to as much as a 25-percent dip in the jobless rate—without changing eligibility rules.

Obviously, weeding out cheaters and loafers would be an almost impossible task. Tough regulations for proving job search can be easily manipulated. In my case, I could furnish written proof from 200 newspapers that I had applied for a job, knowing full well that a *pro forma* application never landed anyone a newspaper job. If a person doesn't want to work, he'll figure out a way to comply with the law and still get his unemployment check. If worse comes to worse, he can always blow the interview. I've done it so many times when I really wanted to work, that I could easily duplicate some of my previous performances. Seedy clothing, long hair, shaky hands—it's amazing how a few minor quirks can keep you on the unemployment line. To cut out the free-loaders, there would have to be a cop at every mailbox, spies in all the personnel offices, and weekly lie-detector tests. For 12 million annual recipients, that's quite a large administrative budget.

Now, except for a few publicized scandals, fraud enforcement is largely haphazard. It's easy to catch a Florida vacationer who confesses on *60 Minutes* to using Michigan benefits to subsidize his golf practice. What's not so easy is doing something about the routine ease with which recipients get benefits while avoiding work. Equally difficult is catching those who collect off-the-books cash income while getting their unemployment checks. Denial of benefits is one tool that's relatively unused—in 1976, only .8 per cent of America's 155,000,000 unemployment claims were denied because the claimants were not looking for work. Criminal prosecutions are even rarer. Fewer than 6,500 people were convicted for unemployment-related fraud last year. Another sign that the government is now on top of the situation is its estimate that less than one per cent of claims are illegitimate. The State employment services, of course, could easily boost denial numbers as a way to get more staff and look tough, but give the way the agencies are run, they'd never make a dent in the problem, while hurting a lot of people unjustly in the process.

The federal government is making a slight move to shake out the system, but it's at the cost of some important personal rights. The proposed extension of Federal Supplemental Benefits tightens eligibility in several ways, while cutting the maximum benefits to an additional 13 weeks, instead of the present 26. It's reasonable to ask recipients, as the proposal would, to supply "tangible evidence" that they're conducting a sustained job search. What's not so pleasant is the requirement that people accept newly defined "suitable labor," even if it pays less or requires fewer skills than their customary jobs. That requirement only goes into effect when the state determines that your prospects for obtaining work in your field are poor.

Naturally, this provision was attacked by a group of 800 chanting unemployed who streamed to Washington recently to protest the new bill. While their leaders spoke from a church pulpit, they cried out, "No Cuts! No Way!" They called the bill "slave labor." Although their language was strong, they had a valid point: if people would rather barely scrape by than do work they find odious, they should have that right. Of course I wondered why they had enough energy to protest but not enough to find a job.

The protestors' attitude is not the kind that sits easily with most Americans—after all, what have they done to deserve a free ride? But the free ride of unemployment compensation is hardly a luxurious one; it provides you with enough money to scrape by, and that, in most cases, is it. If our society is willing to allow people the explicit tradeoff that unemployment benefits imply—if you really don't want a boring, degrading, even dangerous job, the government will maintain you at a subsistence level—that's fine. If it's not, people like me will always find ways to cut the corners and get what we want. There is, like it or not, a group of people in this country for whom the material comforts a job brings are simply less important than doing something interesting, creative, or useful—even just restful. Most people aren't willing to live poor, but we are—and I feel strongly that we're not just leeches on society. I think we're making America a better place. Something like 90 per cent of the actors in this country get unemployment, as well as a sizable chunk of the artists and writers.

While living off my unemployment checks, I was contributing to society by writing short stories and remaining cheerful. If forced to work, I'd have become surly and depressed, gone on wild drinking sprees, crashed into government-owned highway dividers and wasted the time of ambulance drivers, policemen, and emergency-room doctors. Admittedly, I'm an extreme case, but the social cost of forced labor is truly too high for all of us. The price I paid for my freedom was that I barely had enough money to pay my rent, food, and other expenses. Others in the country were also willing to make that bargain.

By this point, those half-dozen readers still following along might be impatient for the stirring cries for reform that usually conclude such articles. How can we make the unemployment system work again? Actually, for my purposes, it works fine. It's better than the Irish sweepstakes and the chances for winning are much greater. It's one of the few programs left in America where any citizen, no matter how unlucky or downtrodden, can get something for nothing. The conservative proposals for making the system pay for itself—higher tax penalties on unstable industries, taxable benefits, tough enforcement—could cause unnecessary human suffering and further unemployment, without closing the revenue gap. To achieve either sound financing or an end to fraud would never be worth the cost we'd have to pay.

What's needed is a dismantling of the entire apparatus of government subsidies to individuals. The subsidies will cost an estimated $192 billion this year, or 46 per cent of the federal budget. We should replace them all with a guaranteed annual income. The current system is unfair and uneven, penalizing the working poor, families with able-bodied adult males, individuals, and childless couples. One person's income is inflated by a wide range of government checks, while another has to survive on social security. It's open to waste and fraud, too. Repeated scandals, hearings and investigations have changed nothing. The Welfare Queen, Linda Taylor of Chicago, is only the ultimate symbol of how rotten the system is. She allegedly used 26 aliases to collect $150,000 a year from welfare programs. She took from nearly a dozen different programs. There are still needy people in this country, but only the hustlers know how to use the programs, while the rest of us pay for it.

A negative income tax might not remedy everything, but it could go a long way towards ending abuses and helping those who really need help. Administered through the IRS it would take all income into account—including gifts and winnings—and provide a bare minimum on which to live. The mechanism is already there, and the necessary fear and respect is there as well. And if you wanted to earn more money, you'd have to go out and work for it. The initial jump in the federal budget would likely lead to long-term savings following the cutting of all the other programs.

Would everyone quit his dull, menial, low-paying job the next day? That would be unlikely, but the threat of that could have an enormous impact on the workplace. Most of the miserable jobs our society parcels out to the under-classes are made available with the boss's confident knowledge that otherwise the people who take them would starve to death. With the small cushion of a guaranteed annual income, workers could begin to demand higher wages, more power, and better conditions. The economic resources now directed upwards to pay the high costs of movie stars, athletes, corporate lawyers, and others with enjoyable jobs might be shifted back down to typists, janitors, and short-order cooks. The *Walden II* economic system could take hold here: we'd pay high prices for the work no one wanted to do.

Even with a negative income tax, work would get done. The leading study in the subject shows that Americans won't stay home in droves even if given free cash. An $8 million, three-year experiment by the Office of Economic Opportunity found that a negative income tax barely affected the work habits of the heads of low-income families. A range of cash guarantees and tax breaks were offered to about 1,300 families in New Jersey and Pennsylvania, who were assigned to either experimental or control groups. White heads of families ended up working only 5 per cent less, and among blacks and Spanish-Americans there was virtually no reduction at all. Another recent study showed that 80 per cent of working people would work even if they were given enough money to live comfortably.

And a guaranteed annual income would allow for only the barest necessities. For me, it would be like a year-round unemployment check. I would still stay home and write my stories. But I wouldn't have to cheat anyone or bankrupt any treasuries to do it.

Bureaucracy:
The Biggest Crisis of All

Michael Nelson

The hallmark of the company town is that it provides its people with not just jobs, but everything else, including entertainment. In Washington, of course, the bureaucracy is the company, and not surprisingly Washingtonians find its foibles to be an endless source of merriment. *The Washington Star* daily runs a "great moments in bureaucratese" feature called Gobbledygook; *The Washington Monthly* has its "Memo of the Month"; and Senator Proxmire grabs headlines with his monthly Golden Fleece Award, uncovering government-funded studies on "the sex life of the fern" and the like.

Washingtonians also seem to assume that if they are laughing at bureaucracy, the whole world must be laughing with them—when it's time for Americans to get serious about politics, they, like their brethren in Washington, surely must drop bureaucracy and start talking about "issues." But to the rest of the country, bureaucracy really isn't the least bit funny. It *is* the issue.

In fact it is not too much to say that out where the services of the government are delivered, the performance of the bureaucracy constitutes the biggest crisis facing our country today. It grows in each of the millions of direct, "routine" contacts that take place every day between citizens and the agencies of their government, many of which are supposed to be helping them. In contrast to Watergate and Vietnam, this crisis is neither readily identified nor easily cured; it is insidious, the more so because it manifests itself in such ordinary ways.

Michael Nelson is a contributing editor of *The Washington Monthly* and teaches political science at Vanderbilt University. Douglas Goralski assisted in the research for this article.

Bureaucracy isn't limited to government, of course, or to the United States. In China, it concerned Chairman Mao more than any other problem, enough so that he plunged his country into near-chaos in an attempt to deal with it. In this country we haven't had a Mao, and with any luck we will never need one, but we do have to recognize that the problem is as serious here as it was in China.

I began to find this out a couple of years ago, after I decided to try to learn what politics and government look like from a citizen's-eye view— what people think about when they think about the political system. I did so by going to three towns to talk with three classes of people—poor whites in Augusta, Georgia, professionals and businessmen in Towson, Maryland, and blue-collar workers in New Milford, New Jersey. I drew people's names randomly from the phone book, wrote to tell them I was interested in finding out what was on their minds concerning politics, and asked to come visit for a couple of evenings with them and a few of their friends and families. I didn't bring in a long list of questions; instead, when I got to their homes, I repeated my interest in hearing about their concerns, then sat back and listened as they talked, partly to me, but mostly with each other. Unlike a pollster, I was as interested in what people chose to talk about then they talked politics as in the specific opinions they expressed.

As the conversations rambled along, these people began to paint a verbal picture of the political world as they saw it. To my surprise, what loomed largest in that portrait was not presidents or elections or issues or the rest of the stuff we usually think of as "politics." In fact, when people spoke of current affairs and the like (mostly I suspect, because they thought it would please me), they did so stiffly, with uncomfortable pauses and lags in the conversation. The subject they warmed to with raised-vioce, table-thumping intensity was the bureaucracy—not the anonymous, bloated, big-B Bureaucracy of Chamber of Commerce after-dinner speeches, but rather the specific agencies of government they felt intruding into their personal lives.

As one might expect, each class of people dealt with somewhat different groups of agencies—the well-off with, for example, the IRS, the blue-collar families with the unemployment office, the poor with the Social Security Administration. But regardless of their class, almost all saw little connection between political issues and their own lives. They saw a great deal of connection, however, between bureaucracy and their daily concerns— and most of what they saw they didn't like.

Further, they didn't like that intimacy, those intrusions. It meant dealing with organizations that were not only large and impersonal, but whose actions sometimes seemed to defy all reason. For example, Frank, a prosperous middle-aged lawyer, told of trying to find out from the IRS how his purchase of a condominium would bear on his taxes. "I went all the way to the IRS district director before I could get anybody to listen to what I was saying. The district director finally says, 'Well, I can't help you; you have to talk to the agent of the day'—you know, call a number and agent so-and-so answers. So when I finally reach him, he says, 'Does your company subscribe to Prentice-Hall and Commerce Clearinghouse and different tax services?' I said yeah. He says, 'Well, you better look it up there because that's more help than we can give you.' "

Martha, a retired spinster, had been supporting herself with a small social security check. Ordinarily, that would have entitled her to get additional Supplemental Security Income (SSI) benefits. But because she had saved over the years for her burial, she told me, she had accumulated more in the bank than SSI recipients were allowed to have. Thus, the local office turned down her application, though a sympathetic caseworker advised her that if she went out and spent her savings, she would become eligible.

RANDOM AND ARBITRARY

Bureaucrats' behavior also seemed random and arbitrary, though for those who were shrewd enough, it could be gotten around. A real estate dealer explained that "It's very difficult to get the right information out of the government in my business. Trying to get a decent appraisal out of a government official—the VA or the FHA—is unbelievable. The red tape. If he appraised it, that's the last word—that's it. And the only way we could rectify two of the things that came in grossly underappraised was to go to our congressman, who used to be a neighbor. He helped us out."

All too often, though, an inept agency action gave the appearance of being malicious. Curiously, many of the poor whites were certain that the government now discriminated against them, using evidence like Homer and Viola's. "I know a black man who used to work at the truckstop," complained Homer, a young part-time school janitor. "His wife went down there and said him and her was separated and had two young'uns. And at that time she's been drawing welfare and food stamps for two years and she said they never had so much as come to her house." "And that woman came down here and went through every cabinet I got, that welfare woman," added Viola.

'IN 30 DAYS I'D BE STARVING'

For some, the inherently complicated nature of bureaucratic procedures was a source of anger and confusion. After Willie's husband Fred, a mechanic, broke his arm, she went down to the food stamp office. "I had a note from the doctor saying he'd have to stay out of work for ten months. They told me I could get the stamps but I'd have to wait 30 days. I told her that in 30 days I'd be starving and she could forget about it." Ron, an unemployed landscaper, dreaded going down to the unemployment office. "You have to get on one line for this and another line for that, and the people behind the counter—they're busy, I know—but they treat you like you're probably a rip-off artist or something. You know, guilty until proven innocent."

The impersonal nature of agency contacts further incensed people. Diana, a university press editor, complained about "the computerized courtesy" of form letters from the IRS: "We got a letter saying come down to the IRS at such-and-such a time, blah, blah, blah, and bring all your papers—very impersonal.

"So we go down and it turns out that nothing is wrong. Well, Good Lord, I've been paying taxes for 30 years and nothing's ever been wrong. Why do they need to call me now? Just more big brother."

Even worse was having to rely on a large, anonymous, and hence unpredictable organization for basic sustenance. Gene and Ella, who live off his VA disability payments, got very upset when some bureaucrat waited too long to get the checks out. "If a man is depending on that check," said Gene, "he could be sitting out in the street with his family maybe for ten days if his landlord wants his rent on the first. You can get pretty hungry from the first to the tenth waiting for that check, and they should take that into consideration. Some of them wait until the last minute and foul everybody up, and it can be real costly to people."

What is striking about these complaints, and the scores of similar ones I heard, is not that people don't like bureaucracy. After all, who does? I once taught a course in public administration to a class of government employees, and even they couldn't muster up a kind word for it.

THE NATURE OF THE COMPLAINTS

What is striking is the nature of the complaints. As every scholarly treatise on the subject will tell you, the great advantage bureaucracy is supposed to offer to complex, modern society is efficient, rational, uniform, and courteous treatment for the citizens it deals with. Yet not only did these qualities manage to conceal themselves from the people I talked with, it was their very opposites that seemed more characteristic. People of all classes felt that their treatment had been bungled, not efficient; unpredictable and bizarre, not rational; discriminatory or idiosyncratic, not uniform; and all too often, insensitive or down-right insulting rather than courteous. It was as if they had gotten stuck with a new car that not only did not run when they wanted it to, but that periodically started itself up and drove all around their lawn.

Equally curious, the agencies that drew the most fire were, on the whole, those whose business is supposedly providing benefits to people—social security, food stamps, welfare, tax counseling, and so on. It is not surprising, of course, that people grumble when the government exacts taxes and other burdens from them. But when in the process of supposedly doing something for them it makes them hopping mad, then we have a problem.

SPANNING PARTY LINES

This last point is underscored in a recent report to Jimmy Carter from Richard Pettigrew, a presidential assistant working on reorganization. Pettigrew sent out a letter to every representative and senator asking them which federal programs their constituents thought were "administered least efficiently," "most confusing," "least successful in achieving their stated objectives," involved the most "excessive paper work," and, finally, were "most responsive." Though congressmen, who are at the receiving end of almost all citizen complaints against the government, were the logical ones to ask, evidently no one ever had before. More than 200 of them replied, often in great detail. Their answers, interestingly enough, were quite uniform, spanning party and ideological lines. (The author of a call for "less government involvement in the 'daily lives' of individuals and businesses," for example, was George McGovern.)

Two agencies ranked high in all four "bad" categories: the Department of Labor's Office of Workers' Compensation Programs, which administers the black lung program and workmen's compensation for federal employees, and the Social Security Administration. (It is worth remembering here that the agency's old age insurance program seemed to work fine; it was the disability insurance, Medicare, and Aid for Families with Dependent Children that drew all the flak.)

The Veterans' Administration was next on the list; it scored badly in three categories. The IRS, Immigration and Naturalization Service, and Small Business Administration showed up in two. Among the others that were singled out frequently: the Occupational Safety and Health Administration, the department of Housing and Urban Development, the Civil Service Commission, the Farmers Home Administration, the Postal Service, the Economic Development Administration, and the Employment Retirement Income Security Administration.

Aside from the IRS and, perhaps, OSHA, all of these are, supposedly, benefits agencies. The patterns of complaints Pettigrew found—unnecessary delays in processing cases, agencies' failure to provide people with information, and "outright rudeness"—were very similar to the ones I heard.

Clearly, then, the message Americans are sending—that they feel and resent the weight of government agencies pressing in on their personal lives—is an urgent one; with the benefit of hindsight, it becomes obvious that they have been trying to get it through for some time. It was expressed at Jimmy Carter's town meetings and phone-ins, for example (not to mention his election itself)—in the plea for help from a Cleveland woman who couldn't get her mother's GI Bill benefits straightened out, the complaint of a Lanham, Maryland jobseeker that she had been frozen out of civil service employment, the California man's protest about letters the Post Office takes forever to deliver, and so on. And, most obvious, there is all that congressional mail.

'DEAR ABBY'

Unfortunately, the message generally has been ignored. Though Carter described his town meetings as "a learning process rather than a teaching process," the White House seemed more excited about the public relations benefits of being seen listening to people than the listening itself. The press was alternately miffed and condescending. *Time*, for example, thought the questions asked at the televised phone-in in Los Angeles were "either soft or silly"; columnist Joseph Kraft said the radio program that started it all was "a set of 'Dear Abby' phone calls to the President."

Similarly, though congressmen respond vigorously to the specific complaints of their constituents, they rarely dig deeper to discover the patterns of agency practice that underlie them. In most congressional offices, the legislative staff almost never tries to learn anything from the casework staff, which handles complaints (in fact, there's a powerful status difference between the two, and snobbery often keeps the high-status legislative assistants from even talking to the lowly caseworkers). Putting out fires as they occur translates into votes; finding out why so many fires take place, though, would be not only long and tedious, but difficult to dramatize to the folks back home as well.

Thus, Pettigrew blandly reports, "even the offices of those senators and congressmen with legislative responsibilities for various programs acknowledge the acute need for administrative reform. The office of Senator Harrison Williams, for example, was extremely critical of the Department of Labor's Office of Workers' Compensation Programs, calling the program 'unresponsive, unorganized, and insensitive.'" Representatives John Dent, Phillip Burton, and William Ford were among those equally critical. As all four gentlemen are, and have been for some time, influential members of the congressional committees that are responsible for the OWCP (Williams is chairman of the Senate Labor Committee; Dent, Burton, and Ford are senior Democrats on House Education and Labor), they obviously bear some of the responsibility for the OWCP's shortcomings.

Yet, like most of their colleagues, they have found it easier just to slam away at an agency than to do whatever is necessary to improve it.

'NO JOBS'

Congress not only fails to correct a lot of the problems citizens have with government; it creates a good many of them by writing bad laws. Senator Lawton Chiles' complaint to Pettigrew that many people's SSI payments go down dramatically whenever their VA benefits go up can be traced to a problem in the law, not the agencies. As a VISTA volunteer representing people at social security hearings, I frequently heard vocational experts testify that my clients should be turned down for disability benefits because they were healthy enough to do sit-down jobs like those at a local Borden's plant. The fact that Borden's had had a "no jobs" sign in the window for as long as anyone could remember was irrelevant; the fact that it was irrelevant was due to the way Congress had written the law.

None of this should be taken to mean that agencies are blameless or that there is nothing they could do to make things more pleasant for the people they deal with. For example, the IRS set up a toll-free number that citizens could call for help with their taxes. Fine. But according to Senator William Proxmire, the line is almost always busy during tax season, for 23 consecutive days in one case. Why offer a service and not deliver it? OSHA made it a practice to concentrate its fire on small businesses rather than large ones; where is the sense in that? And what is the justification for outright rudeness in any situation?

Social Security disability hearings again provide an extraordinary case in point. The agency is notorious for having more than half its determinations that applicants are ineligible for disability benefits or SSI overturned if appealed-usually by its own administrative law judges. What is worse, many congressmen reported, in the four to eight months it takes to get a favorable decision, people have lost their homes, spent hundreds of dollars on lawyers, even died. When I asked Michael Naver at Social Security why local bureaucrats made so many wrong determinations in the first place, he pointed out that "the hearing is the first time anyone in the Administration actually sees the applicant—physically sees how he moves, how he talks, how he copes, and so on. Until then, we're just looking at a file." Again, common sense—never mind human decency and courtesy—would seem to cry out for a change in administrative practice here.

As with poor congressional law drafting, obvious deficiencies like these could be remedied with a little more care and concern; for that reason alone they are probably worth reforming. But if bad guys and bad practices were all that there was to the problem, such tinkering with the machinery—the usual activity of reformers—would be all it would take to solve it.

Unfortunately, the problem is far more fundamental than that. It is basic to bureaucracy, built into the relationship between citizens and government in a democratic welfare state. It lies in the simple difference in perspective between agency and citizen, a difference that makes it difficult if not impossible for the two to deal in a mutually satisfactory way. Perhaps it can be best understood by starting with the desk that lies between them.

OF COURSE

On one side of the desk is the citizen, a unique individual with a unique set of circumstances. Think of Matha, the woman who, because she had saved for so many years for her burial, had more money in the bank than the SSI law allowed its beneficiaries to have. She is, of course, a whole person, and wanted to be treated as a whole person. Special consideration? Of course. Bend the rules a little? Certainly; I'm different. And she is different, as is every other person who sits on her side of the desk.

Across from her is the bureaucrat. He is there not as a friend or neighbor, but purely as the hired representative of his agency. As much as possible, that agency is supposed to execute the law as written, that is, to function as an efficient machine. It's not supposed to do whatever it—or one of its employees—wants, or feels is right. That means the bureaucrat, sitting as he does at the bottom of the agency ladder, must function as a cog in that machine. He is empowered only to do certain limited things, and only for those clients who are eligible. By definition, he must not look at the whole person, but only those features that enable him to transform her into a "case," a "file." His first job, then, is to fit this woman before him into a category: eligible or not; if so, for what and on what terms. Once classified, she becomes subject to the same treatment as all the others in her category.

CONSIDER THE ALTERNATIVE

So Martha did not get her SSI check. The fact that her savings are for burial purposes, not high living, could not even be considered. If that sounds horrible, consider the alternative: bureaucrats with the discretion to waive the law at their option. One would like to think they would do so for good-hearted purposes, but our experience with government is that agencies that are free to exercise the most discretion in applying the law —the regulatory boards, contracting agencies, even judges sentencing criminals—tend to use that discretion in ways that harm, not help, the average man. As bad as machine bureaucracy is, the obvious alternative is worse.

Even good intentions can't do very much about this fundamental problem of perspective, as I learned from my experience in a legal aid office in Atlanta. Everyone who worked there was zealously dedicated to "serving the people;" their long hours at low pay proved that. We thought of ourselves as the anti-bureaucracy agency, tilting against the local welfare, food stamp, social security, and VA offices on behalf of our clients.

THE GOOD GUYS AND THE BAD GUYS

Thus, I was amazed to learn that many poor people regarded us as just another bureaucracy—couldn't they tell the good guys from the bad guys? But they were right. We, too, had our eligibility requirements, kept them waiting in the outer office, got impatient when they didn't keep to our schedules or rambled off the subject. We didn't look at them as whole people any more than our fellow federal employees in the other agencies did.

So what is to be done?

First, although there are limits to what we can do to change bureaucracy, there are ways we can cut it down to size, minimizing the number and complexity of contacts between citizens and agencies. For instance, the vast array of government programs designed to give people sustenance (welfare, disability, social security, unemployment, veterans pensions, workmen's compensation, food stamps, Medicare, Medicaid) realy are addressed only to two simple needs: the need for money to live on, and the need to pay for health care. A guaranteed annual wage (with poverty the only measure of eligibility) and a national health care system would take care of those needs far more simply than the present system, and because of the simplicity, at a reduced cost. Caring for people through outright handouts would also vastly reduce that grating citizen-bureaucrat contact. The advantage of this shines through in the experience of the Social Security Administration. The administration of the old-age pension, whatever you might say about its conception, is simple and popular—I heard almost no complaints about it and neither did the congressmen who reported to Pettigrew. It was the highly complicated SSI, disability, and welfare programs that spawned all sorts of problems.

One reason this kind of simplicity isn't more widespread is that the government's intentions are, in a way, too good—we can't bear to give away money without making sure it's well deserved. Any small-town mayor can tell you that if he wants federal money for some well-deserved project, he has to put up with reams and reams of forms and meetings designed to insure that the construction company doesn't discriminate in its hiring, that the plans are perfectly sound, that the environmental impact of the project won't be adverse, and so on. These are all worthy goals, but they create a lot of bitterness and kill a lot of projects. Sometimes it's better for the government just to take a deep breath and *give* away the money, trusting its recipient to spend it in reasonable ways and accepting that there will be some who won't.

WHAT CANNOT BE ELIMINATED

Of course, any simplification will still leave a lot of bureaucracy standing, so it's important to try to reform what bureaucracy cannot be eliminated. The press can play a large role in this, by giving its audience a running commentary on what parts of the government work, what parts don't, and why, so that we can apply the lessons elsewhere. It certainly doesn't do that now—at the Office of Workers' Compensation Programs, they kept waiting for the flock of reporters to descend when Pettigrew's report came out, but nobody called. Exposing Watergates is fine, but these days lawbreaking is the least of the government's problems.

But most of the burden of dealing with these problems should be shouldered by the government itself. For one thing, we need to teach as well as learn about how bureaucracy works in this country. Our present system of civics education in the public schools, sticking as it does to explications of a constitution that doesn't even mention the bureaucracy, tells people almost nothing about how to make agencies work for them. I would bet that for every thousand people in this country who could list the Bill of Rights and name all nine Supreme Court justices, you would be lucky to find one who could explain his rights against federal agencies and name the members of even one regulatory commission. Because we don't teach these things, we shouldn't be surprised that people feel ignorant and overwhelmed when they have to deal with as many agencies as they do.

GROWING MEANS LISTENING

Elected officials also need to learn more than they do, and in a democracy learning means listening. Most politicians do this chiefly by taking polls, but pollsters get their answers by asking people questions about the things the pollsters (or more precisely, the people who hire them) think are important. As a result, we end up with reams and reams of data about what grandma thinks about the Panama Canal, assuming she cares enough to have an opinion, and nothing at all about what is on *her* mind. Forums like Jimmy Carter's phone-ins, where the citizens themselves decide what to talk about, would be far more educational for Washingtonians who venture out into the bush than the latest Caddell poll.

Listening, learning, and reading are only the first steps, of course; the government has also to act to make itself work better. Now and then proposals for accomplishing this come forth, usually involving some sort of "ombudsman" agency. But a new spirit is at least as important as a new agency; in fact, the Office of Management and Budget in the executive branch and the General Accounting Office in the legislative could, under their charters, do as much investigating of the government as anyone could want, but they don't. The point is to care enough about the government's grating inefficiencies to attack them with passion.

MOSTLY ABSENT

That passion is mostly absent today because criticism of big government is the exclusive province of the right, which doesn't want social welfare programs in the first place. So proposals to meet the bureaucratic problem head-on usually involve throwing out the baby with the bath—getting rid not only of the bad apparatus but also of the good program it's supposed to implement.

In fact, the bureaucracy crisis is an ideal issue for liberals, who *want* the government to meet the major problems of the nation. As Pettigrew's study showed, popular dissatisfaction with government stems from its failure to deliver on promised services, not from the regulatory ills you see detailed in the Mobil Oil ads. A 1976 survey by Potomac Associates found that Americans—even self-described conservatives—want the government to do more to help the elderly, make college available to young people, reduce air pollution, improve health care, and so on. Liberals need not worry that any concession to critics of bureaucracy is an invitation to reaction—the New Deal has already been ratified.

If anything does set off a wave of right-wing, anti-government fervor, it will be the failure of liberals to see to it that the government Americans want need not be gargantuan or staggeringly complex, and must be delivered efficiently and courteously. Over the years, liberals have responded to popular demands with an impressive set of promises; now they must be willing to deliver on them. It will be a huge effort—Mao, after all, started a "cultural" revolution toward that end, and even that was only partially successful. But if the effort isn't made, the mood of sullen resentment I found in the people I talked with eventually will turn to angry action. And when it does, expect the worst.